Beginnings &

A Guide for Personal Growth & Adjustment

LAUREL HUGHES
University of Portland

BROOKS/COLE PUBLISHING COMPANY
I(T)P™ An International Thomson Publishing Company

Pacific Grove • Albany • Bonn • Boston • Cincinnati • Detroit • London • Madrid • Melbourne
Mexico City • New York • Paris • San Francisco • Singapore • Tokyo • Toronto • Washington

A CLAIREMONT BOOK

Sponsoring Editor: *Marianne Taflinger*	Interior and Cover Design: *Laurie Albrecht*
Marketing Team: *Gay Meixel, Romy Fineroff*	Art Editor: *Lisa Torri*
Marketing Representative: *Tamy Stenquist*	Photo Researcher: *Robert J. Western*
Editorial Associate: *Patricia Vienneau*	Typesetting: *ETP/Harrison*
Production Editor: *Marjorie Z. Sanders*	Cover Printing: *Lehigh Press Lithographers*
Manuscript Editor: *Helene Wolff*	Printing and Binding: *R. R. Donnelley & Sons Company*
Permissions Editor: *Catherine Gingras*	

Cover art: *Charles Demuth,* Three Acrobats, *1916, watercolor and graphite on paper. 1983. 127, Amon Carter Museum, Fort Worth, Texas.*

COPYRIGHT© 1996 by Brooks/Cole Publishing Company
A division of International Thomson Publishing Inc.
I(T)P The ITP logo is a trademark under license.

For more information, contact:

BROOKS/COLE PUBLISHING COMPANY
511 Forest Lodge Road
Pacific Grove, CA 93950
USA

International Thomson Editores
Campos Eliseos 385, Piso 7
Col. Polanco
11560 México D. F. México

International Thomson Publishing Europe
Berkshire House 168-173
High Holborn
London WC1V 7AA
England

International Thomson Publishing GmbH
Königswinterer Strasse 418
53227 Bonn
Germany

Thomas Nelson Australia
102 Dodds Street
South Melbourne, 3205
Victoria, Australia

International Thomson Publishing Asia
221 Henderson Road
#05-10 Henderson Building
Singapore 0315

Nelson Canada
1120 Birchmount Road
Scarborough, Ontario
Canada M1K 5G4

International Thomson Publishing Japan
Hirakawacho Kyowa Building, 3F
2-2-1 Hirakawacho
Chiyoda-ku, Tokyo 102
Japan

All rights reserved. No part of this work may be reproduced, stored in a retrieval system, or transcribed, in any form or by any means—electronic, mechanical, photocopying, recording or otherwise—without the prior written permission of the publisher, Brooks/Cole Publishing Company, Pacific Grove, California 93950.

Printed in the United States of America

10 9 8 7 6 5 4 3 2 1

Library of Congress Cataloging-in-Publication Data

Hughes, Laurel, [date] —
    Beginnings & beyond : a guide for personal growth & adjustment /
    Laurel Hughes.
        p.   cm.
    Includes bibliographical references and index.
    ISBN 0-534-23658-8
    1. Adjustment (Psychology)   2. Self-actualization (Psychology)
I. Title.
BF335.H835   1995
158—dc20   95-40150
                                              CIP

For all who gather 'round...

Contents

Chapter One
Introduction   1
What Does It Mean to Be "Well-Adjusted?"

Defining Good Adjustment   3
Healthy Adjustment and the Perspectives of Psychology   5
    The Psychodynamic Perspective   7
    The Behavioral Perspective   8
    The Cognitive Perspective   10
    The Existentialist/Humanistic Perspective   11
    The Biological Perspective   13
    A Synthesized Theory of Good Adjustment   14
Investigating Personal Adjustment   15
Am I Normal?   18
The Role of Values   21
Expanding Your Experience   22
Study Questions   24

Chapter Two
Development Thus Far   25
Understanding Where You Came From

Biology   27

Nature-Nurture Theories 28
   Cognitive Development 28
   Psychosocial Development 35
Nurture: Behavioral and Social Learning Theories 40
   Conditioning and Social Learning 40
Development of Self-Concept 42
   Self-Esteem 43
   Choice and Free Will 45
   Gender 47
Expanding Your Experience 51
Study Questions 52

Chapter Three
Development as a Young Adult   54
Transitionings

Recovery from Adolescence 57
The Role of Biology 58
The "Morning of Life" 58
Setting Up an External Life Structure 59
Building an Internal Life Structure 61
Organizing Young Adult Living 66
   Time Management 66
   Using Study Time Effectively 70
   The Collisions of College Living 72
Expanding Your Experience 73
Study Questions 74

Chapter Four
Stress, Anxiety, and Coping   76
Jostling the Jitters

Stress 78
   Sources of Stress 78
   Stress and the Body 82
Anxiety 86
   Types of Anxiety 86
   The Many Bases of Anxiety 86
Coping 89
   Environmental Solutions 91
   Psychodynamic Solutions 92

    Existential/Humanistic Solutions 93
    Cognitive Solutions 99
    Physical Solutions 103
    Social Solutions 105
Expanding Your Experience 110
Study Questions 111

Chapter Five
Anger, Aggression, and Depression   *112*
Taming the Dragons within Us

Anger 113
Aggression 117
Aggression and Today's World 118
    Aggression and the Media 118
    Rape 120
Managing Anger and Aggression 122
    Stress Inoculation Training 122
    Assertiveness 124
    Dealing with Angry People 125
Depression 128
    The Many Facets of Depression 129
    Managing Depression 132
    Suicide 134
Feeling Good 135
Expanding Your Experience 136
Study Questions 137

Chapter Six
Psychopathology and Seeking Professional Help   *139*
Separating the Wheat from the Chaff

The Components of Psychopathology 141
    Abnormality 141
    Maladaptiveness 143
    Personal or Social Distress 143
    An Example of Psychopathology 144
The *DSM*s: What They Are and Are Not 144

Major Disorders of Adulthood 147
    Anxiety Disorders 147
    Depressive Disorders 149
    Dissociative Disorders 151
    Schizophrenia 152
    Somatoform Disorders 153
    Personality Disorders 155
Psychotherapy 156
    Does Psychotherapy Work? 157
    Psychotherapists 158
    Orientations of Psychotherapy 159
    Alternatives to Individual Psychotherapy 162
    Choosing a Therapist 165
Expanding Your Experience 167
Study Questions 167

Chapter Seven
Physical Self-Care   169
Tending the Body, Nurturing the Mind

Exercise 171
Eating 174
    Eating Styles Leading to Obesity 174
    Undereating 177
    Eating/Noneating 179
Sleep 180
Self-Preservation 183
    Causes of Risk-Taking 183
    Risking Reducing Risk 185
Expanding Your Experience 187
Study Questions 187

Chapter Eight
Substance Use and Abuse   189
Weaving through the Mazes of Altering Consciousness

Substance Classifications 191
    Depressants 191
    Stimulants 192
    Hallucinogens 193

Substance Use Patterns   194
    Alcohol   194
    Caffeine   204
    Nicotine   206
    Illicit Drugs   208
Personal Growth and Substance Abuse   210
    Growing Up in a Substance-Abusing Home   211
    Developing Codependency   213
Expanding Your Experience   215
Study Questions   215

Chapter Nine
Sexuality   217
Dancing in the Moonlight

Understanding Your Sexual Identity   218
Defining Sexuality   219
    Erotic Arousal   220
    Genital Responses   223
    Following the Shared Scripts of Society   226
Sexual Dysfunction   232
Contraception   233
Sexually Transmitted Diseases   235
    AIDS   237
Satisfying Sex   239
Expanding Your Experience   241
Study Questions   242

Chapter Ten
Affiliation   243
The Ties That Bind

Biases: How Do I See Thee? Let Me Count the Ways   256
Finding Friends   258
    Proximity   258
    Similarity   259
    Reciprocity   259
Starting Conversations   260
    Generic Comments   260
    Negativistic Attitude   260
    Self-Absorption   260

Know-It-All Attitude 261
Rigidity 261
Silence 261
Building Blocks of Liking and Loving 264
Intimacy 265
Passion 265
Decision and Commitment 265
Different Types of Love 265
Expanding Your Experience 269
Study Questions 271

CHAPTER ELEVEN
Marriage and Alternative Relationship Lifestyles 273
First Comes Love...

Stages of Marriage 275
The New Couple 275
Having Babies 278
In Come the Adolescents 280
The "Empty Nest" 281
Retirement 281
Success at Marital Relationships 282
Success as Longevity 282
Success as Relationship Qualities 285
Success as Satisfaction 290
Divorce 293
Alternative Lifestyles 294
Staying Single 294
Living Together 295
Homosexual Couples 295
Expanding Your Experience 296
Study Questions 297

CHAPTER TWELVE
Parenting and Family Life 299
Personal Growth: The Next Generation

Do I Want to Have Children? 300
Family Structure 304
Structure 304
Subsystems 304

    Boundaries   305
    Family Dysfunction   306
Parenting   307
Parenting Styles   308
    Permissive and Authoritarian Parenting Styles   308
    Authoritative Parenting   313
Current Child-Rearing Issues   315
    When Both Parents Work   315
    Children and Television   317
    Effects of Divorce on Children   319
    Child Abuse: What It Is and How to Avoid It   321
Expanding Your Experience   322
Study Questions   324

Chapter Thirteen
Work and Play   326
In All Things Be Joyous

Work   327
    Job Satisfaction   328
    Choosing a Career   331
    Life as an Employee   335
How to Become a Workaholic   338
The Type A Behavior Pattern   340
Job Burnout   342
Play   343
    What Is Play?   343
    Why Is Play Important?   344
    How Do We Learn to Play?   346
    The Characteristics of Play   346
    Finding Play   348
Expanding Your Experience   348
Study Questions   349

Chapter Fourteen
Middle Adulthood, Aging, and Dying   351
Ultimate Lessons in Existentiality

Midlife   352
    Midlife as a Stage   353
    Midlife as an Experience   355

Working through Midlife Transition 356
Gender Differences at Midlife 357
Becoming a Senior Citizen 360
Changes during Late Adulthood 360
Adjusting to Old Age 362
Returning to Dependency 366
Dying 368
Dying a Good Death 368
Hospice 369
Euthanasia 369
The Living Will 370
Mourning and Bereavement 371
Expanding Your Experience 372
Study Questions 373

Chapter Fifteen
Perspectives and Objectives 375
Where Do I Take It from Here?

Accomplishing Your Goals 378
Defining and Analyzing Your Goals 380
Prioritizing Your Goals 383
Overcoming Obstacles 386
Goal-Striving or Goal Obsession? 389
Overinvolvement 389
The "Staying Syndrome" 390
Avoiding Goal Obsession 391
Do You Believe in Yourself? 392
Expanding Your Experience 394
Study Questions 394

References 396
Name Index 410
Subject Index 413

Preface

The topic of personal growth and adjustment is unique among courses in psychology. More so than in any other psychology course, students are likely to apply what they learn from their studies to their own personal experiences. Indeed, the material has little meaning or purpose if students find they are unable to apply it. Thus, in addition to facing the usual dilemma of deciding which perspective or perspectives class material will reflect, instructors of personal growth and adjustment must also decide how much emphasis they will place on sharing the basic science and its relevant research base and how much guidance they will provide for applying material toward individual learning. Many different instructional formulas for personal growth and adjustment courses emerge as a result of instructors' wide span of options.

Beginnings & Beyond is organized with the applied orientation in mind and addresses the needs of both students and instructors of such an approach. This freshman- and sophomore-level textbook explains basic concepts of psychology sufficiently for students who have had no other exposure to psychology; yet by means of detailed applications, provides more than a student might already have received in an introductory course. Chapters are relatively free-standing, so that instructors can omit chapters or change the order of assignments to suit their own curricula.

The content benefits from the complementary nature of the differing theoretical orientations of psychology, rather than emphasizing any one perspective or analyzing conflicts between theoretical beliefs. This style creates less confusion for the relatively new student of psychology and also allows for consistency with the many differing orientations instructors may choose. The writing style is kept simple, allowing for ease of reading and making the text ideal for ESL students and the wide range of capabilities found among community college students. At the same time, *Beginnings & Beyond* presents the important basics of usual personal growth topics. Detailed analyses are provided as they enhance the application process, rather than critically as academic exercises or exhaustive representations of the personal adjustment research base. This approach frees students to invest more energy into understanding applications rather than simply memorizing extensive details. Each chapter includes study questions as a means of helping students retain the content of the material. I also make a point of closing each chapter with some of my own personal application experiences in order to provide both a model of self-analysis and additional review of chapter concepts.

However, the most unique feature of this book is the accompanying activity manual, *Expanding Your Experience*. Often when instructors decide to use an applied approach for teaching personal adjustment, they are left to fend for themselves as they search for appropriate applicational activities. Instructors sometimes become dissatisfied with the end results, feeling that their applications may be piecemeal or that they are opening "cans of worms" for students without providing sufficient integration or closure of material.

Expanding Your Experience not only provides numerous exercises and activities for both classroom and individual work, but also organizes them around the concept of the ongoing nature of personal adjustment. Self-application exercises for both a beginning point and an "end" point are included. All activities and exercises are provided on tear-out sheets that are three-hole-punched, so that students can remove them and create a personal activity log from the exercises the instructor chooses to assign. Instructors may also want to provide some of their own favorite exercises for inclusion in their students' personal activity logs. The end result is a product that students can keep with them for living their lives.

The instructor also benefits from the reduced preparation necessary. Since *Expanding Your Experience* activities can easily take up large portions of class time, the instructor can focus on developing lecture material or additional activities that represent his or her special focus areas, leaving the more basic material for reading assignments. In this respect, *Beginnings & Beyond* is especially useful for the first-time instructor of personal adjustment.

The issues of gender and culture are relative newcomers to personal adjustment courses. Of the two, gender has been the most extensively researched. Its considerable research base allows for integration and application of gender considerations throughout the book, especially in the chapters on early, young adult, and later adult development, as well as in the chapters on sexuality and affiliation.

Culture, on the other hand, is more difficult to incorporate. As pointed out by MacPhee, Kreutzer, and Fritz (1994), the formation of solid data on multicultural differences as a basic science is just becoming available; as an applied science, investigations have only just begun. Furthermore, the wide variety of differing cultures that may be represented in any specific classroom creates difficulty for selecting which cultures to include in a textbook. However, as MacPhee et al. have demonstrated, infusing some multicultural content here and there is important, since it can reduce ethnocentric attitudes.

This book therefore addresses the issue of culture with a "multicultural perspective" rather than "multicultural expert" approach (see Soo-Hoo, 1995). Mention of culture within the text is limited. However, *Expanding Your Experience* offers a number of exercises addressing the issue of culture, including some designed around using the multicultural population of a specific classroom as a resource (a few examples are Exercises 2.5, 3.1, and 4.5). I suggest instructors familiarize themselves with material available concerning cultures represented in their classrooms and then use the cultural exploration exercises along with any relevant supplemental readings in order to draw out and validate those differences.

There is a test item file available for *Beginnings & Beyond* to help experienced and novice instructors alike. It consists of 350 multiple-choice questions.

I would like to express my thanks to all who contributed to the production of this project: my colleagues at University of Portland and at Professional Offices for their support and intellectual stimulation; my students/future colleagues for their excellent insights; my Spring 1995 Personal Growth students for helping me explore potential titles; Bill Zuelke, Glenn Watson, and Brynne Chamberlain for their unique contributions; and the reviewers and editors who helped mold the direction of the manuscript: Marsha Beauchamp, Mt. San Antonio College; William Brown, University of Wisconsin–Eau Claire; Kathy Carpenter, University of Nebraska at Kearney; William Cheney, Community College of Rhode Island; Bernard Gorman, Nassau Community College;

Peter Gram, Pensacola Junior College; Bob Helm, Transition Services Inc.; William T. Penrod, Middle Tennessee State University; Jana Preble, St. Cloud State University; Sharon C. Thomas, Miami–Dade Community College; and Deborah S. Weber, The University of Akron. Special thanks to Bill, Frank, Ben, and Bridie for being patient and supportive during this developmental detour of mine; and all those who passed before me on my journey, providing the shoulders upon which I stand.

REFERENCES

MacPhee, D., Kreutzer, J., & Fritz, J. (1994). Infusing a diversity perspective into human development courses. *Child Development, 65,* 699–715.

Soo-Hoo, T. (1995). The multicultural perspective vs. the multicultural expert. *The Family Psychologist, 11,* 31–32.

Laurel Hughes

CHAPTER ONE

Introduction

What Does It Mean to Be "Well-Adjusted"?

*Remember how simple
life used to be?*

That's a question likely to cross our minds each time we face the awe, challenge, and frustration of another of life's many changes. Each new stage of living presents us with challenging new life tasks that make our earlier adventures seem low-key. How frighteningly that first bicycle loomed before us until, depending precariously on our sense of balance, we learned to avoid bruised shins and scraped knees! Yet when we reach the time to move away from home and begin new lives, the fears surrounding that childhood bicycle-riding experience pale by comparison. Most of us do eventually master the art of bicycle riding and come to take it for granted as it becomes an enjoyable and exciting part of our early lives. Likewise, enjoying personal independence and appreciating the rewards of our life activities also one day seem natural and expected.

Life also becomes more complex for us as we adjust to the many rapid changes taking place in our society. Technology has progressed so far that fewer and fewer people actually understand the workings of the many contraptions we all have come to depend upon. Our government's operations become more and more complicated with every new administration. Because world travel has become so much easier, we have increased contact with the other societies sharing this planet, and this presents new complications: the need to understand languages and social rules of many different cultures, dependence on a world economy rather than on a local economy, more rapid spread of disease and distribution of illegal drugs, and fear of hostile action from societies far beyond our borders.

Defining Good Adjustment

As we respond to these new challenges, our personal behavior and society itself changes. Thus our lives will always be changing, as we react to the internal pressures of new developmental tasks and tackle the external challenges introduced by our ever-evolving society. **Personal adjustment** is the process of rising to the occasion of these events. We can consider ourselves "well-adjusted" when we are able successfully to "adjust" ourselves to such internal and external developments. When we succeed, we are more likely to find our lives satisfying and rewarding, both for ourselves and for our society.

Personal adjustment is an ongoing affair. Completing a course in personal growth will not enable you to wake up one morning and say, "Look at me! I've made it!" You will always be growing older, and society will always be changing. Personal adjustment is better defined as an adaptation process than as a goal to be met: We continually adapt ourselves to our changing internal needs and external realities.

The concept of ongoing adjustment can be difficult to grasp for those coming of age within current Western culture. Because we live in a goal-oriented society, our choices of behavior are often motivated by focusing on the end product we wish to attain. For example, we try to do well in class in order to get a good grade; we go to work in order to earn money; we try hard to excel at our jobs in order to get raises or promotions; we play the dating game in order to find a significant other. And, when we are reaching for concrete goals such as these, having a goal orientation serves as an excellent form of motivation.

But to become well-adjusted demands a different type of goal. You will not be striving toward a certain set of behaviors, social roles, or personality types that will ensure automatic success at everything you do. Well-adjusted people are not necessarily those who have demonstrated a high level of intelligence, displayed physical attractiveness and magnetic personalities, won the most awards, achieved the greatest accomplishments, or earned the most money and notoriety.

Every generation has seen its share of celebrities who have ended their lives in despair. Witness the early ending to the life of Kurt Cobain of the rock group *Nirvana*. Despite the fact that most of us would love to have had the benefits of his lifestyle, those benefits did not turn out to be enough to keep Cobain living. A poem that was later put to music in the seventies by Simon and Garfunkel also illustrates this confusing contradiction. *Richard Corey* (Robinson, 1950) narrates the observations of a blue-collar worker who envies the position and personal characteristics of Richard Corey, the owner of the factory in which the worker labors. The worker believes Mr. Corey must be happy, considering all he has attained and is stunned when he hears that Mr. Corey has committed suicide. Nevertheless, the worker goes on to curse his own life and wish he could be like Richard Corey. Of course, what the worker fails to note is that he himself is still living–dreaming, working, and aspiring–whereas Richard Corey's life has ended.

While "fame, fun, and fortune" can abolish a number of the worries that can make living difficult, they cannot make life *worth* living. Happiness, contentment, and life satisfaction are experienced in the here and now as a result of feeling whole, self-accepting, personally competent, and able to meet life's challenges as they arise, regardless of current social accomplishments and predicaments. Richard Corey had every concrete acquisition we might desire. However, he had not developed the internal stability that motivated his factory worker to continue living and striving in spite of all the externals he wished he had but did not.

Consistent with such a process-oriented view of adjustment is the Global Assessment of Functioning Scale from the *Diagnostic and Statistical Manual of Mental Disorders* (American Psychiatric Association, 1994) (see Figure 1.1). This scale presents personal adjustment as a continuum, observing a person's psychological, social, and occupational functioning. As you can see, it does not focus on a certain personality type or static set of personal characteristics. Instead, it describes how a person is functioning at a particular moment, given the individual's internal experience and how that experience expresses itself as the person interacts with his or her environment.

This book is organized not only around helping you understand personal growth and adjustment but also toward applying what you learn to your own growth process. During your pursuit of personal adjustment you will be striving toward a healthy internal experience, a way of "being." You will be developing a repertoire of personal behaviors, coping mechanisms, attitudes, and beliefs that can be applied during the changes that occur throughout your life span to provide you with a sense of personal competence, as well as meaning and purpose for your life pursuits.

Healthy Adjustment and the Perspectives of Psychology

If you have already taken an introductory psychology course, you are aware that there are different orientations of psychology. These differing orientations look at the same phenomena from different angles—often referred to as "perspectives"—and, as a result, come up with many alternative ways of explaining human thinking and behavior. As might be expected, the differing perspectives of psychology offer different descriptions of healthy adjustment. The following sections explain these different ways of looking at a healthy state of being. Future chapters will show how the different perspectives of psychology contribute to other personal adjustment concepts as well.

Global Assessment of Functioning (GAF) Scale

Consider psychological, social, and occupational functioning on a hypothetical continuum of mental health-illness. Do not include impairment in functioning due to physical (or environmental) limitations.

Code (Note: Use intermediate codes when appropriate, e.g., 45, 68, 72.)

100 | **Superior functioning in a wide range of activities, life's problems never seem to get out of hand, is sought out by others because of his or her many positive qualities. No symptoms.**
91

90 | Absent or minimal symptoms (e.g., mild anxiety before an exam), **good functioning in all areas, interested and involved in a wide range of activities, socially effective, generally satisfied with life, no more than everyday problems or concerns** (e.g., an occasional argument with family members).
81

80 | If symptoms are present, they are transient and expectable reactions to psychosocial stressors (e.g., difficulty concentrating after family argument); **no more than slight impairment in social, occupational, or school functioning** (e.g., temporarily falling behind in schoolwork).
71

70 | Some mild symptoms (e.g., depressed mood and mild insomnia) **OR some difficulty in social, occupational, or school functioning** (e.g., occasional truancy, or theft within the household), **but generally functioning pretty well, has some meaningful interpersonal relationships.**
61

60 | Moderate symptoms (e.g., flat affect and circumstantial speech, occasional panic attacks) **OR moderate difficulty in social, occupational, or school functioning** (e.g., few friends, conflicts with peers or co-workers).
51

50 | Serious symptoms (e.g., suicidal ideation, severe obsessional rituals, frequent shoplifting) **OR any serious impairment in social, occupational, or school functioning** (e.g., no friends, unable to keep a job).
41

40 | Some impairment in reality testing or communication (e.g., speech is at times illogical, obscure, or irrelevant) **OR major impairment in several areas, such as work or school, family relations, judgment, thinking, or mood** (e.g., depressed man avoids friends, neglects family, and is unable to work; child frequently beats up younger children, is defiant at home, and is failing at school).
31

30 | Behavior is considerably influenced by delusions or hallucinations **OR serious impairment in communication or judgment** (e.g., sometimes incoherent, acts grossly inappropriately, suicidal preoccupation) **OR inability to function in almost all areas** (e.g., stays in bed all day; no job, home, or friends).
21

20 | Some danger of hurting self or others (e.g., suicide attempts without clear expectation of death; frequently violent; manic excitement) **OR occasionally fails to maintain minimal personal hygiene** (e.g., smears feces) **OR gross impairment in communication** (e.g., largely incoherent or mute).
11

10 | **Persistent danger of severely hurting self or others** (e.g., recurrent violence) **OR persistent inability to maintain minimal personal hygiene OR serious suicidal act with clear expectation of death.**
1

0 | Inadequate information.

FIGURE 1.1

Reprinted by permission of the American Psychiatric Association (1994).

The Psychodynamic Perspective

The psychodynamic model of mental health originated with the theories of Sigmund Freud (1914). He believed that how well we get along in the world depends on how well we deal with internal conflicts. These internal conflicts arise due to interactions between three systems of the mind, which he called id, superego, and ego.

According to psychodynamic theory, the **id** is the biologically determined part of our personality. It is for the most part made up of instincts, one of the most important ones being the **libido.** The libido encourages us to work toward self-preservation and was believed by Freud to be sexually driven. The id is completely self-centered and unsocialized. Like an infant, the id thinks only of its own needs. While the workings of the id are always unconscious, id impulses nevertheless insistently and indiscriminately seek some kind of expression in the outside world. The id does serve a positive purpose, since we need a sense of self-preservation in order to survive. But if left unchecked, our id impulses could cause our behavior to become very immature, self-centered, and unsocialized.

The **superego** is made up of the societal values we have chosen to adopt. It is made up of two main components: the **conscience** and the **ego-ideal.** Your conscience is a collection of moral values you have either consciously or subconsciously identified as being your own. As a result, your conscience makes you feel guilty when you have done something you believe to be wrong. Your ego-ideal is what you aspire to be, what you would judge to be the ideal person. When you succeed in behaving consistently with the characteristics of your ego-ideal, you feel good about yourself.

The main function of the superego is to counterbalance the urges of the id and strive toward positive personal goals. Although this is for the most part a positive function, it also has its drawbacks. Some people can develop a **severe superego,** having standards that are excessively high. They often torment themselves over any perceived slight failure, unrelentingly driving on toward unrealistic perfectionism, or perhaps they decide to just give up.

The **ego** mediates between the id's impulses and the superego's moralism as it chooses solutions on the basis of current realities in the environment. As conflict arises between the id and superego, we experience anxiety. We cope with this anxiety by developing a variety of **defense mechanisms,** which serve the purpose of reducing anxiety, as well as defining our personal styles of reaction and adaptation. Our logic and ability to reason reside within the ego and help us select defense mechanisms and other styles of coping as we deal with our own unique id impulses, superego demands, and the restrictions of reality.

So, according to Freud, a healthy person is one whose defense mechanisms are sufficiently numerous, sophisticated, and appropriately applied. When this is the case, the person is able to meet the variety of challenges created by the internal demands of the id, the societal demands represented by the superego, and the realities currently presenting themselves in the environment. When the conflicts, anxieties, and challenges are successfully managed, Freud believed, happiness and contentment are found, and the person is able to successfully pursue both loving and working.

THE BEHAVIORAL PERSPECTIVE

The behavioral perspective looks at those aspects of mental health that involve learned ways of reacting. Thus being well-adjusted is a form of being well-behaved, or learning to react in ways that are adaptive. We learn behaviors by means of several types of learning processes. Three main behavioral learning strategies are classical conditioning, operant conditioning, and observational learning.

The discovery of **classical conditioning** is usually credited to Ivan Pavlov (1928). He was feeding dogs at intervals as he was performing some experiments involving salivation. He used a bell to signify when it was time for his subjects to be fed and found that after a while all he had to do was ring the bell for the dogs to start salivating. In other words, he discovered that if one stimulus (such as food) is paired with a second stimulus (such as a bell) the second stimulus will produce the same response (salivation in this case) as the first stimulus.

Most fears are believed to have their roots in unfortunate pairings of this nature. John Watson and Rosalie Rayner (1920) looked at the origins of learned fears in a collection of studies best known as "Albert and the White Rat." Albert, a 1-year-old boy, was allowed to play with a tame white rat, which he thoroughly enjoyed. During subsequent trials, the experimenters frightened Albert with a loud noise every time the rat was presented. After a while Albert began to act fearful whenever the rat appeared, even though the scary noise was absent. They also found Albert would act fearful when they presented him with other white furry objects, such as a wad of cotton or a Santa Claus mask. This phenomenon became known as **stimulus generalization.**

We often have a hard time figuring out how we became afraid of an object or situation. The experience that caused the fear can be too far back in the past for us to remember it. Also, because of the role played by stimulus generalization, the original conditioning may be too dissimilar from the current stimulus for us to be able to recognize the connection.

Good feelings also can result from classical conditioning. One example is the popularity that "Golden Oldie" music holds with people who came of age during the music's original era. The periods of adolescence and young adulthood involve exciting, stimulating experiences. Each new generation of young people in our culture listens to their own style of music as they make their passage into adulthood. In later years, listening to that music lets many people—no longer young—recapture those early feelings of excitement.

Operant conditioning, most extensively studied by B. F. Skinner (1938), shows how behavior is learned through reinforcers and punishers. A **reinforcer** is anything that gets us to repeat a behavior. If you study hard for a test and get a good grade, you will likely study hard for future tests, since you have learned that studying can earn the reinforcer of a good grade. This is known as **positive reinforcement.** We also repeat behaviors that get rid of something we find unpleasant. If the alarm clock buzzes and you find that the buzzing stops when you push a certain button, you will continue to push that button whenever the alarm goes off. This is known as **negative reinforcement. Punishers,** on the other hand, are stimuli that cause us to avoid certain behaviors. For example, if you break the speed limit and receive a traffic ticket resulting in a hefty fine, you are more likely to avoid speeding in the future.

Observational learning, as described by Albert Bandura (1973), is learning by means of watching others. Bandura performed many studies involving children watching role models and copying their actions. For example, when he showed children films of a person acting aggressively, he found that they were much more likely to perform those same acts of aggression themselves. He also discovered that the children were observing more than just the acts of aggression. They also made note of what happened to the role model after the aggressive behavior. If the role model was shown as receiving punishment, the children were less likely to copy the aggressive behavior. This is called **vicarious punishment.** Likewise, if the role model was shown earning rewards for the aggression, the children were more likely to try the behavior themselves. This is called **vicarious reinforcement.**

Much of our everyday learning centers on observing others. We copy the behavior of people we admire, hoping to become more like them. While in school we learn procedures such as mathematical calculations and diagramming sentences by watching the instructor do them first.

Throughout life, whenever we want to learn something new, one of the first things we are likely to do is find someone who already has the desired skills, so we can benefit by observing him or her.

So from a behavioral point of view, well-adjusted people are those who have learned a sufficient number of adaptive behaviors and can apply them appropriately. Several factors affect our ability to learn and apply adaptive behavior. First, we need to have an awareness of the consequences of our actions, so we can judge whether our behavior gets us what we want or helps us avoid what we don't want. Second, we need to be observant enough to recognize how the reinforcers in our environments are actually earned. Third, we need to have a certain degree of self-control, so that we can make ourselves perform the behaviors that get us the rewards and avoid behaviors that cause us unpleasantness. When these variables are in place, we can both learn new behaviors and effectively use them to achieve our goals in an adaptive, well-adjusted manner.

The Cognitive Perspective

Cognitive psychologists study how our thought processes can affect how we feel and behave. One of the earliest cognitive psychologists, George Kelly (1955), believed that our minds are made up of **constructs,** each construct evaluating the world according to two poles of a single dimension. For example, using the dimension of justice, we can evaluate a behavior as fair or unfair. Using the dimension of intelligence, we might evaluate a person as being either bright or lacking in substance.

Kelly believed that our personalities are a collection of these types of evaluating constructs. We appear to function better when we use a wide variety of them. When we use fewer constructs, our reasoning processes become limited. We are more likely to automatically assume that others think the same way we do, and we also tend to be less accurate in our predictions about the future (Bieri, 1955). Having few available constructs can also lead us to view things in terms of extremes, thus leaving us less able to consider the more usual gray areas (Linville, 1982).

Cognitive psychotherapists focus on how the extreme polarizations of some of these dimensions can affect our state of mind. Aaron Beck (1976) explains how the polar direction we use when we interpret our surroundings can cause us to experience certain emotions. Suppose you passed a friend on the street and she did not return your greeting. You could tell yourself, "she really doesn't like me," and as a result feel depressed. You have no proof that this is what she is thinking; you are simply interpreting the situation in the negative direction. According to Beck, you could just as easily decide to interpret the event in a positive light, perhaps saying to yourself, "she surely must be preoccupied with something to not notice me," and as a result not have such feelings of depression. The ability to stand back, look at how we are interpreting a situation, and question the validity of our interpretations can therefore be an asset to our emotional well-being.

Albert Ellis (1971) points out that how we philosophically evaluate such situations also can affect how we feel. If you endorse such philosophies as "people must treat me fairly," and "this is awful, and I must never experience such discomfort," you are likely to feel miserable when your friend does not respond to your greeting. A more positive and accepting philosophy, such as one emphasizing the fact that we all really can cope with and accept the occasional adversities of daily living, will not result in those same miserable feelings.

Cognitive-behavioral psychologists, such as Donald Meichenbaum (1977), look at how our feelings then intermingle with our choices of behavior. If you sit around and stew about how your friend has drastically wronged you, you might choose from a selection of behaviors such as telling her off, ignoring her the next time you see her, or angrily complaining to everyone else about how rude she is. If you decide she is simply preoccupied, you will probably forget about the incident; or you may become concerned about her distractedness and ask her about it. Thus how we interpret what is going on around us affects not only our internal state of being but also the adaptiveness of the behaviors we choose as we interact with our world.

So the cognitive perspective assesses personal adjustment in terms of how we organize our thought lives. Developing a positive attitude, expanding the number of evaluative constructs we use, and making use of our ability to question and rearrange our beliefs in an objective manner all contribute to a well-adjusted state of being.

The Existentialist/Humanistic Perspective

The existentialist and humanistic psychologies focus on the immediate human experience. This perspective respects the effects of past experience on who we become and how we behave, as is taught by other orientations. However, the humanistic and existentialist psychologies place their emphasis on what we are experiencing in the present. How we see ourselves, our decision-making processes, and what we experience as being personally fulfilling are all experienced in the here and now. And, after all, life takes place in the present.

Carl Rogers (1951, 1959) taught that, in spite of the various forms of past learning that might affect our internal impulses or behavioral choices, we ultimately have the free will to choose what we will believe or do. We feel best about ourselves when our choices are consistent with our "ideal selves," the persons we would like to be. When our "real selves" are consistent with our ideal selves, we experience a state of inner **congruence.** Depending too much on past or present opinions and expectations of others can interfere with our ability to trust our perceptions of what *we* believe or would like for ourselves, as well as our ability to experience congruence.

Our sense of congruence develops from several influences. First, we must experience awareness of who we are at the moment, such as how we currently express our personalities, how we feel at any given moment, our personal values, and our likes and dislikes. Second, we need to experience our **potentialities,** the basic inborn capacities within which our abilities are framed. Once we experience our sense of potential and become aware of its consistencies and inconsistencies with our current state of being, our **actualizing tendency** drives us toward growing into our potentialities and becoming more like our ideal selves, ultimately striving toward **self-actualization.**

Abraham Maslow (1970) describes in detail the characteristics of self-actualized individuals. Those who are self-actualized experience others, the self, and the world with an attitude of acceptance. They experience a deep caring for the human race, have a strong sense of right and wrong, and do not feel bound by cultural conventions as they behave independently and consistently with their values. Self-actualized individuals enjoy solitude and have a need for privacy but also enjoy having profound and deeply felt relationships with a relatively small number of close friends. Because of their objectivity, self-actualized individuals perceive people and situations accurately, and are effective problem solvers. Their internal experience is characterized by a continued freshness of appreciation for the simple pleasures of living, as well as a sense of awe over the complexities and potentialities of the human experience.

Our spirituality is closely tied to the existential perspective. The concept of spirituality has been given a "bad rap" in recent years, mainly because people often interpret it as being synonymous with going to church, believing in God, and so on. It appears not everyone is cut out for stereotypical organized religion. However, church involvement and organized worship are only one way of experiencing spirituality. **Spirituality** is our ability to transcend our individual day-to-day strivings and instead experience our feelings of connectedness with others of our species, with life in general, or with existence itself. You have most likely experienced your own spirituality on a number of occasions, perhaps when you have been out in the wilderness, performed an act of altruism, or had an especially meaningful meeting of the minds with another person.

Our spirituality's state of health parallels a portion of the congruence between our real and ideal selves. If the practice of our faith—whatever form it may take—begins to feel inconsistent with what our spiritual selves are telling us, we will struggle. Also, spiritual difficulties can erupt when we lose, or begin questioning, aspects of our practice of spirituality; converting to a new religion or being introduced to a new set of spiritual values can cause a temporary loss of the spiritually whole feeling.

So the existentialist/humanistic perspective focuses on those aspects of good adjustment that involve how we experience ourselves in the here and now. Well-adjusted individuals are those who strive toward self-actualization and freely seek congruency between who they are and who they would like to be. And they have the ability to experience a general sense of acceptance and contentment, regardless of their current circumstances.

The Biological Perspective

Personal adjustment research is currently in hot pursuit of the answer to the question of how much an individual's eventual personal growth and adjustment is influenced by biological factors. **Heritability,** or the likelihood that you will have certain growth experiences based on the set of genes you inherited, is appearing more and more to play a role in certain aspects of emotional development and personality traits. Another branch of research has been investigating the presence of hormones, enzymes, and other physiological substances in relation to our psychological responding, as well as studying actual differences found in the brain itself. Yet other research has been turning the telescope around and looking at the biological changes that occur in response to our behaviors and thinking patterns. The fruits of these investigations will be described in many of the upcoming chapters of this text.

The biological perspective has not focused much on developing a model of good mental health adjustment. It is probably most useful in helping us successfully apply our understanding of mind-body connections and becoming familiar with the individual attributes we may have at our disposal as we work through personal growth challenges.

A Synthesized Theory of Good Adjustment

The varying perspectives of psychology though conflicting in how they explain how we function are nevertheless complementary in their explanations of personal adjustment. When the teachings of the psychodynamic, behavioral, cognitive, and existentialist/humanistic perspectives are combined, four dimensions to personal adjustment appear to emerge: the inner self, the outer or public self, the interpersonal self, and the spiritual self.

The inner self, represented by our thoughts and feelings, is the most important component of healthy adjustment. Well-adjusted individuals experience a strong sense of identity—they know who they are and have a sense of what they would like to become. As they strive in the direction of their potential, they have a positive, rather than pessimistic or fearful, attitude toward themselves. They maintain healthy flexibility and are willing to question their own beliefs in ways that make room for learning, growth, and striving throughout their lives.

The outer self, or how we interact with the environment, is characterized by independence of the will. While factors in the environment may teach us to think, feel, and behave in certain ways, we all have the ability to choose which teachings of the environment we accept and which we reject. Well-adjusted individuals, rather than finding themselves bound by the environment, rely on their objectivity and their own internal standards and values. They therefore make decisions and choose appropriate behaviors effectively.

The interpersonal self relates to others with sensitivity and perceives them as who they are rather than creations of a rigid set of biases. Well-adjusted individuals are able to love, work, and play with others. They are skilled at interacting with those who share their environment in ways that both meet their own needs and respect the rights and needs of others.

Spiritually, the well-adjusted person can set aside hurts of the past and goals of the future long enough to experience existence in the here and now. It can come in the form of being in awe of the vastness and power of the ocean, becoming entranced by the vibrant colorings of a wild flower, feeling a deep sense of oneness with fellow human beings, or meditating upon the wonder of the grace of God. The well-adjusted person has the ability to transcend the constraints of daily pressures and appreciate this sense of inner peace, continuity, and contentment.

Investigating Personal Adjustment

As should be clear by now, my approach to studying personal adjustment is based upon investigations within the field of psychology. Psychology has built its knowledge base by using the investigative powers of scientific method. Since most of this text is based on the scientific findings of the study of psychology, scientific method plays a major role in what will follow.

But why go to all the trouble involved with scientific method? Just by looking around us, we can observe human nature in action. Why do we need fancy methods of data-gathering when everybody can figure out psychological truths just on the basis of their life experiences?

Scientific method is actually little more than systematically learning from common sense and life observations. The advantage of using scientific method is that you can be more certain of what you are observing.

For example, let's say a friend of yours, Harry, decides that doing push-ups before he goes to class will improve his ability to learn. He begins doing push-ups every morning, and over several weeks you notice that he does seem to be getting better grades. You begin to wonder if doing push-ups really does make a difference in the ability to learn.

However, the users of scientific method would still be extremely skeptical. There are many other factors that could explain the apparent improvement in Harry's ability to learn. Using scientific method allows you to **control** your experimental situation so that you will be less likely to be led astray by the effects of these additional factors. Following are some questions that a scientist might ask, having observed Harry's experiment, and some of the adjustments a scientist might make in order to control for unwanted influences.

• *Could it be that Harry's learning would have increased anyway, regardless of his exercising habits?* This question shows the scientist's concern about the effects of **history.** In an experiment, history refers to anything that might have been happening in Harry's life during the time he was doing the push-ups. For example, what if he had started doing the push-ups right after attending a seminar on study skills? The effect of the seminar, rather than the push-ups, could then have been responsible for the improvement. One common method used to control for the effects of history is to test more than one person. While it is indeed possible that attending a study skills seminar could affect the results of Harry's experiment, it is unlikely that a group of 100 subjects would all have attended such a seminar during the time of the experiment. Thus any increase in learning because of the seminar would become negligible when averaged together with measurement of the other 99 subjects.

A scientist asking this question might also be concerned about the effects of **maturation.** Maturation refers to changes that could happen by way of natural growth and learning during the same period of time Harry was performing push-ups. After all, we tend to improve any skill with practice. The longer Harry attends any given class the more likely he will be to figure out the ins and outs of succeeding in it. The effects of maturation are usually controlled for by measuring two groups of subjects: one that does the push-ups, known as the **experimental group,** and one that does not, known as the **control group.** If both groups show the same amount of improvement, Harry would know that the push-ups were not responsible for any increase in learning.

• *Could it be that Harry's improvement in learning occurred because of something unique about Harry rather than something that is true of everybody?* Suppose Harry suffers from a neurological disorder that makes waking up in the morning very difficult for him and doing push-ups stimulates his brain into wakefulness. The improvement in learning would still be a true improvement for Harry, but his findings would be useless for anybody else. Scientists control for such individual differences by using a process called **random selection.** They select subjects out of the population as randomly as they can, such as choosing every other person on a list of volunteers, calling every tenth person listed in the phone book, and so on. This way they can be sure that their findings represent the effects of treatment on a wide variety of individuals and are not dependent upon the idiosyncracies of one particular subject.

- *What makes you so sure that you did see an improvement in learning?* In other words, how much objectivity is involved in your observations? It could be that your observations are being flavored by **experimenter bias,** better known as "you find what you are looking for." If you know that Harry is doing push-ups for the purpose of improving learning, you are likely to look for evidence of learning ability that you might not have been looking for before he started doing the push-ups. It could be that Harry had always been a "quick study," but you had never noticed this trait until you started watching him more closely. A scientist would control for experimenter bias by performing the study **"blind."** In other words, the scientist would not know which subjects in the study were doing the push-ups and which were not. So as the scientist observed the subject's learning ability, his or her observations would not be swayed by personal expectations.

- *Could it be that Harry's beliefs about doing push-ups are responsible for his improvement?* If we believe that something will affect us a certain way, sometimes that faith alone is enough to result in the expected outcome. In experimental research, this is called a **placebo effect.** Scientists can control for placebo effects by performing the experiment in a **"double-blind"** manner. In double-blind experiments, neither the subjects nor the scientists know who is getting the treatment that is expected to produce certain results. Often a **placebo group** is used, where the control group receives some arbitrary treatment other than the one being investigated. Since both groups receive a treatment of some sort, both groups' expectations of improvement should be about equal.

- *How do you know that the improvement was due to the push-ups, and not due to chance?* We all have our good days and bad days. How do we know that Harry's apparent improvement in learning is more than just normal fluctuations in performance? In other words, is the improvement really large enough for us to say that it is significant? Scientists answer these questions by using **predictive statistics.** Predictive statistics, also known as inferential statistics, are designed to tell us the probability of any differences we find being due to the experimental treatment, or due to chance. There are many forms of predictive statistics a scientist might choose from, depending on the experimental design. If the scientist applied the appropriate statistic and found that the results were **statistically significant,** he or she could more accurately infer that the experimental treatment (doing push-ups) does have an effect on the observed outcome (amount of learning).

In summary, scientific method involves human observation, just as all of us observe what is going on around us. However, it organizes our observations so that variables such as history, maturation, experimenter bias, and placebo effects are controlled for, and uses predictive statistics for determining how significant our observations are. Such organization allows for greater accuracy as we try to make sense out of the human experience.

Yet, even though scientific method can help sort out our observations, applying these findings to your personal life is an art form. No scientific method exists that will tell you exactly what is right for you. Facts do not tell you what to do; they simply tell you what is likely to happen if you do it. The knowledge of probabilities of various outcomes provided by scientific method is an aid to developing our life choices, not an end in itself.

Am I Normal?

Many of my psychotherapy clients approach me with this concern. Sometimes I try to explain that the adaptiveness of a person's feelings, attitudes, or behaviors is the most important element of adjustment. Yet no matter how hard I try to be clear on this point, people continue to seek some form of validation of how "normal" they are.

The concept of "normal" is similar to what we find within the principles of **descriptive statistics.** Any human characteristic can be observed and evaluated according to how often or rarely it occurs. Descriptive statistics are designed to systematically evaluate such frequencies.

For example, suppose we were curious about how many hours people typically sleep at night. First, we could perform a telephone survey, asking a large number of people how many hours they generally sleep at night. Then, we could apply our grade-school training of taking an arithmetic average from a set of scores: Add them, then divide the sum by the total number of scores. Let's say we calculated an average, known in statistics as a *mean,* of 7.25 hours of sleep per night. On the basis of this calculation, we can say that, typically, people sleep about 7.25 hours per night.

INTRODUCTION: WHAT DOES IT MEAN TO BE "WELL-ADJUSTED"?   19

But of all the people surveyed, how many actually sleep for 7.25 hours? Perhaps 5%? If we said that the arithmetic average defines what is normal, we would then be saying that 95% of human beings are abnormal, which is neither useful nor accurate.

The statistic is set up so that just about all scores are represented when you look within four standard deviations above or below the mean, as illustrated in Figure 1.2. For example, let's say the standard deviation for data gathered from the sleeping survey was calculated to have a value of 1 hour. This knowledge tells us that most every score in the survey falls somewhere between 3.25 hours (7−4 = 3.25) and 11.25 hours (7 + 4 = 11.25).

But we are looking for what is normal. And since only an extremely rare score will fall outside of four standard deviations from the mean, we need some other way of defining normal scoring. For the sake of argument, let's arbitrarily say that we believe "normal" is what 95% of the population does and that scores falling within the 2.5 percentage points above or below that 95% are considered abnormal. As you can see from Figure 1.2, standard deviations are designed in such a way that we can say 95% of all scores fall within two standard deviations above or below

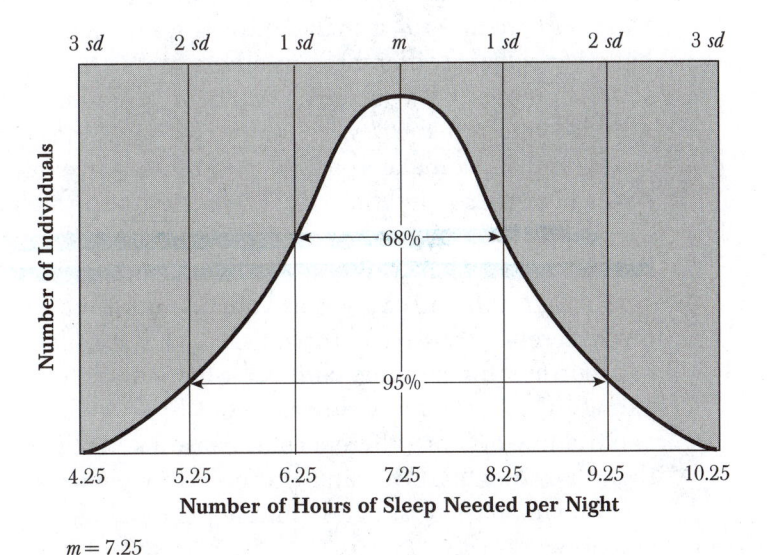

$m = 7.25$
$sd = 1$

FIGURE 1.2
Example of a normal curve.

the mean. By using the 95% rule, we could decide whether any single score is normal by checking to see if it falls within two standard deviations of the mean.

Now, suppose your score falls within one of the bands of scores that we decided to call "abnormal." Is this a good reason to catastrophize, seeing yourself as a reject or misfit of some sort? Certainly not. You see, we all score outside of that middle 95% on at least a few attributes. There are so many diverse ways to classify and evaluate thoughts, feelings, behaviors, and other human attributes, that we're all going to be a little different in some respects. Human beings are not stamped out by templates. Each of us is unique. In fact, despite our concerns about fitting in with everybody else, our unique differences are what we tend to value most about ourselves, as well as about those individuals with whom we choose to develop close relationships. Thus all of us have abnormal traits, but that does not make us abnormal people. We might even go so far as to say that abnormality is in fact normal!

Accompanying this book are a number of scales you can use to measure a variety of personal characteristics. Chances are very good you will find your score within ranges outside of what is normally found. Many students worry that scoring within the normal range makes them "good" and scoring outside the norm makes them somehow "bad." This is a value judgment, and a maladaptive one at that. Discovering that you have a trait that is different from others simply points out one of your personal differences. If you decide that being different is "bad," it is certainly a choice you have the right to make. However, the choice of such a belief is guaranteed to make your life miserable, since you are bound to discover your personal differences as you work through this textbook.

A healthier way to evaluate the personal differences you find is by looking at how adaptively they are fitting into your current lifestyle. Assessing our differences gives us valuable information. To what extent do our differences cause us problems, to what extent are they irrelevant to our current functioning, and to what extent can we view them as strengths? How might we arrange our lifestyles and beliefs in ways that avoid allowing our differences to cause us problems and capitalize on them as strengths? We can't promote our personal growth and adjustment if we do not first figure out the personal ingredients we have available to work with.

As an example, let's say you are one of the people in the sleep experiment who gets by with an abnormally small amount of sleep. This can be an asset when you are trying to put in long hours of studying the week before finals. However, it can become a problem if your roommate is a member of the small percentage of people who need much more sleep than average and your meandering about as you study disturbs his or her sleep. Calling each other "abnormal" and becoming upset will not resolve the difficulty. Neither is it likely that either one of you will be able to significantly change the innate causes of your sleep urges anyway. However, you could use recognition of your individual differences as an impetus to arrange your habits in a way that works out for both of you. For example, you could avoid engaging in activity that disturbs your roommate during periods designated as "sleeping time," and your roommate could refrain from expecting to take undisturbed naps during times that are officially designated as "study time." Or, if worse comes to worst, you can always trade roommates so that you each end up with a roommate whose sleep needs are more like your own. Either way, both of your differing needs are respected and adaptively met.

The Role of Values

Since we are all different, we all have different ideas about what would be the most desirable direction for human striving. Overall goals and what we consider to be important in life are known as **values.** Freedom, honesty, and equality are examples of values that guide many people in the choices they make. Pursuing personal growth, making a lot of money, good health, and becoming famous are goals that reflect individual values. A list of common values is presented in Table 1.1.

Rokeach (1968) believes that our attitudes play a role in our selection of values. He also believes that our value system is designed to enhance our self-regard. By understanding our values, we are better able to consistently design our choices according to what we consider to be important, thus helping us to like and respect ourselves.

While making choices consistent with our values helps develop our sense of congruency, sometimes our hands may be tied. Suppose you are employed by an organization that has an unfair hiring practice. You approach the administrators and explain your position, but they do not agree with you. You do not like working for an organization that you perceive to be unfair, since the work you choose reflects on your own self-perception. You could quit your job, but then you would lose a job you enjoyed; and the unfairness would still be occurring whether you work there or not.

Table 1.1
A List of Common Values

Abstract values	Goals representing values
The work ethic	Having a lot of money
Honesty	Becoming famous
Responsibility	Owning a BMW
Equality	Volunteerism
Intelligence/Logic	Making important contributions
Modesty	Inventing something new
Power	Raising a family
Morality	Worshipping regularly
Individualism	Spending time with nature
Spontaneity	Excelling at work
Creativity	Traveling
Innovation	Having a good time
Personal growth	Finding that special someone
Altruism	Supporting the armed forces
Ambition	Demonstrating against the armed forces
Beauty	Creating an artistic work
Free enterprise	Exercising regularly

Our values are better viewed as standards for guiding our behavior, rather than goals that must be met. We can attempt to change the things that go against our values, but at other times the most adaptive choice will be to accept the situation. We cannot control the choices of others, and demanding that others always do whatever is consistent with our personal values will only become an exercise in frustration. And part of accepting one's self is also being able to accept others for who they are and the choices they make for themselves, regardless of whether their behavior meets our own personal standards. The role of values in personal adjustment is not one of forcing society into behaving consistently with our values. Instead, it is learning to keep peace within ourselves as we make our own personal choices throughout our life spans.

Expanding Your Experience

Psychology is a personal science. One way or another, its findings apply to us all. I made my own personal discovery of psychology when I was about 10. My parents subscribed to a book club that sold a series of volumes covering the various sciences. My favorite volume was the one on psychology. I was fascinated by illustrations depicting the oddities of perception, such as optical illusions. How interesting, I considered, that I can share both perceptions and misperceptions with others.

Later as a graduate student in psychology, cognition and perception were my least-enjoyed fields of study, even though the instructor was one of the most competent and entertaining in the school (which is probably what saved my grade!). However, my original lesson in personal application held fast. I considered whatever I gleaned from my studies as information that applied to me personally, rather than as a collection of facts to be chewed then spewed during finals week.

The fields of personal growth and adjustment are especially tied to personal application. This book will no doubt raise many questions for you concerning who you are, where you are coming from, and where you are heading. As a means of helping you sort out these questions, I have taken two approaches. First, I teach through example. At the conclusion of each chapter I have included some of my own experiences with integrating or personally applying my studies of psychology. Second, I have created a "lab book" of sorts that accompanies the material presented by this book. It contains a number of exercises that are designed to help you apply your learning to observations of yourself and the world around you. Some require individual work, many use a small-group format, and others invite whole-class involvement. These exercises can be saved separately as a journal or "personal activity log," that you can keep with you even if you choose to sell your textbook back to the bookstore.

The exercises for applying Chapter 1 of this text begin by helping you evaluate first impressions as well as get used to your fellow classmates. After all, you are probably going to get to know these individuals more intimately than classmates in most other courses. The second exercise illustrates how many issues, especially those concerning personal beliefs and choices, do not have "right" or "wrong" answers. The third exercise gives you practice with objectively evaluating experiences and observations by examining various "research" findings. The fourth exercise gives you a chance to apply the mechanisms explained by the different perspectives of psychology to your own life experiences. The fifth exercise is a personal essay, designed to help you establish a beginning point for your evaluation of your personal growth. The last exercise is an opportunity for you to examine how you process your values.

Study Questions

1. Define "personal adjustment."
2. How does the concept of personal adjustment conflict with the values of Western culture? Or, if you were raised in a different culture, how do your cultural expectations compare to the concept of personal adjustment as presented in this chapter?
3. Think of someone you believe to be well-adjusted. How would you describe their adjustment in terms of the theories of Freud, Skinner, Beck, and Maslow?
4. How would you describe the inner self of the well-adjusted person? How would you describe the manner in which a well-adjusted person interacts with his or her environment?
5. Is spirituality a personal growth concern? Why or why not?
6. List the advantages that scientific method provides over the use of "common sense."
7. Is there such a thing as a "normal" person? Explain your answer.
8. How can our values play an adaptive role in our personal growth?

CHAPTER TWO

Development Thus Far

Understanding Where You Came From

Mommy, where did I come from?

Many parents struggle with what to say when asked the preceding question. Suppose you were the parent. Looking beyond any personal embarrassment you might feel while discussing human reproduction with a child, how might you go about answering such a question? How much would you expect a member of this child's particular age group to understand? How much will the child remember? How do you present the topic in a way that will not distress the child? How much does a child this age really need to know? Or even, what is the child really *wanting* to know? One mother tried to answer her child's question with a sophisticated discussion of the birds and the bees, only to be interrupted with "No, I just wanted to know if I'm from Chicago, or Los Angeles, or Dallas...."

Perhaps the more appropriate question to ask as we explore personal growth is, How much do I really understand about where I came from? Not only how did I physically come into being but also how did I develop into the unique individual I have become? This question involves more than looking for a particular set of events or circumstances that molded us into some final hardened form. As described in the last chapter, we are constantly becoming who we are throughout our life spans, up until the end of our days. The longer we live, the more unique and interesting we become, as we develop more and more strategies for dealing with the art of being. The field of developmental psychology examines these strategies as four broad areas: biology, nature, nurture, and self-concept.

Biology

Genetic coding is responsible for many of the variations we see in developmental patterns. We have long accepted this reality while observing familial patterns of physical characteristics such as body size, facial features, and hair color. More recently, we have begun to recognize the role of genes in our psychological development, as well.

There have been a number of carefully controlled studies comparing characteristics of parents and their children, taking into account whether the children were reared by biological or by adoptive parents. These studies also look at the amount of genetic material that is shared by individuals. Such studies might compare identical–or **monozygotic**–twins, who both come from the same zygote and therefore share identical genes, with fraternal–or **dizygotic**–twins, who come from two separate zygotes and thus share genes as might any other sibling pair.

One such area of investigation concerns intelligence. When the results of many studies of intelligence and developmental issues are combined and compared, we find that the more closely related two individuals are the more likely they are to share a similar level of intelligence, even when they are reared in different homes. Mental retardation can also be determined by specific genes passed down through the family line. For example, **phenylketonuria,** also referred to as PKU, involves an inherited enzyme deficiency that, if left untreated, is likely to result in mental retardation.

Personal temperament is another human characteristic that appears to be affected by the genes we inherit. **Temperament** is the backbone behind our personalities. It is defined as a more or less stable collection of personal attributes present in a child at birth. These attributes are believed to be caused by inherited unique patterns of physiological processes. These processes influence how we feel or determine what kinds of behavior will feel most comfortable for us. Some more commonly observed temperamental differences are level of inhibition, ability to adapt, activity level, irritability, and frequency of smiling (Kagan, 1989).

Many parents can notice a difference in the temperaments of their children immediately after their arrival. One child might always seem more crabby, another might seem more content, and so on. Research tracking children for years has found that their basic temperaments, especially level of inhibition or disinhibition, remain consistent over time. However, researchers found that despite inherited temperaments, children still seem to learn to behave in ways that do not let temperament get the better of them (Kagan, 1989).

Studies of newborn behavior of various races also suggest an inherited basis of temperament (Freedman, 1974). Infants of some races, such as the Chinese and Navajo, are more willing to put up with physical restrictions such as being carried around on a cradle board. Caucasian babies in the same circumstances tend to raise more of a fuss. Other researchers have made similar observations regarding an inborn basis for temperament in attributes such as shyness, moodiness, activity level, and responsiveness (Thomas et al., 1970).

There are certain mental health complications that also appear to occur more frequently among blood relatives than among those who are not related. These include alcoholism, attention deficit hyperactivity disorder, infantile autism, schizophrenia, and manic-depressive disorder (American Psychiatric Association, 1994). While chemicals and structures within the nervous system are beginning to appear accountable for some of these dramatic conditions, the exact role heritability plays is yet to be determined.

Nature-Nurture Theories

Cognitive Development

Cognitive ability refers to our thinking capacities, such as reasoning, memory, and learning. Children reason differently from adults. In fact, children can reason differently from one another based on their current level of cognitive development.

Jean Piaget (1936) was one of the first to systematically observe these differences. He proposed that the process of cognitive development is facilitated by developing **schemas**—certain ways of reasoning or looking at things. He believed we develop more complicated schemas as we grow older by using the mechanisms of **assimilation** and **accommodation.** Through assimilation, we take in new knowledge. Through accommodation, we adjust what is assimilated to other pieces of learning.

For example, I was playing strenuously with my 3-year-old niece when I informed her I was getting too old to play that kind of game. Her reply was "Then don't be old. Be new." She had assimilated the schema of "new" being the opposite of "old" but had not yet accommodated it to the concept that "new" people are actually referred to as being "young."

We continue this learning procedure throughout our lives. Festinger (1957) calls it a process of **cognitive dissonance.** His theory suggests that we feel stress when presented with a new piece of information that conflicts with a previously held belief. In order to alleviate the stress, we accommodate the beliefs to one another in ways that make sense.

Suppose you oppose the sport of hunting and believe you could never eat wild game because it is harvested in such a violent manner. A classmate invites you over for dinner, serves delicious spaghetti, and later you discover the meat sauce was made from elk. Somehow you will accommodate those two pieces of information in a way that will relieve the discomfort of the discovery. You may decide that it is the sport and not the foodstuff you oppose. Or, you might suspect that it only tasted the way it did because you thought it was beef. You may even decide that hunting isn't so bad after all.

Scientific inquiry itself is a process of assimilation and accommodation. Scientists replicate old findings using different circumstances, as well as alter their theories and predictions based on newer findings. For example, developmental psychologists noticed that infants who were grossly neglected by their mothers usually became withdrawn. Since children who are autistic are also withdrawn, some scientists drew the conclusion that the condition of autism is caused by poor mothering: an assimilation. More recently, studies have shown a biological basis for the condition of autism. Therefore most developmental psychologists have now discarded the notion of autism being created by poor mothering, thus accommodating for a new finding.

Piaget also believed that our cognitive development progresses in stages. He called ages birth to 2 years the period of **sensorimotor intelligence,** so named because the child focuses on what can be taken in by the senses: taste, feel, smell, sight, and hearing. The child learns to move his or her body in space and learns how to interact with the environment, especially in terms of cause and effect. What happens if I shake the rattle? If I start rolling, how will the world look different? If I pull myself forward, what new things can I reach? If I place my foot thus, can I still stay balanced? What happens if I pound the cat?

We learn many things during this stage that we will use for the rest of our lives. Take the ability to walk. Once we learn how, we do not have to stop and think to be able to do it, unless we are coping with unusual circumstances. The mechanisms, through practice, become hardwired. Other types of learning also tend to produce automatic responding. We might discover that a caregiver can be counted on in a time of need, or perhaps we learn that our caregiver is not particularly available. We can therefore learn to automatically assume that people in general are either dependable or undependable, based on our caregivers' reactions to our early cries for attention. Such perceptions can last a lifetime, unless we choose to start looking more closely at evidence suggesting some other conclusion and adjust our beliefs accordingly.

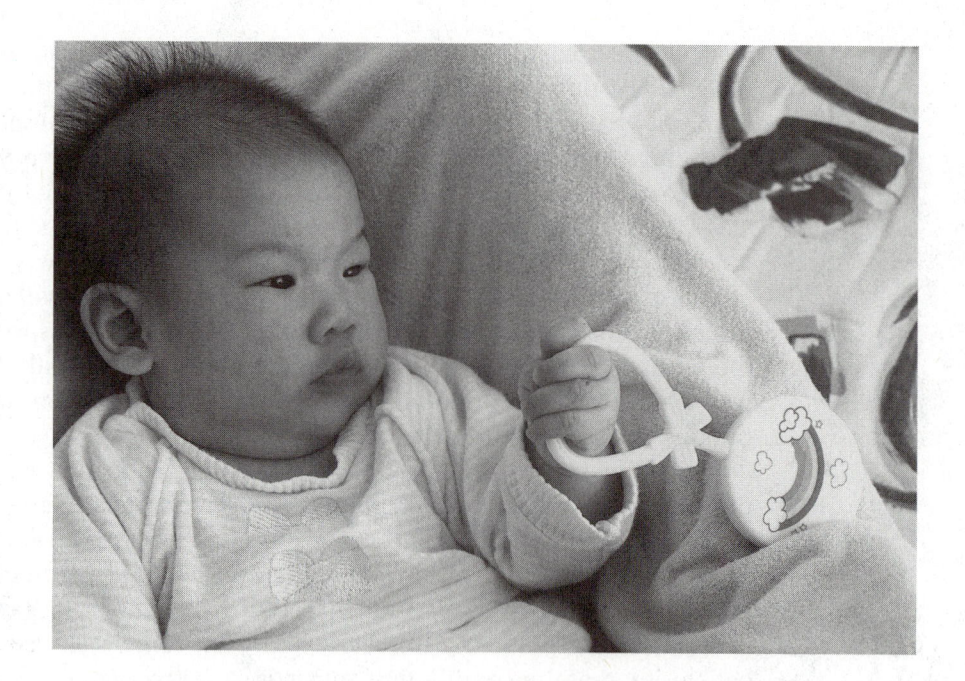

The second stage of cognitive development is called **preoperational thought,** covering the approximate ages of 2 through 6. The term *preoperational* is used because the child has not yet developed the ability to perform many mental *operations* using his or her knowledge. For example, if you tell a preoperational child that Mary is taller than Susan and Susan is taller than Joyce, and then ask who is taller, Mary or Joyce, the child will not be able to apply the logic necessary to solve the problem.

The preoperational child is also unable to "conserve." **Conservation** involves the ability to see that changing the arrangement of an object does not change its content. It also involves the ability to think in terms of more than one variable at a time. Suppose you take two equal glasses of water and pour one into a wide, flat bowl and the other into a tall, thin vase. If you ask the preoperational child which container has more water in it, even having seen that both were filled with equivalent amounts the child will either pick the bowl because it is wider or the vase because it is taller. The concept that one dimension increases in proportion to the others, decreasing involves more variables than the preoperational child can handle at once.

Moral reasoning at this stage depends more on the cause-and-effect consequences of actions than on the intent of the actor. If one child breaks a glass while climbing on a counter to steal a cookie and another drops and breaks a whole tray of glasses while trying to help Mommy, the preoperational child will see the helper as the greater offender. Again, considering intent in addition to outcome involves one too many variables.

While at the preoperational level, children learn to use symbols to represent things. Language is a collection of verbal symbols, and children acquire more language skills during this period than at any other time in their lives. Pretending is another symbolic activity. Considering the past and future, instead of living only in what is sensed in the present, involves the ability to mentally conceptualize past and future events.

Preoperational children are especially **egocentric.** They have difficulty seeing from another's perspective and tend to think that everybody else sees things as they do. They might look at a herd of cattle and say, "See that cow, Daddy?" assuming that Daddy will know which cow he is supposed to be looking at. Egocentrism at this stage also leads children to attribute life to inanimate objects—treating Teddy Bear as though it has feelings, or drawing a face on the sun. Egocentrism also has the unfortunate effect of children seeing themselves as being responsible for traumas in their lives—their parents divorcing, for instance—and subsequently blaming themselves. And we may go back to using our early egocentric thinking as we react to our present-day traumas. People often have feelings of guilt after the death of a loved one or being victimized by a crime, even when there is nothing they could have done to avoid it.

The third stage of cognitive development is called **concrete operations,** covering ages 7 through 11. At this stage, children learn to use a variety of mental operations, but they do so in a concrete manner. They can solve the problem of who is taller, Mary or Joyce, but do so by mentally envisioning the three girls and their heights. They can consider more than one relevant variable and are thus able to conserve. They also have the ability to reverse a procedure, such as seeing that a subtraction problem is addition in reverse.

However, children at this age still have difficulty with abstract thought. Math problems that deal with the abstract—like calculus and more advanced forms of algebra—are difficult for them to comprehend. They also do not yet reason scientifically. In the practice of science, we exhaust all possible hypotheses, looking at every possible explanation for why a set of data turned out the way it did. Concrete operational children will look for one or two explanations, then give up.

The fourth stage, **formal operations,** reflects a capacity found in people age 12 through adulthood. Those who are formal operational can reason in the abstract in addition to the concrete. They have the ability to consider all the possibilities, and can look for ways to test the validity of these possibilities.

Whether or not we use our formal operational ability depends a good deal on our life experiences. Some primitive cultures find no use for it whatsoever, and their members never develop these skills. Most likely, if you grew up in an environment that did not make use of abstract reasoning or hypothesis testing, you will not be skilled at using your formal operational ability either. This tendency is illustrated by the fictional character "Bud" on the television sitcom *Married . . . With Children.* "Bud" is portrayed as someone who is bright enough to get excellent grades in school but whose reasoning schemas within his home environment are extremely limited and concrete. Perhaps as a result, he regularly muddles his way through interpersonal relationships, struggling with his lack of exposure to considering alternative ways of viewing the world and relating to others. However, such a childhood deficit need not be a life sentence. Formal operational reasoning can be taught at a later age, even though it may have been neglected during early training (Scribner, 1977).

A college education is in some ways a training field for the use of formal operations. Suppose your instructor gives you a study guide for an upcoming test. If you rely only on your concrete operational ability, your studying style will most likely involve scrounging through your book or lecture notes and ending your search when you find material that addresses study guide suggestions. You might also learn rote definitions of important vocabulary words. Unfortunately, these strategies alone may not be enough to pass the typical college exam.

Keeping formal operational procedures in mind as you study would prove beneficial. You could apply your formal operational ability by investigating study questions with an exhaustive search, looking for all possible right answers within all of the material presented. You could practice making up your own examples to demonstrate your understanding of the meanings of vocabulary words and important concepts. Through the use of such tactics, you force yourself to come to an understanding of the actual concept—an abstraction—rather than parroting back a concrete definition. Most examinations test such knowledge within the context of an example anyway. So a concrete definition alone may not help you if you do not also understand the concept. And, of course, understanding the concept is an absolute necessity if you plan to apply any new knowledge to your own life!

Moral reasoning. Our moral reasoning abilities become more sophisticated as we progress in our cognitive development. What sort of internal guidelines might we use to help us decide what is right or wrong? Lawrence Kohlberg (1976) describes moral decision making in six stages. Children develop their capacity to use different moral reasoning schemas in concert with their level of cognitive ability.

Very young children are **preconventional** in their thinking. In other words, they are not as likely to consider the conventions of society as they sort out their moral motivations. Reflecting their preoperational stage of cognitive development, children at this age have difficulty considering more than one variable as they make decisions. Instead, they focus on the variable that sticks out most in their early egocentric lives: What's in it for me?

Preconventional moral reasoning occurs during the first two moral reasoning stages. The first level, a **punishment and obedience** orientation, centers on avoiding punishment. Suppose David and Susan, who are living in poverty and have had nothing to eat all day, pass by an apple tree laden with ripe fruit. Unfortunately, it is in a fenced yard posted with a big sign–Keep Out! No Exceptions. Susan decides to climb the fence anyway and pick up a few dropped apples, but she cannot safely do so unless David helps boost her over. Should David help her? Children at the punishment and obedience level of reasoning resolve this dilemma according to how they perceive the possibility of punishment:

"He shouldn't help her steal the apples. They might get in trouble."

Or, "He should help boost her over. He might get in trouble if she got hurt because he didn't help."

At the second level of moral reasoning, **instrumental relativist,** children consider what sorts of rewards might be available as a result of their choices:

"He shouldn't help her steal apples. His mother will be happy with him because he did what she says is the right thing."

Or, "He should help her climb over, and some day she will help him when he needs it."

The next two levels of moral reasoning involve **conventional** considerations. Children take into account the biases, preferences, and dictates of society as they reason. This is consistent with the concrete operational level of cognitive development, since rules and regulations are concrete structures. At the third level, **good boy/nice girl,** children shape their reasoning according to how they think society defines a "good" person:

"A good boy wouldn't help steal apples."

Or, "A good boy would help a girl if she needed it."

At the fourth level, **law and order,** children consider the rules to be the rules, and proper behavior conforms to those rules:

"He shouldn't help her steal apples. It's against the law."

Or, "He should help her get over the fence. That's what friendship is all about."

The last two stages are **postconventional.** They go beyond societal conventions and look at the reasons why rules and regulations were developed in the first place. These reasons take the form of moral principles, such as justice, fairness, and caring about our fellow human beings. Since moral principles are abstractions rather than concrete rules or structures, children have the capacity to effectively utilize this type of reasoning only when their cognitive ability becomes formal operational.

The fifth stage, **social contract,** stresses that we develop rules and regulations as a society in order to support moral principles. So even though rules are important, we can alter them to better fit the moral principles:

"They shouldn't take apples unless they first find the owners of the yard and try to get them to change their minds. Then it would be all right for him to help her."

Or, "The people who own the tree probably wouldn't mind, if they knew that the apples would be going to someone who was truly hungry."

The sixth stage, **universal moral principles,** places the importance of the principles above that of the rules. So if a higher principle is involved, rules might be ignored:

"He should help her get over the fence. Her need to eat is more important than a keep out sign."

Or, "He shouldn't help her. We all have the right to determine the use of our property, and the owners have the right to keep us out if they so choose."

Although our moral reasoning capacity increases with age, we do not do away with earlier styles of reasoning as we grow older. If you were driving along the highway, approaching a known speed trap, and suddenly discovered that your speed had sneaked up to 12 miles over the limit, you would probably immediately let your foot up off the gas pedal. If you examine your motivation for doing so, you will probably discover a primitive reasoning schema: a desire not to get a ticket. In general, it could be that you drive at conventional speeds because of your desire not to cause harm to self or others—a more sophisticated moral reasoning schema. But fear of punishment still remains as one factor that can motivate our moral choices.

Carol Gilligan (1982) did not agree with some of Kohlberg's conclusions. Specifically, she took issue with his view that justice and fairness are the epitome of moral reasoning. Since Kohlberg's early work examined only men and boys, his observations might not be especially relevant for evaluating feminine moral decision making. Cold-blooded logic, which is devoid of feeling, excludes the morality of caring about others.

Gilligan's research emphasized the importance of the roles of caring, as well as of feeling responsibility toward the well-being of our fellow human beings, as we make moral decisions. In her studies, she found that women's moral reasoning tended to progress according to such considerations as compassion, personal responsibility, and feeling a need to reduce human suffering. She pointed out that women tend to draw their conclusions after following pathways of feelings that are not easy to describe in objective terms. Rather than following set outlines of logic, they listen to what she calls their "distinctive voices," feeling voices that guide them toward moral decision making that is congruent with their inner experience.

Kohlberg had drawn the conclusion that since women did not report the same higher-level reasoning processes as men, women are not as well developed in moral reasoning as are men. Actually, there is considerable evidence of a greater inclination toward empathy and moral internalization in girls and women than in men and boys (Hoffman, 1977). We also need to keep in mind that, while one gender uses certain strategies more often than the other, both strategies are observed in both genders' moral decision making. So rather than looking at one or the other gender as being "superior" at moral reasoning, it is more useful to consider that men and women may process their morals differently. Both methods produce moral decisions. They simply get there using different routes.

Psychosocial Development

As with reasoning skills, we also assimilate and accommodate as we learn to relate to others. John Bowlby (1969) studied how infants seem to attach so easily to others, especially their primary caretakers. Clinging, crying, babbling, smiling, following, and sucking are all other-oriented behaviors that are common to almost all infants, without their being conditioned to perform these actions. Attachment to a caretaker is of course vital to an infant's survival. However, the quality of the attachment appears to be important as well. Infants who do not receive much stimulation from their caretakers may not fare as well as those who are securely attached, and they may sometimes show emotional, physical, or intellectual deficits (Casler, 1965).

More-recent studies suggest that, rather than attachment, the most important aspect of an infant's early social life is something called **attunement.** Daniel Stern (1985) describes attunement as a tendency for infant and primary caretaker to adjust their reactions so that their behaviors complement one another. For example, a mother with a baby that does not seem to like being held close may adjust by holding the baby facing away from her. An infant who discovers its primary caretaker is awkward in handling him or her may learn to reflexively tense up while being handled. It is like two puzzle pieces constantly altering their shapes so that the two can fit together. Through this process of both nature and nurture, we learn specific ways of relating to others at a very early age.

Freud (1920/1935) proposed one of the earliest theories of social development. Many theorists have pooh-poohed his ideas because of their preoccupation with "psychosexual" stages of development. Nevertheless, these stages still provide an interesting sequential framework for how we can learn to relate to others. Freud suggests that our stages of social development are a progression of various internal needs or conflicts. Our personal development is a reflection of how we resolve these needs at each stage. If a particular stage is inadequately resolved, we become **fixated** at that stage, and develop certain personality characteristics as a result of the particular fixation.

Freud called our first year of life the **oral stage**, since so much of an infant's activity involves the mouth. Infants spend a good deal of time eating and sucking. As they become more coordinated, they explore their world by trying to stick everything in their mouths. Neurologically speaking, the developmental sophistication of an infant's mouth wins hands-down over the development of its other physical abilities.

According to Freud, our future personality depends in part on how we gratify these oral needs during infancy. He believed that if we are overindulged or overly frustrated we can develop specific long-standing personality traits. If an infant is constantly orally indulged, regardless of the infant's actual need, the child learns to take things in indiscriminately. As an adult, we would expect this person to be overly trusting and gullible. On the other hand, if the child often feels frustrated by the amount of oral gratification he or she receives, we would expect the person to become unduly suspicious of others, not trusting others to be concerned with his or her needs.

The second and third years of life are referred to as the **anal stage**. The main arena of battle between parent and child at this age, as Freud saw it, is toilet training. If toilet training was too pushy, he expected the child would become stubborn, stingy, and preoccupied with orderliness.

If the toilet training was too laid-back, he predicted a child would develop characteristics such as passivity, messiness, and overgenerosity.

The third stage, the **phallic stage**, lasts from about age 3 to age 5 or 6. Freud believed that during these years children are particularly interested in their genitals and begin noticing gender differences as well. He proposed that they also develop an interest in possessing their opposite-gender parents in a sexual manner. He believed that girls and boys resolve this phase of development differently.

Boys go through the **Oedipus complex**, supposedly competing with their fathers for the affection of their mothers. However, a boy recognizes that his father is much bigger and more powerful than he is and develops a phenomenon called **castration anxiety**, fearing that the father will retaliate by physically castrating him. The boy resolves this fear through **identification** with the father. In other words, he incorporates his father's male characteristics into his own personality and is thus able to be more accepting of him.

Girls were thought to go through an equivalent process that Freud called the **Electra complex**. This stage is characterized by **penis envy**, whereby the girl recognizes that she does not have a penis, wishes that she did, and becomes resentful of her mother for not having provided her with one. As with boys, girls resolve the conflict by identifying with the mother's gender and becoming accepting of their mutual predicament.

Many a chuckle has occurred at the expense of these aspects of Freudian developmental theory, but if you replace the genital terminology with words more related to having power, his proposals are not quite so far-fetched. We all feel safer when we have some control over our lives, and control is found by looking to sources of power. Our society, despite the efforts of feminists, is still for the most part patriarchal. Most observable power tends to be held by men. Boys strive to eventually have the power they see held by their fathers–a form of competition or rivalry. Likewise, at some point in their lives most girls can see how their options might have been more expansive had they been born male–which can be seen as a form of envy.

Freud called the fourth stage–ages 6 through 12–**latency** because he believed that we put psychosexual development on hold during this period. The last stage, **the genital stage**, covers adolescence and adulthood. During this stage we develop meaningful, mature heterosexual relationships. While we certainly still experience conflicts as adolescents and adults, we do not develop new fixations. However, we may continue to play out the fixations we developed during earlier stages, such as oral and anal.

Erik Erikson (1963) expanded upon Freud's early ideas. He wasn't as concerned about psychosexual aspects of early personality development but focused instead on developmental tasks covering social development throughout the life span. He also looked beyond the potential for developing mental disorders and addressed healthy resolution of stages of development. He proposed eight psychosocial stages, five occurring during childhood. Like Freud, he believed that how we handled each stage of development would affect our basic personality.

The first year, or first stage, which Erickson called **trust versus mistrust**, is much like Freud's oral stage. By means of their dependency on others, infants learn to either trust that others will be sensitive to their needs or, through frustration, learn to mistrust others.

The second stage, **autonomy versus shame and doubt**, covers the same period as Freud's anal stage. While Freud looked more exclusively to the issues of toilet training, Erikson saw these second 2 years as a time when children discover their ability to do some things for themselves. They can move around more independently and communicate more, giving them many more opportunities to either go along with or go against the wishes of their caretakers. Mastery of this sense of separateness results in feelings of autonomy. Failure to feel mastery of one's will results in feelings of shame and doubt.

The third stage, **initiative versus guilt**, involves preschool children, ages 4 and 5. At these ages children realize they can initiate their own behavior and make independent decisions. Naturally, some of these choices will work out and some will not. How such successes and failures are handled by others has an effect on how children incorporate the findings of their social experimentation. Acceptable decisions are generally rewarded by others; unacceptable choices are generally punished. Discovering the magic formulas for success or failure helps children feel successful in understanding how to assert their wills in a socially acceptable manner and results in a strong sense of initiative. However, if caretakers are critical of all efforts or accepting of any behavioral choices, the path toward successful assertion is less clear, and children instead learn to feel excessive guilt.

The fourth stage, **industry versus inferiority**, covers ages 6 through 11, Freud's latency period. Rather than seeing children as being "on hold" during this period, Erikson saw them as being very busy and productive. School work, sports, and other skills are sharpened. If children feel rewarded for their efforts, they experience a sense of accomplishment and personal industry. If they do not think they are doing well, because of either inadequate direction or excessive criticism, they learn instead to feel inferior.

The fifth stage, **identity versus identity confusion**, covers adolescence. During this time we attempt to develop a full sense of selfhood, including our chosen values, sexuality, and vocation. Successfully finding the parameters of these pieces of self-expression results in a firm sense of identity. Receiving excessively contradictory, overcontrolled, or fragmented messages concerning identity leads to identity confusion.

Alfred Adler (1927) also believed we had inborn tendencies toward psychosocial growth, but he did not see them as occurring in stages. His individuality theory suggests that we develop in accordance with two sources: our **inferiority-superiority complex** and **social striving**.

As children, we grow up among powerful giants—adults—who almost magically seem to possess knowledge, strength, and skills that are far superior to our own. Perhaps appropriately so, we feel intimidated and inferior in comparison. We react to these intense feelings of inferiority by striving to feel more superior through our own learning and achievements. Adler called this the inferiority-superiority complex because the more we feel inferior to others, the more we try to **compensate** by acting or becoming superior. In extreme circumstances, we may **overcompensate**—driving ourselves to unnecessary degrees of performance in order to make up for our perceived inferiority. For example, a child inheriting a large body frame may react to his or her perceived "fatness" with excessive dieting, perhaps even destructively. A child who feels excessively bossed by other siblings might overcompensate by seeking out an overwhelming number of leadership positions.

In addition to our individual striving, Adler believed, we are also driven by **social striving**. He proposed that we experience a connectedness or relatedness to our fellow human beings and that we strive to contribute to the well-being of our communal group. We find happiness when our efforts are guided by social striving because it allows us to feel more compassion, understanding, and acceptance toward our fellow human beings, regardless of their normal foibles and apparent foolishness. The more we are able to experience and work in concert with this form of "brotherly love," the more we are able to experience joy and cheerfulness.

Thus psychosocial development appears to be a microcosm of nature and nurture working hand in hand. We are born with certain potentialities and capacities, and the feedback we receive from the environment plays a role in determining how we develop our abilities in interpersonal relatedness.

Nurture: Behavioral and Social Learning Theories

CONDITIONING AND SOCIAL LEARNING

Behavioral and social learning theories are not concerned with specific stages/ages when children may learn specific things but focus on the role of the environment and learning in the developing child, looking at learning processes that remain more or less consistent throughout the life span.

Conditioning. The discussion of behaviorism in the last chapter described the ways we repeat behaviors we experience as reinforcing and avoid behaviors we experience as punishing. As children, we learn a variety of skills and behaviors through these basic processes. Sometimes learning is immediate. For example, you discover that if you pound the cat, you are likely to be clawed or bitten and you avoid that behavior in the future.

Other learning can be spread out over time, such as happens during **shaping**. Shaping involves learning acquired in bits and pieces, slowly but surely coming closer to the desired form. A professional baseball player's first exposure to the sport likely was as a young child, playing with a toy ball in the backyard, then learning to toss the ball back and forth with another person, and when older learning to play ball in groups. With school came T-ball, then perhaps softball, and eventually Little League. Next came high school baseball, then college teams, and eventually professional baseball. At each step of the way, new and more-complex skills were introduced and learned. The player experienced this as either internally or externally rewarding and felt encouraged to go on.

In addition to explaining how we learn, behaviorism also points out how we can "unlearn." Behavioral changes only stay in effect if they continue to be experienced as reinforcing or avoiding punishment. Once the reinforcers and punishers are removed, unless some new motivation has taken over, the behavioral change will eventually go away. This process is called **extinction**. So while our childhood learning may have taught us many useful things, our later behavior is likely to become reshaped by the reinforcers and punishers we experience in the adult world.

Likewise, any detrimental learning we might have picked up during childhood need not follow us around forever. Suppose as a child you felt overcriticized for your efforts, which you experienced as punishing. In order to avoid this punisher you learned to avoid trying out new things. You feared being criticized for imperfections. Later, as an adult and no longer around the people who put down your efforts, you risk trying something new and do not experience the expected punisher. In fact, you may even experience pleasure or some other reinforcer as you practice your new skill. Or perhaps you still have overcritical people around you, but as an adult, you have learned how to tune them out. Your avoidant behavior becomes extinguished because the punisher, excessive criticism, is either no longer present or has lost its potency.

Social learning. Chapter 1 also brought up how we learn many behaviors through modeling. We appear to be prewired at birth for this style of learning. Infants only a few weeks old are able to copy the smiling expressions they see on their caregivers' faces and may also be able to imitate other facial expressions, such as indicating surprise or sticking out their tongues (Field et al., 1982). You can see babies not even a year old copy behaviors such as head shaking, babbling certain sounds, and table patting. As they become toddlers, you can almost see the wheels turning as they watch another child perform a behavior and then try it themselves. As they approach preschool age they play dress-up, at first trying out the clothes and grooming utensils of both parents, then eventually becoming more gender specific in their modeling. Throughout childhood, they continue to learn a good deal of their behavior, perhaps as much as 80%, by watching others (Bandura, 1973).

We observe a number of different behaviors during our formative years. Why do we choose to copy some but not others? Bandura suggests that there are four variables guiding our modeling choices:

1. *Attention.* A behavior must capture our attention before we can learn it. We must also observe the important cues, or **discriminative stimuli**, involved with successfully reproducing a behavior. Getting money from a cash machine may look like a worthwhile venture. However, before we can successfully reproduce this behavior we must also make sure that we have put enough money into our bank accounts, as well as know which machine is appropriate and how to operate it.

2. *Retention.* We code our learning into symbolic form, such as words or images, and hang on to it for further use. In other words, we must remember what we saw before we can imitate it.

3. *Reproduction.* We must have the ability to actually reproduce the behavior. We can watch someone knit, play a musical instrument, or shoot baskets and get a general idea of how it is done. But we must also have the coordination, patience, and physical abilities necessary to be able to successfully copy what we have observed. We may need to practice many times before actually succeeding at reproducing a behavior to our satisfaction.

4. *Motivation.* We try out new behaviors for a reason. Vicarious reinforcers and punishers play a big role, as do direct reinforcement and punishment. Perhaps satisfying our curiosity as to whether we can do something and what would happen if we did is the only reinforcer. Or maybe a more concrete reward is involved, such as writing a term paper well enough to get a good grade.

Another mediator of whether or not we copy observed behavior is our sense of **self-efficacy**. To what extent do we believe that we can try something and actually have it turn out right? What is our level of self-confidence? If we do not believe we have the ability to try something new and succeed, we are less likely to pay close attention. We may make little effort toward retention. We may not have the self-confidence necessary to successfully reproduce the behavior. And we will certainly not feel motivated if we believe we are facing the punishment of failure for our efforts. Thus our self-concept plays a major role in our individual styles of observational learning.

Development of Self-Concept

How do you view yourself? What kind of person do you see yourself as being? What personality traits, abilities, and mental processes do you recognize as part of your uniqueness? In what ways do you see yourself as existing separately from others? Questions on this order relate to the realm of self-concept. Gordon Allport (1961) proposes that we develop our self-concept in stages and, while the stages may have their beginning points, continue to develop characteristics of selfhood throughout our lives.

During the first stage, **early infancy**, we do not appear to have any self-concept. Instead, our sense of self is merged with our primary caretaker's, and we experience the two as one. The second stage occurs during the second half of infancy, as we become aware of a sense of **bodily self**. We begin to recognize hunger, dampness, softness, brightness, noise, and other bodily sensations as being personal experiences.

The third stage, **self-identity**, occurs during the second year. We learn that our selfhood is continuous: We have a past, present, and future, and we continue to be who we are in spite of any lifestyle or behavioral changes that may occur over time. During the third year, the fourth stage of development, we develop a sense of **self-esteem**. We see our successes, failures, accomplishments, and life pursuits as being ours alone. We begin to evaluate ourselves on the basis of the observations and learn how to feel good about ourselves.

During ages 4 and 5, the fifth stage, **extension of self**, introduces relatedness to others. We incorporate parts of our environment, such as family and household activity, into our sense of self. This contributes toward providing the basis for our internal guidelines. At the same time, we begin to develop our sense of **self-image.** We accept some expectations of us by the environment as our own and begin to define ourselves in terms of such environmental feedback.

During ages 6 to 12, the sixth stage, we begin to appreciate the uniqueness and value of our thought processes. We work toward becoming **rational copers**. We learn that we can mentally evaluate situations and problems to come up with answers without needing to act them out first. The last stage occurs during adolescence, when we begin **propriate striving**. As we transition from childhood to adulthood, we plan life goals that both preserve our sense of selfhood and are consistent with our ever-evolving personal striving.

Self-Esteem

One of the most important aspects of the developing self-concept is self-esteem, the importance of which is evident as we examine the perspectives of psychology. The concept of self-esteem is addressed one way or another by most of the theories of adjustment we have covered thus far. The psychodynamic orientation looks at self-esteem in terms of our behaving in ways that please our conscience and ego-ideal. Rogers (1980) points out the importance of our self-actualizing tendency and searching for congruence between our real and ideal selves. Social learning theory addresses self-esteem in the form of self-efficacy. Adler (1927) defines it within an inferiority-superiority complex. Even most of Erikson's (1963) psychosocial stages are formulated in terms of high or low self-esteem possibilities, such as initiative versus guilt or industry versus inferiority.

Clearly, whether or not we believe in ourselves is going to affect the developmental direction of our lives. Individuals with high or low self-esteem differ in their views not only of themselves but of others and the world in general.

Self-view. Individuals with high self-esteem perceive themselves as valuable, worthwhile human beings. They are independent and self-sufficient, and willing to risk failure as they try new things and strive toward personal growth. They enjoy doing for the joy of doing, even if they do not do as well as others. They recognize their strengths, and are nonjudgmentally accepting of their weaknesses. They take responsibility for their behavior, recognizing that they alone are responsible for the direction they choose for their lives. They tend to be happy and content.

Individuals with low self-esteem assign themselves **conditions of worth** (Rogers, 1980). Rather than seeing themselves as intrinsically worthwhile, they believe their worth is based on the quality of their skills or attributes. They are often perfectionistic. If they are not perfect, they judge themselves harshly. They therefore focus more on their negatives and tend to ignore their strengths. They cannot tolerate losing at anything and will go to any lengths to "win" an argument, competitive sport, or anything that remotely resembles competition. They see change, creativity, decision making, and trying new skills as threatening, since there is potential for failure, and avoid the risks of changing or trying something new. They tend to be more concerned with how things look than how they are. They may strive to hang out with an "in" crowd or try to keep up with fads and stylish possessions. They may miss out on presenting themselves authentically in order to present what they think others will admire.

View of others. People with high self-esteem enjoy other people and consider others worthwhile and valuable, just as they see themselves as worthwhile and valuable. While high self-esteem individuals may become frustrated with others' behavior, they are capable of forgiving and forgetting, accepting others for who they are rather than for what they do. They value interpersonal relationships and organize their lives so that such relationships do not get lost as they pursue other important parts of their lives. They work well in groups, having the flexibility to adjust to others' input and feel comfortable taking the risk of asserting their own views when necessary.

Low self-esteem individuals feel competitive toward others. They are critical of others, seeing only their faults and little of their strengths, as they attempt to look better themselves by comparison. Relationships with others are often strained, as low self-esteem individuals have difficulty dealing with others' shortcomings. Their relationships are also impaired by their difficulty in taking the risk of sharing their vulnerabilities with others. They may take a domineering attitude toward others, because they do not trust others enough to share the powers of control and relating. Or, they may take an excessively submissive position with others, because they do not trust their own abilities to make relationship decisions.

Worldview. Individuals with high self-esteem enjoy the world, see it as a delightful challenge, and do not feel unduly threatened by its inevitable faults and injustices. They appreciate opportunity as it presents itself. Bob Keeshan (1989), better known as "Captain Kangaroo," points out that life is a series of opportunities. Our life patterns and satisfactions follow the paths created as we choose which opportunities we will take advantage of. People with high self-esteem can take the risk of tackling a new opportunity.

On the other hand, those with low self-esteem feel threatened by the world and its unpredictable nature. Opportunities look more like potential failures and scary unknowns than possibilities for challenge and excitement. When adversity comes, they have trouble letting go of their unpleasant emotional reactions. They may cope by developing an inflated view of their own importance and superiority as they deal with their feelings of powerlessness.

Typically, we experience both high and low self-esteem. Healthy adjustment progresses when we can appreciate our episodes of high self-esteem and recover or effectively deal with our episodes of low self-esteem. A later chapter will cover methods of coping with assaults to our self-esteem. Some of us seem to be blessed with frequent high self-esteem, others cursed with chronic low self-esteem. What plays a role in this? Actually, there seem to be many reasons, again based on biology, nature, and nurture. We may be born with favorable attributes that lead to our feeling good about ourselves or with a deficiency or deformity that starts us out as feeling substandard. Or we might inherit a sensitive temperament so we feel the stings of failure more intensely than a less sensitive person and therefore have a more intense struggle with self-esteem.

From the nurture standpoint, we might learn to feel good or bad about ourselves according to the feedback we receive from those around us. Part of developing self-concept includes systematically internalizing the world's concept of us. If significant others seem to think well of us, we learn to think well of ourselves. If we believe the world holds us in low esteem, we learn also to hold ourselves in low esteem.

The developmental stages of nature/nurture are potential breeding grounds for self-esteem development. Successful progression through any developmental task lends support to our self-esteem. Incomplete or destructive processing of developmental tasks can lead to low self-esteem.

CHOICE AND FREE WILL

Another important theme of self-concept development is our capacity for choice and change. Some extreme behavioral theorists believe that we do not have *any* personal choices over our lives, that all of our responding and experiences are simply part of an unfolding sequence of stimulus/response pairings. How depressing! Most theories of adjustment agree that we do have some form of free will and that we can make choices consistent with our personal strivings.

O'Connell and O'Connell (1992) describe our capacity for choosing and changing from a **growth psychology** perspective. Growth psychology emphasizes the ongoing nature of our developing selfhood. O'Connell and O'Connell list seven tenets or assumptions grounding their position on freedom to choose and change.

1. *The process of living has more meaning than any particular goal.* We live within a day-by-day process of experiencing. Life objectives are important, but we must not lose ourselves in the process of pursuing our goals. As we preserve our state of being, we preserve our rights to choice and change.

2. *Labeling situations makes more sense than labeling people.* We all encounter our share of bad situations. Given certain sets of circumstances, we all at one time or another experience impulses to do things and say things we may later wish we did not do or say. If we choose to give in to those impulses, it does not make us "bad people." Though we all may occasionally make unfortunate choices that turn out not to be in the best interests of ourselves or others, there are no bad people.

3. *Unpleasant emotions and mental states are normal and expected rather than evidence of illness.* We are designed to experience sadness at times of loss or disappointment, anxiety in the presence of stressors, and irrationality when overwhelmed or confused. These states are reactions to living. Rather than dreading and hiding from any life circumstance that has potential to put us in touch with such experiencing, we must embrace our internal states, even when they feel uncomfortable. After all, they are just as much a part of us as our more enjoyable inner experiences. They can teach us about ourselves, and provide information for guiding our future choices.

4. *Our unique differences are more valuable than our similarities.* While we need to remain mindful of the needs and dictates of our society, we must also remember that our choosing and changing is an individualized, creative process. We mold our individual paths according to our own perceptions, needs, and life objectives, given what options are available. Creativity comes from uniqueness, rather than conformity to the norm. Our society benefits from our unique abilities as well, having reached its current advanced state because of individuals willing to look beyond those who had gone before.

5. *We alone are responsible for the consequences of our choices.* We alone make our choices, and we alone are responsible for their creative or unfortunate outcomes. Thus we alone direct the pattern and flavor of our lives, and choices need to reflect our chosen direction. As you go through this textbook, some ideas will make sense to you, while others may not. It is your responsibility to sift through the various theories and perspectives and find what is useful. However, do not burn your bridges behind you by discarding ideas that do not fit your current mindset. Our mindsets change, and you may want to return to those ideas at some other time.

6. *Healthy choosing takes into account both the humanistic and holistic dimensions of human experiencing.* Humanism values the experience of the person and emphasizes staying in touch with the human experience as a research tool for future choosing and striving. The holistic approach focuses on every aspect of a person's experience, including physical, mental, emotional, and spiritual.

7. *Choosing and changing is our inalienable right.* No matter what our past experiences or restrictions of circumstance, our capacity for choice and change cannot be taken away. Our internal lives are ours alone, and choice and change is a part of that internal process.

Thus our self-concept presents itself as a constantly rotating kaleidoscope of needs, dreams, beliefs, values, feelings, previous experiences, judgments, attitudes, goals, and potential choices. While the patterns and designs can seem unpredictable and even mysterious, we can delight in their beauty and creativity as they emerge. And, throughout our lifetimes the reflections of our self-concepts continue to color the progression of our development.

Gender

Gender, another aspect of our self-concept, has important meaning in our society. When a new child is born, one of the first questions out of the parents' mouths is usually "Is it a boy or a girl?"–sometimes even before they ask if the child is all right. As we proceed through life in Western culture, our gender will affect our attitudes toward ourselves as well as our choices and opportunities.

Gender issues concern how we perceive ourselves and one another as being male or female, men or women. The first, most basic gender issue is **gender identity**: Which gender do we identify with? What is the inner experience of being male or female? The second gender issue involves how we define the behaviors, attitudes, and other observable attributes of men and women, a broad area that concerns **gender roles**–what we should be like, given that we are men or women.

Gender identity.   Gender identity seems relatively simple to address: Those born with the XX chromosomal combination identify with women, and those with an XY combination identify with men. Kohlberg explains that as children mature they go through a progression of gender acceptance:

- *Gender identity* Recognition of sexual assignment–by age 3 years
- *Gender stability* Realization that gender will not change with age–at around 4 or 5 years
- *Gender constancy* Recognition that gender does not change with modification of dress or behavior–at around 7 or 8 years

The more difficult task of gender identity involves the qualities of the experience. We incorporate our inner experiencing and environmental feedback as we discover what it actually feels like to be male or female.

An exception to the rules of gender identification is a condition called **transsexualism**. Transsexualism occurs when a person feels as if he or she is trapped in an opposite-sex body. Such individuals recognize that they have the external characteristics of one gender, but that their inner experiencing is more like that of the opposite gender. The condition does not go away with the passage of time or psychotherapy, and its origins are still unclear. Some may resolve this conflict by dressing and seeking roles as their inner identity. Others may seek sex-change operations. Others may resign themselves to their predicament and accept it as a frustration of their lives.

Gender roles.   The issue of gender roles reflects a much more complex blending of nature and nurture. Children begin developing the conceptual schema of gender roles at a very young age as they try to sort out how they should live within their identities as boys or girls. Many of their assumptions concerning masculinity and femininity are learned through observation and imitation. Little girls tend to copy the behaviors of Mommy and of other little girls, and little boys tend to copy the behaviors of Daddy and of other little boys. Masculinity is usually assigned such attributes as independence, aggressiveness, being a hard worker and good provider, nonemotionality, strength, and athletic ability. On the other hand, passivity, sensitivity, nurturance, emotional expressiveness, dependence, fragility, and vulnerability are generally incorporated into a child's schema of femininity.

In addition to the behavioral differences adopted by boys and girls, there is some evidence of differences in their cognitive development. Girls begin talking earlier than boys and as a group appear to maintain superior verbal abilities throughout their lives (Hyde, 1981). Boys, beginning around age 8, begin to show superior ability in spatial reasoning tasks, such as mentally rotating a figure in space (Linn & Peterson, 1986). Around age 12, boys also begin to show superiority in mathematical problem solving (Benbow & Stanley, 1980).

Are these behavioral and cognitive differences due to nature or nurture? Some evidence suggests that we may actually teach boys and girls to behave differently through how we interact with them. Parents tend to engage in more rough-and-tumble play with baby boys and use more verbalizations and cuddling with baby girls (Brigham, 1986). Throughout childhood, boys are reinforced more for being active and independent, while girls are reinforced more for being delicate and reserved. Even in the classroom, boys are given more slack when talking out, while girls are more likely to be reprimanded. Likewise, girls are more likely to receive neutral, less-confrontive input from teachers regarding their academic efforts, while boys receive more positive feedback and exhortations to do even better (Sadker & Sadker, 1985). Girls enter the school system with a higher level of reading and computing readiness than boys, but by the time they graduate boys are ahead of girls. Are girls innately booby-trapped to intellectually self-destruct during school years, or is it more likely that boys and girls differ because of their differing educational experiences? There is some indication that even the differences between boys' and girls' performances on SAT-math scores are more due to exposure than ability (Byrnes & Takahira, 1993).

How children interact with their peers also reinforces their perceptions of gender-typed behavior. As mentioned earlier, young children are concrete and relatively inflexible as they apply their schemas. Those who deviate from these schemas are asking for it. Boys who are nonathletic or express interpersonal sensitivity are labeled by their playmates as "wimps," "homos," "nerds," and the like. Girls who play aggressive games and get dirty and messed up are called "tomboys" or some other pejorative that is less than feminine. During the teen years, the young man who is an empathic conversationalist may have girls as good friends. But the young man who is allowed to romantically pursue these girls and enjoy other forms of peer popularity is generally the athlete, student body leader, or other young man holding a more "macho" social role. Likewise, the high school cheerleader or homecoming queen typically has less trouble getting a date than the young woman who is captain of the debate team or excels in track and field. Thus children reinforce one another for staying within their gender expectations.

Although the effects of this type of selective reinforcement would appear to indicate that nurture is responsible for gender biases, we must also remember the original template of attunement that goes on between child and caretaker. A caretaker does whatever it takes to get baby to smile, or at least to stop fussing. Do we really treat young children differently because of our *own* gender biases and expectations? Or do the individual children themselves stimulate a lifelong pattern of selective reinforcement by responding differently to significant others, in part because of inborn gender differences? Also, epinephrine and testosterone are both associated with increased activity and aggressiveness. Could these traits be more evident in boys because of the additional epinephrine and testosterone entering their systems during the gender-determination phase of their fetal development?

When you look a little closer at the specific research focusing on gender differences, another observation emerges. One study of 50 personality traits showed differences between men and women on only seven of those traits, and some did not go along with societal expectations (Steinberg & Shapiro, 1982). Furthermore, closer analysis of similar studies combined finds that whatever differences are found account at most for only 6% of the variance among people, and usually much less.

In other words, even though these studies found differences among men and women as groups, the vast majority of differences found between individuals can be accounted for by reasons other than gender.

Regardless of the origins or extent of gender differences, both young men and young women of Western culture often leave childhood with a confused sense of self. Both are leaving behind a part of themselves as they attempt to fit into their expected gender role. Men learn to dissociate themselves from their feelings of intimacy, vulnerability, and dependency in the pursuit of power and control, the hallmarks of the "real man" (Kupers, 1993). Women learn to disconnect from any tendencies toward assertiveness and learn to distrust their inner experience, since it is so foreign to what is valued or desired by a male power-oriented society (Brown & Gilligan, 1992). Dealing with these internal conflicts continues as they adjust to young adulthood.

Expanding Your Experience

Studying the findings of developmental research can help us understand some of our own childhood experiences. For example, when I was in the sixth grade, I had a teacher who rewarded exceptional classroom participation with the contents of a sack she kept in her bottom desk drawer. The sack was filled with candy bars—not the little snack-sized jobbies, but a variety of the really "big" ones.

One day for discussion, she posed the question, "What sorts of things do people shy away from doing?" The class fell silent. After a while, the teacher repeated the question. Having inherited an inhibited temperament, I tended not to contribute much to classroom discussions anyway and did not find this extended silence to be terribly distressing. However, it was agonizing for the class extroverts, who squirmed uncomfortably in their seats and looked as if they felt downright guilty.

I began to feel for the discomfort of my classmates. I bit the bullet, raised my hand, and shared: "People shy away from saying what they really think." Knowing my introverted nature, my teacher recognized the significance of what I had said beyond its surface meaning. She told me to go get a candy bar.

However, her offer did not feel right. Why? I did not know. I only knew that if I accepted the candy bar, I would feel like my contribution was being devalued. To the amazement of everyone in the room—including myself—I declined the offer. Something more important than a candy bar was directing that I not take a concrete reward for this particular contribution.

After becoming a student of developmental psychology, I came to understand what I had experienced so many years earlier. I had shared a very personal discussion response out of empathy and caring for my fellow classmates. Most likely I had been experiencing the early pangs of internalized and principled moral reasoning and felt a concrete reward would encourage regression back to more primitive, externally oriented motivations. Even though I had not known what I was doing at the time, I had been intuitively protecting my personal growth.

I have included some activities and exercises that I hope will help you similarly assess the experience of childhood. I call the first exercise a "developmental debate," as it gives you the opportunity to explore how you have intellectually processed certain variables of childhood development thus far. The second exercise looks at the differing perspectives of psychology and how they explain the development of our experience of anxiety. The third exercise is designed to help you assess how you identify with your feelings of being male or female. The fourth exercise provides practice at analyzing the various levels of moral reasoning. The last two exercises are a temperamental analysis and a self-esteem rating scale.

STUDY QUESTIONS

1. What is meant by "temperament," and what evidence suggests that it is inherited?
2. Explain the role of assimilation and accommodation in cognitive schema development.
3. What types of learning take place during sensorimotor development?
4. Describe the abilities and limitations of the preoperational child.
5. Suppose a new CD is out that you would really like, but it is very hard to find. How might you go about looking for it if you were (a) concrete operational, or (b) formal operational?
6. What relationship do you see between Kohlberg's stages of moral development and a person's tendency to look inside or outside for direction and guidance?
7. What differences are sometimes found among the moral reasoning schemas of men and women?
8. What is meant by infant "attunement," and what role can it play in our future interpersonal relationships?
9. How did Erikson see child development differently from Freud?

10. What roles do the inferiority-superiority complex and social striving play in child development?
11. Describe how you might use "shaping" to teach a child to write.
12. According to behavioral theory, if you learned to be afraid of dogs as a child, will you be afraid of dogs for life? Explain your answer.
13. Think of a time when you mimicked the behavior of someone you admire, such as a style of dress or a manner of responding. How were the four components of observational learning involved?
14. How might Allport explain why a 2-year-old believes everything is "mine"?
15. Describe the differences in self-view, view of others, and worldview of high and low self-esteem individuals.
16. How can nature and nurture affect the development of self-esteem?
17. How can personal choice affect personal growth?
18. What is the difference between gender identity and gender roles?
19. Do you think cognitive and behavioral differences between boys and girls are due more to nature or nurture? Explain your answer.
20. Are men and women more similar than they are different? Explain your answer.

Chapter Three

Development as a Young Adult

Transitionings

Are We There Yet?

Development as a Young Adult: Transitionings

The shift from childhood to adulthood is a murky one. When does adulthood actually begin? Is it at age 18, when we reach legal majority? Is it when we graduate from high school or college? Perhaps adulthood begins when we are able to live separately from our parents and support ourselves. Maybe the right to drive, vote, drink alcohol, or be drafted into the armed forces is the sign that adulthood has been achieved. Or is it when we are physically able to reproduce? Does getting married signify adulthood?

Obviously, those questions do not help much. Many 18-year-olds are still financially dependent on their parents, even if they have reached legal majority. Likewise, teenagers younger than 18 have struck out on their own, yet they do not have all of the rights of adulthood. Twelve-year-old girls often have the capacity to reproduce, yet in years past it was not unusual for women over the age of 18 to still be waiting for menstruation to begin. Teenage marriages occur with some regularity, yet some individuals go through their entire lives without marrying.

Western culture has complicated the issue by introducing a period of time that has come to be known as "adolescence." Adolescence seems to have been invented so that personal development complements our industrialized culture. We can no longer enter self-sufficiency in our society without a significant amount of specialized education and training. While in earlier days teenagers would become apprentices within various trades and make preparations for running households, today's teenagers go on to middle school, high school, college, and perhaps even professional and graduate schools before they enter the "real world."

Simultaneously, teenagers are physically maturing much earlier than previous generations. Reproductive capacity, attraction to the opposite sex, the desire to produce and start a home, and more-sophisticated reasoning processes are experienced by young people who are still far from prepared for the consequences of following through on those urges and abilities. The end result is a substantial amount of friction between the adolescent's inner experience and how it can be adaptively expressed in his or her outer world.

The outer world itself is not as promising for young people as it used to be. Our economy has recessed to the point where most young couples will need two incomes to be able to get by and even so may never be able to afford to own a house. The environment has suffered many forms of pollution and is working its way toward becoming depleted of necessary resources. Technology has become so advanced that the percentage of workings of our world that we can actually understand is vastly reduced. The threat of AIDS casts its shadow over the pursuit of a significant other. In spite of the toning down of the capitalist/communist battle in recent years, the political world still looks pretty bleak as the media plays up the existence of poverty, violated human rights, and civil wars. Some styles of rock music have capitalized on these frustrations and pump them up as they musically express feelings such as futility.

Not surprisingly, adolescence in our culture is experienced as a tumultuous time of life. Little wonder that teenagers rebel against society's expectations—society rebels against addressing teenagers' changing developmental needs! The teen generation appears to act as a barometer for our society's ills as it wrestles with this internal/external conflict. Most unwanted pregnancies occur among teenagers. Experimentation with street drugs and alcohol is also prevalent, as teenagers numb themselves to conflict and frustration. The crime rate rises as those who are not cut out for higher education or cannot afford to pay for additional training turn to other means of making their way. Interpersonal violence increases as teenagers physically act out their frustration.

With the above as a backdrop, today's teenagers are going through the usual developmental progressions of their phase of life. They delve into formulating an identity, begin developing many important new skills, learn to express their sexuality in socially acceptable ways, and apply their capacity for formal operational reasoning to their pursuits. They also begin recognizing themselves as unique and independently functioning human beings. And within that recognition they will not only find answers to the unique ills of this era, but also their unique solutions to the challenge of living fulfilling lives.

Recovery from Adolescence

Within many cultures, movements from one stage of life to another are marked by some form of traditional public celebration commemorating the events, often referred to as **rites of passage** (van Gennep, 1908). Rituals such as marriages, graduations, bar and bat mitzvahs, baptisms, and funerals are all designed to show the world that a person is moving from one state of being to another. Once the ceremony has taken place, the change is generally accepted as an irrefutable reality by both the individual and his or her society.

There are no consistently recognized rites of passage for moving into adulthood in our culture. For instance, as Robert Bly (1990) points out, in earlier cultures, as boys were maturing toward the edge of the accepted boundaries of childhood, they would be separated, instructed, and ceremonially initiated toward their society's perception of manhood. Having been acknowledged as an adult, the young man would then enjoy the rights and privileges of the status, as well as hold its responsibilities. Bly believes that much of our current gender identity confusion evolved not so much because of changing gender roles but because of the disintegration of the initiation process into the status of manhood, or of womanhood.

Our industrialized, impersonal, "sophisticated" society has become too preoccupied for such rites of passage. As a result, young people are left to struggle with the changeover to adulthood issue by issue, transforming it into a collection of concrete tasks rather than adoption of an identity. And whether or not the collection of tasks has been successfully completed is to a certain degree subjective—not to mention the subjectivity of what constitutes the definition of adulthood in the first place!

Thus the timing of when we arrive at adulthood is more or less up to ourselves. It is an act of the will: Do you accept—irrefutably—that you are now an adult? And since we cannot depend on society to systematically provide us with that definitive status, we must find our own way to establish it. In other words, how do we choose to leave childhood behind and become young adults, how do we move into the experience of adulthood, and what might we find when we get there? The remainder of this chapter explores these questions.

The Role of Biology

Our adult physical structure is determined more by nature than by choice. By the end of adolescence, we have experienced **puberty** and have gone through drastic physical changes from how we looked as children. While as youngsters our basic body shapes looked almost unisexual, our physical characteristics now vary depending on our gender. Young women become softer and develop a curved body shape, while young men become more muscular and angular. Puberty also marks the beginning of our ability to reproduce.

During young adulthood, we reach a **physical peak**. Typically during our twenties our bodies reach their most productive physical potential. We are stronger, faster, better coordinated, and at the height of our capacity for endurance. Our mental capacities also appear to peak during young adulthood. Most scientists make their major research contributions before they reach the age of 40 (Rebok, 1987). Since young adulthood is a busy, active time of our lives, the physical and mental peaks are not only a convenience but also a necessity. We need considerable strength to work our way through the change and stress of adapting to adult roles, establishing ourselves financially, and developing independent lifestyles.

The "Morning of Life"

We begin our adult lives through recognition of our separateness and independence. We learn to make choices that reflect our own dreams and desires. If we simply drift along through young adulthood, going along with the desires of our parents or spouses or following the life direction of our peers, we are psychologically still adolescents. We are also more likely to find ourselves in a state of crisis as we reach midlife!

Carl Jung (1955) conceptualized young adulthood as a time of **individuation**. We define who we are, separate from family and peers. Young adulthood is an entry point into living, the "morning of life." He saw the tasks of young adulthood as falling within two structures: the **acquisition of possessions** and the development of an **ego complex**. The acquisition of possessions represents the building of our external life structures. What will our careers consist of? Who will our spouses be, and what about children? What material needs must be met as a requirement for our feeling happy? What do we need to accomplish in our lives in order to feel as if we are a "success"?

The ego complex represents the development of our internal life structures. During young adulthood we refine our self-identity, transforming our childhood personalities as we experienced them into adult forms, yet not losing our authenticity in the process. In other words, we maintain contact with who we are as we develop conceptualizations of and plans for who we want to be and what we want out of our lives.

Setting Up an External Life Structure

Freud's stages of development ended more or less at adulthood. He felt that any significant development occurred by the end of adolescence, and from that point forward we simply replay or recover from previous life experiences. Daniel Levinson disagrees (Levinson et al., 1978). He and his colleagues suggest that adulthood is a series of structurings and restructurings of our lives. As we enter each phase of adult living, such as marriage and parenting, career establishment, and so forth, we try out our plan for living and then reevaluate it as we move into new phases, and restructure if necessary.

Levinson defined young adulthood as approximately ages 22 to 30. Young adulthood is our first crack at creating a stable life structure. We formulate a "life dream" and work toward making that life dream come true. We develop our love relationships and, usually, start building a family. We see an end to formal training and move on to establishing a career. We seek out a relationship with a **mentor**–someone older and more experienced than ourselves–who shows us the ropes of living. Mentors act as role models and help facilitate our life dreams.

Havighurst (1972) conceptualizes the tasks of young adulthood within eight broad areas:

1. *Choosing a mate.* We learn to approach potential mates, evaluate them, and decide upon a life partner.
2. *Learning to live with a mate.* As our lives become intertwined with those of our spouses, we develop strategies for getting along with one another, including development of joint life goals in addition to our individual goals.
3. *Becoming a parent.* We have children and begin taking into account the needs of the family as we arrange our household, finances, and activities.
4. *Child-rearing.* We develop parenting strategies, in hopes of helping our children grow up to be healthy, happy, and well-adjusted.
5. *Home management.* We set up a structure for running a household, defining tasks, and dividing up responsibilities among its members.
6. *Beginning a career.* We seek out desired training, find employment, and begin developing and working toward long-term career goals.
7. *Finding a role in society.* We find our place in the community, such as within civic groups, churches, and neighborhood activity.
8. *Developing a social life.* We begin forming long-term adult friendships, and define their context in our lives.

This structuring varies depending upon our individual differences. For example, **gender-splitting** is especially evident at this stage (Levinson, 1990). Traditionally, men went off to work while women stayed at home to take care of the children, clean house, and take responsibility for household management. Currently most women work outside the home as well, in many cases because of financial necessity. While some men have started pitching in and sharing household and child care responsibilities, in the vast majority of homes this is not the case, leaving the woman of the household with an exhausting schedule (Rogan, 1984). Therefore women need to carefully evaluate the timing of career and home-related activities in ways that men typically do not.

Likewise, women appear to set up and work toward goals differently than men. Women are less likely than men to set up firmly held long-term goals (Levinson, 1990). This may be due to the extent that chance plays in women's lives. If you suddenly discover you are pregnant, your life plans may be necessarily altered—at least for the next 18 years! Likewise, if there is a chance you might fall in love and marry someone who will expect you to adopt the traditional wifely position of dropping everything in order to run a household or move around in support of his career, setting up firm goals early on can seem unrealistic. Thus, women currently find it more adaptive to maintain flexibility in their life goals.

While sorting out life plans, women tend to seek different mentors and role models. Men typically find mentors within their career fields. Women, on the other hand, are more likely to look for role models outside of their place of employment (Reinke et al., 1983). Since women need role models who help them sort out their multiple-career juggling act, a mentor for only one of those careers may not be adequate.

Many other individual differences can affect the primacy of Havighurst's eight structural areas. Some people choose to remain single rather than enter a committed relationship. Others do not have children. Some play only limited roles in home management, and some do not have careers outside the home at all. Expectations of your particular subculture, race, religion, and socioeconomic status can also play a dramatic role in the extent to which you address these structural areas.

As is evident from the above, during early adulthood we make a lot of choices that will affect our entire life structures. There will be second chances as we make use of opportunities presented in later adulthood, but early choices such as who we marry, the presence and absence of children, the degree of education and training we seek, how well we take care of our health, and our early life dreams themselves will all have a lingering impact on the remainder of our lives.

BUILDING AN INTERNAL LIFE STRUCTURE

Erikson (1963) conceptualized early adulthood as the years 18 to 22. This stage, which he called **intimacy versus isolation**, is a time of learning to share ourselves with others. If we progress successfully through this stage, we achieve the capacity for intimacy. During adolescence our interpersonal identity was more of a reflection bounced off of our significant peer groups; as young adults we feel secure enough in ourselves and our own identity to form relationships based on our true attributes, rather than through smoke and mirrors. We can be close to others without losing ourselves in them. We learn to love, have close friendships, develop adult relationships with our families of origin, and feel responsible for the direction of our interpersonal lives. Erikson believed that if we have a difficult time struggling through this stage we will develop feelings of isolation instead: we will feel lonely, unappreciated by those around us or perhaps even exploited, and generally short-changed by life.

Erikson's studies of development tended to focus more on men than women. Later studies suggest that adolescence, young adulthood, and the development of an identity may be different for women (Gilligan, 1982). While young men's development appears to be guided by issues of autonomy and individuation, young women appear to be guided more by changing patterns of caring and connectedness to others. Recent research findings suggest that women establish the capacity for intimate relationships by the time of young adulthood, whereas this trait still appears to be developing in young men (Reis et al., 1993). Thus adolescence of women may be characterized more by the interpersonal nature of intimacy versus isolation, with the struggles of identity versus role confusion addressed as a young adult.

Individuation. Gould (1978) sees the **individuation** process of young adulthood as a time of letting go of false assumptions about those who raised us. When we were little, we had tremendous, even magical, faith in our parents. We believed they could fix any problem, that they would always be there, and recognized that they were ultimately responsible to society for our behavior and well-being. As young adults, we see that parents do not always have all the answers and may not be able to solve all our problems for us. Likewise, we realize that we are ultimately responsible for our behavior, taking care of ourselves, and developing our own values and morals.

However, separating our internal experience from our parents does not mean that we lose that particular internal function entirely. One way we continue to "parent" ourselves is explained by a form of therapy called **transactional analysis** (Goulding & Goulding, 1979). This theory suggests that our egos are made up of an adult, child, and parent self. The parent self is our perception of our parents—their beliefs, morals, values, and perhaps even physical mannerisms. However, we balance the impact of the parent self's influence with the child self—our impulsive, emotional, and hedonistic self-interests—and the adult self—our objectivity and logic. So although we may hear tapes of our parents' "shoulds" and "oughts" for the rest of our lives, as adults we temper that learning with the reasoning and self-awareness of maturity.

Who's in control? Another way of looking at our young adult individuation process is the concept of **locus of control** (Rotter, 1966). What controls the outcome of our lives? Some people believe that everything is due to chance, that we are slaves to the whims and dictates of others and society, and that there is not much we can do to change this state of affairs. If this describes your attitude, you have an **external locus of control**, since you believe your life is directed by external factors. On the other hand, if you believe you have an impact on the events that affect you, or that we all make our own "luck," you have an **internal locus of control**, since you recognize your own ability to guide your life situation. As you might suspect, we get along better when we have an internal locus of control. If we are still looking outside ourselves for magical control, then psychologically, we are still depending on parents and others for our destiny. Suppose you were looking at someone across the room that you would really like to get to know. If you have an external locus of control, you would most likely be standing around waiting for the other person to place himself or herself in your proximity and initiate some sort of interaction. After all, if you do not believe your efforts are going to make any difference, there is no point in trying to start something yourself. If you have an internal locus of control, you would most likely walk over and introduce yourself, since you understand that your behavior will have an effect on developing a relationship with the person. Either way, a relationship may or may not work out. But with an internal locus of control as a motivator you would at least have more to depend upon than chance.

Subjective well-being. As we define a separate identity, redefine it within the context of interpersonal relationships, and take responsibility for the direction of our lives, we hope to structure ourselves in the direction of life satisfaction. In other words, we strive to be happy. Diener (1984) refers to this as developing a sense of **subjective well-being**.

Subjective well-being is a matter of perception, rather than objective reality. And it appears to be a matter of how often rather than how intensely you feel that way. In general, subjective well-being is present if you are experiencing good feelings, are not experiencing unpleasant feelings, and are for the most part satisfied with the direction your life is taking. Subjective well-being is more likely to be found among those who are married, have good self-esteem, are more extroverted than introverted, and have a positive outlook on life. During young adulthood women tend to be happier than men, but in later years this trend reverses itself.

Refining gender expectations. As we progress through young adulthood, we firm up our concepts of being a man or woman. Since the cultural expectations for these traits seem to be changing yearly, flexibility and adaptiveness are in order as we form the adult version of our gender identity.

Sandra Bem (1981) has studied extensively the concepts of masculinity and femininity. She points out that while there are certain attributes that are traditionally considered female and others that are considered male, we are not necessarily better off when we go along with cultural gender-role expectations.

Individuals of either gender can have varying levels of so-called masculine and feminine traits. Figure 3.1 illustrates the different possibilities. Those who are high in masculine traits and low in feminine traits are the traditional macho males, such as characters typically played by John

	Low in Masculine Traits	High in Masculine Traits
Low in Feminine Traits	Undifferentiated	Traditional Masculine
High in Feminine Traits	Traditional Feminine	Androgynous

FIGURE 3.1
Matrix illustrating the various combinations of traditional masculine and feminine traits.

Wayne or Clint Eastwood. Those high in feminine traits and low in masculine traits are like the more traditional feminine types, such as early "June Cleaver" of *Leave It to Beaver* or "Melanie Wilkes" of *Gone With the Wind*. Those who are low in both sets of traits are called "undifferentiated," as we observe in *Roseanne*'s sister "Jackie," most Woody Allen characters, and the "Pat" character of *Saturday Night Live*. Those showing high presentation of both masculine and feminine traits are called **androgynous**. More and more androgynous movie characters are surfacing who demonstrate both healthy strengths and healthy vulnerabilities, as in characters typically played by Sigourney Weaver and Harrison Ford.

Bem proposed that the most well-adjusted individuals were those whose personalities are androgynous. After many studies, this idea was not supported. Instead, research discovered that the most well-adjusted individuals were men or women who were high in so-called masculine traits (Taylor & Hall, 1982). In view of these findings, Bem (1985) suggests that we move away from the concept of gender role dichotomies and move toward **gender transcendence**. Rather than assign roles and activities to each gender that have nothing to do with inheritance of X and Y chromosomes, she proposes we simply become the people we are and not worry so much about specific gender expectations. In concert with her research, we are currently sorting out the issue of reduction of sexism in societal roles.

Organizing Young Adult Living

As children and adolescents we depend on others for organization and management of how to spend our time. As we emancipate into young adulthood we take on the task of doing those things for ourselves. Exactly what is it we want to do? How will we go about doing it? When and where will it happen? Since you are reading this text, it is probably safe to assume that a college education currently fits in with your plans. The rest of this section describes techniques for increasing the likelihood of meeting your college goals.

Time Management

While we were youngsters, a good deal of our time management was taken care of by authority figures. We were required to be in school during certain hours of the day. Curfews ensured our being home at night. Meals were often structured around family living, requiring that we be present at the table at specific times. Usually we were required to check with parents before doing anything, in the event that we may have overlooked other commitments.

As adults, we take over our own time management. At first, we may be so grateful to be outside of parental control and free from societal requirements of minority that we throw all caution to the wind and do everything we felt like we had been deprived of earlier. Whether or not this strategy works out depends on how excessive our impulses are, what sorts of goals we have for ourselves, and how many internal controls we have developed for reconciling the two.

Effective time management takes organization. It asks the following:

- What are your current time-expenditure goals? You probably have many, both short- and long-term. You want to have time to attend classes and do homework, enjoy college social activities, make enough money

Time	Sunday	Monday	Tuesday	Wednesday	Thursday	Friday	Saturday
6–7 AM							
7–8							
8–9							
9–10	Biology homework	PY 102		PY 102		PY 102	
10–11		WR 122	LEISURE	WR 122		WR 122	
11–12			LEISURE				
12–1 PM	Lunch	Lunch	Lunch	Lunch	Lunch	Lunch	Lunch
1–2	LEISURE	MTH 205	PE 323	MTH 205	PE 323	Weekly quiz MTH 205	Football game
2–3	LEISURE	Math homework	PE 323	Math homework	PE 323	Math homework	
3–4	WORK SHIFT			WORK SHIFT		WORK SHIFT	
4–5		LEISURE	BIO 101		LEISURE		
5–6		LEISURE	BIO 101		LEISURE		
6–7	Sack dinner	Dinner	BIO 101	Sack dinner	Dinner	Sack dinner	Dinner
7–8		PY 102 readings	Sack dinner				Party at Smith Hall
8–9			WR122 homework		Study for Math quiz		
9–10				LEISURE		LEISURE	
10–11				LEISURE		LEISURE	
11–12							

FIGURE 3.2
Example of time scheduling.

to meet your financial needs, spend time with your significant other and your friends, and also participate in some favorite pastimes.

• What are the constraints on your time? The timing of some activities is more or less etched in granite, such as needing to attend classes at certain times, being scheduled to work certain hours, needing regular sleep hours, having time to eat, and attending social activities such as spectator sports, rallies, and parties.

• What are your priorities? In other words, what do you feel or believe you must do, what is less important, and which goals are of relatively little significance?

Having decided on the answers to the above questions, set up a schedule of all your waking hours. Figure 3.2 shows how this can be designed. Then, fill in all hours that cannot be changed, such as school, work, sports practices, and any one-shot social events that are going on during the week. Next, consider high-priority tasks that have a certain amount of flexibility, such as homework. After looking over the study requirements of your courses, estimate the amount of time you will need to complete assignments or study for tests and fill in time slots that will be both long enough and soon enough to meet your deadlines. Your goal is to assign study time adequately enough so that you can still attend major social activities. However, if the only free time you have for writing your report is during the big kegger, you may need to miss that kegger. Careful planning—such as starting your report a little earlier—can help you avoid such conflicts of time interest. Having time for dating or spending time with the significant others in your life may also rate high-priority status within your flexible time slots. Making time to eat during the hours the dining hall is open may be another factor to consider.

Some students plan to use all of their free time during the week for goofing off, then schedule all day Saturday or Sunday for studying. This usually does not work out very well. First of all, you will probably burn out before you get everything done. Second, the hours the library and other school resources are open are often more restricted on those days. Third, many social occasions and extracurricular activities are scheduled on weekends. If you decide one of these is too important to miss, there goes a whole week's worth of studying. Fourth, your friends are going to do a lot of major-league partying and carrying on during the weekend, which will create a tremendous distraction and pull you toward doing the same yourself. Spreading homework over the whole week causes fewer conflicts. If you do end up having a lot of study time on certain days, make sure you include scheduled breaks so you do not run out of steam.

After filling in the flexible high priorities, start filling in moderate and low priorities. You can jostle these things around depending on how much flexibility they have, how important they are to you, and how much free time you find you have left. Remember the following important points as you do so:

• Arrange your schedule in ways that take advantage of your "peak performance" times. I usually work best in the early part of the day, but other people get their best work done in the evening or even into the wee hours of the morning. Arrange your schedule so that you can get the most out of your more productive hours.

• Always include time for leisure. Unless it is scheduled, you may end up going AWOL and not get other important time-expenditure goals met. Also, scheduling nonconflictual leisure time allows you to truly relax and enjoy yourself, since you know you have time scheduled for the high-pressure activities. Making sure you have leisure time provides an added bonus of helping you feel refreshed when you return to more demanding pursuits.

• Once you make a schedule, try hard to stick to it. Despite your best efforts, however, last minute priorities will no doubt present themselves on a regular basis. When you do find the need to make last minute changes, make sure you realistically reschedule the high-priority activities.

• If you find a task or homework assignment seems like too much to do, break it up. For example, writing major papers can seem overwhelming. Not so if you look at the various parts and address them one at a time: deciding on a topic, doing a little library research and refining your topic, choosing your materials and references, putting tidbits of information on 3×5 cards, grouping and organizing cards as they seem related, creating an outline for your paper, writing the first section, the second, the third, and so on. It's still a lot of work. But if you break it up and do it bit by bit over the time allotted, the small pieces by themselves seem much more manageable. A good rule is to begin work on papers the day they are assigned. Putting them off until the last minute is not worth the pressure and anxiety.

• If you have trouble getting into studying, start with something that is interesting or takes little effort. Once you get rolling it gets easier.

• Group together small nitpicky tasks and do them all at once: minor forms to fill out and mail, "administrative" phone calls, and so on. If you have tasks that take you away from home, try to do them all at once, such as doing some necessary shopping and picking up a book at the library on the same morning you have to go to a dental appointment.

These same principles of time management apply to life beyond the university setting. You are likely to always have multiple obligations and interests. Instead of juggling study and socializing, you will most likely be juggling career, family, household management, and personal interests. Young adult school days may suddenly seem a lot easier!

Some of you courageous folks are attending school while also having a family, and you may be working full-time as well. Your schedules are going to fill up a lot faster. Balancing school with child-rearing is especially challenging, since children don't look at schedules before they get ill, hurt, or whiny, or just want some attention. Try to schedule parent-child time when you think it will most satisfy your child. School-age children tend to be most interested in having contact with parents right after they get home from school; infants and toddlers appreciate the most individual attention just before they get tired or hungry and when they first get up from sleeping. Plan your time according to your children's apparent needs. Another good strategy is to spend individual time with the children just before you want to study, so they will feel "filled up" and therefore less likely to interrupt you. And don't forget about leisure time. Be sure to arrange some personal space—even if it is only 15 minutes a day—when you stop being Mommy, Daddy, husband, wife, student, employee, and your other social roles long enough to return to feeling like you.

Using Study Time Effectively

Different academic tasks require study of different levels of intensity. During low-intensity study periods you might be sitting back in a recliner with a can of your favorite beverage at your elbow, partaking in a little channel-surfing on the side. More intense studying might include sitting at your desk poring over your notes, sweat beading on your brow, and a pot of coffee at hand to fortify your all-night vigil.

The first step in organizing your study time is deciding which type of studying you need to do. Is it casual general studying, such as reading chapters that will be covered in lecture the next day, skimming through potential references for a term paper, working your way through a study guide, or some other low-pressure activity? Or is it the type of intense study necessary for preparing for exams, writing papers, or figuring out difficult or complex concepts?

Organize your study environment according to which type of studying time you need. Casual studying requires minimal structuring, as long as you succeed in eventually completing the task. But if you need to get into some quality studying, you will need to do some planning. Interruptions must be minimized, otherwise you will find yourself devoting precious study time to getting back to the level of depth of study you had attained before the interruption. If there are a lot of interruptions, you may not get anywhere. You benefit from getting rid of distractions. Don't take phone calls, turn off or move away from the television, and let your roommate and friends know you need quality study time and request that they not interrupt you. Go to the library to study if your living environment is excessively noisy or chaotic.

When going over material for the first time, a study technique that is both popular and effective is known as the **SQ3R** method (Robinson, 1970). SQ3R is an acronym standing for Survey, Question, Read, Recite, and Review. First you **survey**, skimming over the entire chapter, article, or collection of material you intend to study during that period. Thus you have an idea of what you are dealing with. Then you go through it a second time, asking yourself **questions** that seem to be presented by subheadings or italicized terms, such as "What is *SQ3R*?" It may be helpful to actually write down your questions. Then go ahead and **read** the material, trying to answer your questions as you go along. After each segment, **recite** what you have learned without looking at the text. At the end of your study period, or even a day or two later, **review** the material by requizzing yourself and going over the parts you couldn't remember.

When studying for examinations, there are a number of techniques that can help you memorize material. **Mnemonic devices** such as **acronyms** are especially helpful for remembering lists or collections of concepts. For example, if you remember SQ3R and recall what each letter of the acronym stands for, memorizing SQ3R will lead to your ability to recite the five steps of studying without having to stop and individually retrieve five separate concepts from memory.

Overlearning is also helpful as you commit material to memory. Instead of studying until you can successfully quiz yourself once, you continue to quiz yourself beyond the point of initial mastery. This way you not only learn the material, but also get practice retrieving it, which is what you will have to do when you take the examination.

A common college campus test-preparation technique—which you have probably already tried—is to wait until the night before the test and then cram. You may pass the test after using this strategy, but you are more likely to do well by distributing study over a longer period of time (Wickelgren, 1981). Distributed practice is also more likely to ensure that you will remember something after the test, as is less likely to be the case with the "chew and spew" method of learning.

Another extremely useful skill for enhancing your study time, as well as your overall educational experience, is typing ability. Naturally, building up a good typing speed is most useful when it comes time to type term papers and other written assignments. However, there are other advantages as well. Instructors are usually more impressed with an assignment that has been neatly typed than with one that has been written in longhand. The increased ease in reading also allows the instructor to spend less time trying to decipher your handwriting and more time analyzing what you have written and giving you useful feedback. Typing your lecture notes the night after you take them serves as an excellent means of reviewing and reconceptualizing what you have learned. If you have access to a word processor, you can organize papers and some other written assignments as you go along, rather than waiting until the end stages. Regardless of how you make use of your typing skill as a student, it is nonetheless an ability that can serve as an asset no matter where you go. There are few jobs in our modern technological society that do not require us to be able to make use of a keyboard.

The Collisions of College Living

College life is unique. There is no other lifestyle in Western culture that is quite the same. It has its own sets of unwritten rules, challenges, conflicts, and possibilities; and usually students are left to figure out a lot on their own. Spethman (1992) offers a number of useful trivia that may help you as you adjust to college living:

- Your attitude will make or break your school performance. Try not to procrastinate: The more the work builds up, the worse your attitude will become. When you do endure some "failure," whether it be academic-, social-, or sports-related, do not sit around and mope. Find something productive to do, so you can show yourself that your one screw-up is not the sum total of who you are.

- Find a physical activity you can engage in regularly. Physical activity is refreshing, and it clears the mind. (Chapters 4 and 7 of this text will review some of the benefits of exercise.)

- When meeting people for the first time, spend a lot of time listening. In this manner you are more likely to pick out the "ne'er-do-wells" who are likely to drag you down with them and interfere with your goal attainment.

- Remember that just as there are quality and nonquality study times, there are quality and nonquality parties. You do not have to go to every party you hear about, and some of them are not worth your valuable leisure time. One thing you can always be sure of is that there will be another party. Choose carefully.

- If the purpose of going to school is to prepare for a job, major or take classes in an area that prepares you for one. This may seem like stating the obvious. However many people go to college and major in subjects they enjoy or do well in but by themselves will not get them into related employment. For example, if you are interested in English literature and want to major in it that is all well and good, but make sure you also get a teaching certificate or take journalism classes so you will be able to do something with your skills once you graduate.

- A lot of lending and borrowing goes on in dormitories, fraternities, and sororities. For minimum frustration and conflict always ask before you borrow, and return things when you said you would. No matter how friendly or enmeshed your living situation, people appreciate these common courtesies.

- Avoid "one-night-stands." They are potentially bad for your physical well-being, do not promote healthy mutual respect, and aren't anywhere near as satisfying as sex with someone you really know and care about. You will like yourself better if you manage your sexuality.

- Remember that the transition between reading something and actually understanding and knowing it takes time.

- Learn how libraries work, if possible before you even arrive on your college campus.

- Never miss a review class the day before a test.
- Never take your books on breaks.
- Never drink and drive.

And no matter how difficult things seem to be, hang on to the motto "this, too, shall pass!"

Expanding Your Experience

Our personal uniqueness results in each of us finding our own way to successfully transition into adulthood. For example, I have always looked young for my age, and I was also usually the youngest person in class. Because I was both young and small of stature, my high school classmates treated me differently. Other girls had a tendency to "mother" me, and boys treated me as this frail little thing that needed their protection. It was as if I were the "baby" of the class. While in some ways it was nice to be cared for, I also felt personally stifled, as well as lonely for relating to others on an equal footing.

By the time I finished high school, I had more or less caught up with my cohorts, at least in terms of height. However, I still felt like the "baby," the one that nobody took very seriously, or certainly never viewed as a young adult. Part of my solution to this dilemma was to create a new "identity" by enrolling in a university located on the opposite side of the state. Few people there would be aware of the role I had played during my growing years.

To a certain extent, my solution worked. Adjustment to living 300 miles from home in itself produced feelings of independence. I made new friends, and shifted gears into the behaviors of young adulthood, leaving behind the roles and playthings of my past. I eventually discovered that becoming a young adult was actually an effort of the heart, rather than a role to be played.

The discovery of my internal locus of control was fortunate. Since I still had a slight build and youthful facial features, I looked about 12 years old. I was repeatedly assumed to be a local high school student who was enhancing her education with a few college courses. Had I not come to the conclusion that entering young adulthood is an internal event, I still would have felt like the "baby" and probably would have begun acting-out that role as well.

The last time I was "carded" was when I was 36. When I proudly produced my driver's license, the vendor was somewhat embarrassed—especially when my gigantic 15-year-old son walked up behind me and addressed me as "Mom." As you might suspect, this experience did not result in my feeling like the "baby." It made my day.

The first exercise for this chapter is an opportunity for you to design your own "rites of passage" into young adulthood. The second exercise will help you evaluate your sense of internal or external locus of control. The third exercise will give you a chance to practice time-scheduling.

Study Questions

1. Why is the transition from childhood to adulthood so hard to define?
2. Compare television programs such as *Leave It to Beaver* and *Father Knows Best* to current sitcoms such as *Roseanne* and *Beverly Hills 90210*. What challenges do today's young people face that may not have been issues for earlier generations?

3. What are "rites of passage," and what role do they play in becoming an adult? Describe any "rites of passage" you may have already experienced.
4. What are the biological differences between childhood and young adulthood?
5. Explain Carl Jung's concepts of young adult "acquisition of possessions" and developing an "ego complex."
6. How does Daniel Levinson's concept of young adulthood differ from Freud's?
7. Explain how individual differences can affect completion of Havighurst's tasks of early adulthood.
8. How do Erikson's stages of adolescence and young adulthood appear to be different for men and women?
9. What is meant by "individuation"?
10. Explain the concepts behind transactional analysis.
11. What is meant by internal and external locus of control? Which tends to be healthier in Western culture, and why?
12. Describe Bem's work in the area of stereotypical masculine and feminine traits. What do you think she would suggest we do in order to attain maximum subjective well-being concerning our gender roles?
13. Describe the process of how you could go about effectively organizing your time during a given week.
14. What is the difference between quality and nonquality study time, and how would you organize your study environment to best suit each study need?
15. Describe techniques and strategies you could use that can assist you as you (1) study new material, (2) study for a test, and (3) write a term paper.
16. Familiarize yourself with Spethman's college-life "trivia."

Chapter Four
Stress, Anxiety, and Coping
Jostling the Jitters

You want it . . . when?

One morning you walk into your psychology classroom expecting to sit down with your colleagues and engage in the usual social banter as you await the professor's arrival. However, instead of conversing, your classmates are either silently sitting behind a cleared desk space with pencil in hand or are scanning a few pages of notes.

"Oh, no!" you groan internally. "There must be a test today! How could I let this happen? I'll never be able to pass—I haven't even read Chapter 11 yet. What if I fail the course? There goes my scholarship. What a screw-up I turned out to be."

Your stomach begins doing flip-flops. You break out in a cold sweat. As you take your seat and put down your books, you notice that your hands are shaking. Your head feels as if it is spinning as you struggle to think of ways to handle your predicament. As your internal turmoil is about to reduce you to a puddle of goo, your dorm chum leans over and whispers, "We're playing an April Fool's joke on the prof. Act like you're getting ready for a test—we're going to try to convince him he hasn't given the midterm yet and it's supposed to be today."

You breathe an audible sigh of relief, lean back in your chair and mop your brow. After a few moments of recollecting yourself you clear your desk, take out a pencil, and join your peers with occasional conspiratorial sideways glances.

The preceding scenario illustrates how quickly and easily our lives can be affected by events as we experience them. We react emotionally, physically, cognitively, and behaviorally as the everyday human drama unfolds before us. Stress, anxiety, and coping are all part of reacting to this drama. Typically, stress and anxiety are anticipatory phenomena, involving concerns about future events or fears of what might happen in the future if we are not adequately prepared.

What is the difference between stress and anxiety? Often people use the two terms interchangeably. There are many ways of compartmentalizing stress, anxiety, the interaction between the two, and the related behavioral choices. However, the following discussion will define **stress** as any factor that leads us to feel pressured to act. **Anxiety**, on the other hand, is one of the emotional states we experience in reaction to stress. **Coping** involves how we deal with stress, anxiety, or both as they affect our lives. We will look at each of these terms separately.

Stress

Stress involves individuality and subjectivity. What one person finds stressful may not bother another person at all. Personally I do not feel uncomfortable talking in front of most large groups, since my experience doing so as a psychologist and instructor has desensitized me to many of the usual concerns. However, many people panic at the thought of having to give a public presentation. They experience it as a major stressor, while for myself and others like me it is relatively minor.

Participating in a competitive sport such as a friendly game of softball, however, feels much more stressful for me since my experience in competitive sports is relatively limited. My students who play on the school baseball team—and perhaps even those who are on soccer, tennis, or golf teams—find the prospect of a little back-lot softball much less stressful, since they are accustomed to pitting their physical skills against those of others.

SOURCES OF STRESS

The reasons why we might experience stress for either the softball game or the speech vary. The level of experience we have handling certain situations can reduce the amount of stress we perceive because it reduces our **performance anxiety**. Performance anxiety involves concerns we have over how others will evaluate us as we publicize how well we can actually do something. However, other factors can be responsible as well, such as worrying about reinjuring a bad back during the softball game or being concerned about finishing your speech within the time allotted and still getting your point across. Thus potential sources of stress are not only events themselves, but also how we perceive them and how they interact with our individual differences.

Traumatic events. Often when we think of stress, we think of some aversive event, such as finding out about a test at the last minute. The more severely aversive events are experienced as more than stress and in fact cause physical and emotional trauma. Traumatic events can be due to natural disasters such as hurricanes and floods or human-made disasters such as wars and riots, sudden or violent deaths of loved ones, and near brushes with death of self. Such experiences typically produce a **post-traumatic stress reaction** (American Red Cross, 1993). These reactions can include extreme moodiness, disorientation and numbing, anger, apathy, depression, anxiety, and numerous physical ailments. If these symptoms are not effectively dealt with at the time of the trauma, a person can develop **post-traumatic stress disorder** (American Psychiatric Association, 1994)–a legacy of continuing to reexperience the trauma, which will be discussed in greater detail in Chapter 6.

Life changes. We human beings are creatures of habit. When our lives and environments are in a state of order, we feel more comfortable than when we are dealing with chaos. Our brains are designed to habituate to ongoing stimuli and to become alert when we notice something new. Continuity in our lives allows our brains to habituate and relax. But if we are experiencing a lot of changes in our lives, our brain stems will repeatedly alert us to that fact. This is stressful. So when we develop new friendships, start new schools, get married, move to a new house, have children, or start a new career, in addition to the rewards of the life change, we can also expect to experience a certain amount of stress.

Conflict. One type of uncertainty that our brains struggle to settle is conflict. Conflict can come in the form of disagreements with acquaintances, or even outright arguments with significant others. It can stem from feeling pressured to go along with something inconsistent with our values or what we believe to be the most efficient way to proceed. Frustration is another type of conflict: We know what we want to happen or accomplish, but something is blocking our way.

In addition to conflict with the environment, we can experience conflict within the self. Decision making involves looking at opposing variables and trying to decide which option will work out best for us. We feel off balance during the time we spend trying to make a decision between various conflicting options. There are four main types of decision-making conflict:

1. *Approach-approach.* More than one desirable option is available, but you can only have one. For example, perhaps you have a choice of your two favorite kinds of ice cream. You can only afford one. Whichever you choose you will enjoy, but choosing one means you will also have to go without the other.

2. *Avoidance-avoidance.* There are two undesirable options, and you would rather do without either, but you must choose one in order to meet your goal. "Pay me now, or pay me later" as you purchase a new stereo

is an example of an avoidance-avoidance conflict. Either way, you still have to pay.

3. *Approach-avoidance.* Most goals have both desirable and undesirable features. For example, choosing to get married has many advantages but also the disadvantages of losing freedom and privacy and dealing with the stress of the new relationship. Thus we are presented with a choice of either doing without the advantages or putting up with the disadvantages.

4. *Multiple approach-avoidance.* Most decisions involve a choice between multiple goals, and there are usually both desirable and undesirable features about each goal. For example, you may be faced with the decision to either buy a house in town or buy a house in the country. The house in the country is quieter and less expensive, but then you would have a long commute into town. A house in the city may be closer to work and shopping malls, but it also includes dealing with a higher incident of crime and less privacy. Multiple approach-avoidance decisions can seem overwhelming as we sort out all of the relevant issues and try to decide what is most important to us.

Hassles of daily living.
Just getting through the course of a usual day involves stumbling over a variety of minor stressors. Finishing a difficult homework assignment, the toaster breaking down, trying to think of something to fix for dinner, not being able to find a favorite pair of socks, dealing with a cranky child, and trying to get to work on time all create stress.

Environmental stressors.
In recent years, researchers have been looking at ongoing circumstances in the environment that can create a state of chronic stress. Crowding is one example of an environmental stressor. When the social density of an area becomes too high, we appear to feel the effects of stress, often in the form of an increase of aggressiveness (Fleming et al., 1987). Ongoing excessive noise appears to stress us to the point of interfering with cognitive ability and task completion, as well as increasing our blood pressure (Cohen et al., 1981). Air pollution has been associated with increased interpersonal aggression (Rotton et al., 1979) and decreased interpersonal attraction (Rotton et al., 1978). Ongoing excessively high temperatures have also been associated with increased levels of arousal and aggression (Anderson, 1987).

Other so-called environmental pressures are actually internal ones. When we perceive ourselves as being under pressure to perform over a long period of time, we feel stress (Weiten, 1988). And when we feel out of control of stressors, we feel even more stress (Breier et al., 1987).

Stress and the Body

As our bodies react to stress, we go through a process known as the **general adaptation syndrome** (Selye, 1976). First, the reticular activating system alerts us that something is amiss, or at least deserving of arousal. During this alarm stage it signals the autonomic nervous system by means of hormones, especially **epinephrine** (also known as adrenaline) and **norepinephrine** (also known as noradrenalin). These hormones pump up the heart rate, blood pressure, rate of respiration, blood sugar level, speed of message transmission through the nervous system, and generally organize the system for **fight-or-flight** (Cannon, 1929) reacting. In other words, our bodies physically prepare to deal with the stressor, which may involve running, doing battle, or some other form of quick thinking or behaving.

The body's initial reaction to stress is actually an asset. If you are about to be attacked by a mugger or are being chased by an angry dog, you are going to welcome a little extra energy and thinking speed. The increased arousal can also motivate you to take care of other stressors, such as encouraging you to prepare for an upcoming test, organize your morning so you will not be late for work, and practice shooting baskets before the big game.

We all need a certain level of arousal for optimal performance. The **Yerkes-Dodson law** of arousal points out that if we experience very little arousal or a high degree of arousal, our performance suffers (Hebb, 1955). However, a moderate amount of arousal seems to be necessary to produce good results. Furthermore, we are better at performing simple tasks with a higher degree of arousal, while we perform complex tasks better during lower arousal. Figure 4.1 shows the "inverted U" relationship between arousal and performance.

The Yerkes-Dodson law has no doubt played a role in your test-taking behavior. If you could not care less about a test, or think the test will be a breeze, you are not going to feel stressed and you will most likely have a hard time motivating yourself to study. On the other hand, if you are extremely anxious about an examination, your anxiety may interfere with your ability to think clearly, and your test-taking performance will suffer.

So after the alarm stage of the general adaptation syndrome you deal with the stressor, use up the energy pumped up by your body, and your system returns to normal. However, some stressors cannot be dealt with

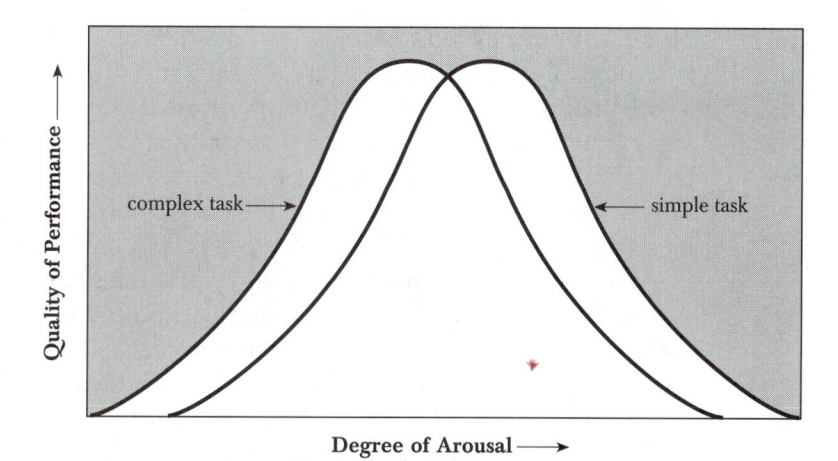

FIGURE 4.1

Illustration of the inverted-U relationship between arousal and performance.

---

by fight or flight. If your roommates drive you up a wall, punching them out or moving might take care of the stressor. However, physical altercations tend to produce other undesirable outcomes, and moving may be either impossible or extremely inconvenient. Thus when limited to only fight and flight options, you may find yourself trying to live within a continual state of stress. This can also be the case when stressors involve uncontrollable environmental factors, ongoing conflicts, and an unusually large collection of daily hassles.

When stressors are continual, our bodies move from the alarm stage into the resistance or adaptation stage. Epinephrine and norepinephrine are still surging through our systems, but in lesser quantities. During this stage the body repairs itself from the effects of the stress and attempts to restore the lost energy. Another set of hormones, known as **corticosteroids**, stimulate mechanisms responsible for fighting inflammation, releasing energy, and other support systems that aid the body as it reacts to the assault of stress.

Unfortunately, our bodies cannot keep this up forever. After prolonged periods of chronic stress we experience exhaustion, the third stage of the general adaptation syndrome. When this happens, our bodies have depleted themselves of the resources necessary to continue coping with the stressors. As a result, we find ourselves lacking in energy and motivation. In addition, the corticosteroids that have been faithfully aiding the body's defense against stress also interfere with the effectiveness of the **immune system** (Antoni et al., 1990). Since the immune system is responsible for fighting off disease, ongoing stress can result in illness as the body moves toward exhaustion. Research continues to uncover a very tight relationship between behavior, the brain, and our immune systems (Maier et al., 1994). Furthermore, the prolonged increases in heart rate and blood pressure caused by the excess norepinephrine are associated with heart disease (Krantz et al., 1988).

Recent years have produced a flurry of studies concerning stress and illness. Table 4.1 lists a number of physical conditions that have been associated with stress. Table 4.2 is a questionnaire developed by Holmes and Rahe (1967) that assesses stress due to life changes. On the basis of this questionnaire, researchers have been able to predict who will be likely to suffer a significant illness within the next couple of years. In addition, individuals suffering from prolonged stress appear more likely to be accident-prone (Thoits, 1983). This is not surprising. If you are forgetful, spaced out, or preoccupied and worn out due to physical ailments, you are much more likely to miss important details–like oncoming traffic–that could spare you from significant injury.

In addition to physical problems, stress can produce many forms of psychological distress. The next section addresses the most common form of stress-induced distress: anxiety.

TABLE 4.1
Common Physical Complaints Caused by Stress

Back pain	Muscle cramps
Jaw tension	Migraine headaches
Asthma	Allergies
Tension headaches	Panic attacks
Stomach pain	High blood pressure
Skin problems	Cold hands and feet
Constipation	Frequent colds
Diarrhea	Insomnia
Fatigue	Profuse perspiration
Depression	Ulcers
Irritable bowel syndrome	Irregular heartbeat
Hyperventilation	Chronic pain
Infectious diseases	Substance abuse
Overeating	Sexual dysfunction
Loss of appetite	Nausea

TABLE 4.2
The Social Readjustment Scale

Circle the number value preceding each stressful life event that you have experienced in the last 12 months.

100	Death of spouse
73	Divorce
65	Marital separation
63	Jail term
63	Death of a close family member
53	Personal injury or illness
50	Marriage
47	Fired from job
45	Marital reconciliation
45	Retirement
44	Change in health of family member
40	Pregnancy
39	Sex difficulties
39	Gain of new family member
39	Business readjustment
38	Change in financial state
37	Death of a close friend
36	Change to a different line of work
35	Change in number of arguments with significant other
31	Mortgage over $10,000
30	Foreclosure of mortgage or loan
29	Change in responsibilities at work
29	Son or daughter leaving home
29	Trouble with in-laws
28	Outstanding personal achievement
26	Wife (husband) begins or stops work
26	Begin or end school
25	Change in living conditions
25	Revision of personal habits
23	Trouble with boss
20	Change in hours or work conditions
20	Change in residence
20	Change in schools
19	Change in recreation
19	Change in church activities
18	Change in social activities
17	Mortgage or loan less than $10,000
16	Change in sleeping habits
15	Change in number of family get-togethers
15	Change in eating habits
13	Vacation
12	Christmas
11	Minor violations of the law

Developed by T. Holmes and R. Rahe (1967), The social readjustment rating scale, *Journal of Psychosomatic Research, 11,* 213–218.

Anxiety

Anxiety is a feeling of dread. Sometimes you know what it is you fear will happen, at other times you may not have a clue. You may sense it as a threat to your personal safety or security, or perhaps you are anticipating a threat to your self-esteem. In any event, you feel motivated to protect yourself from some potential harm.

Types of Anxiety

Anxiety has been studied as both a state and a trait. **State anxiety** occurs as a reaction to stressors. It is usually a temporary condition preceding an anticipated event, such as a trip to the dentist, a visit from relatives, or a first try at hang-gliding. Once the stressor is gone, the anxiety is typically gone as well.

Trait anxiety is a personality descriptor. Some people seem to be chronically anxious. No matter what is happening in their lives, they can always find something to worry about, certain that something terrible is about to happen.

The Many Bases of Anxiety

The different perspectives of psychology offer differing explanations for why the phenomenon of anxiety occurs. The general adaptation syndrome is an example of the biological basis of anxiety, pointing out the neurochemistry behind arousing mechanisms that can eventually be transformed into a state of anxiety. Biology can also contribute to trait anxiety, as our inherited temperament can predispose us to react with more or less emotionality than others (Buss & Plomin, 1975). Other perspectives address how our mental processes can play a role in the experience of anxiety and also offer explanations of why some people seem more vulnerable to anxiety than others.

Psychodynamic view. Freud (1926/1948) evaluated anxiety in three forms, relating back to the ego, id, and superego: **reality anxiety**, **neurotic anxiety**, and **moral anxiety**. Reality anxiety, a function of the ego, is consistent with the general adaptation syndrome. When we perceive ourselves to be in some form of real danger, our egos strive to protect us, motivated in part by feelings of anxiety. Neurotic anxiety is the fear of our own impulses. As you recall, the id is responsible for our more hedonistic self-centered interests. Acting out on many impulses can cause us a lot of problems. Thus we may fear not being able to control our id impulses well enough to avoid being punished by society. Moral anxiety is a function of the superego. When we behave in ways that are inconsistent with our conscience or ego-ideal, we feel anxiety in the form of internal punishment—guilt or shame. If we have severe superegos or excessively impulsive id functions, we are likely to experience ongoing anxiety. Thus when new stressors are introduced, we may be limited in our ability to cope.

All three types of anxiety can occur during the same event. Suppose you are thinking about buying a new sports car. Reality anxiety may come in the form of worrying about whether or not you can make the payments. Neurotic anxiety occurs as you consider how well you will be able to make yourself stick to the speed limit. Moral anxiety checks in as you feel a few pangs of guilt over the thought of spending money on such an extravagance.

While reality anxiety is consistent with state anxiety, moral anxiety and neurotic anxiety explain some underpinnings of trait anxiety. If we have severe superegos or have difficulty curbing our impulsive id functions, we are likely to experience anxiety as an ongoing condition. And whenever we experience a new stressor, we are likely to be less successful at coping with it than others, since our general adaptation functions will already be working overtime.

Existential/humanistic view. One of the greatest of all existential crises is the end of existence. Existentialists link anxieties to **death anxiety**, the fear of nonexistence (Becker, 1973). Anything that exposes us to the potential meaninglessness and nothingness of death or nonbeing causes anxiety. Stressors, as potential dangers to the self, put us in touch with the fear of nonbeing.

On the other hand, humanists explain that although life cannot be free of anxiety, this is not necessarily because we are dominated by death anxiety. As we follow the course of healthy being and growing, we try new things and stay open to new experiencing. Anything new carries with it a certain amount of anxiety, but that anxiety can be translated into an excitement for further exploration rather than a fear of nonbeing (Rogers, 1961). Yet anxiety can result when we feel threats to our self-concept, an implication of nothingness.

Thus the existential and humanistic perspectives suggest that individuals who are unsure of their identities or deal with their anxiety through escape rather than resolution are going to experience more ongoing anxiety and most likely will have a more difficult time coping with the more mundane stressors that pop up from day to day. On the other hand, all of us experience anxiety as a state when we are faced with **actualization anxiety**—the anxiety that accompanies critical incidences of growth and change (Moustakas, 1967).

Behavioral view. Behaviorists believe that anxiety is a learned response. We learn to feel anxious in the presence of various situations, objects, and people because in the past, they had been linked with something unpleasant. For example, if you watch one of your classmates answer a question and the professor tears the answer to shreds, you will feel anxious when the professor next calls on you to respond, since you anticipate being similarly punished.

Classical conditioning also produces anxieties, as stimuli connected with previous experiences of anxiety then produce anxiety all by themselves. Using the same example, you may begin feeling anxious any time you enter that particular classroom—even when it is being used for a different class with a less hostile instructor! **Learned helplessness**, which will be discussed later as a behavioral component of depression, can also lead to feelings of anxiety, as we doubt our ability to cope with stressors.

So according to the behavioral standpoint, we vary in our abilities to cope with stress on the basis of our varying previous experiences. The more confidence we have learned to experience during past endeavors, the less anxiety we will experience during current situations. These mechanisms affect our levels of anxiety as both a state and a trait.

Cognitive view. We are unlikely to feel anxious if we do not believe we are in any kind of danger. Whether a danger is real or imagined, the sequence of stress and anxiety is only going to be set in motion if our brains have alerted us that such a possibility exists. Suppose you are driving on a highway in a flood zone, and as you come around a corner you see standing water up ahead. You perceive yourself as being in danger of driving into the flood waters, and as your stress response surges into action, you prepare to brake. However, as you get closer the image of water dissipates, and you realize that you were only seeing an optical illusion. Later, when the illusion repeats itself, the stress response is not so likely to occur, since you no longer perceive that stimulus as a potential threat.

Cognitive psychologists explain that a key variable in the experience of anxiety is the appraisal of threat—at some point, we decide we really are in danger (Lazarus & Averill, 1972). We can even become anxious over events that we fear might happen but never will, as in the case of the optical illusion of water on the road.

We can also take an anxiety-provoking situation and encourage it to provoke even more anxiety. Table 4.3 is a list of irrational beliefs drawn up by Ellis. The beliefs usually are not the actual thoughts we have but are the philosophies behind the thoughts. For example, suppose you endorse the philosophy of "I must be perfect at everything I do." This is likely to produce thoughts such as "It will be absolutely terrible if I don't do well at this," and you will feel exceptionally anxious on any occasion when you need to perform. If you believe "It is awful, horrible, and catastrophic when things don't work out the way I think they should," everyday frustrations will turn into major-league frustrations as "shouldistic" and "musturbatory" thinking abounds.

Our differing attitudes and belief systems can therefore play a role in how much anxiety we will experience. If we believe ourselves to be incompetent, that others are nonsupportive, or that the world is threatening, we are likely to experience more anxiety in general as we interpret almost everything as a potential threat. And whether we perceive specific situations as threatening contributes to our levels of state anxiety as we react to individual stressors.

Coping

As is implied by the above descriptions of stress and anxiety, there will always be problems in living impacting us. No matter how psychologically healthy we are, we can all expect to have to cope with stressors and adversity occasionally. How psychologically healthy we remain depends in part upon how well we learn to cope. The more coping skills we have, and the better we become at applying them, the better off we will be.

Coping is most simply defined as getting through the situation one way or the other. Coping mechanisms themselves are neither good nor bad. However, how you go about applying them is another story. A single coping strategy might be adaptive for some situations but just cause more problems when used for others. So rather than endorsing some kinds of coping as good and others as bad, we will evaluate them here according to how well they work out.

The biological structure for coping, as described by the general adaptation syndrome, is the fight-or-flight response. At times fight or flight works out for our best interests. But of course, the complexity of human living prescribes that many times it will not. Fortunately, there are many other strategies we can use when classic fight-or-flight responding is unrealistic. Successful strategies can involve managing the emotions surrounding the stressor or dealing directly with the stressor itself.

TABLE 4.3
Typical Irrational Beliefs and Disputations

Irrational belief	Disputation
I must have everybody's love and approval.	It would be nice if everybody loved me, but that is not realistic. After all, I don't love everybody. And how could I possibly get everybody's approval? You can't please everybody.
I must be perfect at everything I do.	Nobody is perfect. We are all fallible human beings. We can do our best when we so choose, but we can't expect to be perfect.
If people behave poorly, they are bad people and should be punished.	People are not their behavior. They are who they are. We all behave poorly every now and then, since we are all fallible human beings.
It is awful, horrible, and catastrophic when things don't work out the way I think they should.	It is certainly unpleasant when things don't turn out the way we would like, but it is best to just change what we can and accept what we can't change.
Unhappiness is caused by external events, and there is nothing I can do to change that.	Unhappiness is caused by what we believe. I can change how I feel by choosing beliefs that represent a healthier life perspective.
I should be anxious about future events that are either unknown or dangerous.	Getting anxious will resolve nothing. Nobody has yet figured out how to cross a bridge before arriving at it.
It is easiest to just avoid difficulties and responsibilities.	This usually turns out to be more difficult in the long run. We are better off facing such events ourselves, rather than waiting for someone else or fate to decide them for us.
We must have someone strong to depend upon.	It is nice when we have someone we can turn to for occasional direction or support, but ultimately we need to make our own decisions about our lives in order to be happy.
My past must control my present and future.	Learning does not stop with the past. We can learn to live our lives differently as our lives progress.
There is a perfect solution to every problem, and it is awful if I don't find it.	Perfect solutions are rare. We can be satisfied by using the best solution available.
The world should be fair.	It would be nice if the world were fair, but it is not. The world is too complex for events to always meet the criteria of being fair to everyone. We can always work toward fairness when possible, but are better off accepting those events we cannot change.
I should never have to suffer any pain or discomfort.	Pain is uncomfortable, but it is a part of the experience of living. We can tolerate pain or discomfort long enough to work toward the goals that matter to us.

Environmental Solutions

Environmental solutions typically manage the stressors, rather than the anxiety. How might we act upon the environment in ways that will reduce stress?

- *Limit the number of stressors.* One good environmental coping strategy is to add up the number of stressors in your life and examine how reasonable a load you are carrying. If your life is high in stressors, see if you can eliminate a few of them. Likewise, do not take on even more stressors if you already have a full load. Learn to tell yourself "no!"
- *Withdraw physically.* Another strategy, similar to the flight response, is physical withdrawal from stressors, sometimes known as avoidance behaviors. Avoidance behaviors involve finding things to do that let you avoid dealing with a stressor. For example, if you become upset when you hear about wars going on in foreign countries, you could stop listening to the international news for awhile. If you get in a fight with a friend and do not feel ready to deal with him or her yet, you can avoid going to places where you would expect to see that friend. Avoidance behaviors give us the chance to lick our wounds and avoid frustrations over which we have no control. They work fine, as long as they are temporary and you eventually get back to any necessary problem solving. Too much withdrawal and avoidance not only interferes with problem solving and decision making, but also limits the amount of positive feedback you will receive from those around you.
- *Take vacations.* Vacations are an excellent coping strategy. They take you away from the ongoing stress of work, your usual interpersonal conflicts, and daily hassles, and they can also be planned to take you away from specific environmental stressors such as crowding, noise pollution, and extreme temperatures. In addition to temporary escape from stressors, vacations provide an opportunity for us to refuel our energies, self-evaluate, and gain new perspectives.
- *Pursue distractions.* Another well-worn environmental coping strategy is the pursuit of distractions. Most of us have no difficulty finding things to do that will temporarily take our minds off of our problems. Movies, video games, reading, hobbies, recreational sports, and other enjoyable pastimes can remove us from our existential wastelands of routine and focus us on happier pastures.
- *Take advantage of time management.* Time management, as discussed in Chapter 3, is also extremely important for effective environmental coping. Even a small number of stressors can become overwhelming if your lifestyle is poorly structured or disorganized.

Psychodynamic Solutions

The psychodynamic perspective provides solutions that consider anxiety caused by conflict within the ego. The ego comes to terms with various id impulses and superego demands by employing a variety of **defense mechanisms**, which "defend" against the anxiety caused by the battling id and superego. These defense mechanisms are effective because they distort reality in varying degrees, thus altering perception of the source of anxiety. Defense mechanisms do not solve the actual problem leading to the anxiety, but do provide an escape from it.

For example, let's say Herman has just broken up with his girlfriend, and is feeling anxious about the restructuring of his social life. Below are several psychodynamic defense mechanisms he might use to deal with his anxiety.

Denial–Refusing to believe the true nature of a threat: Herman tells himself "Her absence won't make much of a difference in my life."

Projection–Getting rid of undesired impulses by thrusting them onto others, thus presuming that others harbor them instead: Herman tells himself "She's the one that's going to have to worry about coming up with a new partner."

Displacement–Transferring feelings and ideas toward unacceptable objects onto those that feel less threatening: Herman starts stewing over a squeaking sound he hears in his car when he uses his brakes.

Regression–Returning to a form of behavior characteristic of an earlier stage of life: Herman spends much more time at his parents' home, intently hanging on every piece of advice they offer concerning his social life.

Suppression–Consciously choosing to set aside painful material: Herman ignores his anxiety in order to throw himself into his work.

Rationalization–Using inaccurate justifications for unacceptable behavior: Herman decides that he really doesn't want a serious relationship during this stage of his life anyway.

Intellectualization–Cutting off emotions and reacting to painful material with pure logic: Herman assures himself that breaking up was the best thing to do under the circumstances and that, given the probabilities, he will eventually meet someone else with whom he would like to have a relationship.

Sublimation–Channeling primitive impulses into the use of socially acceptable strategies: When Herman's bowling partner complains of difficulties with his girlfriend, Herman offers emotional support and helps him explore possible solutions for adaptively dealing with them.

Humor–Using wit to distract one's self from painful feelings: Herman works at an accounting firm; when his coworkers ask him about his love life he comments that he's still "filing singly."

As the ego selects its coping methods it takes into account the **pleasure principle** and the **reality principle** (Freud, 1911/1958). The pleasure principle is our tendency to avoid pain and seek pleasure. When we experience the discomfort of anxiety, we can seek its dissipation by using defense mechanisms. However, the ego's coping solutions must take into account the confines of reality. Which solutions are going to work out in the real world? Due to the influence of the reality principle, we might actually put off the immediate good feelings or release of tension sought by the pleasure principle in order to gain more long-term pleasures, as we consider the structures of external reality.

In this manner, we can choose to deal with anxiety in adaptive or maladaptive ways. By looking at the preceding illustrations of defense mechanisms, you can see how some solutions might work out better for Herman than others. For example, using denial will result in Herman's sending his feelings underground, and most likely his feelings will in turn pop up at times when they are less than convenient. Denying the existence of the problem also negates chances that he will begin working on more-adaptive long-term solutions.

However, this is not an indication that denial is always a maladaptive response. Suppose you are stuck in an impossible situation over which you have little if any control, such as living in a war zone, being diagnosed with terminal cancer, or being the child in an alcoholic family. Denying that there is a problem under those circumstances may be one of the more adaptive means of keeping from being overwhelmed by feelings of fear, futility, and powerlessness long enough to be able to go on with other facets of living. Denial becomes a liability only if you continue to use it as a coping strategy when more active solutions have become available.

Existential/Humanistic Solutions

The existentialists and humanists describe coping in terms of willingness to grow. We choose to grow and move forward through our anxiety when we believe that confronting it will offer more gains than looking for a means of escape. There are two key elements involved in confronting anxiety: expansion of awareness and personal reeducation (May, 1951).

Expansion of awareness occurs as we examine our own motives and fears and seek out which value or goal feels threatened. During reeducation, we restructure our goals and values in order to better fit reality.

Awareness occurs in the here and now. Anxiety is preoccupied with what might happen in the future. Therefore the more we can sense and stay in touch with our immediate experiencing, the more we can slow our anxiety's impetus. One way of increasing awareness is through the use of relaxation techniques. Our minds have the capacity to slow down certain aspects of our regulatory systems at will (Adler & Adler, 1984). Numerous techniques have been found to help with this process.

Biofeedback–**Biofeedback**, a behavioral therapy, is a system of mechanically monitoring various body functions as we concentrate on altering their patterns. Studies of biofeedback have shown that as we slow down our breathing, brain wave activity, heart rate, and blood pressure and concentrate on lessening muscle tension, we become more relaxed. As we relax, we can let go of anxiety and focus more on the here and now. Biofeedback has in fact been used successfully as a treatment for anxiety (Raskin et al., 1981).

Progressive relaxation–Fortunately, we do not need biofeedback apparatus to be able to teach ourselves to relax. One useful method that meets this end is called **progressive relaxation**, originally developed by Edmond Jacobson (1938). Progressive relaxation involves alternately tensing and relaxing various muscle groups and concentrating on the physical sensations produced under those two conditions. With practice, we become more aware of what relaxation feels like, and are more able to produce that state ourselves.

Many audiotapes are available that coach people through progressive relaxation. Some people even create their own relaxation tapes, recording narratives using their own voices or those of friends whose voices they find relaxing.

Transcendental meditation–**Transcendental meditation** (TM) is another internal focusing strategy that produces a state of relaxation similar to that of the relaxation response. This simplified form of Eastern meditation was brought to the United States in the late fifties by Maharishi Mahesh Yogi. Its roots are within Eastern religion, and its proponents have made dramatic claims concerning its effect on health, interpersonal relationships, and general happiness and well-being. However, scientific studies have shown that results of using TM are no different in their physiology than those of the other relaxation techniques, including that of taking a simple rest (Holmes, 1984). So if you have avoided relaxation techniques involving meditation because of religious ties, you need not worry about needing to be "converted" in order to reap the benefits. Secular methods of meditation are just as beneficial.

Relaxation response—Herbert Benson borrowed some of the ideas from Eastern religion to develop the **relaxation response** (Benson, 1975). When you use this system, you sit quietly in a comfortable position, close your eyes, and progressively relax the various parts of your body. You focus on the feeling of your breathing and concentrate on a word or phrase that helps you keep out distracting thoughts. You continue for about 15 or 20 minutes. If you practice this technique regularly, you may be able to access relaxed feelings just by thinking about them. This process has also been called "mindfulness" (Borysenko, 1987). The more you become mindful of your present experiencing, the less you focus on concerns over the past and worries about the future.

Focusing—Sometimes we get all worked up and are not really sure why we are blowing situations out of proportion. **Focusing** is useful for figuring out exactly what it is you are upset about (Gendlin, 1981). Instead of setting aside all thoughts and feelings, you zero in on a specific difficulty over which you are concerned. As you focus on your "felt sense" of the problem rather than its causes or ramifications, you eventually find a label for it, resulting in a feeling of an "emotional shift." In other words, the longer you focus on how the problem is making you feel and why, the less emotional distress you take back with you.

Problem-solving strategies—Another way of coping with anxiety through both awareness and reeducation is to directly address the anxiety-provoking situation. The following problem-solving strategy can be useful for identifying and restructuring goals and values during conflict, as well as for providing active solutions.

1. Define the problem. Specifically, what is the conflict that is bothering you?

2. Separate out subproblems. Since problems can only be solved one at a time, related difficulties must be set aside in order for you to become more focused. You can always come back to other problems later.

3. Describe how you feel as a result of the problem. Recognizing how you are feeling expands your self-awareness.

4. List possible causes of the problem. Examining the factors that led up to the problem helps expose potential solutions and creates a higher level of personal understanding.

5. Generate a list of possible solutions. Include as many solutions as you can think of, no matter how ridiculous they may seem. The absurd solutions that come to mind are as important to evaluate as the ones that seem more adaptive.

6. List the advantages and disadvantages of each potential solution. How workable is each solution? What could you expect to happen if you followed through on it? This is especially helpful concerning absurd solutions, which we usually just dismiss when they come to mind, thinking no further about possible ramifications. Unfortunately, when people act impulsively or make split-second decisions, they may choose one of the less adaptive solutions simply because they have never thought them all the way through.

7. Select a solution that appears to present the fewest negatives and the most positives. Sometimes identifying the top three solutions is useful, in the event that your preferred solution is in some way blocked.

8. Create a plan of action and follow through. What specifically are you going to do? When are you going to do it? How are you going to evaluate its success?

Here is a step-by-step example using the above strategy.

Jane and Sally work in a veterinary clinic as veterinary assistants. Their jobs are for the most part identical: assisting the veterinarians as they treat the animals. However, Sally is not a "self-initiator." She does not initiate any task until her employer tells her to do something. Jane, on the other hand, does not need to be told what to do before she does her job. The result is that Jane performs many necessary tasks that should have been done by Sally, who is waiting for the veterinarians to tell her to do them. What should Jane do?

1. Define the problem: Jane does not like doing more work than Sally.

2. Separate out the subproblems: Jane also believes that the lunch hour is inequitably arranged with Sally. While this is also an inequity involving Sally, addressing lunch scheduling is not likely to resolve the problem of Jane doing more work. The scheduling difficulty can be addressed as a separate problem later.

3. Describe how you feel: Jane is angry that she works more for the same pay. She is also anxious that she might get in trouble for something not being done because Sally has not followed through. Her self-concept feels threatened, as she does not perceive herself as a person who is easily taken advantage of. She also is experiencing some confusion about her

role in the work environment: Does she really feel like she knows what is going on? This results in even more anxiety.

4. List possible causes of the problem: It could be that Sally is basically lazy and is indeed taking advantage of Jane. Possibly, however, Sally is afraid she will do something wrong if she initiates work on a task without being told to do so. She may not be sure what her job is either. Maybe Sally is depressed and does not initiate much of anything in her life these days. On the other hand, maybe the problem is a matter of Jane's perceptions. Does Sally really do as little as Jane thinks she does? Does Jane really do as much as she thinks she does? Are the work roles really defined in the manner that Jane assumes?

5. List all possible solutions: Jane can
   - Tell Sally off.
   - Sit back and watch things fall apart, and hope she gets in trouble.
   - Continue to pick up after her, so Jane doesn't have to worry about getting in trouble herself.
   - Confront Sally about the inequity.
   - Point out Sally's negligence to their employer.
   - Ignore the problem and hope it goes away.
   - Find a way to get even with Sally for being so self-centered.
   - Kill her.
   - Ask their employer for a clearer delineation between Sally's responsibilities and Jane's responsibilities.
   - Complain to all the other employees about how awful and unfair Sally is.
   - Bribe the vets to fire Sally.
   - Quit her job.

6. Look at the advantages and disadvantages of each solution:
   - Tell her off: Jane might feel good after venting her anger, but Sally's resentment concerning the verbal abuse might lead to her feeling even less likely to consider Jane's needs. Jane may also feel bad about herself afterwards, since verbal abusiveness is not consistent with her self-concept.
   - Sit back and watch things fall apart: Sally might get in trouble and the problem might be addressed, but it could be that Jane would get in trouble as well.
   - Continue to pick up after her: While this lets Jane avoid any form of action or confrontation, her resentment and the ongoing threat to her self-concept will continue to build and the inequity will remain.

- Confront Sally about the inequity: Jane could point out to Sally that she has noticed Sally misses some tasks and that Jane feels compelled to pick up on them in order to keep the office moving smoothly. Jane could then ask Sally if she can think of a way to remedy the problem. If Sally is agreeable to work on the problem and does not feel defensive about the confrontation, this approach could produce some results. However, it does not necessarily clarify what their employer had in mind.
- Point out Sally's negligence to their employer: This approach would be one indirect way to find out exactly how the work load is supposed to be handled. The employer might get on Sally's case, but then Jane would be in the position of having to get along with Sally, who would then know Jane had gone to the boss behind her back.
- Ignore the problem: Denial may provide some temporary relief to the anxiety, but it is not a long-term solution.
- Find a way to get even: While this might feel good in the short run, it does not let Sally know exactly what it is that Jane is angry about and therefore does not increase the likelihood that the problem will be solved. It also involves acting out against another person, which could lead to feelings of guilt and immaturity.
- Kill her: Jane will probably lose her job if she has to go to prison. Seriously, thoughts like "I could just kill him/her" are not unusual. Before automatically discarding the thoughts, it can be helpful to think through exactly why you would not follow through: the moral dilemma, the guilt, the effect on others, the gravity of orchestrating another person's nonbeing.
- Ask the employer for a clearer delineation of tasks: This solution still involves working up the courage to talk to the employer, and Jane would possibly be exposing her ignorance in the matter. However, job roles are indeed the responsibility of employers, and as an employee it is Jane's responsibility to make sure she knows what she is supposed to be doing. This approach also would clarify whether her perceptions of who is doing how much work are accurate. And even if Sally doesn't pitch in more, at least she will be clearer on her own role.
- Complain to the other employees: This is certainly a way to vent emotions and get even, but it will only increase the tension in the work situation. Also, complaining and rabble-rousing is not consistent with Jane's self-perception.
- Bribe the vets to fire Sally: In addition to this solution's low probability of success, bribery is manipulative and dishonest.

Anyway, if Jane had the resources for bribery she probably would not need the job.
- Quit: While quitting would get her out of the anxiety-provoking situation, and she might be able to find just as good a job elsewhere, she likes her other co-workers. She would also have to deal with the hassle of interrupted income, job-hunting, getting used to a new position, etc. Also, she does not believe in quitting when faced with adversity until she has at least tried to remedy the difficulty.

7. Select a solution: Jane decides upon the following hierarchy as her first three choices:
- Ask the employer for a clearer delineation of tasks.
- Confront Sally.
- Quit.

8. Arrange follow-through: Jane makes an appointment to talk with her employer after work the next day concerning her confusion over her responsibilities. She shows up for her appointment and explains her concerns. If her employer's response does not resolve her problem, she begins problem-solving anew!

Cognitive Solutions

Cognitive therapies have demonstrated that our thoughts affect how we feel. A wide variety of coping strategies, both simplistic and complex, are commonly used as cognitive coping.

Brooding. Cognitive coping is sometimes unpleasant. Brooding is one way of passing time while dealing with anxiety. Some people can find benefit in brooding, if it consists of blowing things so out of proportion that they are able to see the humor in it all and then have a good laugh. However, most brooding is unproductive. Discerning whether your worrying is productive or unproductive is not difficult. Active planning and problem solving eventually produce a solution or plan; unproductive worry just keeps going around and around in bigger and bigger circles.

Daydreaming. Our thought processes can also cope with anxiety by heading in a completely different direction: daydreaming. Daydreaming is a classic form of mental escape. It removes you from the stressful situation when you cannot physically remove yourself. Creative people frequently daydream, and sometimes they can even come up with solutions as a product of fantasizing. Of course, to daydream during times when it interferes with necessary activity can become counterproductive.

Forgetting. Another type of instant escape is forgetting. You might have noticed that when you are under a lot of stress, you start forgetting significant details. You may have trouble concentrating or paying attention. A lot of this forgetting is built in. When you experience cognitive overload, pieces of the load start falling out of the wagon. If you forget about a few of the issues you are juggling, your mind can more efficiently handle the smaller load. Forgetting also has the advantage of causing old stimuli to become novel again, which can increase your alertness toward them (Riccio et al., 1994). Forgetting becomes maladaptive if you have not developed supplementary strategies for reminding yourself to do the things you typically forget while you are on cognitive overload.

Cognitive rehearsal. Cognitive rehearsal is another form of coping with anxiety. In our mind's eye, we can practice scenarios that we either know we must face or are afraid might happen. As we mentally walk ourselves through the situation, we experience some of the anxiety. If we do this enough, we defuse some of the anxiety and begin to feel more comfortable with the situation.

Acceptance and perseverance. Deciding to persevere is another form of cognitive coping. It is not the same as giving up, where you throw up your hands, go "oh poor me," and give up all control. Instead, you accept some things as unchangeable and problem-solve in ways that help you cope with the unchangeable. We are often faced with situations that—at least in terms of our best interests—we must simply endure, such as getting through finals, performing our jobs on days we do not really feel like working, or putting up with the faults of parents or in-laws who clearly are not going to change for our convenience. Perseverance becomes maladaptive if you see all problems as something you must endure and avoid actively dealing with difficulties.

Prayer. Another cognitive coping strategy is prayer. Many people find comfort and guidance by seeking contact with a higher power. Prayer also reduces anxiety as it helps increase feelings of control. Unfortunately many people use prayer maladaptively, often in the form of passively praying for magical solutions rather than dealing directly with stressors. Prayer can also become a scapegoat of futility. If things turn out the way you want, you can thank the higher power for throwing the situation your preferred way. If the situation resolves itself undesirably, then it was "God's will." Either way, you are sitting by passively and feeling little control over your life, which contributes toward even more anxiety and depression.

Positive reappraisal. Since anxiety changes shape and intensity depending on appraisal of threat and subsequent evaluations, anxiety can be reduced through cognitive restructuring that reevaluates that appraisal. **Positive reappraisal** is one form of reevaluation. When you find yourself looking at a situation negatively, focus instead on the positive side. For example, suppose you are meeting your boyfriend's or girlfriend's parents for the first time. You are very nervous, sure that you will somehow meet their disapproval. Rather than look at the anxiety-provoking side of the situation, you could focus on the more enjoyable side of the meeting: You have already heard a lot about them and they sound like fun people; you enjoy socializing and meeting new people; you are going to one of your favorite restaurants together; and so on.

Positive reappraisal only becomes maladaptive when we become Pollyanna-ish in our thinking. If you were walking along the beach and a tidal wave suddenly appeared in the distance, thinking "Gee, I was really feeling like taking a dip just now" is not particularly adaptive. Sometimes anxiety is intended to spur us into action.

Raising self-efficacy. Another form of positive reappraisal involves raising self-efficacy. If we tell ourselves we cannot cope, we probably will not cope. This tendency can be counteracted with a technique called **self-instruction** (Meichenbaum, 1977). Let's say you are sitting in your classroom, taking a difficult exam that you had been dreading for weeks. You find yourself thinking, "This is so difficult. How will I ever get through it? I can't afford to fail this class. What if I flunk out of school? What will I do then?" Using self-instruction techniques, you teach yourself to refocus on the task at hand, as well as think more positively: "Let's see, you've done questions 2, 3, and 6 so far and you're doing fine. Now let's do number 4. It covers the material you studied out of Chapter 11. You studied that chapter well; you can come up with a fine answer...." If you have specific worries that are troublesome, you counteract them: "Ignore the fact that nobody else seems as nervous as you feel. You are graded on the quality of your answers, not how your feelings compare with your classmates. You've written acceptable answers so far. Keep up the good work."

Challenging irrational beliefs. Instead of buying into Ellis's irrational beliefs, we can challenge their validity. They have no proof; they are merely maladaptive philosophies that have found their way into our reasoning processes. And why choose beliefs that make us miserable? Table 4.3, in addition to listing Ellis's twelve main irrational beliefs, also illustrates how we can challenge these beliefs.

For example, let's say that while Jennifer is driving to work on the freeway she inadvertently cuts in front of another driver. The other driver expresses her displeasure by honking and shaking her fist. Jennifer reacts by feeling anxious. As she examines her internal workings, she finds she is mainly upset because of the other driver's reaction. What if she keeps honking at me all the way to work? She worries that someone she knows might have seen her or will find out about her mistake. She is probably harboring the following irrational beliefs:

- I must worry.
- I must not experience unpleasantness.
- I must be perfect.
- I must have everyone's love and approval.

Ellis provides an *ABCDE* strategy for challenging such beliefs. *A* stands for "activating event." Specifically, what happened that led to the distress? *B* stands for "beliefs." What irrational beliefs are leading you to blow the situation out of proportion? *C* stands for "consequences." How do you feel as a result of these beliefs? *D* stands for "disputation." If you were to argue with these beliefs, what might you say? And *E* stands for "evaluation." How do you feel when you choose to believe your disputations, rather than the irrational beliefs?

Here's how Jennifer might use Ellis's strategy to deal with her anxiety:

A– Activating event: She made a driving error and another driver became angry with her.

B– Beliefs:
    a. I must worry about whatever might happen next.
    b. I can't tolerate any potential discomfort from this situation.
    c. It is not acceptable that I made this mistake. I should not make mistakes.
    d. The other driver is upset with me. I must not have other people dislike me.

C– Consequences: I feel anxious.

D– Disputation:
    a. Worrying about this will not resolve anything. Nobody has yet succeeded in crossing a bridge before arriving at it.

  b. Sure it doesn't feel good to have this person angry with me and knowing that I blundered. But I can tolerate it–life is full of uncomfortable events, along with the comfortable. I can tolerate it long enough to get to work in one piece. I've lived through other such predicaments.
  c. Nobody is perfect. I did what I felt was best at the time. That's the most anyone can do.
  d. Nobody likes everybody. I don't like everybody, do I? It would be nice if everybody liked me, but that is not realistic.
 E– Evaluation: Jennifer might still be a little embarrassed over her error, but she will not be consumed by anxiety and self-criticism.

Physical Solutions

Physical behaving or reacting also serves as a way of coping. Our bodies will find a way to do this all by themselves as a result of the general adaptation syndrome. As we reach the exhaustion stage, our immune systems wear down and we become ill. Eventually we are forced to stop, withdraw, relax, and refuel because we become unable to go on in such a deteriorated physical condition. However, there are many other physical solutions available we might pursue before the situation becomes this desperate. Physical coping solutions allow us to work off some of the energy we have pent up as a result of our hormonal excesses during stress.

Exercise. Exercise is an excellent physical solution for stress management. It need not be informal exercise programs; it can also come in the form of daily living activities, such as washing the car, doing housework, or digging dirt. Just getting up and moving appears to help. Research has shown numerous mental health benefits by way of physical exercise. It not only reduces anxiety (Long, 1984) but also has been associated with decreases in depression (McCann & Holmes, 1984) and maladaptive acting-out behavior (Roskies et al., 1986). Those who exercise regularly have also demonstrated higher levels of self-esteem (Sonstroem, 1984), self-confidence and self-discipline (Hogan, 1989), and belief in ability to perform physical tasks (Ryckman et al., 1982).

Nervous habits. Nervous habits are ritualistic behaviors that use pent-up energy not being dispelled otherwise. They vary as much as the individuals who use them: nail biting, hair pulling, toe tapping, finger rapping, knee jiggling, lip biting, scalp scratching, doodling, whistling, fidgeting, throat clearing, sniffing, running your hand through your hair, and so on. As long as they are not so severe that you do physical damage to yourself, they are generally harmless and normal. They are also useful as a tool for gauging our level of anxiety, since they provide clues to our inner experience.

Work and play. Work and play both require that we focus on a particular activity. In order to effectively zero in on a single activity, we need to temporarily shut out other concerns. Thus play helps us block out the concerns of our careers, our careers help us temporarily forget about interpersonal difficulties, and so on. The importance of work and play in our lives will be discussed in greater detail in a later chapter.

Creativity. Creativity can be found in all of us. Many of the creative geniuses have been in fact mentally ill, but they maintained their composure and channeled themselves adaptively by expressing themselves through their artistic media (Rothenberg, 1990). Creativity involves taking an inner experience and expressing it as an outer reality. Our creations need not be outstanding or even useful. They are forms of expression, productivity, and affirmation, allowing us to express nonlogical aspects of our being and giving us a sense of personal accomplishment. Creative outlets abound: Writing, composing music, craft work, drawing and painting, designing new inventions, carpentry, gardening, sewing, rebuilding an engine, and even building sand castles are but a few of the many activities that can be used as outlets for creativity.

Substance use and abuse. Using chemical substances as a means of coping with uncomfortable feelings has become increasingly prevalent in our society. Alcohol, tranquilizers and stimulants, nicotine, caffeine, and even street drugs are all commonly used as an escape from the pressures of reality. These substances do indeed temporarily numb the discomfort of stress and anxiety. Unfortunately, the short-term advantages of many of these substances can easily become outweighed by the potential long-term disadvantages. Substance use and abuse will be discussed in greater detail in a later chapter.

Risk-taking, gambling, and other hormonal "highs." As mentioned earlier in the chapter, our bodies react to potential threats with a jolt of epinephrine and norepinephrine. Most people can recognize when these hormones kick in. They provide a rush, regardless of whether we interpret it as excitement, anxiety, or anger. This rush temporarily removes us from our previous state of experiencing and focuses us on an immediate need to act. Currently there are many risky hobbies available, such as hang gliding, bungee jumping, race car driving, skydiving, martial arts, and gambling. Risky situations are sometimes set up spontaneously, as in taking dares, driving recklessly, and picking fights. Obviously, these coping mechanisms present some serious safety concerns, and in many cases can become extremely maladaptive.

Crying. Crying provides an emotional release. It is also a release of the tensions that led up to your feeling like crying. When we give in to a good cry, we are temporarily giving up on keeping our emotional cool, which at stressful times can take a lot of energy. There may be a biological reason why most people report feeling better after crying. One study showed that tears shed during times of distress excrete significantly more protein than tears formed due to eye irritation (Frey et al., 1983).

The exact role crying plays in the release of inner turmoil is still not clear. Another study showed that when people feel like crying, they feel significantly better an hour later regardless of whether they gave in and cried or suppressed the urge (Kraemer & Halstrup, 1986). This is good news for the male population, since our society still clings to a bias of crying not being manly. Apparently we can reap benefits from just getting to the point of feeling like crying without having to go through with the act itself.

Music. "Music has charms to soothe a savage breast." So wrote William Congreve in *The Mourning Bride*. Music is processed in a different part of the brain than cognition. It is more temporally focused, usually conveying emotion rather than logic and analysis. There can be little doubt that music has an effect on our feelings and behavior: Restaurants and stores go to great lengths to pipe in just the right kind of music for producing the desired effect on their clientele.

Most people have specific types of music they like to listen to when they feel stressed. Music can provide a vicarious emotional experience when your own experiencing feels constricted. It also provides a means of escape, shutting out the world in order to concentrate on the song. If you play a musical instrument yourself, you are already familiar with how playing in and of itself can be an emotional outlet.

SOCIAL SOLUTIONS

Situations with which we must cope often involve other people. Coping itself may involve the use of resources that we can only access through the assistance or involvement of others. As such, we commonly draw in other people as we select coping strategies.

Manipulative behavior. Some social solutions are more effective than others. Manipulative behavior as a social solution is likely to cause additional problems, even if it does take care of the initial stressor. For example, George wants to watch a certain television program one night, but it appears opposite a program his wife, Sarah, always watches. George arranges for their daughter to be at a friend's house, needing to be picked up by Sarah right when the conflicting shows are due to be aired. He succeeds in getting to watch his program, but he also has the new stressor of dealing with his wife's anger over being forced to miss her program, as well as impairing his long-term relationship with her. "Getting even," lying, and emotional blackmail are other types of manipulative behavior that may solve the problem in the short run but backfire in the long run.

Complaining. Complaining is a common social coping strategy. We all complain amongst ourselves as we deal with our imperfect world. It is a method of unloading. And if you complain to the right person, a solution may appear at hand. Complaining becomes maladaptive when your complaints would best be directed to the source of the problem, but instead you are passing your disgruntlement around to all the wrong people—popularly referred to as talking behind someone's back if the complaint is about a person. This behavior impairs relationships. Also, if complaints characterize the sum total of your conversations with others, others may learn to run the other direction when they see you coming.

Conflict resolution. Conflict resolution is one of the more effective social coping strategies when situations involve others. It occurs directly, and only, between the people involved. It is most successful when both individuals' perceptions and feelings are shared and acknowledged. Solutions generated are usually most successful when they consist of a negotiated compromise giving both sides something they wanted. It could be so simple as your roommate agreeing not to leave her hair dryer out if you also agree not to leave your shoes lying in the way of the front door. In some cases, others may be willing to go along with your desires simply because they had not previously recognized that what they were doing was irritating or inconveniencing, and you have now pointed that out. This is a key advantage that direct communication has over the more-manipulative behaviors.

Altruistic behavior. Our social connectedness itself can serve as a coping strategy. One form is altruistic behavior. **Altruism** can be defined as doing something for someone else, without expecting something in return. Doing something for someone else feels good, as you observe or imagine their pleasure and get in touch with your sense of social striving. It also takes your mind off your own problems and allows you to act, perhaps at a time you are unable to do something about your own stressor. Altruism becomes maladaptive if you find that you are always running around rescuing people but never working on resolving your own difficulties.

Seeking social support. We are social animals; we find security in numbers. We feel stronger and more able to cope when we feel the supportiveness of our significant others. Research has shown that the presence of a quality social support system can reduce the negative impact of events such as losing a job, giving birth, and other stressful life events (Danish & D'Augeli, 1980).

Different people want different things when they seek social support. Sometimes we have thought out exactly what we would like; at other times we don't know what we want. Clarifying for ourselves what we desire of others helps us know what to look for in a social support network. Do we want a shoulder to cry on, or do we want someone to tell us what we might do? Are we looking for a reality check, or do we want someone to offer to help out in some way? Let's explore these issues by looking at how we might provide support for someone else.

Suppose a close friend of yours is going through a difficult time. He is very upset, and comes to you ranting and raving about perceived injustice in his life. What can you do that would be supportive? Actually, there are a number of strategies you can use that might be helpful. Some suggestions are grouped below within the categories of provision of emotional support, confrontation, advice-giving, and active involvement.

Some forms of supportiveness are helpful because they provide emotional support. For example, you can offer to listen to your friend. Most of the time, people are looking for an opportunity to express their feelings when they look for social support. Your friend may feel better if he can simply unload, without fear of judgment or criticism. You can express understanding of why he might feel the way he does. Even if you do not think it is how you would react, you will most likely be able to see the progression of events, thoughts, and feelings and their logical connections. If you have been in a similar situation, you can commiserate with him: misery loves miserable company (Zimbardo & Formica, 1963). However, remember to say, "I can understand how you feel," rather than "I know how you feel." Nobody truly knows how someone else feels. We can only make educated guesses based on our own experiences. People sometimes feel like their emotions are being trivialized or robbed of their uniqueness and individuality when we imply that we have their internal workings pegged.

Other forms of emotional supportiveness involve encouragement and provision of hope. You could affirm your friend's ability to cope with the unfortunate situation, using evidence from his past coping successes in general, as well as his successes with similar situations in the past: "You've been through this before, you'll make it." Eleanore Roosevelt's observation "this, too, shall pass" is indeed accurate. You can also point out the potential positives of the situation, provided they are realistic. Discuss the negatives with your friend, and then point out the positives. If he is catastrophizing over a potential negative outcome, remind him that not only are there more-positive possible outcomes but also that he has the ability to cope with the outcome whatever it may be.

In some cases, confrontation can serve as social support. You can point out undesirable consequences of emotionally handling the situation in the manner your friend has chosen. "Snap out of it!" would not be a particularly sensitive response, but allowing your friend time to grieve over the situation and then saying, "OK, so now it sounds like it's time to figure out what you want to do. Want some help?" will be better received.

Another form of confrontation involves helping the person see the big picture. You can help your friend put his problem in perspective. How important is it in the big picture of life? He has his friends, his health, his talents and abilities, a family who cares about him, a full stomach and a roof over his head, and everything else that does not happen to be a facet of the problem. However, it is important not to imply to him that he should not feel as he does because of all the blessings he can count. Feelings are never wrong. Counting blessings is a strategy for reducing the intensity of unpleasant emotions, not for eliminating them.

Sometimes you can see that a person is overreacting to a stressor. Occasionally, confrontation can help with overreacting. Suppose you believe that your friend has misinterpreted the actions of others or other environmental occurrences. You can point out that yes indeed, that is one possible way of interpreting the situation. However, you can see others. Such confrontation needs to be approached with caring and gentleness, so that your friend does not feel attacked.

Another form of social support is advice-giving. Some people want more than emotional support; they want someone to help them find strategies for coping. Having read this chapter, you can probably think of a number of suggestions. If the person is dealing with a problem and looking for solutions, the problem-solving strategy discussed earlier in this chapter can be helpful for exploring options. It helps you aid the friend as he selects his own solution, as well as helps you avoid simply telling him what you think he should do, which is generally not as helpful.

Active involvement can also serve as social support. It can be as simple as offering to do something with your friend that would provide a distraction from his woes, such as going out for a hamburger, going for a walk in the park, or playing a little one-on-one. In some cases, there are simple tasks that can help relieve the stress of the problem, such as lending him $10 until Thursday, running a simple errand that has him overwhelmed, or giving him a lift to work for a few days. Caution must be taken, however, not to let active involvement become "rescuing" behavior. If your friend is always coming to you for this kind of support and you are constantly obliging him, his ability to develop his own coping strategies will become undermined.

So what kind of social support do you think is usually most helpful for you? You may prefer one form, or perhaps the type you would like differs according to your situation. As you seek social support, look for a good match for your needs. Nobody likes to be told what to do if all that is desired is a shoulder to cry on. Likewise, we would prefer that our friends not jump in and offer to do things for us if all we are looking for is validation of our reality. Make note of which significant others are most adept at offering which kinds of support. Some friends have the savvy to provide many kinds of support, especially if they are familiar with a narrative similar to the one above.

And when you go to someone for support, let him or her know what kind you would like. If it turns out that what you want is not something the person can give, don't keep beating your head against a brick wall, and don't judge the person poorly because of his or her incongruent supportive style. The adaptive reaction is to seek that form of support elsewhere.

Expanding Your Experience

As a student you are no doubt already well aware of the effects of stress on daily living. The worst year for myself regarding stress and student life was the second year of my doctoral training. Training was intense and year-round. So by the second year, most students' immune systems were shot. As a result, we were able to identify second-year students just by observing how often they were ill. I managed to have three different secondary infections due to illness within 6 months.

In addition to using antibiotics, I was most successful at dealing with the impact of stress by limiting the number of other stressors in my life. I also lowered my expectations of performance. Rather than going the extra mile necessary to earn the ever-important "A," I redirected my energies toward learning and incorporating what I had learned into my practice of psychology. Even though I received more "B's" my second year, my learning experience was ultimately more useful and less stress-producing.

How do you manage your stress and anxiety? The first exercise can help you evaluate how likely it is that your stressors might result in your contracting as many illnesses as I did. The second exercise is an inventory of the sources of stress in your life, which you can compare with those of your classmates. The third exercise gives you an opportunity to examine your experience of anxiety from several psychodynamic standpoints. The fourth exercise helps you evaluate your unique anxiety-producing thoughts. The fifth exercise is a checklist of coping strategies. The sixth exercise gives you practice with the 8-point problem-solving strategy discussed earlier in this chapter. The seventh exercise provides an opportunity to try out Ellis's RET strategy as an anxiety-reducing technique. The last exercise is a relaxation sequence narrative.

Study Questions

1. What is the difference between stress and anxiety?
2. Describe typical sources of stress in Western culture.
3. How is it that even change for the better can be stressful?
4. Describe four types of conflict involving approach and/or avoidance.
5. What is the general adaptation syndrome, and why can it result in physical illness?
6. What are state anxiety and trait anxiety?
7. Describe anxiety from the psychodynamic, existential, behavioral, and cognitive viewpoints.
8. Can coping mechanisms be termed "good" or "bad"? Explain your answer.
9. Suppose you make a comment in class that you believe is brilliant, but a number of your classmates put it down. Describe how you might cope with your resulting feelings through use of the following defense mechanisms: projection, intellectualization, regression, sublimation, displacement. Which do you think have the greatest potential for being adaptive? Maladaptive?
10. How are focusing, biofeedback, meditation, and the relaxation response alike in their abilities to help us cope?
11. Suppose you have some noisy neighbors who repeatedly keep you awake at night. Use the eight-point problem-solving strategy described on pages 95–99 to find a solution for this problem.
12. How might you use self-instruction as a coping mechanism while you are preparing to make a speech?
13. Outline how a student could use Ellis's ABCDE to deal with feelings of anxiety over having to tell his or her parents about plans to move off campus.
14. List the different ways you could provide social support for a friend. Which form do you typically prefer when you are distressed?

CHAPTER FIVE

Anger, Aggression, and Depression

Taming the Dragons within Us

Hostile! Who says I'm hostile?

Anger, Aggression, and Depression

Let's look again at the scenario presented at the beginning of Chapter 4. You walk into the classroom and see everyone preparing to take a test, and you had no idea that a test was going to be given that day. Instead of being a case of a practical joke on the instructor, it turns out there really is a test that day for which you have not prepared. You muddle through the test as best you can. Afterwards, you feel terrible. You know you haven't done very well on it. You may start getting down on yourself, blaming yourself for having been so disorganized, and become depressed. Or, you may start placing blame on your instructor for not having been clearer about when the test was to take place. You become angry.

While anxiety and stress are the emotional consequences stemming from what we are afraid might happen in the future, anger and depression are emotional reactions to events or circumstances that we perceive as already having happened, or as being inevitable. Aggression involves behavioral responses that can occur as a result of our emotional reacting. We will look at the phenomena of anger, aggression, and depression individually.

Anger

The most basic underpinnings of the experience of anger is its physiology. We have little difficulty recognizing when people are in a raging fury because we observe consistent bodily reactions in those whom we suspect to be experiencing it. They may become red in the face, scowl, grit their teeth, frown, flare their nostrils, narrow their eyes to slits, have veins standing out from their necks, clench their fists, stiffen up, and/or become louder or more strained in their vocalizations. Likewise, we are aware of how our own bodies seem to take off on their own when we are angry. We may feel shaky, restless, somewhat choked, nauseous, or numb. We notice that we breathe more rapidly, our hearts pound, we sweat more profusely, and we may begin to feel out of control.

These common reactions are produced by the hormones epinephrine (adrenaline) and norepinephrine (noradrenalin) that appear in our system while we are angry (Tavris, 1982). As you may recall, these same hormones also play a role in the experiences of fear and anxiety. Becoming angry can help fuel the "fight-or-flight" aggression necessary for defending ourselves when we are being attacked. In this respect anger can be very useful. Anger can also motivate us to try to eliminate the social injustices we see, and to work toward a better world (Averill, 1982).

Adrenaline rushes can be experienced numerous ways (Selye, 1976). Whether you experience the sensation as anger, fear, anxiety, or excitement is determined by how you perceive your situation. For example, if a lion is charging in your direction, you will most likely experience fear. If you believe that someone has been stomping on your individual rights, you will be more likely to feel anger. If a young man or woman you have been admiring as a potential love interest turns and smiles at you, your adrenaline rush probably will be experienced as excitement. A single event can itself be experienced in more than one way. You might at first be angry if your boyfriend or girlfriend was tardy in showing up for your birthday dinner. But you would then experience the arousal as excitement as he or she and a number of your friends seemingly jump from the woodwork and yell "Surprise!"

The degree of anger we experience can also be mediated by our thought lives. Often when we become angry we have a personal demand of our world that we do not feel is being met. Ellis (1962) refers to this type of demand as **musturbatory thinking**. The following beliefs are likely to pump up an angry reaction for any situation:

- Others must be considerate and kind toward me.
- The world must be fair.
- I must not experience any personal discomfort.
- Things must go the way I would like them to go.

Beck et al. (1979) also point out how we can sometimes think of the world in an unrealistic manner and make matters worse for ourselves. These **cognitive distortions** can fuel our anger. In addition to the "musts" and "shoulds," cognitive distortions especially prone to produce angry feelings are **labeling**, **magnification**, and **mind reading**.

Labeling involves perceiving people solely on the basis of their undesirable behavior. A person does something that causes you discomfort or inconvenience, and because of this transgression you think of him or her as being a jerk, geek, airhead—or perhaps some other more colorful label. Seeing a person as being a "jerk" puts the person in an entirely negative light. Labeling also involves overgeneralizing, perhaps on the basis of only a single event. In reality, we all perform our share of "jerklike" behaviors. But if we label someone else as the jerk we see ourselves as being somewhat more superior. We then feel more justified in becoming angry with this person, since he or she is the essence of badness, rather than just a person who chose a behavior that we consider to be undesirable.

Magnification occurs when we blow the negative event out of proportion. Instead of recognizing the undesired event as unfortunate, we see it as a major catastrophe. Becoming frustrated or irritated while you are kept waiting an extra half-hour in your physician's waiting room is natural. But if you tell yourself that this is a disaster, it is more than you can stand, and you just can't take it any more, you can fume indefinitely.

Mind reading is a form of making up reality as you go along. Somebody does something you don't like, and you choose to interpret the person's motives as being hostile, inconsiderate, or unfair, thus making yourself even more angry over the situation. The only person who has a chance of accurately knowing the motives involved is the person who experienced them. So we may end up jousting windmills as we pump up our anger over the person's "vendetta" against us, which may in fact be nonexistent.

Where do these cognitive distortions come from? Behaviorists might suggest that they are learned, perhaps through modeling by others or as an effect of rewards and punishers. However, psychodynamically oriented theorists would make reference to the role of frustration in ego-building. Jacobson (1964) explains that reasonable levels of frustration help a young child let go of the magical thinking of infancy, as well as help the ego develop more realistic ways of coping with adverse events throughout the life span. Low levels of anger or frustration therefore act as an impetus toward growth.

Unfortunately, we live in a society that tries to minimize frustration. We must have everything now and experience everything now, even if it means buying on credit until our charge cards are maxed to the limit. When marital relationships develop difficulties we have become more likely to divorce and look for new romantic prospects, rather than deal with the frustrations involved with working problems through. More and more consumables are becoming disposable, ending frustration over the need to clean and reuse. Fast food and instant microwave meals have reduced the need to tolerate waiting through an extended period of food preparation. Spitz (1959) points out that our pharmacological culture may interfere with human development as alcohol, nicotine, psychotropic medications, and street drugs have become so frequently relied upon to numb frustrations. Even television sitcom plots encourage us to believe that our frustrations should be resolved during the course of a 30-minute episode.

Thus, as we avoid frustration, we may cling to more childlike ways of thinking. We must have our way, people are either all good or all bad, others must be nice to us, and everything should be fair. In this manner we may learn to manage our anger maladaptively, rather than in ways that are productive, socially acceptable, and growth producing.

Aggression

While anger is a feeling, aggression is actually a behavior. Aggression is one way of coping with anger, as in fighting off an assailant or taking an aggressive stance toward a controversial social issue. However, it is a choice: You can choose to behave aggressively, or you can choose another form of behavior if you see it as being more adaptive. You can even behave aggressively in the absence of anger, such as playing aggressively in a competitive sport.

Aggression can be defined as any behavior that involves intent to do undesired harm of some sort to another (Baron, 1977). A variety of hypotheses have been used to explain the bases of aggression. The psychodynamic view describes aggression as an instinctual drive that assists us in separation-individuation and ego development (Freud, 1920/1935; Gillespie, 1971). Lorenz (1966), an ethnologist, also believed aggression to be instinctual. By encouraging fighting it serves the purposes of protecting the species from intruders, ensuring that the strongest males will mate, and dispersing the population in ways that maximize utilization of resources. Yet other theorists have seen aggression as a drive that naturally arises when goals are frustrated (Dollard et al., 1939).

The role of hormones and aggression has also been extensively studied, although largely in laboratory animals. The presence of the male sex hormone, **testosterone**, appears to increase the likelihood of aggressive behavior (Rothballer, 1967). Testosterone levels go up in many male species during mating seasons, a time when male aggressive behavior also increases (Conner & Levine, 1969). When testosterone is administered to female guinea pigs or mice, an increase in aggressive behavior is seen (Phoenix et al., 1959; Edwards, 1968). On the other hand, there is an increase in aggressive behavior in female mice during lactation that seems connected to maternal protectiveness; however, this aggressiveness seems to be facilitated by the presence of male partners (Debold & Miczek, 1981).

We might speculate that testosterone also plays a role in human aggression. We certainly observe more physically aggressive behavior among men than women (Averill, 1982). However, when push comes to shove we also see physically aggressive behavior among women, and verbal aggression appears among women with the same frequency as that of men (Reinsch & Saunders, 1986).

The ambiguous role of gender in the occurrence of aggression can be explained in part by social learning theory. While our aggressive drives, instincts, or hormones may influence us one way or the other, we have the advantage over lower animals of a more complex and highly developed cerebral cortex. In other words, we have the ability to make intelligent choices concerning whether or not to follow through on our aggressive impulses, based on what we have learned.

Bandura (1973) demonstrated that aggressive behavior can be learned by seeing it performed by a model and that future performance of the learned behavior can be increased or decreased based on the observed consequences of the behavior. So if a child sees others obtain their pick of the playground equipment by bullying other children, and these cohorts are not perceived to receive unpleasant consequences for such behavior, the child will be likely to try bullying as well. However, if an observed aggressive behavior would place a person at odds with the perceived gender role he or she has adopted, the unpleasant feeling involved with such an internal conflict would reduce the likelihood that the person will copy the behavior. Thus in a culture that prescribes male aggressiveness, we would expect gender role learning to inhibit physical aggression in women and facilitate physical aggression in men.

Aggression and Today's World

The level of acceptability of various types of aggressive behavior is constantly changing. The increase in environmental stressors—noise, crowding, air pollution—has also seen a corresponding escalation of aggression. Thus in recent years some types of aggressive behavior have met with increased perceived acceptability, especially if you put stock in media presentations of aggression.

Aggression and the Media

If you are interested in being exposed to aggressive behavior, you need not go any further than your television screen. Violence abounds on television. It stimulates and arouses us, which is often why we turn the television on in the first place. The more we feel stimulated by a television program, the more likely we are to watch it. The sponsors love this, and the television network executives are more likely to bring in increased revenue if they can please sponsors. So thanks to the effects of positive reinforcement, aggressive behavior on television proliferates.

Unfortunately, there appears to be a connection between aggressive behavior and television viewing. Numerous studies, especially with children, have found a relationship between viewing television violence and behaving aggressively (Singer & Singer, 1986). This research, however, is correlational, so we don't know which causes which. Does viewing aggression on television cause more aggressive behavior, or do aggressive people choose to watch violent television?

This is a complex question that is still being sorted out. For now, we can speculate that both are probably true. The tendency of our brains to habituate to ongoing stimuli applies to viewing violence as well. People who typically behave aggressively create plenty of stimulation in their lives. Since this produces a certain amount of desensitization, the television programs that will feel stimulating to these individuals will have to be even more aggressive than their own daily living experiences–programs such as those involving murders, car wrecks, violent fighting, buildings blowing up, hostile humor, and so on. Programming involving more-traditional daily living and adaptive forms of resolving conflict would probably put them to sleep.

Desensitization also can play a role in increasing tolerance of violence by those who happen to see it (Drabman & Thomas, 1974). Again, constant exposure to a stimulus causes our brains to habituate. We may be less likely to feel aroused by aggression or violence in our lives if we have become desensitized to it through our television-viewing habits. As our brains become numbed to violence and aggression, we begin seeing it as a more prevalent, "normal" behavior than it really is.

Viewing television violence can also increase our aggressive behavior because of the effects of social learning theory. We learn aggressive behaviors we would never think up on our own by seeing them portrayed on television. There are numerous incidents of vicious novel acts of aggression portrayed on the media being copied in real life (Geen, 1990). Also, we see "bad guys" get what they want by using violence and forms of inappropriate aggression–which places us in a vicarious reinforcement scenario. In addition, we see the "good guys"–our heroes and potential role models–driving recklessly, hitting others, and killing people right and left in their pursuit of justice.

So how much violence do you expose yourself to during your television-viewing times? It gives one pause for thought. Of course, there are plenty of individuals who watch aggressive behavior on television and would never copy such behaviors themselves. What makes these individuals different? Most likely, they continue to actively remind themselves that these are not appropriate or adaptive real-life behaviors (Huesmann et al., 1983). Perhaps we can protect ourselves from the pervasiveness of violence portrayed in the media by doing likewise: remembering that most television programming is not reality but a fictional creation driven by whatever benefits those who sponsor their existence.

Rape

Rape, which can be defined as forced and unwilling participation in sexual intercourse, most commonly occurs between a male perpetrator and a female victim. It is alarmingly commonplace: If you include all unwanted sexual contact, such as forced kissing and fondling, three-quarters of all college women report being sexually assaulted (Kanin & Parcell, 1977).

Rape is commonly misperceived as an act of sexuality but is actually an act of aggression. Many other myths surround the act of rape. Victims are often seen as having an unconscious desire to be raped, or "deserving" to be raped if they dress revealingly, engage in heavy necking and petting, hitchhike, act stuck-up, get drunk, or go to a man's home on a first date (Burt, 1980). None of these beliefs is true.

Rapists look for victims who appear to be easy marks, those lacking confidence, appearing vulnerable, or acting submissive or passive (Myers et al., 1985). It is indeed unfortunate that these characteristics are often reinforced in women as part of the stereotypical female gender role. However, the within-population similarities of rape victims end there. Anyone, male or female, can become a rape victim.

The profiles of rapists share more similarities than the profiles of rape victims. The typical rapist is a young man between the ages of 15 and 25, who is poor, unskilled, undereducated, and/or below average in intelligence. In many instances, he is married and living with his wife. He usually knows the victim he chooses, and the rape is usually carefully planned rather than being a spontaneous impulse.

Whether or not a rape actually occurs depends entirely upon the rapist. The key variables that appear to play a role are the man's attitude concerning aggression and his level of inhibition. As you may recall, the stereotypical male gender role involves acting macho, aggressive, and domineering. Young men who tightly cling to this stereotype as evidence of their manhood are more likely to find the portrayal of rape to be arousing. In one study, they were found to be aroused to the same degree as convicted rapists (Check & Malamuth, 1983). Disinhibition appears to occur in conjunction with alcohol consumption, observing pornographic violence toward women, and men's feelings of being out of sync with their perception of masculinity (Linz et al., 1988). Researchers believe that the propensity of rape is therefore not a result of sexual need, but instead is a phenomenon that increases along with all acts of violence toward women as certain types of men attempt to control and subordinate women (Donnerstein, 1983).

Date rape, when women are assaulted within the context of a date, is a murkier area. Sometimes date rape occurs for the same reasons as other acquaintance rapes. However, it can also occur as a product of misguided expectations concerning sexuality and poor communication. Our culture prescribes flirting patterns that involve men pursuing women for as much sexual contact as they can get and women teasing and leading men on. At least, this is how it is often portrayed in the media. And in a whirlwind of passion, the two lovers are often shown giving in to their erotic impulsivity amid much female protestation and male pleading. Rare is the movie or television program that shows the other important preliminaries, such as discussing the level and types of sexual contact they feel comfortable with, birth control methods, communicable diseases, and level of commitment to the relationship. Thus it is little wonder that some young men become confused about the validity of their paramours' protests, and find themselves being accused of rape.

Men can protect themselves by communicating up front about what they and the objects of their desires are doing: Get a specific "yes" before you proceed with any sexual contact. If she changes her mind and says "no," stop and get clarification. Always assume that "no" means "no," even if you suspect she is really saying "maybe." If she really wants to be with you, let her know that she must make that preference perfectly clear. Do not presume that previous engagement in sexual intercourse is an ongoing open invitation, even if the woman involved is your wife. And think twice about using alcohol during initial contacts, so you can depend on your ability to inhibit your impulses. Sure, this takes some of the whirlwind of passion out of the moment, but it beats finding yourself in prison blues.

Women can protect themselves from date rape in a number of ways. If you are meeting someone for the first time, agree to meet him in a public place, so you have an opportunity to evaluate him before finding yourself alone with him or revealing to him where you live. You may want to hold off on using alcohol while dating him until you know him well enough to trust him not to take advantage of you in a disinhibited state. Before engaging in sexual activity, decide for yourself how far you want to go, and communicate this preference. Do away with false protestations and tell him exactly what you mean. If things get out of hand and he refuses to stop escalating, do not be afraid to do what you have to do to protect yourself. If all else fails, yell loudly, "What you're doing is rape and I'm calling 911." Responding in this manner has been found to stop most men's unwanted advances (Beal & Muehlenhard, 1987).

Managing Anger and Aggression

While anger and aggression are actually two separate entities, the above descriptions illustrate how complexly intertwined they can become. Learning to deal with anger and aggression involves sorting out all of these variables so that you can plan and choose in ways that enhance, rather than complicate, your life.

Novaco (1979) shows how the components of anger interrelate: (1) We experience an aversive event, (2) We appraise the event or develop expectations on the basis of it, (3) We experience the feeling of anger, and (4) We choose a behavioral reaction to the event. For example, suppose your instructor hands back your term paper, informing you that you only earned a "C−." Having thought the paper deserved a better grade, you feel annoyed, frustrated, insulted, or perhaps even picked on. You have thoughts about the event: He shouldn't have given me such a low grade! This isn't fair. I can't stand it when things turn out this way. These cognitions arouse you, turning your annoyance into full-fledged anger. Based on this anger, you decide to tell your instructor what you really think about him or her. While for many the above seems like a natural progression of events, telling off your instructor probably isn't going to work for your best interests.

Stress Inoculation Training

Stress inoculation training (Meichenbaum & Novaco, 1978) can be used to deal with all four determinants of the progression of anger and aggression. It consists of three phases: education and self-exploration, coping skills development, and application of these skills to the real world.

Experiencing the aversive event. Aversive events happen to everyone. However, different events are especially aversive to different people. Education and self-exploration during this initial stage of anger involves brainstorming exactly which situations seem to be most arousing to you in particular. Are there particular circumstances? Particular people? Particular places? Is there a particular mood you might be in that could contribute? A particular time of day? Be as specific as possible.

The major coping skills at this level involve keeping yourself out of trouble at the start. If you always lose your temper when you go to hockey games, settle for watching hockey on television. If you blow up a lot later in the evening as you are becoming tired, find ways to limit your stressors during that time of day. If you always seem to get into arguments when you are around Susan, analyze the progression of these arguments so you can discover how you allow yourself to be drawn in or what Susan is doing that leads to your feeling compelled to challenge her.

For application of these strategies to the real world, some people educate themselves to their aversive events by keeping an "anger diary." They write down the episodes of anger experienced during the day, noting the people, place, circumstances, and time of day, watching for patterns. This strategy helps them learn to recognize problem situations as they occur; and by stopping to observe the situation, they are learning to react with a certain degree of detachment from their angry feelings.

Appraisals and expectations. The last chapter described how we can cope with anxiety by addressing our thoughts and beliefs. These same strategies can be used while coping with anger. What sorts of "should's," "must's," and demands for fairness do you see behind your anger? Also, how realistic is your appraisal of the aversive event? Did the driver who cut in front of you really do so as a personal attack, or was it because the driver discovered some other need to change lanes quickly? Did your boss assign you an undesirable task because he does not care about your preferences, or because he thought you were the best person for the job?

You could educate yourself by exploring the particular beliefs fueling your anger and learning to recognize them as they occur. Ellis's RET or Beck's CBT strategies can help you learn to cope with the beliefs. Once identified, you can practice challenging irrational beliefs and automatic thoughts. Application of cognitive learning to actual situations can come about by role-playing typical anger-provoking scenarios, and reminding yourself of less anger-provoking beliefs as you do so.

Experience of anger and arousal. No matter how much cognitive restructuring we do, we cannot completely escape feelings of anger. After all, there will be times when that anger will motivate us to look out for our best interests. However, we also want to be sure that the experience is not so profound that our behavior becomes misguided and maladaptive.

First, anger can be modulated by learning to recognize when you are in fact experiencing anger. Sometimes people react aggressively and blame their behavior on the situation, not realizing that anger plays a more significant role in their choices of behavior. Learn to recognize your own physiological responding when you are angry: Is your respiration and heart rate up? Do you feel shaky? Is your mind racing? What cues can you use to recognize that anger, and possibly aggression, is around the corner?

Second, you can cope with anger by applying the same relaxation techniques that are useful with anxiety. Deep breathing and progressive relaxation both help reduce the physiological arousal behind anger. Practice is possible by imagining yourself in an anger-provoking situation, feeling the arousal, then using the relaxation technique. Third, you can apply your learning by actively attempting to produce the same relaxation response when real-life situations arise. Since you cannot experience arousal and relaxation at the same time, the more skilled you are at applying the relaxation response, the lower your arousal—and level of anger—will become.

Behavioral reaction. Our options for behavioral reactions to anger, like all behavioral reactions, depend on what we have learned. If someone takes your seat in the movie theater and you can only think of responses such as insulting him, punching him out, dumping your beverage over his head, or creating some other embarrassing scene, you are likely to choose to react aggressively. Thus the first step in managing behavioral reactions to anger is learning alternative methods of responding. In other words, we must know how to react assertively.

Assertiveness

Responses to anger and frustration can be viewed as either **assertive** or nonassertive (Alberti & Emmons, 1978). Assertive behaviors can be defined as those that allow a person to stand up for his or her rights, while not violating the rights of others. Nonassertive behaviors, on the other hand, can be actively aggressive, passively aggressive, or passively inactive.

Using the movie theater example, the insults and physical attacks would be considered actively aggressive. The disadvantages of aggressive behaviors are obvious: They invite retaliation, they alienate others, and they usually leave us feeling not very good about ourselves.

Passive-aggressive behaviors are those that do not openly express anger but do serve the purpose of venting anger by "getting even." For example, you might take the seat directly in front of the offender and put your hat on. Or perhaps sit behind him and "accidentally" kick the back of the seat every now and then. Or maybe you know which car is his, so you make a long scratch mark on the driver's-side door.

A major problem with passive-aggressive behavior is that it does not let the offender know that he or she has offended. Had the person known he was sitting in your spot, he might have been willing to move. Another problem with passive-aggressive behavior is that it is not so likely to get you what you want. Suppose your roommate, who occasionally borrows your clothes, always returns them unlaundered. You decide that instead of dealing openly with the problem, you will start returning clothes you borrowed from her unlaundered. This arrangement might be fine with your friend, in which case the irritating circumstances could go on indefinitely.

Passive-inactive behaviors typically involve sitting back and taking it. When someone takes your seat at the movies, you meekly find another. If your friend returns your clothing unlaundered you say nothing and launder it yourself. Patterns of passivity can lead to depression, since you do not stand up for your rights, treating yourself and your own needs as if they are unimportant. Furthermore, there is some indication that people who seem to constantly end up being victimized become so because of chronic use of passive-inactive behavior (Schwartz et al., 1993).

When you handle situations assertively, you clarify that your needs are indeed as important as anyone else's yet acknowledge others' rights to be treated fairly:

"Excuse me, I was sitting here. Would you mind finding another seat?" (using a calm, friendly tone)

"I would appreciate it if when you borrow my clothes you would launder them before you return them. And I will certainly be happy to do the same for you."

If you know you are about to enter a situation that typically results in your acting angrily, you can practice assertiveness ahead of time. Plan what you will say, and practice in front of a mirror or with a friend.

Dealing with Angry People

A major impediment to managing our angry and aggressive responding is the natural protective reaction we experience when faced with someone else who is angry. Albert Bernstein (1993) reminds us that angry responding has its bases in the most primitive part of the brain, the fight-or-flight mechanisms we share with lower animal species. He refers to this part of our brain as our "dinosaur brain." When others become angry with us, our dinosaur brains perceive their anger as an attack and we begin experiencing fight-or-flight responding. This is often escalatory and may not resolve the situation effectively.

When we react on the basis of what our dinosaur brains are telling us to do, we are not using much of our cerebral cortexes, where higher forms of thought and logic occur. Likewise, when others become angry with us, they are less likely to be using their cerebral cortexes. If we can bypass our dinosaur brains and use our cerebral cortexes when others act angrily toward us, we have a substantial IQ advantage over our adversaries. We can use this advantage to help resolve the situation, rather than let our dinosaur brains roar back and forth at each other.

Awareness. First, examine your own internal state, and guide yourself toward using your cerebral cortex and ignoring your dinosaur brain:

1. *Become aware of your physiological reactivity.* If you feel your heart pounding, you know that your dinosaur brain has been alerted. Do whatever you need to do to calm yourself—take deep breaths, count to 10, or use any of the other appropriate techniques described in the last chapter for relaxing yourself.

2. *Ask the other person for a moment to stop and think.* This creates a "time-out" for both of you. Attempting to think instead of react puts you more into your cerebral cortex and distracts you from your dinosaur brain. It also has a calming effect on the other person, since you have made it clear you are taking the situation seriously and are willing to attempt to work out a solution.

3. *Decide what you would like to see happen.* Think of possible options and the ramifications of following through on them as you decide.

Do's and don'ts of dinosaur brain management. Once you have placed your cerebral cortex closer to the driver's seat, you are ready to begin helping others out of their dinosaur brains and into more-advanced thinking patterns. There are a number of do's and don'ts for proceeding. First, the don'ts:

Don't do anything while the other person is still yelling. His or her dinosaur brain is in an attack mode and is more likely to interpret whatever you do as a form of counterattack, rather than take it at face value.

There are a variety of techniques you can use to promote an end to the attack mode. One method is illustrated by the pack behavior of wild dogs. When a dominant member of the pack acts offended by the behavior of a more submissive member, the lesser of the two will concede by crouching, looking away, and perhaps even whining. In this manner the dog has adopted a very nonthreatening stance, which helps defuse the dominant dog's fight-or-flight responding. While crouching in a corner, covering your head, and whining may not work out during human conflict, there are other ways you can make yourself appear nonthreatening. Remember how you typically appear physically when you are angry and attempt to do the opposite, such as relaxing your body as much as possible, lowering your voice, moving and speaking more slowly, and attempting to wear a neutral facial expression.

Likewise, you can indirectly request that the other person adopt a more nonthreatening posture. Try asking the person to speak more slowly so you can understand. In order to do so, the person will need to ignore the rousings of his or her dinosaur brain in order to actively manipulate rate of speech. Speaking more slowly can also become a contradictory response to aroused responding, meaning the person will have difficulty feeling aroused if he or she is simultaneously behaving in a laid-back manner.

There are other distractions you can use to help guide the other person back to his or her cerebral cortex. Distractions are useful because they help break up typical attack/counterattack patterns. Bernstein describes using the "uh-huh rule" and the "Bugs Bunny approach." The "uh-huh rule" concerns our use of the expression "uh-huh" when listening to someone talk for a long time. Usually, we say it whenever the person stops to take a breath. If you refrain from saying "uh-huh," you break up the normal pattern of responding. If you remain silent, the angry person will run out of steam more quickly. In fact, if you are talking on the telephone, the person may stop and ask if you are still there.

Bugs Bunny is the Muhammad Ali of nonresponse. After Bugs drops an anvil on Elmer Fudd's head, or performs some other act of violence, Elmer typically picks up his shotgun and chases after Bugs, displaying classic dinosaur brain reacting. When he catches up with Bugs, Elmer finds him calmly leaning against a tree, munching on a carrot, and saying something inconsistent with the scenario, such as "What's up, Doc?" At other times, Bugs uses flattery–"Gee, Doc, that's a great-looking hat you're wearing"–and Elmer responds by pulling out of the aggressive stance, blushing and pshawing, and talking about the merits of his hat.

While such blatant flattery would appear transparent in the real world, there are other ways of using the Bugs Bunny approach to break up the attack/counterattack pattern. For example, you can say something like "It's clear you've given this a lot of thought." Far from being a counterattack, it acknowledges that you have listened to the person and given some merit to what he or she has said, regardless of whether or not you agree with the person's position. Bernstein suggests saying "You're obviously an intelligent person." He points out that nobody is going to argue with such a statement, nor are they likely to feel counterattacked, unless of course you are using a sarcastic or condescending tone of voice.

Don't make "you are" statements to describe the person's responding. They are perceived as a form of attack, and the person is likely to launch into a defensive counterattack. Such responses also sidetrack the discussion into the accuracy of the "you are" statement, rather than sticking to the topic at hand.

Don't dive into explanations of your own point of view. Since your own point of view is probably contradictory to the angry person's point of view, it implies that the other person is "wrong." This can be perceived as yet another attack, which further stimulates the person's dinosaur brain into defensive maneuvers.

When you have done some defusing and have guarded against further provocation, there are techniques you can use to help the person move toward problem-solving.

Do let the other person know that you hear what he or she is saying. Adopt a stance and facial expression that looks interested, as if you are listening intently. State back to the person what you believe he or she has said, and express understanding of why the person is upset. You may not agree with the angry person's reasoning or position, but their explanations will most likely clarify for you why the person is upset. Once you show understanding and acceptance, the person's dinosaur brain feels less compulsion to attack and protect.

Do ask what the angry person would like you to do, making sure you sound interested rather than sarcastic or exasperated as you do so. The person may not have given it much thought yet, and possibly what he or she wants is not far from what you had in mind in the first place. Furthermore, asking the person to think in this manner forces him or her to use thinking ability, distracting the person away from dinosaur-brain reacting.

Do let the angry person know what you would like to see happen, with the emphasis on this being what you would like, not something etched in granite and thus unchangeable.

Do let the angry person know that you would be interested in negotiating. Reiterate what the angry person wants and what you want, and suggest generating options for solutions. In this manner you move into a problem-solving mode.

Do set up a time for follow-up. As with any problem-solving strategy, get verbal acknowledgment of the solution you have selected together and decide upon a time for reevaluation so you can check on how the solution is working.

Depression

Depression is often referred to as the "common cold" of mental health. Everyone experiences depression. Like anger, depression occurs when we perceive a stressor or some feared event as having happened or being inevitable. But rather than turning our energies outward and engaging in protective and counterattack maneuvers, we turn the anger inward. We accuse ourselves of some form of failure or inadequacy concerning the event, and react emotionally with feelings of depression.

Depressed people can be easy to identify. They often withdraw from social contact, seem uninterested in the activities they usually enjoy, or seem oversensitive and easily teary-eyed. They may not take their usual care of their physical appearance and may neglect or alter their sleeping and eating needs as well.

We usually become clued in to our own depressions through the corresponding uncomfortable inner experiences. We may feel lethargic, unmotivated, irritable, and slowed in our thoughts and movements. Even the simplest tasks may seem too difficult to tackle. We usually feel bad about ourselves, that our situations are hopeless, or perhaps that others do not like us. Guilt, brooding, and anxiety are also common symptoms of depression.

While the experience of depression is unpleasant, it actually can be an adaptive phenomenon. Depression follows or coincides with significant stressors. When we slow down and withdraw from usual activity, we conserve energy that can be applied toward rebuilding our inner resources and recovering from the impact of the stress in our lives. Furthermore, withdrawal helps reduce the chances that we take on even more stressors during a time when we are already stretched to our limits. It appears to be our bodies' natural way of telling us "time out!"

The Many Facets of Depression

The different perspectives of psychology address different aspects of the experience of depression.

Biological perspective.

The biological perspective focuses on the neurochemical and genetic differences between depressed and nondepressed individuals. Seriously depressed people tend to have lower levels of serotonin or norepinephrine (McNeal & Cimbolic, 1986). The presence of these substances is important for feelings of subjective well-being.

Also, research suggests that the tendency to become depressed may in fact be an inherited trait (Egeland et al., 1987). Chronic depression is more likely to be experienced among members of the same biological family than among those who are not blood relatives.

Psychodynamic perspective. The psychodynamic perspective notes the role of loss in depression. The earliest traditional psychodynamic views related all depression back to the original attachment between parent and child. Depression was seen as a reaction to perceived rejection by or loss of a primary caretaker, which amounts to a loss of support and affirmation. Thus any adult depression was considered to be a replay of such early experiences.

Grief reactions are obvious reactions to loss. When we lose a loved one, we can feel overwhelmingly depressed. However, grief reactions can also occur from other losses, such as the loss of friends as we move from one part of the country to another, the loss of a way of life when we cross over from student living to the working world, or even the loss of an ideology as we grow and develop more complex ways of interpreting our life experience.

Depression also occurs as the result of loss of self-esteem or self-worth. Personal failures or perceived shortcomings frequently cause depression. In many ways, depressed people are rejecting themselves and their needs as they neglect their appearance, ignore eating and sleeping needs, and refrain from engaging in enjoyable activity. These self-rejections can be evidence of lack of belief in their basic worth.

Behavioral perspective. Behaviorists explain the feelings of hopelessness experienced by depressed people. Seligman (1974) introduced a concept known as **learned helplessness**. Normally when we see an aversive experience looming ahead of us, we do what we can to escape it. Research on learned helplessness shows that when we see no escape from such negative reinforcers, we sometimes give up and endure the aversive experiences. We feel that the situation is hopeless, and we temporarily lose our faith in our own abilities to cope. Learned helplessness explains why abused individuals can be so difficult to pry loose from their batterers.

Another component of behavior theory that can be responsible for these feelings of hopelessness concerns positive reinforcers. Certain skills are required to obtain social reinforcers, outside of those that occur by chance. An adequately paying job, a significant other, and the respect of those around us are all positive reinforcers provided by society. If we have difficulty with the social skills necessary to obtain the available positive reinforcers, or do not believe we have the skills, we can feel hopeless and depressed. Furthermore, the more we withdraw and avoid social contact, the fewer social reinforcers we receive, which can lead to even more depression (Youngren & Lewinsohn, 1980).

Cognitive perspective. Depression involves a lot of negative thinking. We are down on ourselves, down on the world, and critical of life in general. Our life circumstances may indeed be unpleasant or unfortunate when we experience depression. In fact, depressed people appear to see the world more accurately than those who are not depressed (Alloy & Abramson, 1979). Rather than having inaccurate perceptions, depressed individuals appear to suffer because of the inadequacy of their methods of processing their thoughts (Beck & Emery, 1985). The cognitive processing of depressed individuals is characterized by stability, internality, and globality, often directed toward themselves (Robins, 1988).

"I'll never get this right." This depressing thought is an example of the perception of stability. You failed at something, maybe more than once, and make the deduction that this state of affairs will never change and you will always fail.

"It's all my fault." This example of internality illustrates how when something goes wrong, a depressed person may place all blame on himself or herself, rather than take into consideration the circumstances contributing to the unfortunate situation.

"I can't get anything right." After a perceived failure at a single task, you accept the event as evidence that failure characterizes all of your efforts. This illustrates the globality of depressive thinking.

Humanistic perspective. The humanistic perspective also analyzes self-perception's role in depression. Depression attacks our self-acceptance. Rather than seeing ourselves as intrinsically valuable, regardless of our behaviors, we assign ourselves **conditions of worth** (Rogers, 1961). We become worthy only through our accomplishments and successes, and lack worth if we fail or are less than perfect.

So when we fail at a task and become depressed, the gap between the real and ideal selves has become unacceptable. However, this gap can also be created when our expectations of ourselves are too high. Unrealistic expectations of our abilities can set us up to never experience a comfortable gap between our real and ideal selves (Higgins, 1987).

Managing Depression

Since everybody experiences depression, popular demand has resulted in the development of many strategies for managing it. How you go about tackling your depression depends on how your particular depressive experience is manifesting itself.

Lethargy. You feel sluggish and unmotivated. You drag yourself around from task to task, with little enthusiasm or enjoyment. Or perhaps you just sit like a lump, while even simple daily tasks seem like too much to handle. You feel mentally slow and distracted, occasionally putting your mind on "hold" as an escape from the pressures that seem to be surrounding you.

An effective approach for dealing with **lethargy** is some form of activity. Aerobic exercise has been found to be especially effective in alleviating symptoms of depression (McCann & Holmes, 1984). Why this is so is not yet clear. Some believe that **endorphins** play a role (Hopson, 1988). Endorphins are natural opiates. They can give us a natural "high," similar to the "high" that is artificially induced when we consume opiatelike pain-killing medications. Also, just becoming more physically fit may play a role in our psychological well-being.

Exercise may also be effective because it boosts self-esteem. People feel better about themselves when they are actually accomplishing something or feel like they are taking control of a difficult situation. Or perhaps exercise distracts us from our problems. Focusing on psychological preoccupations is difficult when you are preoccupied with physical challenge. Thus effective activity need not be aerobic exercise. Forcing yourself to do anything—even routine tasks—can help alleviate feelings of depression.

Hopelessness and "self-downing." You find you are perceiving yourself as a failure, worthless, incapable of succeeding. The world and the people in it are unsupportive, uncooperative, and the situation is hopeless. When you find you are verbally abusing yourself in this manner, it is time to start examining your critical thoughts and challenging them. Just as dealing with dysfunctional thoughts and beliefs is useful for dealing with anxiety and anger, challenging such thoughts is extremely useful in the treatment of depression. In fact, research suggests that of all the talking therapies, cognitive therapy is most effective in the treatment of depression (Shapiro & Shapiro, 1982).

As described earlier, depressive thinking is characterized by stability, internality, and globality. For example, let's say you are a member of the basketball team. During the last few seconds of the game, the opposing team is ahead by one point and your teammate throws you the ball. You stop, you aim, you shoot, and you miss. The game is over. Your opponents win. You are hit with a wave of depression, and depressive cognitions begin to roll. Here is how you might challenge them:

Stability: "I'm a terrible basketball player. I don't know how I made the team."

Challenge: "The fact is, you did make the team. You're even a starter. Therefore you must be better than most of the other players who tried out. And this was only one missed shot. Actually you made quite a few shots today. You can't judge your ability on the basis of one shot."

Internality: "It's all my fault. If it weren't for me, we would have won the game."

Challenge: "So who died and made you the god of basketball game outcome? There were other players on your team who also contributed to the score. And the refs seemed to be calling fouls in the other team's favor. Not to mention the fact that you are missing your star center. Or perhaps the other team just played better today—or was more lucky! You played your best; winning just wasn't in the cards this game."

Globality: "No matter how hard I try, I always mess up. I'm a failure at everything."

Challenge: "Ridiculous. You have succeeded at many things. You have several strong friendships. You made it into the school of your choice. You even got an 'A' in that physics class that everyone else complains about. Furthermore, what about the time you blocked a last-minute shot and saved the win? You failed at one shot in a basketball game, not everything."

Brooding and anxiety. You are lying on your bed, staring at the ceiling. You have been trying to get to sleep for two hours, but you keep drifting back to the argument you had over the phone with your mother. Your thoughts continue to go around and around: what she said, what you said, what you could have said, what she might do, what you would really like to do, how she might react, and so on. The brooding and anxiety do not get you anywhere. The only purpose they serve is to keep you from sleeping or doing whatever else you would prefer to be accomplishing at that moment.

Since these thinking patterns do not serve any useful purpose, the most adaptive approach would be one that stops them. One form of thought-stopping, provided by the behavioral approach, is known as the **rubber-band technique**. You wear a rubber band around your wrist. Every time you find yourself uselessly brooding, you snap the rubber band. It hurts. Thanks to classical conditioning and negative reinforcement, the pairing of the pain and the brooding will eventually lead to your automatically avoiding such thoughts.

Another technique is to force yourself to brood. Pick a time of day when it will not interfere with your schedule and tell yourself you will worry for one hour. During the rest of the day, when worrisome thoughts occur, you remind yourself that you have set aside a time for those thoughts, and you return to worrying at the appropriate time. Since worry is one of those activities which you really need to be in the mood for in order to succeed, you find yourself trying to brood during your worry hour but running out of material. This eventually shows you that the events aren't as important or catastrophic as you had originally perceived.

SUICIDE

The most serious potential side effect of depression is suicide. Most people think about suicide at some point in their lives, but only a small minority actually try to carry it out. When people feel suicidal, usually they have come to the conclusion that killing themselves is the only way they can end their psychic pain. If they are in enough pain, all the moral judgments and social stigmas in the world are not going to keep them from choosing self-destruction. Suicidal people have forgotten that "this, too, will pass." Given time, most seemingly unbearable situations will change of their own accord. The elderly make up the age group most likely to commit suicide (U.S. Bureau of the Census, 1992), perhaps because many of the health difficulties, financial problems, and issues of alienation really may not pass for these individuals.

While women are three times more likely to attempt suicide, men are at least five times more likely to actually kill themselves (U.S. Bureau of the Census, 1992). This difference is due in part to the level of lethality of methods chosen by men and women. Men usually choose more aggressive means, such as gunshots to the head or hanging. Women tend to choose more passive methods, such as taking pills or slitting wrists, which allows considerably more time for either being discovered or changing their minds and getting help.

If you have suicidal thoughts, do not become concerned that you are "crazy," considering that most people have been in the same position. However, you do want to safeguard yourself from going any further than a few suicidal ideations. Find someone to talk to. Different from popular mythology, talking about suicide with someone does not encourage him or her to try it. If talking does not help, seek out a mental health professional or someone else who is trained to deal with such situations. There are many crisis hotlines located across the nation—help is only a phone number away. Take advantage of it. You will be glad you did after the crisis has passed.

Feeling Good

Most of us would agree that as long as we can be happy, the rest of our life circumstances are not so important. We all try to feel good. We seek out experiences that are positively reinforcing. We avoid experiences that feel punitive. We may even purposely endure unpleasant periods of time, knowing that our endurance will result in some form of longer-term happiness.

Feeling good can be cultivated. You need not become angry, depressed, or anxious before you can begin working on the frequency of your pleasant feelings. The first step in happiness work is to develop an understanding of the circumstances in which you feel happy. What sorts of events feel pleasant? A walk on the beach? A game of one-on-one? A game of solitaire? Window-shopping? Being in the middle of a really good book? Going dancing? A quiet evening with your significant other?

We are all unique in what pleases us. Create a list of events that you find to be pleasant, including as many as you can think of. Then during times of stress, you can make a point of including these activities in your life before the stressors get the better of you. Also, when we are actively depressed we may not be able to think of what we previously had found to be pleasurable. If you have your "pleasure list" constructed and readily at hand, you can use it to help pull yourself out of your moodiness.

Many people include alcohol or other drugs in their pleasure-seeking activities, whereby they create an artificial feeling of goodness. Unfortunately, alcohol and drug use may not produce these results, and in the long run may result in even more depression and dysfunction. Substance use and abuse will be discussed in further detail in an upcoming chapter. But for now, remember that your "pleasure list" would best exclude activities involving alcohol and drugs.

We can also increase our level of happiness by limiting input of anger- and depression-laced material. There are many forms of entertainment that can subtly restrict our levels of happiness. Television sitcoms and stand-up comics often depend on hostile humor—humor that is based on pointing out imperfections in others or pessimistic futility in living. Movies and television dramas often include a significant amount of violence, anger, and exposure of the less pleasant aspects of life. The most recent generation experiencing the passage through adolescence and young adulthood has spawned some styles of music glorifying themes such as Satan worship, cop killing, death, futility of effort, and hopelessness. While I applaud any generation's success in defining their separateness and uniqueness, research has demonstrated resoundingly that negative cognitions create negative feelings. You may want to consider the effect of bombarding yourself with these forms of entertainment as you capitalize on pleasurable feelings.

Expanding Your Experience

We are all unique in what will most likely fuel our anger and depression. For example, my most troublesome irrational belief has always been "the world must be fair." Sometimes it emerges when I think I'm being taken advantage of. But much of the time, it arises in the form of righteousness and indignation over the unfortunate realities of the human condition.

Somehow I have never managed to completely remove myself from a life stance of trying to save the world.

One approach that has helped me sublimate this belief has been entering the world of volunteerism, such as taking in foster children, teaching Sunday school, providing tutoring at the local grade school, and providing many years of free counseling. These years of massive volunteerism have taught me many things. First of all, saving the world is hard work. Second, you can't save the whole world; you only have enough time and resources to try to save your piece of it. Third, you don't really "save" anyone. At times you can have some influence over others' lives, and if you're lucky you may actually contribute toward putting a dent in a societal problem. Fourth, your best, most diligent efforts may not produce any visible results. The impact of your world-saving efforts may not even appear until you are no longer in a position to see their effects.

But by trying to live out my save the world fantasy, I ultimately developed the three "P's": patience, perseverance, and peace. They resulted from my discovery that fairness is actually a goal or value that we use to gauge our choices of beliefs and behaviors, rather than a final external outcome that we hope to eventually observe. All of these characteristics contributed one way or another toward my ability to become an effective therapist, teacher, writer, and parent, as well as more effectively manage my feelings of anger and depression.

I hope the exercises will help you evaluate and manage your experiences of anger and depression without having to try to live out your irrational beliefs. The first exercise is an example of how to create and use an anger diary. The second exercise is an opportunity to generate some examples of assertive, aggressive, passive-aggressive, and passive-inactive behaviors. The third exercise is a checklist you can use in order to decide whether you need to be evaluated for your depression. The last exercise is a chance to develop your own pleasant events checklist.

Study Questions

1. Explain how our emotional responding can differ, even when the hormonal responses are actually the same.
2. What sorts of thought processes are likely to pump up feelings of anger?
3. Where do you think cognitive distortions come from?
4. What is the difference between anger and aggression?

5. Is aggression instinctual or learned? Explain your answer.
6. Take a look at the violence portrayed in movies such as *Terminator, Boyz n the Hood,* and *Thelma and Louise.* What relationships do you see between violence and aggressive behavior in society?
7. How might you go about reducing the likelihood of television violence affecting your attitudes?
8. Describe the characteristics of those who are most likely to become rapists and those they are most likely to choose as rape victims.
9. How might you protect yourself from date rape, or from being accused of date rape?
10. Describe an anger-provoking situation and how you might use stress inoculation training to address each level of Novaco's description of the progression of anger.
11. Describe passive-inactive, passive-aggressive, active-aggressive, and assertive behaviors.
12. Why do our dinosaur brains have such a hard time managing interpersonal conflict?
13. How could you react toward an angry person in a manner that would be likely to help defuse the anger?
14. How do the various perspectives of psychology explain depression?
15. Describe how you might manage your own depression if your primary symptoms were (1) feeling sluggish and unmotivated, (2) feeling bad about yourself, and (3) excessive brooding.
16. Is suicide a moral phenomenon? Explain your answer.
17. Describe how you might go about encouraging the frequency of your good moods.

CHAPTER SIX

Psychopathology and Seeking Professional Help

Separating the Wheat from the Chaff

Crazy Is as Crazy Does

What is really meant by mental illness, or what the person on the street might call "crazy"? The term seems to be used loosely, usually as a pejorative rather than as a clinical diagnosis:

"He's a few ingredients short of a sandwich."

"Her world view is definitely located 'round the bend."

"The tinsel ain't hangin' straight on his Christmas tree."

"Crazy" is also used to characterize a person as someone who is less inhibited than most people: "What a wild and crazy character!" Or, we might use the term to describe excessive enthusiasm: "I'm crazy about chocolate!" However, these popular uses of this term do not help much as we try to decide what constitutes severe or significant mental or emotional problems.

Another popular term for defining mental illness is "insane." **Insanity** is actually a legal term. A judge rules individuals as insane when they cannot be held legally responsible for their behavior due to an inability to understand or distinguish right from wrong, or because their mental conditions render them unable to conform their behavior to the law. Thus an individual who has perpetrated a crime may be found "not guilty by reason of insanity," and is likely to be sent to a mental institution for treatment rather than serve a prison sentence. Mental health professionals provide evidence used by lawyers as such a defense is pleaded, but "insane" is not a clinically derived term for describing disabling mental conditions.

So how, then, does mental illness–or **psychopathology**–fit in? Defining psychopathology can be as difficult as defining normality. Some have even gone so far as to say that mental illness does not exist (Szasz, 1974). When we feel severe emotional disturbances we do not say we feel "mentally ill," though when suffering physically we are likely to say we feel physically ill. Typically it is those who observe a distraught person who assign the label of mental illness.

While popular terms do not give us a clear understanding, they do hint at some of the basic criteria. Psychopathology is a matter of degree. The symptoms we might call "crazy" or "insane" are actually reaction styles that we all use more or less. Psychopathology becomes a relevant term when these reaction styles get out of hand.

The Components of Psychopathology

A person can be described as suffering from psychopathology when three criteria are met: the behavior or reaction style is abnormal, it is maladaptive, and it causes personal or social distress. As these criteria are elaborated upon, you will see how all three are necessary before a person can be described as suffering from a significant mental disorder.

Abnormality

Abnormality is evident when a behavior deviates from the norm. In other words, the vast majority of people do not typically experience that particular thought, feeling, or behavior. The abnormality can be a matter of quantity. Crying occasionally is considered normal; crying every day for an hour or so is considered outside the norm. Abnormality can also be judged because of the quality of the thought, feeling, or behavior. Trying to convince people that phone calls received in a certain phone booth are actually messages from God, as well as other psychotic ideations, are examples of having an abnormal quality of thinking.

The context of the reaction must also be taken into account when assessing abnormality. That which is normal for one setting can be abnormal for another. Wearing sticks, bones, and other large objects through holes in your nose, earlobes, or lower lip is judged as significantly abnormal by Western cultural standards but considered not only acceptable but attractive by some African cultures. Likewise, stating intentions and needs directly is a normal Western behavior but might be considered abnormal or even an insult in Japanese society, which relies more on nonverbal behavior for many communication needs.

Normality can also differ according to individualized contexts. A person feeling severely depressed after the death of a loved one is experiencing a normal emotional reaction. Feeling severely depressed because your watch is broken is considered excessive.

However, abnormality alone is not evidence of psychopathology. As was presented in Chapter 1, we all have behaviors, feelings, and thoughts at one time or another that are significantly different from those experienced by others. Such experiences can be evidence of our personal uniqueness and are not necessarily indicative of the presence of psychopathology.

Maladaptiveness

An experience is maladaptive if it significantly interferes with our lives. Perhaps it keeps us from getting along with others, disables our school achievement, impairs our ability to do our jobs, or even gets in the way of basic self-care. The quality of the experience itself is irrelevant; how it affects functioning and survival is most important. For example, a fear of small enclosed places does not present much of a problem if you live and work on a ranch. However, it would be tremendously maladaptive if your profession involved operating elevators.

But again, by itself maladaptiveness does not constitute psychopathology. We all demonstrate our ability to "mess up" every now and then by doing things that are not in our best interests. We occasionally eat too much or too little. We "lose our cool" under various idiosyncratic circumstances. We might find ourselves driving a little too fast for safety. We sometimes harbor beliefs that only serve the purpose of getting us worked up. In many other ways we occasionally fail to cooperate with the dictates of common sense. Such imperfections of behavior alone are not necessarily evidence of psychopathology.

Personal or Social Distress

Psychological disorders cause us distress. The distress is usually experienced by the person exhibiting the symptom, as in states of severe depression or extreme confusion. However, the distress can also occur for those who must deal with the person. Individuals experiencing a manic high often feel exhilarated rather than upset, yet they cause significant problems for their families. A delusional person might feel righteous and purposeful as he or she obeys a "message from God," climbs to the top of a building, and opens fire on the people below.

The distressing experience need not be a novel one. A person might have always had a fear of public speaking. But not until the person began a career in teaching did this fear become significantly distressing. Or, perhaps a person had always been unusually aggressive. This attribute did not become distressing to society until the person moved to a highly populated area.

An Example of Psychopathology

Mary is a nursing student. During her training, she learns about many types of common bacteria and how to keep them from infecting treatment procedures. She starts using similar procedures at home, just to be sure she does not become infected there. After a while, she finds that she feels more comfortable washing all of her dishes and laundry in alcohol. She begins washing herself several times a day, since she touches so many things that may have come in contact with bacteria. Since others carry bacteria, she decides she will no longer allow others to enter her home unless they have systematically washed themselves upon arrival. She eventually drops out of her nursing school, since it required her to come into contact with "germy places" like hospitals. She spends all her time at home by herself, worrying about bacteria she might have missed and about how she is going to support herself, feeling lonely and isolated.

Mary's behavior is certainly abnormal. Most people do not go to such extreme lengths to refrain from contacting bacteria. Her behavior is maladaptive because it is interfering with her ability to even train for a job, let alone leave home long enough to go to work. And since she is lonely and struggling with many worries, we can also surmise that she is experiencing significant distress. Mary can therefore be diagnosed as suffering from psychopathology.

The DSMs: What They Are and Are Not

In an effort to better understand psychopathology and pinpoint means of treating it, professionals developed—and still are developing—a system of classifications. The earliest classifications were arranged by those trained within the psychoanalytic perspective, which was closely tied to the medical model of treatment. Originally, two broad categories were used to describe all mental dysfunctioning: **psychotic**, which referred to the more severe disturbances such as impaired reality testing, bizarre behavior, and impoverished social relationships; and **neurotic**, referring to the rest of us and our more common anxiety-related difficulties. Obviously, these categorizations are far too broad to be of much use. In fact, the term "neurotic" is currently almost never used in clinical practice.

More recently, the American Psychiatric Association has developed a series of editions of the *Diagnostic and Statistic Manual of Mental Disorders,* better known as the *DSM*s. These documents have been widely accepted as the most currently accurate classifications of mental illness. Each new edition updates the classifications so they will be consistent with newer research findings. Each classification typically lists a number of criteria that must be met before the diagnosis can be made. Sometimes there are multiple lists, and the diagnosis requires observations of a certain number of symptoms from each list, much like selecting a meal off of a Chinese menu.

The *DSM*s are extremely useful for mental health professionals. They provide a consistent means of communication. For example, if one therapist informs another that a client suffers from borderline personality disorder, the therapist can conceptualize an immediate thumbnail sketch of the types of difficulties involved, without needing an exhaustive run-down on the individual person's symptoms. The classifications also can indicate an appropriate course of treatment, such as prescribing lithium for those diagnosed as manic-depressive.

Unfortunately, the document also has a number of drawbacks. Since it is controlled by the medical community, it is tied very closely to the medical model of treatment. In other words, it focuses on looking for a specific form of dysfunction that is labeled as "illness" and will supposedly indicate the appropriate course of therapy. Sometimes this is true, but often it is not. Often those conditions that can be treated through medical means—such as drugs and hospitalization—are those more likely to be labeled as mental illness. Difficulties that respond well to psychotherapy, which is practiced by many different types of mental health practitioners, do not necessarily fit into such neat psychopathological packages and instead are categorized under such labels as "adjustment disorders" and "V-codes."

By itself, the lesser emphasis on nonmedically related disorders is not so great a problem. But when you throw in the influence of the insurance companies, it becomes extremely important to all of us. Insurance companies will pay for your therapy only if your therapist has assigned a diagnosis that the insurance company has decided is worthy of being treated as an illness. Thus diagnoses such as adjustment disorders and V-codes can put severe limitations upon how much therapy they will pay for, if they pay for it at all. Most insurance companies also avoid paying for personality disorders, a collection of debilitating conditions that are treatable with long-term psychotherapy but are not responsive to medical treatment. Since most people cannot afford the expense of psychotherapy without the help of their insurance companies, the *DSM*s have come to determine who among us will receive treatment and who will not.

Another problem with the *DSM*s is the downside of labeling a condition as mental illness. Labels are useful if they indicate a course of treatment. The *DSM*s can also be useful for patients by more accurately defining the conditions they observe in themselves, when they may have been thinking of themselves as a "psycho" or a "bad person," thus providing hope as the appropriate course of therapy takes place. However, there is also the problem of patients seeing themselves as a diagnosis rather than as persons, or judging themselves harshly because of the stigma our society has attached to mental illness.

A related difficulty is the nature of what is considered to be psychopathology. Some professionals believe the categories have sexist overtones. For example, the symptoms of dependent personality disorder describe the traditional submissive model of femininity that has often been encouraged in little girls, especially in years past. Thus women can be considered psychopathological just for following societal norms. Defenders of the diagnosis say it is only relevant if the symptoms become extreme. However, critics are quick to note that excessive independence—which in some ways describes the traditional "macho" model of masculinity—can become just as dysfunctional, yet there is no diagnostic category known as "independent personality disorder."

Also, developers of *DSM-III-R* suggested further research to determine whether or not there is a personality disorder that could be called the "self-defeating personality disorder," terminology that describes psychological symptoms suffered by battered spouses, typically women. Yet a category for the perpetrators of the crimes, the typically male batterers, was not proposed. Thus the proposers were suggesting that battered women—the victims—eventually be labeled as mentally ill, rather than that the batterers be diagnosed. After being picketed by activist groups they decided to include as a category for further research—a possible "sadistic personality disorder," which describes the psychological symptoms of batterers.

These examples suggest that there may be a bias toward labeling the feminine condition as psychopathological, which certainly does not contribute to fair treatment of women's needs and values. If such a bias exists, men also lose out, since genuine psychological conditions causing significant distress and more commonly found among men may be inappropriately diagnosed or ignored, resulting in inadequate or even nonexistent treatment.

As you can see, the *DSM*s describe classifications that have evolved from professional, personal, and societal biases, as well as the leanings of current research in clinical psychiatry. But in spite of their shortcomings, the *DSM*s are a vast improvement over past efforts to define psychopathology. The authors continue to refine and attempt to improve upon their descriptions of the various forms of psychopathology with each new edition. The following descriptions of the major disorders of adulthood are drawn mainly from *DSM-IV* observations (APA, 1994), not because *DSM-IV* has come to define reality, but because it provides a framework for describing psychological syndromes that you may one day wish to bring to the attention of your own health service provider.

Major Disorders of Adulthood

Anxiety Disorders

As described in Chapter 4, we all suffer from anxiety as a function of daily living. Our anxieties are defined as disorders when they become very pronounced, frequent, or debilitating. There are many different kinds of anxiety disorders, and it is not uncommon for an anxiety-disordered person to experience more than one.

Phobias. **Phobias** are irrational fears, typically of certain objects or situations. In other words, we are more fearful of a situation than is warranted by the potential threat. We all have some irrational fears, and they are especially common during childhood. They only become significant to our mental health if they interfere with our daily functioning. Examples of **simple phobias** include fears of heights, spiders, snakes, flying, and small enclosed spaces. Table 6.1 lists a number of common phobias.

Fears involving situations where public scrutiny may occur are called **social phobias**. These fears are significant if they interfere with the functions of your social life, such as your ability to attend social gatherings where you do not know anyone or to give speeches before audiences. Individuals suffering from social phobias fear that they may do or say something resulting in their being humiliated or embarrassed. They either avoid being in a feared situation or experience intense anxiety when they must endure one.

Another form of phobia is called **obsessive-compulsive disorder**. Individuals who cannot get certain thoughts out of their heads, no matter how hard they try, are suffering from **obsessions**. They are suffering from **compulsions** if they repeatedly make themselves perform certain acts or behaviors. Even though they know these actions are not necessary, they cannot stop themselves without experiencing extreme anxiety.

For example, a person with obsessive-compulsive disorder may not be able to get the thought of the door being unlocked out of his or her mind and will repeatedly go back to check the door, even though the person knows the door has already been checked. Or, such an individual may fear some substance, such as germs, dirt, or pesticides, and will repeatedly and often ritualistically wash anything that could conceivably have come into contact with them. Such an individual may spend the entire day compulsively cleaning and not have any time left for normal daily living, as occurred in the example of "Mary."

Panic disorders. Some individuals react so strongly to certain forms of anxiety that their bodies demonstrate unusually severe symptoms. These reactions are called **panic attacks**. First, they feel a sudden surge of fear or a sense of impending doom. Then they notice several of a variety of unpleasant physical sensations: shortness of breath, dizziness, heart palpitations, nausea, sweating, choking, shaking, numbness, hot flashes or chills, or chest discomfort. They may also find themselves thinking they are going to die, go crazy, or do something uncouth which they cannot control, such as wetting their pants, throwing up, or passing out.

Panic attacks are not unusual. In fact, most people do experience a panic attack at some point in their lives. It becomes a disorder when the frequency and severity begins to interfere with a person's life. Some people with panic disorder also experience **agoraphobia**, the fear of being in places where there is no easy escape route or a companion to help in the event of a panic attack. Typically persons suffering from agoraphobia

TABLE 6.1
Some Simple Phobias

Name	*Feared object/situation*
Acrophobia	Heights
Aerophobia	Flying
Arachnophobia	Spiders
Claustrophobia	Small, enclosed areas
Hematophobia	Blood
Hydrophobia	Water
Monophobia	Being alone
Mysophobia	Dirt
Nyctophobia	Darkness
Ocholophobia	Being in a crowd of people
Ophidiophobia	Snakes
Thanatophobia	Death

avoid going to public places alone and may even avoid ever leaving their homes at all.

Post-traumatic stress disorder. Some individuals, after experiencing an extremely traumatic event, will continue to reexperience it through dreams, recollections, or **flashbacks**—suddenly feeling as if they were back in the traumatic experience. They may also feel a sense of emotional "numbness," as if their bodies have shut down in order to protect them from further emotional damage. They may avoid any stimuli that remind them of the traumatic event. This collection of symptoms is called **post-traumatic stress disorder** (**PTSD**). PTSD is best known because of its association with the Vietnam War veterans. However, it is also often found in individuals who have been victimized by violent crimes such as rape or extreme child abuse or who have endured natural or manmade disasters such as earthquakes and airplane crashes.

Generalized anxiety disorder. Some individuals are especially excessive in their worrying. They are suffering from **generalized anxiety disorder** if their worries are both continuous and unrealistic, such as constantly fearing their children might be in danger, fearing their academic performance may be unacceptable, or worrying about money even when they are financially secure. Perfectionism and fear of failure are common among these individuals.

Depressive Disorders

As was explained in Chapter 5, depression itself is normal. At what point then does depression become a clinical consideration? This section will explore the various types of depression that go beyond normal reacting to the "downs" of daily living.

Major depression. **Major depressive episodes** involve symptoms common to normal depression: feeling sad or irritable, losing interest or pleasure in activities that had previously seemed enjoyable, having difficulties with sleeping and eating, entertaining thoughts of death or suicide, or feeling constantly lethargic or fatigued, preoccupied or indecisive, or having a sense of worthlessness or guilt. Major depression is diagnosed when many of these symptoms continue to be present over a period of 2 weeks or more. Typically, social activity and ability to perform usual tasks are also slowed or impaired. Sometimes anxiety and a form of hyperactivity called **psychomotor agitation** are present.

In extreme forms, some individuals suffering from major depressive episodes experience psychotic symptoms such as **delusions**—obviously untrue beliefs from which the sufferer cannot be swayed no matter how much evidence is provided, and **hallucinations**—sensory experiences occurring without the usual necessary physical sensory stimulation. The content of the hallucinations or delusions is usually consistent with depressive themes of guilt and deserved punishment, disease and death, and personal inadequacy; but in some cases they may take other forms. However, the most serious side effect of major depression is still suicidal feelings and impulses.

While major depression is a common phenomenon, it is much more likely to occur when blood relatives of an afflicted individual also have had the disorder. Thus there is considerable speculation that vulnerability for the disorder may be in part genetically determined.

Bipolar disorder. Manic-depressive disorder, also known as **bipolar disorder**, also involves becoming clinically depressed but can also involve feeling extremely "high." These extreme feelings of expansiveness are called **manic episodes**. In some ways, manic episodes mimic the symptoms of individuals who take mood-inflating street drugs. The afflicted person experiences a feeling of inflated self-esteem and high energy and can get by on very little sleep. These individuals may take on activities that are extremely risky, are enjoyable but have painful consequences, or are more than the person can realistically handle. They may become very goal-directed, but often the goals are ill-advised or directed by psychotic features. Others may have difficulty understanding what the sufferer is trying to communicate, since he or she may speak very quickly and express a rapid progression of ideas that are only loosely associated with one another.

The disorder is called "bipolar" because the symptoms can swing back and forth between feeling extremely high and feeling extremely low. These swings are called "cycling." However, some individuals with bipolar disorder experience only depressive or only manic episodes.

Bipolar disorder is believed to be genetically determined. Physiologically, those afflicted show an imbalance in a naturally occurring salt known as **lithium**. Most individuals suffering from bipolar disorder can be successfully treated with supplements of lithium.

Dysthymia and cyclothymia. These disorders though similar to major depression and bipolar disorder differ in that the symptoms are more frequently present and are typically less intense. **Dysthymia** involves depressive symptoms that are experienced by the person more days than not. While the depression is not as severe as in a major depressive episode, the experience goes on indefinitely, and with little reprieve. **Cyclothymia** is a watered-down version of bipolar disorder, but again, the milder symptoms are almost constantly present, rather than occurring in occasional cycles.

Dysthymia and cyclothymia usually do not have the extreme debilitative nature of major depression and bipolar disorder. However, there is evidence that a person with dysthymia or cyclothymia is more likely to have a blood relative who suffers from major depression or bipolar disorder, suggesting the existence of a genetic link among the various depressive disorders.

Dissociative Disorders

Dissociation is a process by which individuals separate part of their consciousness from the rest of their psychological experiencing. We all dissociate in some form. Daydreaming is a mild form of separating our mental experience from our current physical surroundings. "Spacing out" when you are bored with somebody can also be the result of dissociation. Forgetting details that you would rather not remember–like a dental appointment–may also occur as one part of your consciousness avoids contact with another.

Most **dissociative disorders** occur as a result of severe psychological trauma. Usually the inconvenience of the dissociative processes is not anywhere near as unpleasant or traumatic as experiencing or reliving the event or events that resulted in the development of the dissociative disorder, at least at first. Thus it is a protective device, and our ability to dissociate is actually a blessing in disguise. But when dissociative processes become severe and begin to cause difficulties in individuals' lives, they may be suffering from dissociative problems that need intervention. The rest of this section describes these disorders.

Psychogenic amnesia. Sometimes when individuals encounter a traumatic event, they forget parts or all of it. Most commonly, individuals forget everything that happened right after the traumatic event. This is called **psychogenic amnesia**. With **selective amnesia**, only certain aspects of that period of time are forgotten. For example, you might remember being mugged but not remember what the assailant looked like. Sometimes these lost memories can be retrieved through hypnosis, or the memories can be spontaneously triggered by stimuli that simulate certain aspects of the traumatic event.

Psychogenic fugue. A rarer and more extensive form of dissociative forgetting is called **psychogenic fugue**. After the traumatic event you forget who you are, and during this period of time you adopt another identity. Some people suffering from psychogenic fugue travel to another location or engage in some other purposeful behavior that takes them away from the triggering event. When they finally recollect who they are, they cannot remember what happened during that time period, which usually lasts for a period of hours or perhaps days but may last longer. Recovery is usually rapid, and the psychogenic fugue generally does not recur.

Multiple personality disorder. In the most extreme cases of dissociation, individuals can split themselves up into several personalities, each personality having its own set of characteristics, memories, thoughts, and feelings. The new personalities, known as "alters," emerge in order to deal with whatever trauma is presented. In this manner the weaker alters need not continue to be traumatized. Such individuals are said to have **multiple personality disorder** (**MPD**). This disorder is now recognized as occurring more frequently than previously believed, although it still meets with skepticism in some psychiatric circles. It typically develops during childhood when children are severely and continuously abused, usually sexually.

Individuals with MPD may learn to develop such a good sense of cooperation and communication among their alters that nobody other than their closest friends are aware of their multiplicity. However, others may not even have awareness of their own alters, aware only that they have lost periods of time. Or perhaps the alters are generally aware of each other but dislike each other or have no sense of teamwork as they work toward conflicting life goals. These multiples often have tumultuously dysfunctional lives, as alters battle for control and punish one another for their lack of cooperation or perceived shortcomings.

MPD is usually chronic, but through intensive psychotherapy alters can learn to get along with each other in a more productive manner. In some cases, alters have been able to reintegrate into a single personality.

SCHIZOPHRENIA

Schizophrenia is actually a whole set of disorders. They generally involve losing touch with reality and having a fractured sense of self and thoughts or feelings that are severely disturbed. Originally, anybody who showed psychotic or severely detached functioning was diagnosed as schizophrenic. Currently, it is a waste-can term for psychotic-like disorders that have not yet been weeded out as separate disorders, as has happened with manic-depressive disorder, autism, brain damage, and temporal lobe epilepsy. What remains can be divided into two sets of symptoms: positive and negative. Schizophrenics may have just one of these sets of symptoms, or they may have symptoms from both sets.

Positive schizophrenia occurs when certain unusual characteristics appear to be tacked onto the patient's psychological makeup. These characteristics include delusions, hallucinations, and bizarre behaviors. Positive symptoms have been found to be connected with an overabundance of dopamine, a neurotransmitter. Medications such as thorazine are usually successful in treating these psychotic symptoms. *DSM-IV's* **paranoid type schizophrenia** describes more positive than negative symptoms. The diagnosed individual becomes preoccupied with systematic delusions and auditory hallucinations, usually surrounding a persecutory theme.

In instances of **negative schizophrenia**, something found in normal functioning seems to have been subtracted from the person's psychological makeup. For example, rather than showing normal variation in mood and voice intonation, the individual with negative schizophrenia often has a **flat affect**, speaking in a monotone and portraying a seemingly blank mood state. Another negative schizophrenic symptom, **anhedonia**, is present when the person loses the ability to experience the sensation of pleasure. The thinking of individuals with negative schizophrenia also loses its quality, usually becoming disorganized or illogical, and the person may lose self-direction and organization of even the most basic functions.

Negative schizophrenia correlates with the presence of enlarged ventricles of the brain, which suggests that it is a form of brain atrophy or deterioration. Usually negative schizophrenia does not improve when antipsychotic medications are prescribed.

DSM-IV describes two types of schizophrenia that are consistent with negative schizophrenia. **Disorganized** type involves an almost total loss of coherent thought or organized behavior. **Catatonic** type is characterized by extreme withdrawal, perhaps by demonstrating a continual blank stupor, ongoing unreasonable negativity toward all efforts of assistance, or taking on unusual rigid postures.

Somatoform Disorders

Somatoform disorders are those that involve the experience of a physical disorder when no physical cause can be found, usually in the form of pain, paralysis, or a specific sense or body function. It can often be traced to a specific stressor, such as in the case of experiencing too much "pain" to be able to study for finals. Somatoform disorders are not to be confused with **malingering**. With malingering, the person knows that he or she is not really sick but is seeking to gain something by being recognized as impaired, such as receiving special attention, getting out of certain tasks, and other forms of secondary gain. When a person has a somatoform disorder, the physical symptoms are really experienced.

Hypochondriasis. One of the most common somatoform disorders is **hypochondriasis**. Individuals with this disorder believe they are sick when they are not. They are either preoccupied with this belief, or preoccupied with the suspicion that some minor body sensation is evidence of a serious problem. Even when doctors assure such patients that nothing is wrong with them, they still believe they are ill, often going from physician to physician until they succeed in being assigned a diagnosis. Most individuals with hypochondriasis refuse to see mental health professionals, because they do not believe the difficulties have anything to do with their mental functioning. As far as they are concerned, they are experiencing physical illness.

Somatoform pain disorder. Some people become preoccupied with sensations of pain for which no physical explanation can be found. This is called **somatoform pain disorder**. This reaction often develops after such a person experiences a physical trauma. However, over time physicians discover they can find no physiological reasons for the pain to persist.

Conversion disorder. **Conversion disorder** involves some loss of physical functioning, such as being unable to walk, talk, see, hear, use one arm, and so on. It used to be called "hysteria," as in "hysterical blindness." It usually occurs after a psychosocial stressor is involved with the physical function that has become "lost," such as losing the ability to make a fist after hitting someone during an episode of rage. The symptoms also provide secondary gain, because they help the person avoid dealing with the emotional conflict behind their physical reaction. The symptoms often also make it impossible for them to follow through on the dictates of their conflictual impulses.

The disorder is seen much less now than in earlier decades, probably because people know more about how their bodies function. If you recognize that it is impossible for your specific symptoms to occur due to physical explanations, you suspect that the unexplainable loss of body functioning must be psychological. This recognition diminishes the disorder's ability to protect the psyche from the inner conflict it is trying to avoid addressing. Thus conversion disorders have become less common as people realize that having such symptoms would have to be "all in your head."

Personality Disorders

Personality disorders involve character traits that are both maladaptive and inflexible. Usually, these traits restrict or impair a person's overall functioning. The traits may be strange or eccentric, overemotional or unpredictable, or involve some extreme fear. Lying beneath this turmoil hides a weak or poorly functioning sense of self. Many different types of personality disorders have been identified or suggested, but differentiating one from the other is difficult for even the seasoned professional. Typically, professionals will agree that a person has a personality disorder, but they will often disagree on which one it is.

Two forms of personality disorder have emerged that seem to hold some consistency among the diagnostic opinions of clinicians. One is called the **borderline personality disorder**, so named because afflicted individuals appear to lack recognition of boundaries between the self and others, as well as lack the ability to conform to expected social boundaries. They engage in a number of destructive behaviors such as promiscuity, impulsive spending, and emotional acting out, since they are not in touch with the social boundaries that prohibit such behavior.

In addition, they place very rigid boundaries around the concepts of "good" and "bad." All people who go along with the needs and desires of the afflicted individual are considered "good"; in fact, almost saintlike and omnipotent in their perfection. Anyone who disagrees with or does not cooperate with the desires of the borderline individual is considered "bad": an enemy, the scum of the earth, the essence of evil and wrongdoing. Borderline personality disorder usually develops in individuals who have been sexually abused—which, after all, is one of the most profound personal boundary violations. Not surprisingly, most individuals with borderline personality disorder are women, since they appear more likely to be sexually assaulted than men.

On the other hand, the **antisocial personality disorder** is more commonly found among men. These individuals appear to lack a conscience or sense of morality. They feel no remorse about how their behavior affects others and tend not to learn from the consequences of their experiences. They often engage in criminal behavior, since they only have respect for the law or social requirements if they see some kind of external consequences forthcoming. This disorder usually begins in childhood. Many factors have been associated with its development, such as childhood attention deficit disorders or conduct disorders, absence of consistent parental discipline, and being abused as a child.

DSM-IV suggests the existence of a number of other specific personality disorders. For example, the **schizoid personality disorder** is used to describe individuals who experience little emotion and have little interest or pleasure in developing relationships with others. The **narcissistic personality disorder** applies to individuals who are missing a sense of empathy toward others and who develop an unrealistically inflated view of themselves as a defense against their limited sense of self. Individuals with **paranoid personality disorder** feel their sense of self as being unrealistically vulnerable and therefore perceive themselves to be constantly threatened by others. However, these personality disorders are more difficult to single out from the others than are the borderline and antisocial personality disorders. Other such personality disorders include schizotypal, histrionic, avoidant, dependent, and obsessive-compulsive.

Personality disorders can be extremely debilitating. Those with antisocial personality disorder find themselves spending most of their lives in prison; those with borderline personality disorder ruin their interpersonal relationships because they lack respect for social boundaries. However, personality disorders are treatable. With long-term therapy, personality-disordered individuals can rework their sense of self through their relationship with the acceptance and empathy of their therapists.

Psychotherapy

What is **psychotherapy**? Specifically defined, psychotherapy is a formal relationship between a client and a trained person that centers on bringing about behavioral or personality changes that will promote personal development. It differs from counseling, which tends to be more problem solving oriented. Sometimes counseling alone is sufficient to deal with life problems. However, there are other times when psychotherapy is more appropriate. The following indicators are clues that you may need psychotherapy instead of counseling:

- You find that you have multiple problems, such that you are becoming emotionally overwhelmed.

- A problem is extremely severe in nature, such that you feel that your selfhood is in some way being assaulted.
- As soon as you fix one major problem, another mysteriously seems to appear.
- Your difficulties seem related to your personality style, and thus are impairing most or all aspects of your life.
- You experience emotional disturbance that is quite severe, such that you do not seem to be functioning in many or all areas of your life.

Does Psychotherapy Work?

Early research examining the efficacy of psychotherapy was not promising. While improvement was found in two-thirds of the individuals receiving therapy, improvement was also found in two-thirds of those who were on a waiting list (Eysenck, 1952). Since this study raised its initial cloud of dust, the lack of significantly better improvement shown by therapy patients has been attributed to a number of variables, largely sloppy experimental controls. More recent major analyses of psychological treatment results indicate that therapy does indeed provide more benefits for its recipients than sitting around in a control group (e.g., Lipsey & Wilson, 1993).

Psychotherapists

Who provides psychotherapy? A number of different mental health professionals are trained to provide this service.

Clinical psychologists and **counseling psychologists** have the most formal training in psychotherapy as well as in basic psychology. They usually have a doctoral degree in psychology or a closely related field. Their degree titles are typically Ph.D., Psy.D., or Ed.D. "Psychologist" is a licensed term. Psychologists are required to do at least 1 year of internship and 1 year of residency training as requirements for becoming licensed, as well as pass a national licensing exam and state licensing exams in the states in which they wish to practice. There are also psychotherapists who have Master's degrees and perform psychotherapy under the supervision of a clinical or counseling psychologist, but their training is usually not as extensive.

Clinical and counseling psychologists tend to wear many hats. In addition to being highly trained as psychotherapists, they are also the most heavily trained in psychological assessment. They often give seminars, teach, do research, write, and engage in other professional activities other than working with clients.

Psychiatrists are medical doctors who have gone on to get training in mental health. They have the usual M.D. or D.O. degrees earned by all physicians and do a 3- or 4-year residency in psychiatry in a mental health hospital. Preferably, they also become "board certified," meaning they go through a certification process during which they are evaluated by their peers for their competency in psychiatry. A physician can announce that he or she has a "practice limited to psychiatry," but this is usually an indication that the physician has not become board certified.

Since psychiatrists are medical doctors, they can prescribe psychotropic medications, which psychologists are not allowed to do. Because of their ability to prescribe, as well as their more direct access to hospitals, psychiatrists are more likely to deal with the severe psychopathologies, such as schizophrenia, manic-depressive illness, and other disorders that may require medication or hospitalization.

Social workers differ from other therapists in that they may involve themselves more extensively in their patients' lives, such as making home visits and networking with various social service agencies involved with the case. Social workers usually begin with an M.S.W. degree, and may go on to get a Ph.D. or D.S.W. Some also get specialized training in a mental health or hospital setting in order to become psychiatric social workers.

Social workers' credentials change as a function of the amount of experience and postgraduate training they receive. The next step up from M.S.W. is licensed clinical social worker (L.C.S.W.), then registered clinical social worker (R.C.S.W.). In terms of ability to provide psychotherapy, R.C.S.W.s are often as well trained as many clinical and counseling psychologists.

Orientations of Psychotherapy

The different perspectives of psychology offer differing styles of psychotherapy. All of these major styles have merit. However, how they address the problem can differ significantly. Each uses its own agent of change, based on the philosophical grounding of the therapist. If you are deciding whom to see for your problem, you might begin by considering which style of therapy best fits your own philosophical beliefs and problem-solving style.

Psychodynamic psychotherapy.

This style is also sometimes referred to as ego psychology, object relations, and psychoanalytic therapy. It focuses on how past relationships, especially childhood relationships with parents, affect our personalities and problems we have in the present. It operates under the assumption that we **project** our parents onto those around us. We then react to others in the same way we reacted to our parents because we expect them to behave as our parents did. Usually we are not completely aware of the patterns of interaction we have picked up; nor are we completely aware of when we are applying them.

During the course of therapy, the client eventually projects his or her parent onto the therapist. This is called **transference**. As this happens, past conflicts concerning parental relationships are worked out in the present through this relationship with the therapist. By resolving inner conflicts concerning past childhood experiences, the client can resolve certain types of emotional distress.

The process of psychodynamic psychotherapy maximizes input from the client and minimizes verbalizations by the therapist. The client is encouraged to talk a lot about childhood experiences and important relationships in the past. The therapist may encourage the client to **free associate**, an organized form of saying whatever comes to mind. The therapist may also want to talk about the client's dreams and fantasies. As the material is presented, the therapist notes significant patterns and provides **interpretations** of why the client may be feeling or behaving in such a manner. Therapy is considered to be completed when the client can recognize his or her projections, interpret them, and experience a change in emotional reacting as a result without the assistance of the therapist.

Behavioral therapy. Behaviorists focus on maladaptive behavior, rather than personality and emotional life. Typically, the therapist helps the client identify the problem behavior, then helps the client learn more adaptive ways of reacting. Most behavior therapists will require clients to do homework, working on specific aspects of their behavior outside of the therapy session.

One method of behavioral therapy is called **behavior modification**. This method is based on the principles of positive reinforcement. Typically, the client is assisted in setting up a system whereby he or she is rewarded for engaging in more of the desired behavior, or less of the undesired behavior. The therapist begins by gathering a **baseline**—in other words, how often does the behavior seem to occur? Then the therapist helps the client pick a realistic reward for improved behavior. Together they create a **schedule of reinforcement** that requires the client to slowly engage in more and more of the adaptive behavior in order to earn the rewards.

Similar principles are involved in **token economies**. This strategy is usually used in classrooms, mental health wards, and other types of controlled environments, rather than in outpatient therapy. Typically patients are allowed to "buy" all privileges with tokens that are earned by performing various appropriate behaviors. While behavior therapists usually do not recommend token economies during individual psychotherapy, they might assist a client in setting up such a program in order to deal with a parent-child problem.

A behavioral therapy that is very successful in the treatment of phobias is called **systematic desensitization**. During the therapy session, the therapist teaches the client how to relax. Simultaneously, they work on identifying a list of feared situations related to the phobia. The client organizes the list of fear situations according to which is least anxiety-provoking and which is most anxiety-provoking. Together therapist and client work their way up the hierarchy, teaching the client to experience the relaxed feelings for situations that are more and more anxiety-provoking. Since relaxation and anxiety cannot happen at the same time, the anxiety eventually dissipates. The therapist and client may choose to work through the hierarchy using **imaging**, where the client simply imagines being in the anxiety-provoking situation, or **in vivo**, where the client purposely creates the feared events.

Other forms of behavior therapy are based on the principles of punishment and negative reinforcement. One is called **aversion therapy**. The client learns to administer some form of unpleasantness in order to discourage his or her undesired behavior. The technique discussed earlier concerning snapping a rubber band on your wrist when you have undesired thoughts is a form of aversion therapy. Another common aversion therapy is the use of **antabuse** for alcoholics. The drug makes treated individuals feel ill if they consume alcohol, which is experienced as a punisher for the undesired behavior of drinking. Individuals who wet the bed sometimes place a special pad under their sheets that delivers a shock or causes a bell or buzzer to go off at the first dab of wetness. The unpleasantness of the stimuli leads to these heavy sleepers eventually waking up when they need to go to the bathroom.

Another therapeutic technique that uses aversive events is called **flooding** or **implosion**. The technique is especially helpful for individuals experiencing obsessive-compulsive disorder. The client purposely places himself in an extremely anxiety-provoking situation until the anxiety eventually wears down. For example, a compulsive hand-washer may be prevented from washing all day. Or, a compulsive door-checker may be allowed to check one time that doors are locked, and then not allowed to check for the rest of the evening. The client eventually learns to experience the less-anxious feelings without needing to engage in the compulsive behavior.

Role-playing is a form of behavior therapy that provides actual practice for handling difficult situations, especially those involving interactions with others. The client and therapist pretend they are in the situation, taking turns playing the role of either the client or the other person involved. The two of them play out what the client might say or how he or she might act. Assertiveness training often makes use of role-playing.

Cognitive therapy.

The cognitive approach emphasizes how thought lives affect emotional lives. In other words, clients are taught that the way you look at a situation, rather than the situation itself, makes you feel good or bad. Cognitive therapists help their clients identify dysfunctional thinking and irrational beliefs and teach them how to deal with them. The process usually involves homework, as clients learn to challenge dysfunctional thinking and apply more-adaptive thinking to their daily lives. Cognitive-behavioral therapy appears to be one of the most successful therapies for treating mild to moderate depression and anxiety (Giles, 1983). However, we must note that cognitive and behavioral treatment outcome is easier to objectify than the other therapies, which may account for any experimentally demonstrated superiority over other methods.

Existential and humanistic therapies. These styles emphasize learning to deal with one's self in the here and now since, after all, emotions are experienced in the here and now. The therapist assumes that the answers are within the client, and the client is helped by becoming more skilled at introspection. The therapist facilitates introspection by exhibiting unconditional positive regard toward the client, becoming nondirective, and behaving in an accepting manner toward whatever inner experience the client reports. Expanding inner awareness and taking responsibility for personal feelings and behavior are a big part of this perspective, as clients learn to develop a more internal locus of control.

Eclectic therapy. **Eclectic** therapists develop courses of therapy that borrow from the many different orientations. As you have probably noticed, the different types of therapy complement and do not necessarily contradict one another. Currently, more therapists identify themselves as being eclectic than as practicing any other individual orientation.

Eclectic therapists make use of the interrelatedness of the many therapies and apply them in ways that fit the unique needs of the particular client. For example, the therapist might use principles from the humanistic approach, such as unconditional positive regard and nondirectiveness, as a means of establishing a good working relationship with the person. The roles of psychodynamics and learning may be considered as the therapist develops hypotheses regarding how the client arrived at his or her current state of being. Cognitive strategies and biological solutions such as drug therapy may be applied as the therapist helps the client deal with the particular difficulty.

However, an eclectic orientation is not an indication that a therapist can treat everything. All therapists have their limitations and will refer certain types of patients when they consider these patients' needs to be outside of their areas of expertise.

Alternatives to Individual Psychotherapy

Individual psychotherapy can be a draining experience, both emotionally and financially. While in many cases it is an excellent choice of intervention, there may be other means by which you can resolve your difficulties without putting in such a huge personal investment. Following are some alternative methods for intervening upon psychological distress.

Counseling.   Many different types of counseling are available: marital, family, religious, alcohol, vocational, and so on. Counseling may be adequate if you are dealing with one of the many generic problems that counselors are commonly trained to handle. Counselors tend to work with individuals over shorter periods of time and charge significantly less for their services than other therapists.

The main difficulty with counseling is the murkiness surrounding the criteria of what qualifies a person for being a counselor. In some states, "counselor" is a certified term that can only be used if the candidate has received the proper training and assessment. In other states, anybody can hang out a shingle and say "I'm a counselor." If you are going to use a counselor, make sure you ask about his or her qualifications and fields of training before signing your name on the dotted line.

Drug therapy.   Psychotropic medications are often prescribed for emotional disturbances. For example, antidepressants are often as successful as cognitive therapy in the treatment of mild to moderate depression (Klerman, 1986). For the treatment of more severe depression, a combination of the two appears to get better results than either one individually (Beckham & Leber, 1985). Lithium is helpful in treating manic-depressive disorder, antipsychotic medications are useful for schizophrenic disorders, antianxiety medications are useful for the treatment of anxiety disorders, and so on.

However, most therapists agree that medication alone generally does not solve the problem. The problems in living that originally led to the emotional disturbance are not necessarily altered by taking drugs. Even individuals suffering from schizophrenia need more than antipsychotic medications to be able to function in the world. They especially need training in social skills to help them become more able to cope with life stressors and less likely to decompensate and need medication adjustments again. Drugs also have side effects, some causing conditions that can be debilitating.

Group therapy.   Different groups vary in what problems they address and how they progress. Group therapy usually involves learning to deal with difficulties through the relationships developed within the therapy group. It can be very intense, but it is also very effective in addressing issues involving interpersonal life. Group therapy is usually less expensive than individual therapy, since a number of people are splitting up the cost of the therapist's time. If you are thinking of entering group therapy, make sure the credentials of the leader of the group include training and experience in group therapy.

Support groups. Support groups are different from group therapy groups. They typically center on a common problem, such as being the relative of an alcoholic, having a child with special needs, or having difficulty with weight loss. Support groups typically do not provide psychotherapy. Instead, members help one another through mutual education, sharing common experiences and ways of dealing with a problem, and providing support.

Bibliotherapy. There are many self-help books available that address specific problems. However, evaluate such books carefully before taking them seriously. Just because authors succeeded in getting their words into print does not mean they know what they are talking about. For example, many books are still being circulated that claim a change in diet will calm hyperactive children. Unfortunately, controlled studies have not substantiated these claims (Mash & Barkley, 1989). Nevertheless, book sales abound.

Ask yourself the following questions about any book you are considering:

- What are the credentials and background of the author? Are they consistent with the subject about which he or she is offering advice?
- Is the author affiliated with reputable institutions?
- Does the author provide evidence of what is being proposed, beyond the author's personal observations, such as professional books and journal articles?
- Does the author's thesis make dramatic claims of success, far beyond what can be reasonably expected of any method? If so, look out for snake oil.
- Does the author's thesis hang together? In other words, does the author make sense to you?
- Is the author's thesis far afield from what other experts in the area propose? Fringy types sometimes play fast and loose with marginal or nonexistent research findings.

If you do not feel comfortable with your own ability to evaluate the legitimacy of self-help books, try contacting a local therapist or specialist in the field and ask for the name of an appropriate book.

Choosing a Therapist

Your relationship with your therapist is one of the most intimate ones you will experience in your life. Therefore, you need to take care in selecting one with whom you believe you can forge a successful therapeutic relationship.

First, try to formulate just why it is you think you need professional help. It is helpful if you can pinpoint exactly what is wrong. Perhaps you are trying to recover from a specific traumatic event. Maybe you have excessive unpleasant feelings that you can't seem to shake. Or perhaps you find you are mired in an ongoing interpersonal problem that has become more than you can handle on your own.

On the basis of the nature of the problem, decide what sort of intervention you would like to try. Some specialized problems, such as dealing with parenting or relationship issues, are adequately resolved by simply going through a good self-help book. Or perhaps you feel what you really need is the moral support that can be provided by a self-help group of individuals with similar difficulties. Maybe you are concerned that your feelings of depression could be related to a medical difficulty and a visit to your physician is in order.

However, you may decide that you would prefer to have a supportive objective observer help you evaluate and work through your difficulties, in which case you will be seeking out the services of a psychotherapist. Naturally, you will want to check to see if your potential therapist has the appropriate credentials. One good way to find a competent therapist is to contact state associations and ask for a referral to a therapist who deals with your type of difficulty. Most community mental health centers are also aware of where you might find the type of therapist you are looking for. Also, your personal physician may recommend someone. Seeing someone with whom your physician has a professional connection can also become very expedient should the issue of medications arise and the two need to work together. A friend who has been through successful psychotherapy may also be able to provide you with the name of a good psychotherapist.

As a last resort, you can always check the yellow pages. However, this is really not the best way to evaluate the competence or appropriateness of a potential therapist. The therapists with the biggest advertisements are not necessarily the most competent; they simply spend enough money to buy more space. Unless the therapist is just starting out in a new area, the consumer may appropriately wonder why the therapist is needing to resort to yellow pages advertisements to build up his or her practice, rather than get by on referrals from more professionally based sources.

You may want to initially choose more than one potential therapist. Most therapists are willing to let the first session serve as a trial run, so the client can size them up and decide whether or not the client can work with them. After all, not all combinations of people can work well together, regardless of the type of relationship involved. Psychotherapists are human beings, too, and differ in their personality characteristics the same as everybody else. Select one who feels most comfortable for *you*. Just because a certain therapist turned out to be the right one for a friend of yours does not mean that the particular therapist will also be right for you.

Other things you should watch for during your initial interview concern how the therapist handles the session:

- Does the therapist explain what type of therapy he or she uses? If not, be sure to ask. The therapist may mistakenly assume that whoever referred you filled you in.
- Does the therapist fill you in on the business aspects of the therapy arrangements, such as office policy, fee arrangements, and limits of confidentiality?
- Does the therapist seem to listen?
- Does the therapist seem to understand you?
- Does the therapist mention goals, or ideas of what might be going on?
- Remember that you are a consumer. If you decide that a particular therapist is not going to work out, feel free to try another. However, keep in mind that after a couple of months or so, as therapy becomes challenging, people often get angry with their therapist or frustrated with therapy. This is normal, and not necessarily a reason to change therapists. On the other hand, if something comes up that you suspect involves unprofessional behavior, and you do not like the explanations you are getting from your therapist, consider having a one-time consultation with another therapist in order to assess how your therapy is progressing.

Expanding Your Experience

As I was getting ready to take my first course in abnormal psychology, a school chum warned me to "watch my head." As I waded through the academics of psychological functioning versus dysfunctioning, I began to understand what he had meant. I discovered that I suffered from every mental illness in the book! Fortunately, I didn't let this discovery push me over the deep end. I didn't have time to think about it. The following term had me investing my existential energies into thrashing about in the whirlpools of experimental design. It wasn't until I was well into my clinical training that this personal conflict resurfaced, at which time I realized that all my worrying had been for naught.

Whenever I teach abnormal psychology, one of the first things I point out to students is that they may begin to suspect that they have every disorder they study. Then I inform them that, to a certain degree, their observations are correct. We all make use of the behavioral, cognitive, and emotional styles of functioning that under certain circumstances can also make up forms of psychopathology. But as the first part of this chapter pointed out, psychopathology is a matter of degree. Is the person's experience or behavior significantly different from the norm? Is it maladaptive? And is it also causing subjective distress?

The first exercise I have included for this chapter will provide practice at sorting out these three components of psychopathology. The second exercise is an opportunity for you to explore how you would go about finding a psychotherapist and which orientation of psychotherapy you think would fit in with your worldview. The last exercise is a creative venture you and your classmates can use to explore the tenets of transactional analysis.

STUDY QUESTIONS

1. What is the difference between being diagnosed with a mental illness and being given the label of "insane"?
2. Describe the three components involved with psychopathology.
3. How is *DSM-IV* useful? On the other hand, what have therapists criticized about it?
4. Describe the following symptoms: phobia, hallucination, dissociation, panic attack, obsession, delusion, flashback, compulsion, manic episode.

5. Think of three fictional characters you believe show the characteristics of any of the following disorders:

   Obsessive-compulsive disorder   Agoraphobia
   Post-traumatic stress disorder   Major depression
   Borderline personality disorder   Bipolar disorder
   Antisocial personality disorder   Hypochondriasis
   Multiple personality disorder   Conversion disorder
   Positive or negative schizophrenia

6. How are psychologists, psychiatrists, social workers, and counselors alike? What advantages does each have over the other alternatives?

7. John is depressed. What changes would you most likely see in him if he were treated with psychodynamic therapy? Cognitive therapy? Behavioral therapy? Humanistic psychotherapy?

8. Describe the advantages and disadvantages of drug therapy.

9. What questions might you ask yourself as you evaluate the legitimacy of a self-help book?

10. What characteristics and behaviors would you look for if you were in the process of choosing a psychotherapist for yourself?

CHAPTER SEVEN

Physical Self-Care
Tending the Body, Nurturing the Mind

You want fries with that?

It's well into the month of January, and you are beginning to feel the winter blahs. Your enthusiasm for your coursework is dwindling, and the length of the road toward the end of the term seems discouragingly long. You find yourself behaving more irritably than you did during the holiday season. You still spend some time socializing, but you tend to spend more time alone than you did earlier in the year. The grayness of the weather seems to weigh down on you. You may even become mildly depressed.

Some people experience these symptoms as a result of **seasonal affective disorder.** The shorter days, especially the lack of early morning sunlight, appear to cause these individuals to become depressed. However, you note that you did not have this problem last month, when the days were even shorter.

Why has your daily experience become so lackluster? If you examine your self-care habits, you might discover some significant differences in how you are treating your body. Because of less favorable weather, you are not as active and are getting less exercise than usual. During the holiday season there were abundant goodies to devour, and you ate rather well. However, now that you are back to the usual winter fare, your enthusiasm for eating has dwindled, and you find yourself just poking food around on your plate. You might just order the fries and forget about the sandwich altogether. The blanket of grayness in the sky makes you feel bundled in a cocoon, resulting in afternoon drowsiness and more naps than usual. Unfortunately, these naps disrupt your ability to sleep through the night. So how much of your winter blahs might be accounted for by lack of exercise, poor eating habits, and disrupted sleep?

Early theorists of the mind at one point concluded that mind and body functioned separately, a concept known as **dualism.** But as the above example points out, as does the entire chapter on stress and coping, there is actually quite a bit of interconnection and interaction between the two. Emotionally distressing and elating events have a direct hormonal effect on our bodies. At the same time, our physical health appears to have an effect on our emotional and mental states.

How we take care of our bodies thus becomes a point of interest as we monitor our personal growth. This chapter will discuss four areas: exercise, eating, sleeping, and self-preservation.

Exercise

Even while in grade school, we were instructed about the importance of staying physically fit. Physical fitness can be defined from several standpoints—strength, endurance, and flexibility, for example. Different exercise programs address different areas of fitness, depending on what is most important to the individual. All areas of fitness are important, but this section will focus on exercise as it pertains to our health and sense of well-being.

Aerobic exercise appears to best suit the purpose. Aerobic exercise is any activity that improves the ability of the lungs, heart, and arteries to use oxygen during times of physical exertion. Typically, aerobic exercise programs involve activity that is strenuous enough to result in our breaking into a sweat and breathing hard for 15 or 20 minutes. In order to have the most beneficial impact on our cardiovascular systems, the activity needs to take place at least three times a week. And while aerobic exercise is best, even sustained low aerobic activity can provide some benefit.

The types of activity that result in aerobic benefit are unlimited. Heavy-duty exercise such as running, swimming, racquetball, and aerobic workout videotapes are all popularly known aerobic activities. However, moderate exercise is equally successful in producing an aerobic effect. A brisk walk in the park, along the beach, or even through the neighborhood can be much more pleasant than pushing yourself to some competitive extreme.

When looking for evidence of aerobic benefit, you do not hover over a graph of how fast you went, what distance you covered, how many games you won, or how many push-ups you can do. Although such graphing can serve as evidence of progress, it does not necessarily demonstrate aerobic improvement. The best way to monitor your improvement is to measure your heart rate. In order to have an aerobic effect, your pulse rate should approach at least 50% of your predicted maximum heart rate. Predicted maximum heart rate is calculated by subtracting your age from 220. Any exercise that involves your larger muscles and gets your heart rate up to this level will provide aerobic benefit. Be careful not to exceed 80%–this would be overdoing it.

In addition to improving our physical fitness, aerobic exercise impacts our sense of emotional well-being. People often say that they feel good right after exercising, which is probably in part due to our bodies producing endorphins during times of strenuous physical activity. However, people also report that they feel better overall when they are on an exercise program. Sonstroem (1984) points out many possible reasons for this, including general feelings of well-being and improved physical health, the positive feelings that occur when we achieve a set goal, feeling more control over what is happening with our bodies, and even enjoying the social support of our exercise partners.

Some people avoid strenuous exercise programs because they have heard of people dying from heart attacks, strokes, and the likes while running or otherwise physically exerting themselves. Our chances of experiencing these mishaps do indeed go up during extreme exercise, no matter how fit we are. However, what is important to remember is that the more fit we are, the *less* likely we are to experience some cardiovascular accident during exertion. In other words, a person who runs regularly is *twice* as likely to have a heart attack during physical exertion than during a resting state. However, someone who never exercises can be *many* times more likely to have a heart attack during physical exertion than during a resting state.

If you live a life that involves absolutely no physical exertion, you might argue that an aerobic exercise program is not worth the risk. But such individuals are few and far between. If you wanted to pursue such a lifestyle, you would need to avoid any strenuous yard work or housework, never need to climb several flights of stairs at once, shovel snow, participate in various sports, run or otherwise move quickly when late or trying to catch up with someone, become extremely excited, or even be sexually active. This does not sound like much of a life, even if you could find a way to create it.

However, such observations suggest that we do need to remain mindful of whether or not we are overdoing it. Work your way slowly into any new exercise program. Remember to monitor your heart rate, rather than the quantity or quality of your exercising. Even when you are fit, you will vary in your day-to-day physical endurance level. Also, if you get away from your exercise program, do not try to reenter it at the same level you had achieved earlier. Tone it down to whatever gives you the appropriate heart rate and push yourself no further.

Some individuals set up an exercise regimen but are sporadic in how often they implement it. Perhaps they do nothing all week then "make up for it" by running five miles Sunday morning. This type of exercising actually does more harm than good. The exercise is not frequent enough to actually provide aerobic benefit, yet since it physically exerts you it places you at higher risk of having a cardiovascular accident.

Based on this discussion of exercise, here are some basic guidelines for setting up an aerobic exercise program:

- Before starting any exercise regimen, consult with your physician.
- Find a strenuous physical activity that you enjoy—anything that uses large muscles, gets you breathing heavily, and eventually results in your breaking into a sweat.
- Arrange to have at least three times a week when you can engage in this activity.

- Take part in your activity in such a way that you approach 80% of your predicted maximum heart rate, and maintain this rate for 15–20 minutes.
- Remember to breathe deeply as you exercise. However, if your breathing becomes so labored that you cannot even talk, or you become dizzy, slow down your physical activity. You are pushing yourself too hard, and will not be getting enough oxygen into your system to be able to receive aerobic benefit.
- If possible, find exercise partners. Your program will be more enjoyable if you have someone else along for the ride, and you will also be more likely to follow through.

Eating

The media continually tune us in to how diet affects our physical well-being. Nutritional factors play a role in our mental and emotional health as well. As time goes by, more and more evidence has accumulated suggesting that various foods can have an effect on the biochemistry of the brain, including the neurotransmitters that play a role in depression, dementia, and other mental malfunctions (Campbell, 1985).

All through our early lives, parents and educational systems instructed us on what constitutes good nutrition. We know we should include fruits and vegetables, proteins, whole-grain carbohydrates, and dairy or other calcium-rich foods in our daily diet. We also know we should limit fats, salt, and sweets and make sure we get plenty of fiber and fluids. Unfortunately, the North American culture and lifestyle does not necessarily support such eating habits. Following are some of the unhealthy eating styles that have emerged, as well as their drawbacks.

Eating Styles Leading to Obesity

First of all, **obesity**—whether you define it by cultural standards or from a medical standpoint—is not necessarily due to poor eating habits. Body weight appears to be more closely tied to genetics than to learned eating patterns. Identical twins raised apart tend to end up with body weights more like one another than fraternal twins who have even been raised in the same home environment (Stunkard et al., 1986). In addition, the number of fat cells we are born with is probably an inherited trait (Bogardus et al., 1986). Since fat cells only collapse rather than disappear during weight-loss diets, we are more or less stuck with them for life, increasing our chances for future weight gain.

However, anyone who owns a bathroom scale can tell you that what you eat and how much of it you eat does affect your weight. Whether or not your diet is relatively balanced, if it is high in fat and calories and you do not engage in enough physical exercise to burn them off, your body will store them as body fat. Thus such an eating pattern is likely to eventually result in weight gain.

Weight gain itself is not necessarily bad. People who engage in muscle-building exercises regularly gain weight. Muscle weighs more than fat; so as your waistline goes down your weight may actually go up! Thus bathroom scales are not necessarily the best monitors of healthy weight gain or loss. Instead, we need to learn to take some control over the percentage of our body weight that consists of fat.

The tastier foods American culture offers are frequently high in fat. Almost everything from fast food restaurants is loaded with it, often deep-fried. And fat's slippery nature can result in just about anything going down a little more nicely with the addition of a dab of butter. Most popular desserts, packaged foods, and preprepared foods are also high in fat.

One way we can take control of our percentages of body fat is to control how much fat we eat. Consumed fat is slow to digest, taking relatively longer to burn up than other nutrients. The idea is not to completely cut out fat, but to limit the number of calories we have each day that come from fat. Nutritionists recommend that no more than 30% of our total caloric intake consists of fat. Some manufacturers have begun listing the number of calories from fat in their product, along with the other nutritional information. If they do not, you can calculate it yourself by multiplying nine times the number of grams of fat, and dividing the product by the total number of calories.

For example, suppose you are going to eat a packaged cookie. On the box it says there are 5 grams of fat and 90 calories per cookie. Nine times five is 45; and 45 is 50% of 90. Therefore you know that 50% of the calories in the cookie come from fat.

Does this mean you do not eat the cookie, since more than 30% of the calories come from fat? Of course not! It means that you need to balance out your diet that day with some other food that does not contain so much fat but has an equivalent number of calories. A small apple should do the trick—it has around the same number of calories but no fat. Top it off with a sandwich that rounds out to about 30% fat calories, and you have a fat-healthy lunch!

Another way to take some control over your body fat is to get regular physical exercise. Physical activity burns calories, resulting in fewer of them converting into stored fat. You need not set up an actual exercise program as a means of burning calories. Many occupations already involve regular physical labor; yours may be one of them. You may have favorite pastimes that take a lot of energy, such as gardening, sports, biking, or hiking.

Another factor concerns individual differences in how quickly or slowly we burn up calories. This is in part due to our **metabolic rate.** If you were lucky enough to inherit a high metabolism, you burn calories relatively quickly. Thus you often eat as much as you want but do not put on excess fat. On the other hand, if you inherited a slow metabolism you use up calories slowly; you are much more likely to develop an overfat body if you do not balance your eating with a sufficient amount of physical activity. And as you age, your metabolic rate will go down if you do not pursue an adequate amount of physical activity.

Furthermore, we also appear to inherit something called a **set point.** The set point influences the percentage of calories that are converted into fat by speeding up or slowing down the metabolism. If the set point detects that you are starving or even significantly undereating, it will slow down your body's metabolism. This is a protective device. If we truly were starving, we would want our bodies to conserve calories as much as possible.

Unfortunately, our set points are not particularly concerned with producing a socially desirable weight level. Your set point is more interested in keeping you alive. The result is that if you go on a starvation-type diet, you will probably lose weight at first. But as your set point slows your metabolism, you will have more and more difficulty losing weight. Furthermore, your set point will stay put for some time after you reach your desired weight. So even if you went back to normal, healthy eating you would be likely to start putting weight on.

This is why many people who go on diets first lose the weight and then end up even heavier than when they started. As they diet again, then gain again, diet again, then gain again, they become increasingly more overfat. This result is sometimes called "yo-yo dieting" (Brownell, 1988). For this reason, very low calorie diets, such as those involving liquid diet meals, are generally ill-advised.

The many reams of research on dieting have come to the general conclusion that dieting may work for some but there are more costs than benefits to others (Brownell & Rodin, 1994). So if you really do need to lose some weight, here are some general suggestions:

- See your physician before making any drastic changes in your eating habits.

- Eat a normally balanced diet, with only a small reduction in the number of calories recommended for a person of your age and gender.

- Keep the percentage of calories from fat well below 30%. You will probably find that you can get by with eating a lot more once you cut out some of the fat calories.
- Do not skip meals, especially breakfast. The more time that passes between meals, the more your body will try to conserve calories.
- Exercise regularly when you lower your caloric intake. This can help prevent the set point from changing, since your metabolism will need to keep up with the energy being expended through activity. Also, your body will be less tempted to digest muscle tissue instead of fat if the muscle tissue is being used.

UNDEREATING

During the last few decades, American culture has promoted an absurd image of what constitutes a socially desirable weight level. Models, actors, and others who are informally elected to appear before the masses tend to be stick thin. Past generations did not share this value. If you look at works of classical artists, their female models looked downright obese by today's standards. Even one of the greatest sex symbols of recent times, Marilyn Monroe, looks chunky when compared to her contemporary counterparts.

Only a small percentage of the population is born with a frame and metabolism that will healthily support the stick-thin image presented by the media. Those who attempt to battle this inevitability are often doomed to creating health problems for themselves. Keeping yourself underweight and undernourished can put you at risk for both disease and injury.

Another unfortunate malady of undereating that has increased in proportion with our society's preoccupation with overthinness is **anorexia.** Those suffering from anorexia seem to others as if they are trying to starve themselves to death. They eat as little as possible, and when they do eat, they may try to vomit up whatever they have consumed. They sometimes control their appetite feelings with diet pills. They often use diuretics to help quickly rid themselves of anything containing calories. They may exercise for several hours a day, hoping to quickly burn off any calories that may have found the way into their systems.

The typical person who becomes anorexic usually begins with a desire to lose some weight. The person may actually need to lose a little weight. Often the normal pudginess that adolescents develop just before their growth spurts is interpreted by the teen as a need to diet. Or, the person may be involved in activities that encourage underweight, as is true for dancers, actors, models, some athletes, and beauty pageant participants. Or the person may just want to look more like his or her favorite media personality.

Most anorexic individuals are female. This is probably due to our culture and the media placing so much worth and value on how women look, and especially how much they weigh. Our culture is not so concerned with assigning value and worth according to what men might weigh. One look at the tabloids confirms this hypothesis. You frequently see articles describing the latest diets of women who battle their body size, such as Oprah Winfrey and Roseanne. However, you rarely see stories about the dieting activities of overweight men, such as John Goodman and the late John Candy, no matter how obese they may become.

At any rate, the future victim of anorexia starts dieting, loses a little weight, and likes the results. She enjoys the compliments she gets from others, and perhaps the additional attention she gets from the opposite sex. She begins to fear obesity, since it would take away her new-found social rewards. So she decides to lose a few more pounds, just for insurance. But for these individuals, enough is never enough. No matter how much they lose, they do not feel like they have created enough of a buffer to avoid becoming "too heavy" again. Their perceptions of how their bodies look become inaccurate, and they have difficulty understanding why everyone is so upset about their dieting.

Why do some people who diet become anorexic and others do not? There are a number of personality and environmental factors that appear to predispose some dieters for anorexia (Sandbek, 1986). They tend to be excessively concerned about what others think about them. They have a poor self-image and poor self-esteem. They are perfectionistic, and worry a lot about being good enough. They are excessively attached to routine and become uptight if their routines are disrupted. They are especially prone to emotions such as depression, guilt, helplessness, resentment, excessive anxiety, and unreasonable fears. They have considerable stress in their lives, and may feel like they are losing control or are being excessively controlled by others.

In addition to being underweight, there are many medical side effects to anorexia. These include fatigue and lack of energy, loss of menstruation in women, skin problems, and inability to sweat. Sufferers develop circulation problems and may begin feeling cold even in hot weather, or even develop gangrene of the fingertips. They can experience swelling in the face, hot flashes, rapid heartbeat, and breathlessness. Those who vomit regularly develop rotting teeth and ulcers of the esophagus.

The final outcome of anorexia is death. Anorexia is a fatal disease. Most fatalities occur as a result of nocturnal cardiac arrest, which occurs as the poor diet creates a low potassium level, causing an electrolyte imbalance. So if you see yourself falling into this particular eating pattern, it is essential that you seek medical attention at once. Anorexia is not "just dieting." It can be a death sentence.

Eating/Noneating

Another maladaptive eating pattern developed by some individuals who diet is known as **bulimia.** These individuals eat in binges—eating a massive amount of food over a short period of time. In our youth most of us participated in some form of binge eating, such as pizza or ice cream feeds, pie-eating competitions, and the like. We usually leave such events feeling overfull and wishing that we had not eaten quite so much, but generally we do not suffer any other unusual consequences.

This is not so with bulimic activity. Bulimic bingeing typically takes place when the sufferer is at home alone, and it occurs on a regular basis, usually at least once a week. The binge ends when the sufferer is actually in pain due to the fullness of his or her stomach. Then the person usually induces vomiting, also known as "purging."

Unlike anorexic sufferers, those who binge and purge are aware that their eating pattern is abnormal. They are ashamed of it, and make a point of trying to hide it from others. After a binge/purge cycle they feel depressed and judge themselves harshly. They try to make up for any weight gain caused by bingeing through fasting. Their eating habits are characterized by swings between eating nothing or eating everything they can get their hands on, usually foods that are high in fat and go down easily.

What type of individual is likely to become bulimic? Some individuals who binge and purge begin as anorexic, thus having the same predispositional factors as those who are anorexic. Others appear to be suffering more from a disorder of impulse control. Once they start eating, their "fullness" cues are not sufficient to make them stop. They often have other problems with impulse control, as is involved with compulsive stealing, chemical dependency, and alcohol abuse. They tend to have difficulties with interpersonal relationships. Often these individuals have family members with histories of depression, and they may in fact be depressed themselves (Halmi, 1985).

Individuals who develop bulimia also seem to use a specific all-or-nothing thinking pattern, one you may recall from the discussion in Chapter 5 concerning those who suffer from depression. When these individuals diet, they are either fasting or eating an extremely limited amount of food. If they consume anything that is not on their diet, as far as they are concerned, they have "blown it." According to their logic, they then may as well eat whatever they feel like eating, since eating one potato chip or a whole bag equally violates their perfectionistic standard.

The medical consequences of bulimia are similar to those of anorexia, including the possibility of nocturnal cardiac arrest. So even though it may feel embarrassing, if you see yourself in the above description, find professional help.

Sleep

When we do not get enough sleep, we do not perform as well as usual—physically, mentally, or emotionally. Who among us has not at some time rationalized away poor personal performance with "I just didn't get enough sleep last night"? With some variation, we all seem to need somewhere between 5 and 10 hours of sleep every 24 hours. Furthermore, we do best if that sleep occurs at about the same time each day, so that our circadian rhythms are not disrupted.

The importance of sleep is most clearly demonstrated by individuals who have been deprived of it. For example, **sleep apnea** is a sleep disorder that causes the sufferer to stop breathing while sleeping. When this occurs, the brain stem alerts the body to wake up enough for the somatic nervous system to do something about it. Usually the person will then make a sudden snorting noise, or throw himself or herself around in order to get some air, then go back into a deeper state of sleep. Often the only way sufferers even learn they do this is by hearing the complaints of bed partners and roommates regarding their "snoring."

However, the person often does complain of having trouble sleeping and/or being drowsy all the time. The drowsiness occurs because of the lack of **REM sleep.** REM stands for "rapid eye movement." During this stage of sleep our eyes dart back and forth under our lids. If you wake sleepers during REM sleep, they usually say that they have been dreaming. We seem to need a certain amount of REM sleep to keep from feeling drowsy and to perform well during wakefulness. In fact, if you keep waking up a person during REM sleep during one sleep period, they will make up for lost REM time during the following sleep period. If deprived of REM sleep indefinitely, we can actually begin experiencing symptoms of delirium, such as stupor, hallucinations, delusions, or extreme agitation (Wells, 1985).

However, when most of us have interruptions in our REM sleep, the cause is much more mundane. The most common sleep problem is

insomnia. Insomnia is the inability to fall asleep or stay asleep. It can occur as difficulty getting to sleep when you first go to bed. Or perhaps you wake up in the middle of the night, then have difficulty getting back to sleep. Or maybe you wake up early and then stay awake. All of these are forms of insomnia. Just about everybody experiences it from time to time, especially when excited or anxious about something.

Some people use sleeping pills or alcohol as they try to get to sleep on a restless night. These may actually help them fall asleep, but they may also find that they are still tired the next day. This is because drugged sleep is not the same as normal sleep. For example, using large quantities of alcohol does indeed eventually result in unconsciousness and a form of sleep. However, the alcohol consumer's first half of the night will consist of an extremely deep sleep that does not make it back up to the lighter REM pattern. The second half of the night, the sleeper often wakes up and sleeps fitfully for the next several hours (APA, 1994).

Another drawback to using drugs and alcohol to fall asleep is that your body becomes accustomed to them. Your body may sense that you contain enough "downers" to do the job and stop producing its own forms. Thus you find yourself virtually unable to go to sleep unless you either continue to use the substances or go through the process of withdrawal (Kandel & Schwartz, 1985).

If you are having difficulty getting to sleep at night, here are some suggestions that may help:

- Make a point of going to bed and getting up at the same time every night. Do not sleep in if you were up late tossing and turning. Get up at your usual time, and resist the temptation to take a nap during the day.

- Find a way to relax before bedtime. Relaxation tapes or other techniques can be useful for this purpose. *Do not* use drugs or alcohol to relax before sleep.

- Avoid eating rich foods just before bedtime. You might try warm milk instead, since it has a tendency to produce drowsiness (notice how babies usually fall asleep after polishing off a meal of warm milk). A light carbohydrate snack just before bed can also help produce drowsiness, much as our high-carbohydrate lunches tend to cause difficulty staying awake during 1 P.M. classes!

- Light exercise a couple hours before going to bed, such as taking a walk or doing light housework, also aids sleep. Avoid engaging in heavy exercise late in the evening, as it can be energizing and impair your ability to fall asleep.

- If you are lying awake stewing about things, use thought-stopping techniques such as the rubber band technique discussed in Chapter 4. Also, do not create secondary stress for yourself by worrying over the fact that you are experiencing insomnia. Occasional insomnia will not harm you. Most likely, you will make up for any lost REM sleep during the following night's sleep.

- If you have been lying awake for more than 15 minutes, get up and find something else to do until you feel drowsy, then try again. This way you do not create conditioning that accustoms you to lying awake while in bed.

- If you have frequent insomnia, stop using the bed for superfluous activities like reading, watching television, or eating. Like lying in bed awake, these activities may teach you to associate being in bed with wakefulness.

Following these guidelines will most likely take care of any normal insomnia you may experience. However, ongoing insomnia is most commonly caused by some form of emotional disturbance (Kandel & Schwartz, 1985). If you continue having difficulty getting a good night's sleep, consult with professionals.

Self-Preservation

One of the few adult human behaviors still attributed to instinct is self-preservation. Obviously, if it were not present, our species would not be likely to last very long. Presenting it as a necessary personal growth topic at first may even sound absurd. However, in spite of its importance, many people engage in activities that defy the logic of self-preservation. Young adult men are especially at risk for such behavior—have you noticed how hard it is for individuals of this age and gender to purchase insurance? And as the feminist movement has carried us "forward," young women are also beginning to be considered a higher insurance risk than in previous years.

Following is a list of 1990s-style activities that demonstrate limited respect for our physical vulnerabilities:

- Reckless driving
- Unprotected sexual activity
- Drinking alcohol to a state of unconsciousness
- Joining street gangs
- Using street drugs
- Hanging around in bars, waiting for a fistfight
- Hang gliding, bungee jumping, race car driving, free-climbing cliffs, deep-sea diving, rattlesnake hunting, alligator wrestling, and other high-risk sports

CAUSES OF RISK-TAKING

Why do we pursue activities that propose such high risk to life and limb? Chapter 4 points out that the adrenaline rush produced can at times be a way of coping with stress. Thus some of us may use these activities for escapism purposes.

For others, high-risk behavior has more to do with inborn temperament, as discussed in Chapter 2. Those of us who were born with an introverted temperament are not so likely to try risky behavior; the excessive stimulation feels too uncomfortable. However, those of us with extroverted temperaments can handle significantly more stimulation before we begin to feel uncomfortable; in fact, we may start feeling bored without excessive stimulation. Dangerous activity is one way to create enough stimulation to escape boredom. Those who are high in this "sensation-seeking" temperament tend to view risky events as less threatening than those who are low in sensation-seeking and are therefore more likely to take part in them (Zuckerman et al., 1978).

During adolescence, some risk-taking occurs as a result of developmental tasks. At this stage in our lives we are trying to "spread our wings" and establish our individual identities. We pursue a variety of new experiences as part of the exploration of who we are, and some of these experiences involve high risk. Also, we may knowingly choose risky activities not so much because we enjoy the danger but because others have been telling us for so long that we should not do these things. Some have suggested that a personal myth of "I am invulnerable" is not unusual during young adolescence (Elkind, 1967). Notice how much more carefully you must drive by the junior high school as classes are let out, as students seem to wander out into the street with little regard for the vehicles that pass by!

However, recent research has suggested that it is not so much adolescents' less realistic assessment of risk as it is their choice to act in spite of perceived risks. Adolescents and adults do not appear to differ that much in their ability to realistically assess risk (Beyth-Marom et al., 1993). No matter what our age, for some reason we seem to see ourselves as less vulnerable in a risky situation than we would predict for somebody else (Quadrel et al., 1993). We also seem to be overconfident in what we know (Yates, 1992), which could push us even closer to engaging in unnecessary risks.

For many of us, peer pressure plays a major role in our risk-taking behavior. We do things that are ill-advised, but we perceive them as being necessary in order to fit in with the crowd. Or, we may engage in risky behavior in order to attract the crowd's acceptance. Ironically, being accepted by a social structure is actually another requirement for human survival, as will be covered in greater detail in Chapter 10. However, this need is being misapplied if we follow along in activities that threaten our physical existence.

Another social reason we may engage in high-risk behaviors is the value sometimes placed on "spontaneity." Doing things on the spur of the moment and giving in to various whims produces the image of being a "free spirit," a personality description typically smiled upon by our culture. Actually, the existential perspective would applaud being so in touch with experiencing the moment.

However, there is a big difference between being spontaneous and being impulsive, and sometimes the two are confused. Spontaneity has been run through the sifter of common sense: "What will the consequences be if I follow through on this whim of the moment? Is the risk of danger or consequences that are sure to follow worth the experience of being able to give in and let loose?" On the other hand, impulsiveness is simply letting your whims take control, without regard for what might happen. Spontaneity acts only on whims and feelings that will not be likely to produce unwanted consequences.

For some, risk-taking may in fact represent self-destructive tendencies (Holinger & Luke, 1984). Many "accidental" deaths, and even some homicides, actually involved risks knowingly taken by individuals who did not value their lives. Some individuals may give in to the thrills of risk-taking not so much because of direct suicidal inclinations but because their lives feel so tumultuous or hopeless that they do not feel they have that much to lose.

Risking Reducing Risk

Our lives will always include the presentation of risks. The risks typically encountered during adolescence and young adulthood, however, can have unusually drastic and long-term consequences. The experimentation of youth has always included dangerous activities. However, there are currently many new dangers that were not as prevalent during previous generations, such as street drugs, sexually transmitted diseases, street gangs, death-defying "sports," or traveling through the inner city.

By the time we reach later adulthood, we have already sifted through most of these dangers in the process of discovering our identities and finding our social niches. Just by means of experience and the passage of time we develop habits that keep us out of some risky situations. We still find ourselves presented with risk, but the situations tend not to have as potentially life-threatening consequences as those we encountered in our youth. Thus teenagers and young adults need to be especially careful of how they approach high-risk activity.

Obviously, the results of taking multiple high risks could spell disaster. So how do we protect ourselves from the mechanisms that interfere with self-preservation? Here are some guidelines you might consider:

- Learn as much as you can about the high-risk situations you feel you are likely to encounter and the ways to reduce the risk. For example, familiarize yourself with the discussions on "intentional drinking" in Chapter 8, and "safer sex" in Chapter 9.
- When you discover you are in a high-risk situation, remind yourself of this fact. When we are aware of risk, we are more likely to use extra care.
- Always evaluate the potential consequences of taking risks. And since you are likely to underestimate the probability of those consequences happening to you, consider instead the likelihood of such consequences happening to your best friend in similar circumstances.
- If your crowd is constantly getting you into unnecessarily risky situations, reconsider your current choice of friends.
- Remember that you are a human "being," not a human "doing." You are who you are, not what you do. In other words, you need not prove either your identity or your autonomy by engaging in risky behavior.
- If you are going to take up a potentially dangerous sport, get the best training you can. Use good-quality equipment and be sure to take all the advised necessary safety precautions. Even stunt men typically do not take unnecessary risks for the sake of the thrill; as trained professionals, they do everything they can to ensure that they perform their stunts safely (Piet, 1987).
- If you are one of those individuals who needs a lot of stimulation to feel alive, try some of these safer means of sensation-seeking:
  - Watch stimulating movies.
  - Try adventuresome new foods.
  - Go places you have never been before.
  - Decorate your home with an unusual high-stimulation decor.
  - Try occasional "shame attacks" à la Ellis, such as riding the elevator to the top of a building and calling off the floor number at each stop.
  - Arrange for social gatherings with individuals who are very (safely!) different from your usual crowd.

- Get involved with politics or social interest groups.
- Try *safe* social experiments, such as wearing your clothes inside out and seeing who notices.
- Do not engage in high-risk activities when you are depressed. You will not be as likely to take necessary safety precautions, especially if you are having subconscious suicidal ideations.

Expanding Your Experience

Risk-taking was not one of my favorite pastimes during my youth. I was unusually conservative. When I signed up to vote, I couldn't even let myself face the potential risks of political party identification. To this day, I am still listed as "independent."

However, even though I may have scored within the abnormal range of risk-taking, I recognize that most other people take significantly greater risks. The first exercise is designed to explore and compare your risk-taking behavior with that of your other small group members, as well as to look for alternative ways of handling high-risk situations. The second exercise not only helps you assess your particular health orientation but also introduces you to the joys, frustrations, and complications of assessment scoring—an activity you may eventually do a lot of if you are taking this course as a part of entering a psychologically related field. The last exercise is a checklist of eating disorder symptoms.

STUDY QUESTIONS

1. How is aerobic exercise different from other types of exercise? What are its benefits?
2. Why might charting and regularly increasing your running speed and distance not necessarily increase your aerobic fitness?
3. What reasons can you give for the general feelings of well-being that people experience while on a regular exercise program?
4. Jim Fixx died of a heart attack while running. Why shouldn't we use this as evidence that exercise is a bad idea?
5. List several reasons why obesity may be more of an inherited condition than a product of learned behavior patterns.

6. Explain how reducing caloric intake alone may not help you in attaining a permanent weight loss.
7. How do your metabolic rate and set point affect your weight?
8. What is "yo-yo dieting"?
9. Why is exercise important when you diet?
10. Describe a person who would be likely to become anorexic after dieting.
11. Why do you think women are more likely to become anorexic than men?
12. What is meant by the "binge and purge" cycle?
13. What are the medical side effects to anorexia and bulimia?
14. List six ways to help yourself deal with insomnia.
15. List several reasons why we sometimes take unnecessarily high risks, even though they have the potential to be life-threatening.
16. Why does it appear to be more important that young people monitor their risk-taking behavior than older individuals?
17. List several ways you can protect yourself when faced with high-risk situations.

CHAPTER EIGHT

Substance Use and Abuse

Weaving through the Mazes of Altering Consciousness

A man walks into a bar with a duck under his arm...

Tami was a college freshman living on a large college campus. Her dormitory was known as the "party dorm." On any given night of the week—and sometimes during the day, as well—there was a party of some sort taking place. Alcohol was almost always present at these events. Tami had not had much experience with alcohol during high school, so she generally stayed away from these parties. As she made her way through her first term, she kept her nose to the grindstone and breezed through finals.

"Now I'm ready to celebrate!" she decided. Down the hall, there was a drinking game in progress involving several older students. Participants were downing small glasses of beer based on whether they rolled certain numbers on the dice or correctly answered certain questions. "That sounds like fun!" thought Tami, feeling confident in her ability to succeed at any brand of test-taking. She joined them.

At first, she hardly missed any questions. But as the evening wore on and the alcohol began to take effect, her ability to retrieve the information she wanted became muddled. She started feeling relaxed and "devil-may-care." Her responding became goofy and very entertaining for the older students, who were already experienced in managing their drinking and were not yet quite so impaired. They arranged that Tami received the lion's share of the game's questioning and drinking episodes, increasing their level of entertainment. Tami felt flattered by the extra attention she was receiving from older students, which upped her enthusiasm—as well as her drinking—even more.

The next morning Tami woke up in her own room, but could not recall how she got there. She felt ill. Several dorm members poked their heads in to see how she was doing, as well as to fill her in on some of the things she had done the night before. She was so embarrassed that she didn't show her face around campus again until after the break.

Few of us have been formally trained or indoctrinated into the appropriate use of consciousness-altering substances, in spite of the fact almost everybody uses them in one form or another. We appear to have a greater anthology of jokes about substance use than we do useful guidelines. The story of Tami illustrates the informal way that training is more likely to happen—by hit and miss, and with the potential for unwanted consequences. While this chapter cannot tell you all the idiosyncracies of how various substances will be utilized specifically by your own body, it will nonetheless provide some information and guidelines that will help you make intelligent choices concerning your own substance use.

Our culture has adopted the use of a variety of substances that serve the purpose of altering states of consciousness. Drugs that alter your perceptions and moods are called **psychoactive**. Most of them are used recreationally, and some are used for medicinal purposes; but generally speaking they all have the potential to be misused. Using drugs maladaptively is called **substance abuse**.

When used regularly, most psychoactive drugs will produce a state of **tolerance**. This means that your body has adjusted itself to the drug's effect and you need more and more of it to achieve the same effect. When tolerance becomes so severe that you become physically dependent on the drug and are unable to function normally without it, you have the beginnings of an addiction. Drug **dependence** means not only has your body accustomed itself to the presence of the drug but also if you stop taking it you will experience **withdrawal**—feelings of illness until your body readjusts. Dependency may also be psychological, where there may be no physical addiction yet you believe you cannot function without the drug.

Substance Classifications

Psychoactive substances can be classified into three main categories: depressants, stimulants, and hallucinogens.

Depressants

Depressants are so-named because they depress, or reduce the responding of, the normally invigorating sympathetic nervous system. Thus a drugged individual feels more relaxed, experiences less anxiety and fewer inhibitions, exhibits some slowed or impaired coordination and mental functioning, and may experience mood swings. The most widely used depressant is alcohol. Another group of depressant drugs is known as **barbiturates**. These include sleeping pills and many tranquilizers; they are usually obtained with a physician's prescription. Barbiturates can be very lethal, especially if you take too many or combine them with alcohol.

Opiates are another type of depressant. These include opium, morphine, heroin, and a variety of prescription painkillers. These depressants typically replace pain and anxiety with feelings of euphoria and relaxation, similar to the "natural high" we experience from our own endorphins. They are thus highly addictive. If opiates are introduced artificially, our bodies temporarily stop producing natural endorphins. So if we use them for a long time and then stop taking them, we will feel pretty miserable. Addiction is unfortunately a common side effect of the therapeutic use of painkillers, as well as of the use of alcohol and barbiturates.

Stimulants

Stimulants speed up body functions and create a "rush" of heightened consciousness. After the drug wears off the user "crashes," feeling somewhat depressed and irritable. **Amphetamines**, one type of stimulant, were once used to treat depression, but they were later found to cause more problems than they solved because of the crash after the "high." Now amphetamines are typically used for the treatment of attention deficit disorders, Parkinson's disease, and some sleep disorders (Bezchlibnyk-Butler et al., 1994). They are also popular as street drugs because of the high they produce.

The most widely used illegal street stimulant is cocaine. It produces feelings of excitement, energy, elation, and increased alertness. The user feels as if he or she can do anything—a little like a manic high or delusions of grandeur. The risk of addiction to cocaine is very high, as well as is the risk of overdose.

However, the most widely used and seemingly socially sanctioned stimulants are **nicotine** and **caffeine**. Nicotine, one of the most addictive of all psychoactive substances, is the active substance found in tobacco products. Caffeine is found in coffee, tea, and chocolate, and is added to many forms of soda. Some over-the-counter medications such as pain relievers, diet pills, and cold remedies also contain caffeine.

Caffeine is contained in so many commonly used products that many of us are addicted without realizing it. Withdrawal from caffeine is characterized largely by a headache that only goes away if you consume more caffeine. Perhaps this is why caffeine has found its way into over-the-counter pain relievers!

Hallucinogens

Hallucinogens are most noted for creating distorted perceptions and sensory experiences. The actual effects vary widely from person to person and from use to use. One person may experience a wonderful euphoria and another absolute terror. A person may experience euphoria one time and terror the next. Hallucinogens are generally not physically addictive, although some individuals may become psychologically addicted.

LSD (lysergic acid diethylamide) is a laboratory-produced hallucinogen of the 1960s that seems to be experiencing a new surge of popularity. Its effect usually begins by pumping up whatever mood you were in when you took it. You see patterns and bright colors, often taking on a tunnel or funnel configuration. As your "trip" progresses, your hallucinations and delusions take on more of a story line and you begin to feel detached from your body.

While this experience may sound intriguing, it is in fact very scary and can be very dangerous. You have little way to predict whether your trip will be good or bad. Furthermore, you are at risk of causing bodily harm to yourself if your delusions encourage you to believe you can fly, you are immortal, or that an actual stream of heavy traffic is a stream of mountain water. "Flashbacks" can be a problem: You may suddenly find yourself back in a trip when you have not retaken the drug. While LSD is not physically addictive, psychological dependence can develop.

Psylocybin is a hallucinogenic substance found in a certain mushroom. Its hallucinogenic effects are very similar to LSD. In fact, if you have developed tolerance for LSD, you are also likely to find that you have tolerance for psylocybin.

Mescaline is a natural hallucinogen found in peyote. Its effects are generally not as severe as those of laboratory-produced hallucinogens. Peyote has been smoked in some Native American cultures for centuries as part of their religious rituals.

Cannabis is the psychoactive substance found in marijuana and hashish. It is difficult to classify because it not only creates a mild version of the altered perceptions of the hallucinogens but also causes the relaxed feelings that are typically produced by depressants. While use of cannabis is still illegal, it does appear to have medicinal properties of reducing nausea in chemotherapy patients and of being useful in the treatment of glaucoma. Whether marijuana use should be legalized—at least for certain medicinal purposes—is an ongoing topic of debate. However, experts point out that legalizing marijuana might encourage chronic use, which has been found to produce such effects as weight gain, loss of energy, apathy, slow and confused thinking, impaired judgment, and reduced reproductive potency in men (Bezchlibnyk-Butler et al., 1994).

PCP (phencyclidine hydrochloride) is a hallucinogen that also has effects similar to those of sedatives and depressants. Phencyclidine is used legitimately as a general anesthetic in veterinary medicine. When used as a recreational drug, the effects begin almost immediately and can last for days or weeks. Since it is somewhat easy to synthesize, many "cookers" try their hand at it; unfortunately, it is also easy to make mistakes that result in the user becoming extremely ill, comatose, or expired. The effects are similar to those of LSD only more extreme, more prone to produce bad trips, and more likely to result in death or serious injury. As with LSD, flashbacks may occur, and psychological dependence sometimes develops.

Substance Use Patterns

The differing effects and consequences of using psychoactive substances dictate different patterns of use and abuse. Following are discussions of substance use patterns and ways to exercise control over them for alcohol, caffeine, nicotine, and street drugs.

Alcohol

Alcohol is an extremely popular substance on most college campuses. In fact, young adults attending college consume more alcohol than those of that age group who do not go to school. However, in spite of alcohol's popularity, the average person tends not to be aware of what it is and the extent of its effects on the body.

What is alcohol? Alcohol is chemically known as **ethanol**. It is produced through the process of fermentation. When yeast is added to aging fruits and watery starches, it survives by digesting any available carbohydrates. As a by-product of the digestion process, the yeast produces ethanol. It produces more and more of this alcohol within its medium of residence until the concentration of alcohol becomes about 14%. Since alcohol is a toxin, such a high concentration kills off the yeast. Thus the highest concentration of alcohol that can be created by natural means is 14%, or 28 proof. Most beer and wine derives its relatively lower alcoholic content solely through fermentation.

As you have probably noticed, there are many forms of alcoholic beverages that are higher than 28 proof, especially those called "hard" liquor, such as rum, vodka, gin, whiskey. Their higher concentrations of alcohol are produced by means of distillation. Through the use of a "still," water is removed from the concoction until the desired concentration of alcohol is attained.

In spite of the differing amounts of alcohol found in various beverages, standard served drinks all tend to contain about the same amount of alcohol. A 12-ounce beer, 4- or 5-ounce glass of wine, and a mixed drink containing a single jigger of alcohol all contain somewhere around two-thirds of an ounce of pure alcohol. Thus any one of these drinks is likely to produce a relatively similar effect for the average person.

What is the effect of alcohol on the brain? As classified earlier, alcohol is a depressant. After we drink it, it enters our bloodstream and works on the brain as an anesthetic (Miller & Munoz, 1976). Beginning with the outer, more sophisticated structures it seeps in toward the inner, more primitive structures, and the brain becomes more and more anesthetized.

Therefore the first functions of the brain to be affected are our more advanced ones. At first we feel a little more relaxed, as any tendencies toward anxiety or hypervigilance are counteracted by the alcohol's depressant nature. Our reaction times become slowed, as we feel less pressured to act upon stressors. As the alcohol penetrates further into our cerebral cortexes we become less alert, and our judgment becomes less stringent. As judgment goes, so do varying degrees of our self-control. We begin to say things we would not normally say and do things we would not do while sober.

As we continue to drink, the alcohol makes its way toward those structures of the brain that affect movement. First, fine motor control is affected: Speech becomes less precise and we stumble over words; our handwriting becomes sloppier; we may inadvertently nick a finger preparing vegetables for dinner. Then gross motor functions become impaired: We weave, stumble, and otherwise become less effective at negotiating the terrain; coordination and balance become more difficult.

Alcohol also interferes with the process of storing memories. Thus the more you drink, the more your recent memory may be impaired. After periods of extreme intoxication, you may experience "blackouts," whereby you have no memory of what you did the night before, how you got home, and so on, simply because the capacity to create memories had become completely anesthetized.

The alcohol's last stop is the center of the brain, where our most basic functions are regulated. The autonomic nervous system controls those activities that carry on by themselves without our having to think about them—such as staying conscious, breathing, and heart beat. "Passing out" occurs as this part of our brain becomes partially anesthetized. If we manage to consume even greater amounts of alcohol we can anesthetize the part of our brain that reminds us to breathe, resulting in death.

Fortunately, we generally do not die as a result of the alcohol we have consumed on any given evening. Our bodies have mechanisms that help rid themselves of the substance. A small amount of the alcohol leaves our bodies through our lungs as we breathe. This is why it is so easy to tell if others have been drinking by smelling their breath. All the mouthwash and breath mints in town are not going to do away with an odor that is actually emanating from the lungs. The rest of the alcohol is digested, metabolized by our livers at the rate of about one drink per hour. Thus an hour after you have a drink, most likely there will not be any alcohol left in your system.

Another less glamorous protective mechanism is the vomiting response. When we consume substances that our bodies find to be toxic we reflexively throw up, thus removing the substance from our systems. Unfortunately, this reflex can also lead to your demise. If you drink to the point of passing out, are lying on your back, and then vomit, you stand a good chance of inhaling it and drowning.

Consequences of excessive alcohol use. Drowning in your own vomit is certainly one inconvenient drawback of excessive alcohol use. However, there are other higher-probability problems that tend to arise when drinking gets out of control, especially for college students. One major concern is the effect that excessive drinking can have on grades. Since alcohol impairs memory processing, having any alcohol in your system during times of learning, studying, and testing can be detrimental. You are also likely to miss class more often and reduce your test-taking effectiveness if you find yourself hung over after a big night of partying.

Another problem from drinking during the college years is the fact that many college students are under drinking age. For many of you, drinking is illegal. Engaging in illegal activity has its own set of consequences, especially if you are caught drinking and driving. In some states, underage drinkers can lose their driver's licenses if they are found driving while they have *any* alcohol in their systems, regardless of the actual percentage. Higher percentages of alcohol in your system while driving—no matter what your age—can result in DUIs (driving under the influence), accidents, permanent injuries, and death; as well as the possibility of spending the rest of your life carrying around the guilt of having caused harm to someone else as a result of your drinking and driving.

Since our judgment and self-control become impaired with excessive drinking, we may participate in a number of other ill-advised activities. Perhaps, while intoxicated, we could muster up enough moral inhibition to keep ourselves from driving but not from getting into a car with some other drinker who should not be driving. Or due to our released inhibitions, we might follow through on impulses we would normally inhibit, such as telling friends and family what we really think of them. Such behaviors can destroy interpersonal relationships. Not surprisingly, general family dysfunction is commonly found in families where one of the adult members uses alcohol excessively (Heath & Stanton, 1991).

Released inhibitions might also result in our engaging in unprotected sex or sexual behavior we do not really want, an especially scary possibility considering the looming shadow of HIV. We might take other ill-advised risks, such as walking across a questionable part of town in the middle of the night or taking "dares," activities we would consider too dangerous if we were thinking clearly. A significant percentage of violent and criminal behavior can also be connected to the released inhibitions created by excessive alcohol use (McCord, 1992). Around 30% of all suicides and over 50% of all homicides have been found to be related to the use of alcohol (Institute of Medicine, 1987).

Long-term excessive use of alcohol can result in many health problems, especially damage to the liver, cardiovascular system, immune system, digestive system, and nervous system (National Institute of Alcohol Abuse & Alcoholism, 1990). A health problem that receives a lot of press is the potential for developing alcoholism. Around 10% of the population appears to be genetically or otherwise predisposed toward becoming alcoholic after making use of alcohol (Goodwin, 1985).

The joys of intentional drinking. Statistically, 10% of the population drinks on an alcoholic level, 60% on a light or moderate basis, and 30% not at all (Levin, 1990). If you are among the 30% who abstain from drinking, the rest of this section will probably not have much meaning for you, unless you decide to change that status or to share these ideas with your drinking acquaintances. If you are among the 70% who do use alcohol, most likely at this point you are beginning to wonder how you can arrange your alcohol use so that you can enjoy its pleasant effects yet not fall victim to the many unpleasant consequences of uncontrolled drinking.

Bill Zuelke (1995) calls such an arrangement of drinking behavior **intentional drinking**. Intentional drinking can be defined as drinking in ways that do not cause you problems. The amount of alcohol you drink is not necessarily the issue; rather, whether you can drink that amount and not end up in trouble is essential. The idea behind intentional drinking is that it have a low impact on your daily functioning, regardless of how much or how often you imbibe.

Before we can take charge over our levels of impairment due to alcohol consumption, we need to have an understanding of how alcohol affects each of us individually. How much can we drink before it can be expected to affect us one way or another? On a concrete level, we are looking at blood alcohol level. Different levels of blood alcohol usually account for the varying effects on our behavior. For example, if you attain a blood alcohol concentration of 0.03% or less, you are still relatively sober. You will probably feel a little more relaxed, find it easier to forget about the day's hassles, lose a few minor inhibitions, and feel a bit of a "buzz." If your blood alcohol level is between 0.04 and 0.07%, you are beginning to become impaired in your behavior and judgment. You will probably start mispronouncing words, laugh uproariously at jokes that you normally would not find to be so funny, and will have released enough inhibitions to start becoming a "life of the party" type. Even though you are still not legally drunk, your driving behavior is likely to be affected, as you take chances you would not normally take or fail to make note of all important variables of safe driving.

In most states, you are considered to be legally drunk if your blood alcohol concentration is 0.08% or higher. At this point you have probably begun stumbling around, your vision is impaired, and your judgment has become highly questionable. You are likely to begin engaging in behaviors you will be embarrassed about the next morning. If you are caught driving with this blood alcohol level, you can be arrested for driving under the influence.

If you continue to drink even after reaching a blood alcohol concentration of 0.08% you will eventually suffer from the more extreme symptoms of intoxication, such as blackouts, throwing up, passing out, and severe hangovers. If you manage to consume enough alcohol to achieve a blood alcohol concentration between 0.40% and 0.50%, you will probably be dead due to the effects of respiratory depression.

The concentration of alcohol that develops in your bloodstream varies in accordance with your individual differences. One important variable is body size. The bigger your body, the more blood you have in your system and the lower the concentration of blood alcohol you will have after drinking a given amount. For example, a person who weighs 125 pounds is much more likely to feel the effect of a single drink than a person who weighs 250.

Another important variable is how close together your drinks are. Your liver busily metabolizes alcohol at the rate of about 0.015% blood alcohol level per hour (Olson & Gerstein, 1985). Thus if you have had several drinks in quick succession, your liver will have had little chance to go to work, and your blood alcohol level will be much higher than if you had spread the same number of drinks over several hours.

In addition to the influences of body weight and pace of drinking, your level of intoxication is affected by many factors involving the rate at which your body absorbs the alcohol. If you have an empty stomach, the alcohol will be absorbed much more quickly. Carbonation also has a tendency to speed things along. Having a lot of body fat slows absorption. If you are female or approaching old age, you will absorb alcohol faster than someone who is male or relatively young. Illness and fatigue can also increase the rate of absorption. We even appear to inherit differing metabolic rates that can affect our individual rates of alcohol absorption.

How you experience your level of intoxication can vary even when your blood alcohol level does not. If you are expecting to become intoxicated, you will feel the effects of alcohol more quickly. Even the expectations of your drinking companions can affect how intoxicated you feel.

The first half of intentional drinking involves achieving the level of alcohol effect you had planned on a given evening. Perhaps you are the designated driver that night and you choose to drink diet cola instead. Or perhaps you plan on studying later in the evening, and just have a single drink with your dinner. Or maybe there is a party going on down the hall, you don't have any pressing tasks to do that evening, and you decide to drink enough to have a "really good time." Or maybe you have had a horrible week, it's Friday night, and you decide to get bombed (probably not the greatest choice, but it is still a choice). Given the information in the last few paragraphs regarding how alcohol affects the body, in addition to remembering how alcohol has affected you in the past, how much can you drink over how long a period of time and achieve your original intention? Plan your drinking accordingly, and stick to your plan.

The second half of intentional drinking involves taking responsibility for yourself and your state of impairment. You take control over any variables that might interfere with sticking to your drinking plan. For example, make sure you have a general idea of the amount of alcohol present in whatever you drink. Ordinary beer is about 3% or 4% alcohol, but some of the classy designer-type beers can be anywhere from 6% to 8% alcohol. Most wines are around 10% to 12% alcohol, but fortified wines—such as dessert-type wines that have had additional alcohol added—can be as much as 20%. The hard liquors come in a variety of proofs. Know the percentage in your beverage so you can calculate how much of it you can drink. And if you are having mixed drinks someplace other than in a cocktail lounge, mix them yourself or tell your host or hostess how you would like your drink to be measured. You may want to bring along your own measuring jigger until you find you are able to judge the proper amount by sight.

Another important factor is the size of the drink itself. Exactly how big is that glass you are holding? Remember that your calculations are based on a 12-ounce beer, a 5-ounce glass of wine, or one jigger of hard liquor. If you are drinking your beer out of a 16-ounce tumbler, or are drinking wine or mass-mixed drinks out of a recycled jelly jar, your calculations may be inaccurate. Bringing your own beer glass to the kegger or providing yourself with a recycled jelly jar that you have premeasured for volume can help ensure that you control the amount of alcohol you consume.

A college campus activity that can interfere with intentional drinking is playing drinking games. The typical drinking game involves downing drinks on the basis of the game rules, such as keeping up with the other drinkers, having to take a drink as a punishment or reward for game performance, or taking some kind of dare. If you are drinking on the basis of game rules, your drinking is being controlled by chance, or by other individuals' criteria for level of drunkenness. Intentional drinking means drinking according to your own plans, not those of chance or of someone else. Drinking games are best avoided. They can become quite dangerous.

If you have chosen to achieve a blood alcohol level that results in your becoming impaired or legally drunk, there are other precautions you will want to take for yourself. Since your judgment will be impaired, it is important that you plan to borrow someone else's frontal lobes during your period of drunkenness. Have a friend or someone else you trust keep tabs on you—someone who is either not drinking or having only a single drink. Plan ahead of time how this person will intervene on your behalf, and under what circumstances he or she will do so. You may want to turn over your car keys to this person. And, of course, make sure you have a sober designated driver if the place of intoxication is outside walking distance from where you plan to spend the night.

What if you find that you can't seem to stick to your plan? There will always be circumstances where you choose to make last-minute adjustments. Perhaps the party down the hall is a dud and you decide to go home after one drink. Or maybe you realize that you have plenty of time to do your studying on some other occasion and decide to have a second drink after your dinner. However, if you find that you frequently end up drinking more than you had planned, have trouble stopping once you get started, have life complications as a result of your drinking, or always choose to drink to the point of significant impairment, you may be on the road toward an abusive or even alcoholic drinking style. Here are some questions you might ask yourself:

- Do significant others in your life complain or express concern about your drinking?
- Have you missed work or lost a job because of your drinking?
- While drinking, have you gotten into fights or had brushes with the law?
- Do you have blackouts or pass out when you drink?

- Are you frequently hung over after a night of drinking? Or, do your hangovers become less severe after equivalent periods of drinking?
- Does your school performance go down in quality or have you been kicked out of school because of your drinking behavior?
- Have you lost friends or alienated yourself from family members because of drinking behavior?
- Have you ever been in an accident or received a DUI because of drinking and driving?

If you answer "yes" to any of these, intentional drinking may not be enough for you to use alcohol adaptively. Some people simply cannot use it without becoming abusive or alcoholic drinkers. A biological predisposition for alcoholism may even be present. If you suspect you may be a member of this group, you may want to join the 30% of the population who abstain from using alcohol.

Treating alcohol addiction. Physical addiction to alcohol is treated through detoxification—an individual is simply isolated from alcohol until the withdrawal symptoms pass. The medical treatment of alcoholism sometimes includes regular administration of **Antabuse**, a drug that causes the alcoholic to become physically ill if he or she consumes any alcohol.

However, treating alcoholism is difficult, not only because of the physical addiction, but also because in the process of becoming alcoholic a person undergoes a number of psychological changes (Maxwell, 1984). Alcohol develops a utilitarian meaning. Rather than using alcohol for social, dietary, ritual, or other more customary reasons, the future alcoholic uses it more and more for the effect: feeling better, relieving stress, entering a different state of consciousness, or being more able to act and feel like the person the future alcoholic would like to be. The "supportiveness" found in the substance encourages the person to develop a relationship with alcohol, as if it were another person, rather than treat it as the object it is.

For the future alcoholic, any rewards coinciding with using alcohol are usually more pronounced. The effect of the very first drink often feels extremely rewarding. The person finds it easier to socially interact, or may find instant personal acceptance within a drinking subculture. Thus the person drinks more often, connects alcohol to more activities, and drinks more and more at a time. As alcohol begins to become the basis of the person's social and emotional life, the future alcoholic becomes more and more preoccupied with drinking, anticipating it more, and seeing it as increasingly more essential. Such individuals are likely to become involved with a social group that supports heavy drinking. And in the process of developing this psychological dependence, the drug itself causes the development of physical dependence and its corresponding undesirable consequences.

Unfortunately, alcohol again comes to the rescue as the alcoholic deals with some of the negative consequences of alcohol addiction. A drink in the morning relieves the physical symptoms of withdrawal. As others get on the alcoholic's case about his or her drinking behavior, consuming more alcohol numbs the emotional fallout of interpersonal strife. The typical alcoholic is actually out of control of when he or she will drink and/or how much will be consumed, but through continued use the alcoholic feels as if he or she is back in control again.

Other problems develop that drinking cannot help. However, the role of alcohol in the person's life has become so important that the thought of leaving it is unthinkable. Instead, the alcoholic learns to deal with such unpleasant consequences through denial and projection. Developing beliefs such as "I could stop any time I want" and making massive and generally unsuccessful efforts to drink in a controlled manner are common forms of denial. Selective memory results in only the pleasant sensations and experiences being remembered, while the memories of undesirable consequences never make their way into long-term memory. "It's everyone/everything else's fault that I drink the way I do" is the usual path of the alcoholic's projective notions, resulting in the person becoming more and more isolated and lonely, as well as feeling as if there is nothing he or she can do about it. In this manner the alcoholic develops a distorted sense of reality, becomes further cut off from the world, and must drink even more in order to cope.

So in addition to treating the physical addiction, alcoholics are faced with the necessity of restructuring their entire self-concept, social life, and basis for emotional functioning. Rare is the person who can take on such an extensive task all on his or her own.

Alcoholics Anonymous (AA) is a grass-roots organization that evolved from alcoholics' need for support as they deal with their addictions. AA groups are made up of recovering alcoholics—anyone who has problems with alcohol consumption and is trying to quit drinking. They are mutually accepting of one another, friendly and caring, open and honest, and respectful of one another. They offer each other hope, as each finds that he or she is not as alone in their problem as they had imagined, and that others have gone before them. Thus AA provides a social network to replace the drinking culture upon which the alcoholic had become dependent for social connectedness.

This atmosphere of acceptance, honesty, and caring also helps the alcoholic cut through denial and projection. The goal of AA members is to eventually recognize, admit, and accept their alcoholism—and their lack of control over it. As they do so, they give their failed efforts at control over to some "higher power," whatever that might represent for any given individual, and take responsibility for any consequences of their drinking behavior. This model has proven to be so successful that almost all current alcohol treatment programs include some form of group support, and patients are usually encouraged to attend regular AA meetings.

In addition, AA provides a source of information on how to avoid falling off the wagon. There are a number of strategies anyone can use to try to take more control over their alcohol use:

• Limit the availability of alcohol. Attend social gatherings that do not include or have very limited emphasis on alcohol use.

• If you are going for a low-use model of drinking, keep only a single bottle of beer in the refrigerator, rather than a six-pack.

• Switch to a brand of beer or kind of drink you do not particularly enjoy.

• Do not connect your alcohol use with television, video games, watching sporting events, reading, a "19th hole," or any other pastime you pursue for enjoyment.

• Develop friendships with individuals who limit their use of alcohol.

• When you are dealing with emotional upset, develop strategies other than drinking to deal with your feelings. Try relaxation techniques, exercise, favorite distractive pastimes, talking it out with a friend—or, in especially troubling circumstances, seek help from a mental health professional.

• Remind yourself that you, not the substance, are in control. You need not give in to your impulses, including those to drink. Learn to challenge any cognitions that attempt to convince you otherwise.

Caffeine

Most people do not think of caffeine as being in the same class as other addictive drugs. It does differ in terms of social acceptability and the severity of impairment it causes. Caffeine consumption is an accepted part of our culture. We are encouraged to use caffeine through peer pressure, advertisements, and by seeing most of the significant people in our lives use caffeine-containing substances. After we try it, we are encouraged to continue by its rewards: feeling energized, having clearer thoughts, and being relieved of drowsiness.

People do not typically expire from overdoses of caffeine. You would need to consume 75–100 cups of brewed coffee before you would have ingested a lethal dose. Usually when people begin to have concerns about their caffeine consumption they are experiencing some of the more undesirable side effects, such as feeling restless or irritable, having difficulty sleeping, depression, nausea, headaches, or frequent trips to the bathroom. There are also medical conditions that are complicated by the use of caffeine, such as gastrointestinal, heart, and kidney ailments. However, there do not appear to be any serious long-term psychiatric problems due to caffeine addiction alone (Graden, 1985).

Treating caffeinism. In the past, one of the greatest difficulties in treating individuals suffering psychological symptoms of caffeine use has been convincing them that caffeine is the cause. As the general public has become more educated, this has become less of a problem. Beverage companies have also complied by marketing a number of popular beverages that do not contain caffeine, such as decaffeinated coffee and soda, herbal teas, mineral waters, and new and creative fruit juice beverages. Thus caffeine users can cut down by substituting part of their daily caffeine consumption with beverages that are at least socially and gustatorily satisfying. The biggest problem in stopping caffeine use altogether is putting up with the major-league headache and depressive symptoms that are likely to last for 2 weeks after quitting.

College students often use a lot of caffeine. "Burning the midnight oil" with a pot or two of coffee is not an unusual dorm room scenario. However, at least one study found that college students who use a lot of caffeine do not do as well as those who use less (Weiss & Laties, 1962). Of course, in a study like this there is the problem of subject selection: rather than caffeine causing students to do less well, it could be that less-skilled students rely on caffeine more in order to get by.

NICOTINE

The problem of nicotine addiction sneaked up on us. Smoking became very popular before we finally realized how damaging it could become. Currently close to half a million people a year die in the United States due to diseases caused or exacerbated by cigarette smoking (CDC, 1991).

Also, currently, more cigarette smoking is found among the poor and less educated (Pierce et al., 1989). The less educated are less likely to be aware of the risks and mechanisms that result in health problems. The poor are more likely to be drawn in by advertising that connects smoking with wealth, power, and glamour; or perhaps they feel they have less to lose. Thanks to aggressive educational campaigns, the number of young people who begin smoking was going down in recent years. This trend continued until 1993, curiously not long after the introduction of "Joe Camel" and other cigarette advertising logos that appeal to children. And, perhaps as misguided efforts toward equality, the percentage of new smokers who are female has increased.

Recent studies have shown that even breathing secondhand smoke can impair our health (DHHS, 1986). This has resulted in antismoking campaigns becoming even more militant. Smoking is no longer allowed in many public areas, cigarettes are seen as fair game for special taxation, and those who smoke tend to be looked down upon by most of society. The inconvenience, expense, and humiliation of being a part of the smoking population often play a role in the smoker's desire to quit, and the overwhelming majority of smokers do wish they could stop (Graden, 1985). Unfortunately, nicotine addiction is extremely powerful, and quitting is difficult.

Most current smokers began smoking while young. New smokers are usually children and teenagers, who begin due to peer pressure. Nobody enjoys his or her first cigarette, but after the new smoker begins to appreciate the burst of energy provided by the nicotine, the distastefulness of inhaling smoke becomes easier to ignore.

Treating nicotine addiction. The best way to avoid nicotine addiction is to never use nicotine at all. Once addicted, you will be fighting an uphill battle, perhaps for the rest of your life. Most people who quit will eventually start up again. However, there are some methods that seem to be more effective or popular than others (Schwartz, 1987).

Most people who decide they no longer wish to smoke simply stop on their own. While their resolve may not last forever, it does increase the feelings of self-efficacy and self-control that encourage further attempts to quit. Another popular method is to seek out groups and clinical programs, which approach nicotine addiction with education, cognitive strategies, and self-monitoring. These have slightly more success than going it alone, probably because of the advantages of group support and education.

Medical interventions have experimented with the use of a number of psychotropic medications. The most effective so far, however, appears to be the use of nicotine gum and patches. These reduce the amount of nicotine the addict is getting but give them enough to be able to deal with withdrawal symptoms. The treatment resulting in the fewest patients returning to smoking appears to be a combination of using nicotine substitutes and teaching cognitive strategies.

If you are trying to cut back on or discontinue nicotine use, here are a number of strategies you might try.

- Quit "cold turkey" rather than cutting back a little at a time. You will be more likely to succeed.
- Arrange to be in settings where you cannot smoke, such as the nonsmoking section of the restaurant, nonsmoking friends' homes, etc.
- Take up activities where smoking is not practical or becomes an impairment, such as physical activities.
- Find something else to do with your hands or mouth during times you previously had smoked, such as shelling and eating sunflower seeds, chewing on a toothpick, doodling, chewing gum, or fiddling with a pencil or carrot stick.
- Change to a brand of cigarettes you do not like.
- If you decide to cut back rather than go "cold turkey," limit the number of cigarettes you have on hand at any given moment.

- Since relapse is usually connected to emotional upset, find something to do other than smoke when you are frustrated. Remember that the "relaxed" feeling you have after smoking is really just removal of nicotine withdrawal symptoms.
- Put away the money you save from reducing your smoking and plan to spend it on something you have always wanted.
- Remind yourself of all the negatives of smoking: chronic coughing, emphysema, risk of lung cancer and other medical complications, smelly clothes and living environment, others not wanting to be around you, the expense, etc.

Illicit Drugs

The potential undesirable consequences of using alcohol, caffeine, and nicotine tend to develop slowly over time, but illicit drug use presents big problems from the start. In most cases, you are engaging in illegal activity with your first use. Some of the faster-acting drugs, such as crack cocaine, can result in immediate addiction. Street drugs are an expensive habit and, if you become an addict, can get in the way of spending money on your other favorite pastimes, or even necessities. Many addicts turn to crime to support their habits; in fact, it is estimated that 25% of property crimes, 15% of violent crimes, and 14% of homicides are directly related to drug use or drug dealing (Beck et al., 1993). Interacting with drug dealers in itself puts you in contact with the criminal element, which can result in additional risky situations. If you carelessly share a needle—which you may be tempted to do if you are in the throes of withdrawal—you increase your chances of becoming infected with a host of deadly illnesses, such as hepatitis and AIDS. And since safety controls do not exist for street drugs, you are at risk for serious illness or even death after using your very first dose.

These drawbacks alone suggest that it would be very difficult to set up a pattern of illicit drug use that is not maladaptive. So why do people do it? There are two separate issues involved: why people get started and why they continue. People who begin drug use are usually in settings where the substances are readily available and that support substance use as a means of stress reduction, socializing, or just fitting in with the crowd. Family problems and low self-esteem are also often correlates.

The high incidence of drug use among inner-city African American citizens has sometimes led to the inaccurate notion that drug addiction is an affliction of minority races and the poor. During the Vietnam War, when many soldiers from all walks of life became addicted to heroin, continuing with the addiction after returning to the United States was associated more with being white, older, and having parents with histories of crime and/or alcoholism (Jaffe, 1985).

Users usually continue to use because of the reward value of the drug itself. In the user's mind the short-term pleasant effects, as well as the addict's immediate desire to escape the unpleasant withdrawal symptoms, often outweigh the long-term dangers involved with acquiring and reusing the drug. The euphoria and feelings of well-being produced by most street drugs prevent the user from experiencing the anxiety we normally feel during inadequate life management, and thus users do not experience one of our major motivators for getting our acts together. And because of the increased availability and reduced price of many street drugs in recent years, expense has become less of a deterrent.

Avoiding illicit drug use. The most effective way to prevent an illicit drug habit is to avoid that first hit. Since peer pressure and drug availability play such major roles, one of the best preventive techniques is to choose your friends carefully. If you go to a party where your entire social circle is passing around a bowl, and they hand it to you, it is going to be extremely hard to resist.

Some individuals become addicts because of drugs that were originally prescribed by their physicians. If your physician suggests using painkillers, amphetamines, minor tranquilizers, or some other psychotropic medication, do not immediately accept a prescription. Carefully discuss the medication's addictive properties. Then weigh the potential benefits of using the drug against the risks of use and abuse.

Treating addiction. The constant changes in the availability of different drugs and which ones enjoy current popularity create difficulty when attempting to develop effective treatment modes. When heroin became a major addiction problem in the 1960s and 1970s, researchers developed **methadone**. Heroin addicts who take methadone are relieved of their craving for heroin; and should they use heroin anyway, the methadone will block its euphoric effects. Methadone therapy appears to be an effective treatment for heroin addiction, although getting off the methadone can pose a new problem (Jaffe, 1985).

Crack cocaine is the fastest-growing addiction of the 1990s, and medical research has yet to come up with a cure for it. Nor are there any medically based cures for dependence on marijuana, LSD, PCP, and most other street drugs. Even the most popular attempted cure for addiction to prescription medications consists of little more than taking away the prescription.

Currently cognitive and behavioral techniques appear to be the most effective aids for dealing with addiction to street drugs. Behaviorally, addicts need to learn how to find social support, acceptance, and a sense of well-being without using. Support groups such as Narcotics Anonymous are useful in this respect. Most clinical treatment programs also include group work, since mutual support is such a big part of getting off drugs. Addicts also need to learn how to avoid situations where they will be likely to use, or be tempted to use. Educational programs—as are also part of most treatment protocols—help addicts learn about their own patterns of use and how to steer clear of them.

Beck and his colleagues (1993) point out how addictive behavior consists largely of having an urge and giving in to it. There are a number of people in this world who try drugs but do not subsequently become addicted. Although they also may experience the urge to use, they are able to resist by conjuring up common sense logic and unpleasant memories of past use. Therefore another useful treatment method is to teach addicts to think like nonaddicts and thus become better skilled at resisting their urges. They can be taught to challenge any irrational beliefs that fuel their drug use, such as

- If I feel an urge, I must satisfy it.
- I *need* the drug in order to stay sane.
- My social/occupational/sexual/academic performance is better when I use.
- Just one more hit won't make any difference.
- The satisfaction I will feel is worth any consequences.
- I can't stand the discomfort of withdrawal.
- I've had a hard day, so I'm entitled.

Personal Growth and Substance Abuse

The preceding discussions point out how psychoactive substances become abused as the user leans on them as a means of coping with stress and producing good feelings. Such strategies for living have a profound effect on the overall developmental process.

For example, Erikson's theory of psychosocial development pointed out how we resolve various conflicts and develop certain competencies during different stages of our lives, such as intimacy versus isolation and identity versus role confusion. Part of the impetus toward building those competencies is the anxiety we experience as we face the new conflict. As substances numb this anxiety, they also numb our motivation toward successful stage resolution.

Likewise, Adler's inferiority/superiority complex and issues of social interest risk inadequate resolution. The substance abuser artificially relieves any feelings of inferiority and therefore has no need to learn to feel more superior through learning, achievements, and self-knowledge. Anesthetizing feelings of social interest results in less need for social striving, thus fewer feelings of social connectedness.

The effect of substance abuse on our capacity for sound judgment can have long-term effects on our personal growth, especially during adolescence and young adulthood. As we enter the adult world we make decisions that will affect the rest of our lives, decisions such as whether or not we will go to school, what career we will choose, whom we will marry, and so on. Substance abuse interferes with using our best judgment as we make these choices. Likewise, it is difficult to let go of Gould's "magical thinking" of childhood if we have anesthetized the intellectual capacity necessary to be able to develop the more realistic beliefs that would normally replace such thinking patterns.

The effect of substance abuse on a person's life is so pervasive that it expectably affects the lives of those around him or her as well. Over the last couple of decades, researchers have closely examined the families and significant others of substance abusers. The next section will share the commonalities these observations have revealed concerning the personal growth patterns of those within social systems of substance abusers.

Growing Up in a Substance-Abusing Home

Regardless of the type of substance a family member might abuse, those who grow up in a substance-abusing home can develop personal growth impairments. Claudia Black (1981) was among the first to extensively describe such an effect in terms of parents' alcoholic habits on their children's development. She points out that the alcoholic home is ruled by inconsistency and unpredictability. The functioning of the home centers on how sober or intoxicated the alcoholic is on a given day, rather than on consistent structure and routine. Since children need structure to feel secure, they find ways of taking control and thus providing it for themselves in an alcoholic home by taking on various roles: the responsible one, the adjuster, the placater, or the acting-out child.

Oldest and only children often adopt the role of being the **responsible one**. They take over the responsibilities that are normally handled by parents. They may care for younger siblings, prepare meals, perform household chores, and even take care of their intoxicated parents as though they were the children.

Younger children are more likely to become **adjusters**. They learn to provide structure for themselves by adapting to whatever circumstances they find when they get home. If there is no food in the house, they either go without or find food elsewhere. If drunken father orders them not to play in the school basketball game that evening, they simply stay home. If mother is in an intoxicated rage, they put on their coats and spend the night at a friend's house. If Dad gives away the family pet, they learn to do without. They tend to keep a low profile, so they will not be noticed. They do not bring friends home because they do not want to risk having their friends see passed-out parents lying on the floor. They learn to turn off their feelings, so that their many disappointments will not create such an overwhelming sting.

Children who tend to be sensitive are likely to become **placaters**. They deal with all the pain and turmoil going on around them by trying to comfort and please those who are distressed. They find ways to distract the intoxicated mother from yelling at another sibling; they get in between their parents as the alcoholic father victimizes the mother; they console the depressed, sobbing parent who is contemplating suicide. Thus they learn to deal with their own pain by denying it as they relieve the pain of others.

Some children organize the chaos by becoming an "acting-out child." They deal with their frustration by retaliating and causing problems of their own. As they do so, they draw attention away from the family alcoholism and draw fire onto themselves. While taking on the role of being the "sick" one in the family provides its own set of discomforts, at least it provides a structure, and it gives the child some sense of control.

Regardless of which role or roles children adopt, they also cope by learning specific rules for living. They learn not to trust: Parents typically are denying the obvious problem of alcohol abuse, making promises they either forget or cannot keep, and cannot be depended upon for support and guidance. They learn not to feel: It is too painful, and the denial system of the alcoholic family does not support expression of feelings anyway. They learn not to talk: The secrecy of the alcoholism does not allow for freedom of expression, and ignoring it makes it easier to deal with anyway. The resulting inner experience is loneliness, ongoing unidentifiable anxiety, and despair.

As children of alcoholics enter adulthood they carry with them whatever rules for living got them through their childhood experiences. As a result they often have difficulty with interpersonal relationships, since they do not trust, are out of touch with their feelings, and do not know sincere self-expression. They are prime candidates for becoming alcoholic themselves, not only because of any possible genetic predisposition, but also because of whatever role they chose to play as children. The responsible ones may find that alcohol is the only means by which they can relax. The adjusters may use alcohol as a means of being able to ignore problems around them or deal with their feelings of powerlessness. The placaters use it to cope with their sensitivity and pain. And the acting-out children continue to take control by becoming acting-out drinkers.

Another unfortunate tendency of children of alcoholics is that of forming relationships with others that allow them to continue to play their childhood roles. The next section discusses this type of dysfunctional relationship.

Developing Codependency

Becoming an adjuster, responsible one, or placater is actually an asset for children of alcoholics when they adopt the roles, since such roles help children cope as they endure horrendous childhood situations. And since the roles' activities relieve pain, they are reinforcing. Thus as such children enter adulthood, these role behaviors are hard to give up. When people continue to behave in this manner even after they have left their dysfunctional environments, they are suffering the effects of continued **codependency**.

At first, most codependent people do not even recognize that their ideas of interrelating are significantly different from anybody else's, their own attitudes and preferred behaviors seeming normal. Over time, however, they find they have difficulties in their more intimate relationships. As they choose significant others, they have the incredibly bad luck of always ending up with another alcoholic, batterer, unfaithful type, or other such dysfunctional partner. They usually do not consciously look for such individuals but do tend to feel more at home with them, since these types allow codependent individuals to continue playing out their learned scripts for living.

Breaking away from codependent behavior patterns involves addressing several symptoms of waylaid personal growth (Mellody & Miller, 1989). One of the most important ones is setting an appropriate level of self-esteem. As a codependent person, you could go either direction. You may not develop any positive self-esteem, perceiving from your parent's alcoholic behavior that you are not worth being loved or taken care of and are probably to blame for whatever goes wrong. Or, you may learn to cope by developing narcissisticly high self-esteem: Since nobody else seems to recognize your worth, you place inflated emphasis on your own ideas, abilities, wants, or needs. Both outcomes are destructive in interpersonal relationships.

How you develop personal boundaries also suffers. The rules for your interpersonal relationships may be extremely rigid, either keeping people at a distance or demanding an exact, unvarying script of behavior. Or, your interpersonal boundaries may become almost nonexistent, as you give up any individuality or self-determination in order to become hopelessly enmeshed with the life or dictates of another person. Appropriate self-expression may not be learned, since the alcoholic home tends to be characterized by either nonassertive or aggressive expression.

Needs and wants are frequently confused, since neither are consistently met. And even if you do recognize the difference, you may not have learned how to go about meeting them appropriately. Relationships suffer as a result of your not being able to tell your significant others what you want or need, or from expecting others to meet an unrealistic proportion of your needs.

The denial ruling the alcoholic home results in difficulty recognizing and defining reality. You learn not to trust your own experiencing. Thus as you enter adult life, you are faced with a dilemma: Is reality what others tell me, what logic tells me, or what I see for myself? Relationships suffer as a result of your inability to sort out what is really happening now and what is part of an old script.

The key to overcoming these symptoms is to break down the denial and become more aware of all that has been denied: who you are, what you feel, what you know, and what you want or need. As you become more self-aware, you can begin to learn new ways of perceiving and interacting. Most alcohol treatment centers include programs for helping family members deal with their codependent behavior. Also Al-Anon, an offshoot of AA, uses principles similar to those of AA as a means of helping people recognize and deal with their codependent dysfunctions. There are now also ACOA (adult children of alcoholics) groups for those who may not currently be involved in codependent relationships but who wish to deal with the baggage they still carry around from previous codependent living.

Expanding Your Experience

During my youth, drug use became romanticized. It was the "in" thing to do. Marijuana was having its first big surge in popularity. Relatively new concoctions such as LSD, heroin, and speed were appearing on the streets. Alcohol, of course, was also still a popular choice. We did not take drug use very seriously—in fact, one of the better-held school secrets was the fraternity-sown marijuana amidst the plants in the concrete structures in front of the student union building.

Unfortunately, romanticizing drug use creates false images. These false images do not project the less-popular potential consequences that users may suffer. As a student I observed a number of individuals whose life goals were necessarily changed, because of the effects substance use had on their grades.

The exercises for this chapter will help you consider the seriousness or nonseriousness of the impact of substance use on your life. The first exercise helps you understand how you can reduce your chances of getting yourself into difficulties with your amount of alcohol consumption. The second gives you an indication of the possibility of being a problem drinker or alcoholic. The third assesses your potential for being or becoming codependent. The fourth exercise gives you a chance to show off your small group's acting skills, as you demonstrate methods of handling an intoxicated friend. With the last exercise, you can test your knowledge of street-drug slang.

Study Questions

1. What are the differences between substance abuse, substance tolerance, and substance dependence?
2. Why are opiates so addictive?
3. What is the most widely used illegal stimulant? Legal stimulants?
4. What dangers are involved with the use of hallucinogens?
5. How would you go about creating an alcoholic concoction that is 50% alcohol?
6. Describe the progressive effects of alcohol intoxication on the brain and behavior.
7. What are the disadvantages of drinking as a college student?

8. What is meant by "intentional drinking"?
9. Describe four different ways in which extreme alcohol intoxication can result in death.
10. What sorts of events occurring in your life might cue you to the fact that you have an alcohol problem?
11. What psychological reasons encourage an alcoholic to keep on drinking?
12. Describe strategies you might use in order to cut down your consumption of alcoholic beverages.
13. Do you think caffeine helps or hinders academic performance? Explain your answer.
14. Describe strategies you could use to help yourself stop smoking.
15. List the risks of using street drugs even once.
16. How can substance abuse in general impair personal growth?
17. Describe the roles children learn to play when they grow up in an alcoholic home. Explain how each of these roles can contribute to the child growing up to become an alcoholic.
18. What is meant by "codependent"? What sorts of rules for interrelating are learned by those who are codependent?

Chapter Nine

Sexuality
Dancing in the Moonlight

That which we call a rose by any other word would smell as sweet.
—Shakespeare, *Romeo and Juliet*

The pragmatic purpose of sexual behavior is continuation of the species. Needless to say, the song and dance of sexuality in our species has become much more complex than simple reproduction. Thanks to our larger cerebral cortexes, we have ensured the likelihood of reproduction by developing many pleasant correlates of reproductive behavior. How we experience and express ourselves sexually is as intertwined with our individuality as any other aspect of our personalities. Arguably, our sexuality is one of the most personal and intimate reflections of who we are as individuals.

Understanding Your Sexual Identity

Sexual identity goes beyond sexual orientation, gender identity, and sexual practice preferences. It is a here-and-now part of our experiencing. It exists regardless of whether or not we are currently expressing ourselves within a sexual relationship. In this respect, we are *all* sexual beings, regardless of our values, attraction patterns, beliefs, or preferred sexual behaviors. However, values, attraction patterns, beliefs, and preferences of behavior do play a significant role in how we actually express our sexuality. When they do not, our "real" and "ideal" selves conflict and our sexual identities suffer. Thus an important part of understanding our sexual identity is understanding who we are as individuals in general.

The emotional bonding that results from sexual activity is another factor to consider as we express our sexuality. Since sexual activity can result in reproduction, our tendency to emotionally bond with our sexual partners is fortunate. Such bonding increases the chances that any children produced will have two parents caring for them, rather than one, usually increasing the resources for child care. As with any other human attribute, the degree of emotional bonding we experience as a result of sexual activity will vary. Yet regardless of its level of intensity, it is still a significant piece of our sexuality.

So how do you experience yourself in general? Are you more driven by your immediate impulses or your values? How do you feel about how you sort out and apply both impulses and values? How much responsibility do you feel as a result of the consequences of your behaviors? Does your behavior feel more comfortable when it contributes to your sense of social striving, or are you more interested in what you get out of any situation for yourself? How important are caring and fairness to you in your choice of behaviors?

Likewise, how do you experience your sexual attitudes and values? Do you view sexual behavior primarily as a body function, like eating and sleeping? Or is it more like the merging of two souls, almost religious in nature? Is it just a "game" between potential sexual partners? Or do you feel that sexual activity without love and commitment is disappointing or even degrading? How important are certain characteristics of potential partners as you experience sexual attraction toward them? Is your sexuality an important part of your life, or is it less important to you than other current life pursuits?

Your answers to the above questions can serve in part as a guideline for how you express your sexuality. The rest of this chapter will describe a collection of aspects of sexual functioning, as well as correlating factors such as contraception and sexually transmitted diseases. As you examine them, consider how these component parts of sexuality fit in with your personal sexual identity and how you can experience and express your sexuality consistently with how you see yourself as a person.

Defining Sexuality

Sexuality incorporates many aspects of our functioning. Zgourides (1995) describes how sexuality is in fact **biopsychosocial**. In other words, biology, psychology, and sociology all play a role. He illustrates the biopsychosocial nature of sexuality with the example of "Sally":

> Sally was raised to believe that "nice" women do not enjoy sex or have orgasms (social). Because she experiences distress about

not having orgasms during intercourse with her husband (psychological), she concentrates too much on her sexual performance, which distracts her from fully immersing herself in sexual activity (psychological). In time, her nervous system becomes so aroused that orgasm is difficult or impossible (biological). Berating herself about not having orgasms (psychological), she makes excessive demands of her husband and inadvertently creates a hostile sexual environment that only adds to her problems (social). (p. 10)

Reiss's formal definition of sexuality also reflects the biopsychosocial perspective, referring to it as "the erotic arousal and genital responses resulting from following the shared scripts of society" (Reiss, 1989). As a means of putting this into everyday English, let's divide up the definition and look at its component parts.

Erotic Arousal

What leads to erotic arousal? The underpinnings of what "turns us on" are complex, intertwined with a number of biological, psychological, and sociological factors. From the biological standpoint, the presence of hormones such as **androgens** appears to play a role in whether or not we experience the feeling of arousal (Urdry & Billy, 1987). Introduction of additional hormones also appears to affect our feelings of sexual arousal. Adolescent girls who have begun menstruating at earlier ages tend to begin having intercourse sooner than those who mature later (Newcomer & Urdry, 1984). Also, women tend to experience more desire for sex around the time they ovulate (Stanislaw & Rice, 1988). So it appears that sexual arousal, like all of our other subjective experiences, has some basis in our physiology.

Sexual scripts. Our **sexual scripts** also play a role in arousal (Gagnon, 1977). A sexual script is a highly personalized collection of environmental, interpersonal, and situational factors that make up a person's ideal sexual encounter. It includes the type of lover the person finds attractive, the most exciting setting, the behaviors and emotions leading up to sexual activity, and the style of sexual activity itself. The closer a real-world situation comes to your sexual script, the more aroused you will feel.

Fantasizing about your sexual script typically leads to arousal. In fact, fantasizing your script during actual sexual activity is likely to enhance the quality of your sexual experience. This is a common practice and is considered normal. Unfortunately, some individuals feel their lovers should be thinking only of them during sex and perceive any fantasies their partners might have as some form of "unfaithfulness." First, sexual fantasies don't necessarily reflect what a person would really like to do; they merely serve the purpose of creating and enhancing arousal (Sue, 1979). Second, you cannot expect your partner to suddenly do away with all the biological, psychological, and sociological factors that led up to the development of his or her sexual script just because your real-life attributes do not fit into the picture. Your partner's private fantasies are therefore not to be taken personally.

Pornography is another way you might come into contact with your sexual script. The more a pornographic presentation resembles your fantasy, the more arousal you are likely to feel. This is probably one of the reasons why pornography continues to meet some social tolerance and proliferate despite the connection found between pornography and devaluation of and violence toward women.

Both men and women appear to be aroused by pornography (Heiman, 1977). Is there anyone out there, male or female, who did not appreciate the arousing qualities of that infamous love scene in the movie *Ghost*? However, there do appear to be some variations in the aspects of sexual depictions men and women find to be exciting (Knoth et al., 1988). Men are much more likely to become aroused by the actual visual stimulus of an attractive person, pictures depicting sexual activity, or narratives that describe the pragmatics of a sexual encounter. Women are more likely to report feelings of arousal when there is some form of romance, affection, or interpersonal sensitivity involved. Since both types of stimulation are present in the *Ghost* love scene, it has succeeded in appealing to almost everyone's erotic sensitivities. This difference between men and women also might explain why women seem to enjoy romance novels more, even when explicit sexual aspects are not included.

Emotions and arousal. Emotions affect our capacity for sexual arousal in numerous ways. In our culture, love is the main emotion linked to sexual feelings. The more intimate a relationship is, and the longer it lasts, the more likely it is that sexual activity will occur (Sprecher, 1989). Such a prerequisite is in fact adaptive. If you are going to have a sexual relationship, it is better to have it with someone who cares enough about you to avoid hurting or taking advantage of you, would stand by you in the event of pregnancy, and would take any precautions necessary to avoid giving you a sexually transmitted disease.

A moderate amount of anxiety can also increase feelings of arousal (Barlow, 1986). The roots of anxiety are numerous, especially for initial sexual encounters:

Will I be able to perform adequately?

Will I enjoy it?

What is it really like?

Will I get dumped if I do (or don't) give in?

Will this cement the commitment of the relationship?

On the other hand, extreme anxiety dampens sexual arousal. Intense anxieties, whether they evolve from daily stress or problems in the relationship, can lead to shunning sexual activity. Anxiety is the cause of many sexual dysfunctions. One reason may be because of its distracting nature. Sexual arousal requires that most of your attention be directed to what you are experiencing; anxiety disrupts attention span.

Depression is also a cause of reduced sexual arousal. Like anxiety, the cause in part may lie in the reduced capacity for concentration that is found among those who are depressed. When compared with nondepressed individuals, those who are depressed have been found to have fewer sexual thoughts and fantasies and less frequent sexual activity and to report feeling less satisfaction and pleasure when they do engage in sexual activity (Reynolds et al., 1988).

Physical stimulation. Touching certain parts of our bodies results in feelings of sexual arousal. Areas of the body that are sexually responsive to touch are called **erogenous zones**. The genital area is the most obvious erogenous zone. Our culture also perceives touching that involves lips, breasts, and buttocks as having sexual potential. However, just about any part of the body can become an erogenous zone, given the particular individual's sensitivities and the nature of the physical stimulation. Likewise, even direct stimulation of the genital area can fail to cause arousal. Perhaps the person is not in the mood. Or perhaps the context is wrong: Rarely does a woman report feeling sexual arousal while receiving a gynecological examination.

Genital Responses

Psychological arousal leads to physical responding. Our bodies follow predictable patterns when we experience sexual arousal. In spite of the remarkable contrast between the physical characteristics of male and female genitalia, men and women appear to share a similar physical experience. The human sexual-response cycle for both men and women proceeds through four phases of sexual responding: **excitement**, **plateau**, **orgasm**, and **resolution** (Masters & Johnson, 1966). However, there are differences between how men and women might experience those phases. The similarities and differences are charted in Figure 9.1 and explained below.

Male physical responding. The most noticeable condition of male sexual arousal is erection of the penis. During the excitement phase, blood flow increases to the man's genital area, leading not only to an erection but also to enlargement of the testicles. The man experiences a rise in heart rate, blood pressure, and respiration, as well as erection of

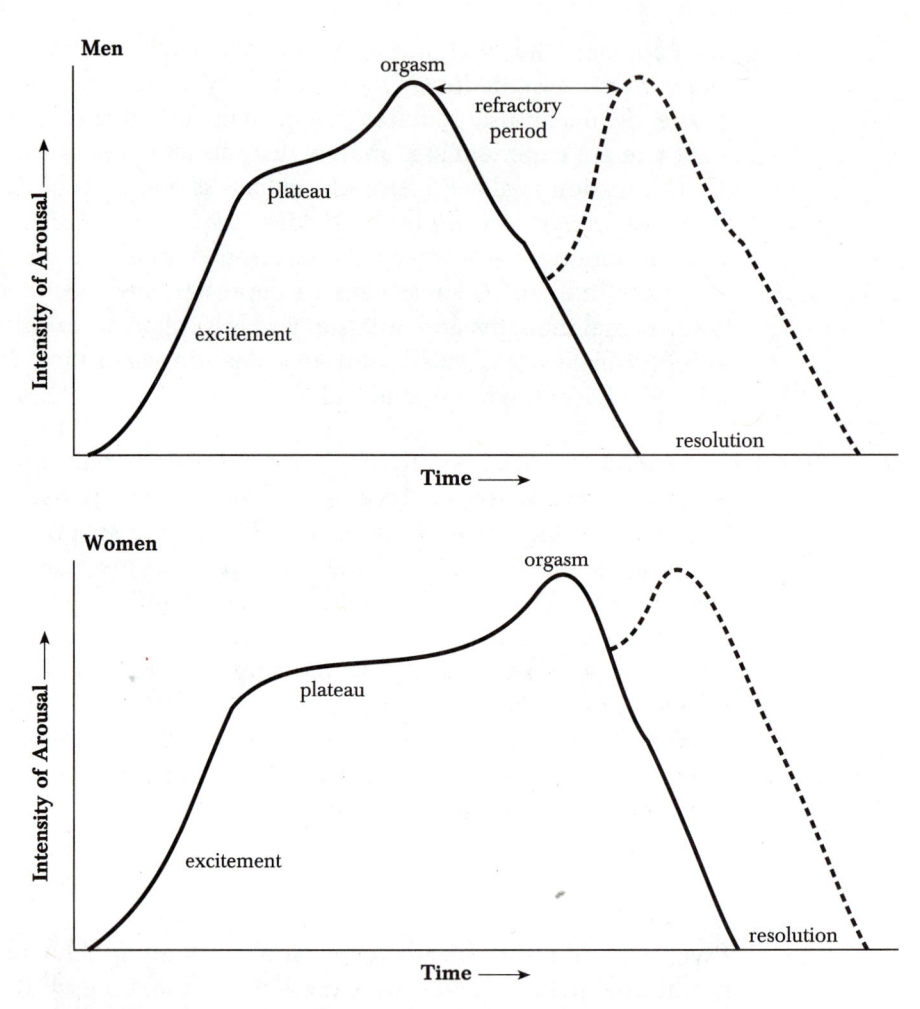

FIGURE 9.1
Sexual response cycles of men and women.

his nipples and numerous other bodily changes. If stimulation ends, the excitement and physical responding also will subside.

If stimulation continues, the man reaches the plateau phase. Excitement becomes more intense, and the man's urge to continue stimulation increases. Semen often begins leaking from the man's penis, as his body prepares for the reproductive programming of sexual behavior. If stimulation ceases, the excitement and physical responding will still subside, but it will take longer–not to mention that the man will experience such an abrupt end as considerably frustrating and uncomfortable.

Prolonged stimulation during the plateau phase typically results in orgasm. Up until orgasm, we still have control over whether we continue stimulation and the corresponding sexual behavior. At the point of orgasm, our bodies take over. Orgasm is a reflexive release of the sexual tension and is subjectively experienced as powerfully pleasurable. During orgasm the man will ejaculate, as contractions of muscles at the base of his penis release the sperm-laden semen.

Immediately following orgasm the man experiences a **refractory period**, during which he is incapable of experiencing either an erection or an orgasm. As the refractory period ends the man may become stimulated to another erection and proceed to orgasm again. If stimulation ends he will go through the resolution phase, returning to lower levels of sexual arousal as the blood engorging his genital area is dispelled throughout his body.

Female sexual responding. As a woman begins experiencing sexual arousal, her body prepares itself for intercourse. Like the man, the woman experiences an increase in heart rate, respiration, and blood pressure during the excitement phase. Her breasts swell and her nipples become erect. As blood rushes to her genital area, it results in some swelling of the **clitoris**—the organ that will allow her to experience orgasm—and surrounding structures. As the woman's vagina prepares itself to accommodate an erect penis it lengthens, dilates, and begins releasing lubrication.

As with men, the characteristic bodily responding intensifies during the plateau phase. However, during traditional heterosexual intercourse women usually need more time to reach the more intense feelings of arousal. Women also may develop a **sex flush**, a mottling of the skin, as stimulation and arousal intensifies. Discontinuing stimulation at this point is as frustrating and uncomfortable for women as it is for men, but as with men, the feelings of arousal and physical responding will eventually subside.

Women also experience orgasm as a series of involuntary muscular contractions. The muscles surrounding the outer third of the vagina reflexively and rhythmically contract, contributing to the pleasurable experience of orgasm. Different from men, women do not have a refractory period following orgasm. So if stimulation continues and the woman is so inclined, she may have a second, third, and fourth orgasm; in rare instances she could have as many as 50. If stimulation ceases, the woman's body proceeds through the resolution phase, returning to a resting state.

Following the Shared Scripts of Society

Different cultures have differing views of what constitutes an acceptable way to express sexuality. These formal and informal rules and regulations have as dramatic an effect on how we express our sexuality as do our individual differences. With whom is it okay to have sex? Where? When? How? Why?

Sex and marriage. In our culture, sexual behavior was originally socially sanctioned only within the context of marriage. One of the main reasons for this requirement was the tendency of sexual activity to produce children. If a woman is married when she has a child, she will be more likely to have the necessary financial backing and other forms of child-rearing support. If a man is married to a woman and her sexual behavior is marital only, he can know for sure whether or not he is the father of any children that are produced.

In the sixties and seventies a number of technological and social changes occurred that resulted in what has been called the **sexual revolution**. Birth control pills came on the market. Abortion became legalized in many states. The feminist movement resulted in women being able to get better-paying jobs and thus depend less on men for an income. Researchers dispelled the myth of Freud's "vaginal orgasm" (it is actually clitoral) and of the belief that women do not have as much sexual potential as men, freeing women to acknowledge the realities of their sexual sensing. The easing up on fetters such as unwanted pregnancies, financial dependency, the "double standard" described in the next section, and sexual misinformation has resulted in women becoming inclined to have sex more freely.

The problem with the sexual revolution is that it became intertwined with the gender revolution. The feminist movement strives to ensure women the same opportunities as men, such as training programs, career paths once predominantly male-occupied, equal pay for equal work, and freedom to take part in other previously male-dominated activities. So as women began writing new sexual scripts, the scenarios that popped to mind were those more common to men.

While it seemed like a new freedom at first, many women have found that it is not a part of their nature to have casual, meaningless sex with the same frequency as is found among men. Furthermore, the sexual revolution seems to have benefited men more than women. Men can more easily find sex partners, without being "trapped" into marriage. The number of pregnancies occurring outside marriage has skyrocketed in recent years, and women still bear most of the brunt of the reproductive consequences of sexual behavior. As cohabitation has become more accepted, men can have not only a live-in sex partner but also someone who will in all likelihood take over the responsibilities of the traditional role of housekeeper. More relaxed attitudes toward sexual activity have resulted in oddities such as "swinging," "wife-swapping," and other "open marriage"-type arrangements, all of which tend to be enjoyed more by the men involved than by the women (Murstein et al., 1985). Some women feel that if they had really won the sexual revolution, men would have moved more toward feminine sexual values!

Gender biases. For centuries many cultures, including our own, have prescribed a double standard for sexual expression by men and women. Men are given more leeway. If men with high sex drives have multiple sex partners, they are simply "sowing their wild oats." If women with high sex drives have a lot of sex partners, they are "promiscuous." Even our slang concerning sexual activity implies a woman's diminished right toward and need for sexual gratification: men "get some," while women "put out."

The sexual revolution has taken a little of the steam out of the double standard. Yet it still remains, not necessarily because men are out to subjugate women but, in part, because of feelings of women themselves. There are basic differences between how men and women approach intimacy. As you may recall from Chapter 3, women tend to express more relationship-oriented concerns than men. These characteristics appear to apply to their sexuality as well, as women show a greater preference toward sexual activity within the context of an intimate relationship.

However, there are societal variables that have gummed up the works even as women attempt to express their sexuality within their own framework. Cassell (1984) points out how the differing cultural expectations have resulted in women applying a **fantasy reflex** when faced with sexual arousal and the potential for sexual activity. Our culture typically views sexuality as more acceptable for women when it is in the context of love and commitment. One way for a woman to be able to allow herself to be sexual in such an atmosphere and not feel like a tramp is to plug into the "swept away" phenomenon. When she feels overwhelming arousal, she interprets it as being "hopelessly in love." She lets herself be swept off her feet, and since she perceives herself as being controlled by a socially sanctioned motivator for women's sexual behavior, she does not judge herself so harshly.

Thus men and women often approach sex with two different sexual scripts. While women typically see love as necessary for being able to enjoy sex, only about 1 in 10 men report that love is a prerequisite for enjoying sexual intercourse (Pietropinto & Siminauer, 1977). The first time a man goes to bed with a woman may mark the end of a competitive, goal-directed series of behaviors. Having reached his goal, unless he had some other reason to pursue the woman, his next step may be to say good-bye. A woman who follows the swept away script typically sees sex as a beginning. Her agreeing to sexual activity is more likely to imply an expectancy of deeper commitment or at least continuing intimacy—the beginning of a beautiful relationship. Even a woman who introduces sexuality into her relationship because of more-genuine, intimate caring—even love—may despair if she discovers her partner has seen the relationship as little more than a potential notch in his belt. Little wonder that women often come away from sexual encounters feeling used, while men may come away feeling pressured and trapped!

Masturbation. **Masturbation** is stimulation of the genitals that produces sexual pleasure and/or orgasm. Men typically masturbate by manipulating their penises by hand, while women usually rub their clitoral areas. It may occur as self-stimulation, or as a result of being physically manipulated by a sex partner.

Society has typically looked askance at this practice, more for perceived moral reasons than anything demonstrated empirically. Referred to as "self-abuse," many of us have grown up hearing rumors that it causes maladies such as sterility, insanity, blindness, hair growing on palms, genitals falling off, and so forth. Some individuals believe masturbation is immoral because of religious prohibitions against "spilling seed." Masturbation has even been purported—erroneously—to lead to homosexuality.

In spite of societal and religious protestations, the vast majority of people masturbate. Even in the 1940s, when sexual attitudes were much more restrictive than they are today, 95% of men and 60% of women reported having masturbated (Kinsey et al., 1948). It is common practice even among married individuals. Around 70% of husbands and wives report continuing masturbation after marriage (Hunt, 1974). Some spouses fear that if their partners masturbate it is because they are not satisfied with the marital sex. This is not true. Only you can know exactly the right pressure at exactly the right time in exactly the right place for maximum pleasure to occur. Desire to experience this pleasure does not indicate lack of interest in marital sex. Furthermore, unless you have experienced orgasm often enough to know how your body responds, you will have a difficult time explaining to your partner how to satisfy you.

There are advantages of masturbation that go beyond immediate pleasure. The concentration necessary for producing, intensifying, and culminating genital responding may need to be learned. Masturbating is one way of training yourself to focus successfully, and it is often included in sex therapy techniques. Mutual masturbation is one of the safer forms of sex, in terms both of preventing pregnancy and of avoiding contraction of sexually transmitted diseases. It also is a means of relieving sexual tension when your partner is not available or during times when you do not wish to deal with the entanglements of a sexual relationship.

Homosexuality. Homosexuality refers to individuals who are sexually attracted toward those of the same gender as themselves. In the past homosexuality has been erroneously referred to as **sexual preference**. Homosexuals do not choose their patterns of arousal, any more than do heterosexuals. And in view of the stigma with which homosexuals live in our culture, why would anyone actively choose a homosexual orientation, even if such a choice were possible?

Society's distaste for homosexuality could in part be a backlash from the behavioral movement. We discovered that much of our behavior can be controlled by learning—and went a little overboard. If you or your parents are left-handed, you might recall how children were at one time frowned upon for this individual difference and disciplined against writing with their left hands—a result of educators assuming even handedness can and should be behaviorally controlled! We also appear to have assumed that homosexual behavior is a product of learning and, being different from the norm, should be discouraged. However, attraction patterns and sexual behaviors are two separate phenomena. Homosexual behavior typically occurs as a result of homosexual attraction, rather than vice versa.

At any rate, homosexuality was once considered to be a mental illness caused by having an overbearing mother and a weak ineffectual father, an inaccurate assumption that also probably contributed significantly to some of society's current attitudes. While this is generally no longer believed, scientists are still curious why this difference develops in certain individuals. Since homosexual individuals are less likely to produce offspring, it is difficult to see how homosexuality could be naturally selected for as a part of continuing the species.

While clear-cut answers have not yet been found, partial clues have emerged. Some twin studies have shown higher concordance rates for homosexual orientation among identical twins than fraternal twins. And among some pairs of identical twins consisting of one homosexual and one heterosexual birth mate, psychological similarities involving sexual and body-image confusion have nevertheless been found in both twins. Other studies have shown some ambivalent findings suggesting hormones and specific brain structures may play a role.

Scientists have hypothesized that some of us might inherit a type of sexual identity vulnerability that causes us to be more easily influenced by environmental variables as we form our sexual identities, whether our eventual identity is heterosexual or homosexual. Thus a person might begin with a condition that starts as biology, but proceeds differently depending on what the person learns during experiences in the environment. However, these ideas are relatively new and complex, and much more research is needed before we will be able to say anything definite about the roles of genetics and environment in homosexuality.

The psychological community now treats homosexuality as an individual difference. Estimates vary as to the actual number of people who are homosexual, but it appears to be around 10% of the population (Hyde, 1990). Obviously, the anatomy of homosexual couples plays a role in what can be included in their sexual activity. Oral and manual manipulation are the most common means of homosexual sexual gratification. However, homosexual couples share more similarities with heterosexual couples than differences in how they express and experience their sexuality (Kurdek, 1991). Satisfaction with their sex lives is positively related to the global relationship with their significant others, just as it is with heterosexuals. The only significant difference appears to be that although many homosexuals, especially lesbians, remain committed to monogamous partners, homosexuals put less emphasis on sexual fidelity in the relationship than do heterosexuals. With the spread of AIDS, though, this difference may become less pronounced.

Sexual deviancies. Sexual deviancies are clinically known as **paraphilias**. Money (1988) defines paraphilia as "a condition occurring in men and women of being compulsively responsive to and obligatively dependent on an unusual and personally or socially unacceptable stimulus, perceived or in the ideation and imagery of fantasy, for optimal initiation and maintenance of erotosexual arousal and the facilitation or attainment of orgasm." In everyday language, a person with a paraphilia requires something others might think of as "kinky" in order to become sexually aroused. It may always need to be present, only occasionally need to be present, or may only show its existence in the form of fantasies. Below are some of the more commonly known paraphilias and their conditions of arousal:

- Exhibitionism: Arousal is brought on by the shock or panic experienced by someone who is visually exposed to the exhibitionist's erotic areas.
- Fetishism: The presence of a particular object or body part is required for arousal.
- Masochism: Arousal is dependent upon receiving abuse, punishment, or some other form of humiliation.
- Pedophilia: Sexual responsiveness occurs in conjunction with children.
- Sadism: Arousal is dependent upon delivering physical or mental pain.
- Voyeurism: Arousal occurs in conjunction with the risk of being discovered while clandestinely watching someone disrobe or engage in sexual activity.

Society is quick to blame pornography for all of the sexual deviancies that seem to be around these days. Activists hope that by getting rid of pornography, both unusual and traditional, they will also get rid of some of the paraphilias. However, Money (1988) suggests they have put the cart before the horse. Unusual pornography is typically pursued by those who have already developed the particular paraphilia involved.

Money (1988) hypothesizes that paraphilias develop as a result of growing up in a climate of negativity toward sex. Physical exploration of the genital areas, playing "doctor," masturbation, and other forms of sexual-rehearsal play are universal and normal for growing children. However, many adults in our society look down on such activity and chastise children as being "bad" or "dirty" when they engage in such behavior. When offered such a stimulus-response chain, children are conditioned to associate sexual thoughts, feelings, and behaviors with conditions our society considers as negative or undesirable, such as those involved with various sexual perversions. Ironically, the campaign of negativizing traditional pornography may do more to create perversions than eradicate them!

Money bemoans the lack of adequate research on normal childhood sexual behavior and development. Establishment of a norm would help clinicians detect future sufferers while they still have a chance of altering their often-disastrous courses. Currently, the only treatment for adult paraphilias that demonstrates consistent effectiveness is administration of Depo-Provera, a synthetic hormone that reduces sexual arousal in general.

Sexual Dysfunction

Just as with any other human function, our sexual functioning may become impaired. *DSM-IV* classifies sexual dysfunctions according to the different phases of the sexual response cycle (APA, 1994). These difficulties are only considered to be dysfunctions if they cause the person distress or interpersonal difficulty.

Some individuals suffer from a sexual dysfunction as early in the sexual response cycle as basic desire. **Hypoactive sexual desire disorder** involves a lack of interest in either sexual fantasies or sexual activity. Similar symptoms can occur in individuals who are taking medications that suppress desire, or they can be caused by intoxication. **Sexual aversion disorder** occurs when individuals feel extreme anxiety, disgust, or fear when presented with sexual opportunity. This might involve just certain aspects of sexual responding or as much as anything remotely related to sexual activity. Some sufferers may even experience panic attacks.

Other problems involve inability to maintain arousal long enough to complete the sexual act. **Female sexual arousal disorder** is characterized by a woman's inability to create or sustain a sufficient lubrication-swelling response, while **male erectile disorder** is a man's inability to maintain an erection. **Female orgasmic disorder** and **male orgasmic disorder** occur when a person can proceed normally through sexual arousal and physically respond to sexual excitement, but has difficulty producing an orgasm. Of course, these problems are not considered to be dysfunctions if they occur as a result of inadequate sexual technique or because of one partner ending sexual activity before the other partner has had sufficient time to become satisfied. **Premature ejaculation** is the term used when men ejaculate before, during, or immediately after penetration.

In addition to dysfunctions associated to certain phases of the sexual response cycle, some conditions involve genital pain that occurs in correspondence with sexual intercourse. Both men and women can suffer from **dyspareunia**, genital pain that may occur before, during, or after intercourse. **Vaginismus** is a condition where the outer third of the vagina, which normally spasms during orgasm, persistently and involuntarily contracts when sexual behavior is imminent. The contracted muscles usually obstruct attempts at penetration, which is experienced as painful if the partner succeeds. Sometimes this disorder can be traced to negative attitudes toward sex, or to having been sexually abused or traumatized.

Sex therapists are mental health professionals who help individuals who suffer from sexual dysfunction. Many of their techniques are behavioral. For example, individuals suffering from problems of sexual desire arousal can be helped with a procedure known as **sensate focus**. The couple sticks with touching each other in ways that are pleasurable, while direct genital stimulation is temporarily forbidden. This removes the pressure to perform, allowing the partners to enjoy the activities that they do find to be stimulating. Eventually, as the couple is allowed more and more physical contact, nature takes its predictable course. For premature ejaculation, a sex therapist might help the couple find ways to maximize female stimulation and minimize male stimulation, at least until the woman is satisfied.

Other techniques concern communication skills. After all, sexual intercourse is a form of interpersonal communication. Most couples find that their sex lives are a mirror image of their ability to communicate in other areas of their relationship. Communication is very important for either partner's ability to experience sexual satisfaction. For example, a woman has a greater chance of experiencing orgasm during traditional intercourse if she can tell her partner what feels the most stimulating or if she can inform her partner of other ways of helping her reach orgasm.

Those who become sexually dysfunctional due to negative attitudes toward sex can be helped through cognitive restructuring. For example, you can reduce anxiety over sex using the same cognitive techniques that you might use to address the irrational beliefs and old tapes that cause anxiety in other areas of your life. Traditional psychotherapy is also useful for dealing with life history issues that may have led to the dysfunction, such as being sexually abused or traumatized. Therefore it is also important to check and be sure when you choose a sex therapist that you are selecting one who has the training and certification requirements appropriate for the state or province in which you seek treatment.

Contraception

While our sexuality does serve the purpose of continuing the species, our sexual arousal patterns usually are not based on the desire to produce a child. Most people take measures aimed at ensuring that pregnancy will not occur as a result of their sexual behavior. Some of these measures, passed along by folklore, do not in fact work. For example, withdrawal of the penis before ejaculation is not usually effective birth control, since semen often leaks out during the plateau phase. Douching was once popular as an attempt to avoid conception; however, douching is actually more likely to encourage conception, since the water pressure will serve the purpose of pushing the sperm even deeper into the woman's reproductive ducts.

Other methods, while effective, have moved to the wayside due to undesired side effects. For example, intrauterine devices–better known as **IUDs**–are foreign objects that are inserted into the uterus by a physician. In addition to preventing pregnancy, however, they also have a tendency to produce heavy menstrual cramping and bleeding, pelvic infections, and the potential of infertility. Because of their fears of lawsuits, most companies no longer distribute IUDs in the United States.

The most effective form of contraception, other than abstinence, is sterilization. Both **vasectomy** in men and **tubal ligation** in women create sterility by preventing sperm from traveling the usual route toward conception. The procedure is usually permanent, but is in some cases reversible. While sterilization does not result in any physical reasons for interference with enjoyment of sexual activity, some men experience a reduced sexual desire due to an adverse psychological reaction.

Another effective and well-known form of contraception is administration of hormones. Birth control pills–when taken regularly–and hormone implants are both highly effective. They require a physician's prescription. There have been some side effects reported, such as headaches, nausea, and high blood pressure, resulting in fewer women using oral contraceptives in recent years.

Diaphragms, cervical caps, and condoms are designed to interfere with conception by placing a physical barrier between the egg and sperm. They average out with a failure rate of about 15%, however. Their contraceptive effectiveness is improved when used in conjunction with spermicides, which destroy sperm before they can reach the egg. The contraceptive sponge, a relative newcomer, operates from both the barrier and spermicide philosophies, but tends not to be as effective as using a condom or diaphragm along with the spermicide.

Those who object to active contraception for religious or other moral reasons can passively avoid pregnancy by using the **rhythm method**. This involves timing sexual activity so that it occurs during the woman's monthly period of low fertility. Of course, this method is dependent upon a woman's ability to predict when she will ovulate, and some women are not so regular that they can rely on their predictions.

No matter what form of contraception you choose, its effectiveness is dependent upon using it correctly. Missed birth control pills and other forms of sloppy handling of contraception are responsible for many unwanted pregnancies. Characteristics of specific contraceptives that can lead to misuse or nonuse include their being messy, interrupting "the moment," being expensive, and prone to mechanical failure–a condom breaking, for example. Here are some guidelines you might consider as you choose your contraception:

- If you are a woman who tends to be forgetful, the pill may not be for you. There are also some health conditions that contraindicate the use of contraceptive hormones. Consider a combination of physical-barrier contraception and a spermicide instead.

- If you do not plan to have any more children, sterilization of yourself or your partner puts an end to pregnancy concerns. However, be very sure that you do not want more children, since the procedures are usually irreversible.

- If condoms appear to be the only option and you cannot talk your male partner into using one, there is a relatively new female condom now marketed under the name "Reality." It looks weird and takes a little learning to figure out how to wear it. However, it is less likely to break than latex condoms, and its more-extensive genital coverage offers more protection against pregnancy and sexually transmitted diseases.

- If money is a problem, diaphragms are relatively inexpensive. The rhythm method is completely expense-free, unless you count dealing with an unwanted pregnancy.

- If you have moral or religious reasons for not using active contraception, your best bet is abstinence. The rhythm method may work for you, but your chances of contraceptive failure are relatively high. You might also consider sticking to sexual activity such as mutual masturbation.

- If you find yourself having difficulty interrupting your sexual activity for a contraception break, choose a form such as birth control pills, implants, and cervical caps, which do not require last-minute application.

Sexually Transmitted Diseases

In earlier decades, the consequence most feared by individuals engaging in sexual activity was the possibility of an unwanted pregnancy. Sexually transmitted diseases were also a concern, but they received much less press than they do now. Currently, the situation has reversed. Thanks to AIDS, people tend to be more concerned about what kind of disease they might pick up as a result of their sexual behavior and are arranging their sex lives correspondingly.

Sexually transmitted diseases (STDs) are those that tend to be passed on mainly by sexual contact. **Gonorrhea**, nicknamed the "clap," is one of the more common STDs. In men, the bacterium causes noticeable symptoms such as pain during urination and a cloudy discharge coming from the penis. It is easily treatable with antibiotics. However, women who have gonorrhea usually have no obvious symptoms. Thus the infection may continue to fester until it produces pelvic inflammatory disease or even infertility. Furthermore, since the woman does not know she has the disease, she may unknowingly infect other partners.

Syphilis is another bacterially caused STD, but its consequences are much more serious than those of gonorrhea. The first noticeable symptom is the appearance of a chancre, which is unusual in that the person does not experience any pain in association with it. After the chancre disappears a skin rash develops, which may eventually disappear. The infected person will then enter a period without noticeable symptoms and may figure that whatever had been causing the chancre and rash has passed. Left untreated, however, the disease progresses to such serious symptoms as blindness, insanity, heart failure, and even death.

Herpes is a viral infection, and thus cannot be treated with antibiotics. Once infected, you have it for life. It causes small red bumps on the mouth, genital area, or other moist areas of the body that eventually rupture into long-lasting sores. The symptoms come and go. Some people may have regular outbreaks, while other infected individuals experience them rarely. Herpes tends to be passed along when an infected area touches the warm, moist area of someone else's body, as happens with intercourse, oral sex, anal sex, or even kissing.

Chlamydia is another bacteria that is typically passed on by sexual contact. Men who are infected usually experience painful urination and a discharge from the penis. Women usually do not experience immediately noticeable symptoms. However, if pelvic inflammatory disease develops, it can result in flulike symptoms, abdominal pain, and disrupted menstrual cycles.

Yeast infection is a common infection that causes women to feel itchy around the vaginal and vulvar areas and produces a white, cheesy-looking discharge. It often develops in women when they take antibiotics, since they kill the bacteria that normally keep yeast under control. However, it can also develop as a result of sexual contact.

Genital warts are virally caused, typically passed along through direct body contact and resulting in wartlike growths on both dry and moist skin areas. **Pubic lice**, also referred to as "crabs," can be spread not only through body contact but also by sharing infested clothing and bedding. **Viral hepatitis** causes mild to severe flulike symptoms, and is spread by means of passing along body fluids such as semen, blood, and saliva. However, the most serious STD to be passed on by body fluids is **acquired immune deficiency syndrome**, a 100% fatal disease popularly known as AIDS.

AIDS

AIDS first proliferated in the United States among the gay population. This is probably because at that time the gay lifestyle involved having multiple sex partners and because of the high likelihood of the virus being passed along by the exchange of semen and anal intercourse. People originally viewed AIDS as a gay disease and did not take necessary precautions to protect themselves. In view of the fact that you can have the virus for years before showing any symptoms, even now most people in the United States who are in the process of dying from the disease are male homosexuals. However, the virus itself is now equally if not more commonly spread through sharing hypodermic needles, infected mothers passing it on to their babies during pregnancy, and heterosexual sex.

The best way to avoid the AIDS virus is to avoid sharing body fluids with other individuals. Of course, this remedy would include complete abstinence from sexual intimacy, not a realistic option for most individuals. The next best way to avoid coming into contact with the virus through sexual activity is to minimize the risks. Below are several guidelines for "safer sex":

• Avoid or be extremely cautious when having sexual relationships with high-risk populations. These include gay or bisexual men, intravenous drug users, people who have multiple sex partners, people who use blood products (such as hemophiliacs and surgery patients), and of course, those who are already infected with the AIDS virus.

• Avoid casual sex. You cannot depend on relative strangers to be honest with you about their sex lives, let alone what current infections they might have.

• Have sex only within the context of a monogamous relationship.

• Have both yourself and your partner tested for STDs before becoming sexually intimate. Since the test for the AIDS virus may not detect its presence until several months after infection, you may want to pursue testing more than once.

• No matter what form of contraception you use, protect yourself against STDs by using latex condoms. They may offer even more protection against the AIDS virus if they are treated with the spermicide **nonoxynol 9**, which, in laboratory conditions, kills the AIDS virus.

• Mutual masturbation is relatively safe sex, since body fluids are not exchanged. Consider using this form of stimulation if you believe you are in a high-risk situation.

Most high schools and middle schools now educate students extensively on how to protect themselves against AIDS. Our education on this topic continues through the media, as famous individuals such as Rock Hudson and Magic Johnson have publicized their illness, and movies such as *Philadelphia* reveal the plight of AIDS patients. Yet in spite of all this publicity, most young people continue to engage in risky sexual practices. Why?

There are a number of possible explanations. It may be a product of the risk-taking nature of youth, flirting with one's own mortality. The media is also in part to blame: How often on television or in the movies do you see STD protection play a role in a romantic encounter? Many of us design our own sexual encounters around what the media have trained us to expect, thus protection does not usually become a part of our sexual scripts.

Another factor is the role of cognitive dissonance. If we take measures to protect ourselves against STDs, it implies that we might possibly become infected by our chosen sexual partner. Common sense tells us that if a behavior presents potentially disastrous risks, we probably shouldn't be pursuing it at all. Furthermore, protecting ourselves implies that our sexual partner is a potential disease carrier. This ideation can be a major sexual turnoff. So in order to resolve or avoid the cognitive dissonance, we may deny the dangers and fail to use protection.

No matter why people take this risk, unprotected sex can result in the end of life itself. Is it really worth dying for?

Satisfying Sex

As you can see, sexuality is highly personal and individualized. Finding a satisfying sex life will be based on these individual differences. Nobody can tell you what is satisfying for you; it is an ultimate experiential experience that you alone learn to discover and appreciate.

A number of variables contribute to satisfying sex. Clearly, satisfaction with the overall relationship with your sexual partner plays a role. How can we expect to enjoy intimacy within our most personal form of experiencing if we cannot even get along and cooperate while dealing with day-to-day surface issues? Good communication also contributes to good sex. One survey showed that 50% of women who were able to discuss their sexual feelings with their partners described their sex lives as being very satisfying; only 9% of those women who did not discuss their sexual feelings reported feeling very satisfied (Tavris & Sadd, 1978). Obviously, your partner cannot satisfy you without knowing what you enjoy or dislike. Furthermore, you need to be receptive to what your partner tells you, without feeling like you are being criticized for previous efforts to please your partner.

Realistic expectations also enhance satisfaction. What do you want out of your sex life? If you are not satisfied unless you can have mutual orgasms, and anything less than that is considered a failure, you are not likely to feel satisfied very often. If you expect your partner to want sex as much or as little as you do, your differing libidos can be expected to experience frequent clashes. If you believe a certain size or shape of sex organ is necessary for you to be satisfying to a partner, you are not only headed for dissatisfaction but are also sadly mistaken. If you expect traditional heterosexual intercourse to produce the same level of stimulation for the woman as it does for the man, you will also be disappointed. None of these individual differences are evidence that your sex life is doomed. They can be worked out one way or another by employing caring, communication, and a spirit of cooperation and compromise.

As mentioned earlier, there are gender differences that will affect sexual satisfaction. Typically women are most satisfied when sexual activity takes care of certain quality aspects, such as love and affection. Men are more likely to avoid dissatisfaction by taking care of quantity concerns, such as frequency, variety, and spontaneity. These differences do seem to diminish with age, however.

We can enhance our sexual satisfaction by allowing ourselves to be aware of our sexual scripts. What are the necessary components of our scripts for arousal? How much of the script is what we would really like in our sex lives and what aspects would we prefer to incorporate into fantasy? We also need to be aware of our bodily responding. What physical sensations do we find to be arousing, how do we experience them, and how can we help our partners succeed in producing these feelings?

A number of roadblocks can interfere with sexual satisfaction. Clearly the most troublesome is the problem of negative attitudes toward sex. In our society, they tend to proliferate. At the very least, such attitudes interfere with healthy self-examination and experimentation; at their worst, such attitudes result in sexual dysfunctions. Social anxieties such as performance anxiety can also interfere. Both of these problems can be addressed by a competent sex therapist.

Adherence to the double standard also diminishes sexual satisfaction. If you are a woman, you may feel dirty or less valuable if you experience your sexuality. If you are a man, you may be tempted to devalue the role of your female partner's sexual satisfaction, or may even devalue your female partner altogether for having joined you in sexual activity. All of these outcomes interfere with sexual satisfaction.

Casual sex almost guarantees some form of dissatisfaction. It may satisfy a need for spontaneity, a particular fantasy, or the desire to be "swept away." But unfortunately, having sex with someone you do not know very well has a number of pitfalls. Since genuine caring has not had a chance to fully develop, you cannot expect to employ the same level of communication and cooperation that you would have with a well-known significant other. You also cannot assume that the person will take appropriate precautions against pregnancy and spreading STDs, which can create a lot of distractive anxiety. And since a relative stranger is not going to be as concerned about protecting your sexual sensitivities, you could end up being coerced into doing something you would rather not do—another major dissatisfier, as well as a potential traumatizer.

Most importantly, let your sexuality flow from who you are as a person. If your standards require that you have sexual intercourse only within the context of a committed relationship, you will be much more satisfied with your sex life if you save that activity for your preferred conditions. And remember not to confuse spontaneity with impulsiveness. Spontaneity takes into account the possible consequences of "spur-of-the-moment" behavior; impulsiveness does not.

Expanding Your Experience

Other generations, including my own, often became sexual before having had much in the way of sex education. Around the sixth grade, girls might have been shown a film or received some other presentation on the topic of menstruation (these days most girls are already menstruating by then!). In the ninth grade the bare basics of reproduction might be explained in biology classes. For seniors in high school, the health classes would have minimal discussions about sexuality, focusing more on reproduction than sexual behavior and feelings. Parents of earlier eras typically did not provide much information, so anything else young people learned came from sources other than home or school. (Personally, I first learned about the "birds and the bees" in the fourth grade during a discussion that took place in the girls' restroom.)

By the time young adults became college freshmen, they were left to exchange their few collective gleanings of information and misinformation. Naturally, it has always been a hot topic in dormitories. As I was passing through this life phase, a book came out entitled *Everything you always wanted to know about sex—but were afraid to ask*. Two of my dorm buddies and I scraped together enough spare change to purchase a copy of the book. Actually, sexuality was underresearched at that time. However, it still provided a lot more "forbidden information" than any of us had ever imagined existed. We devoured it. It became the most passed-around book in the entire dormitory. I suspect this tendency hasn't changed much even now: As I was researching this topic in the University of Portland library, I discovered that the human sexuality books containing all the really explicit, detailed descriptions of sexual behavior are stored in the reserve library.

The exercises I have included in the activity book give you substantially more opportunity to investigate your sexuality than was available for previous generations. The first exercise is an investigation of attraction patterns. The next one is designed to help you figure out how you are going to go about bringing up the topic of protection from AIDS with a potential sex partner. The third is a sexual attitude survey. The last exercise—for the more adventurous types—is a debate on various aspects of sexual behavior.

Study Questions

1. Would you say that sexual arousal is more biological or psychological? Explain your answer.
2. What is a "sexual script"?
3. What role do sexual fantasies play in arousal, and how do they appear to differ between men and women?
4. What role does love play in sexual arousal?
5. In what ways might anxiety affect sexual arousal?
6. What are "erogenous zones"?
7. Describe the human sexual-response cycle for both men and women.
8. Do you believe the "sexual revolution" was a success? Explain your answer.
9. What is the "swept away" phenomenon, and why do you think it developed?
10. What differing agenda do men and women appear to have when they enter into sexual relationships?
11. Describe the advantages and disadvantages of masturbation.
12. Is a homosexual orientation inborn or learned from experience? Explain your answer.
13. What is a "paraphilia"? How do clinicians believe paraphilias develop?
14. Will doing away with pornography put an end to paraphilias? Explain your answer.
15. Describe the disorders of sexual desire, sexual arousal, orgasm, and sexual pain.
16. How might a sex therapist help a couple with the problems of premature ejaculation and female orgasmic disorder?
17. Describe how you would go about choosing your preferred form of contraception.
18. Why do you think people continue to have unsafe sex, even though they know they might pick up a very serious STD?
19. Describe the variables likely to increase your chances of having a satisfying sexual relationship.

CHAPTER TEN

Affiliation
The Ties That Bind

*I get by with a little help
from my friends.*
—THE BEATLES

We earthly creatures differ in our agendas for relationships. Some of us function very independently from other members of our species. For example, bears live relatively solitary lives, coming into contact with other bears only long enough to mate or produce young. We typically do not see large numbers of bears hanging around together and interacting as a group, other than in *The Far Side* cartoons. On the other hand, dogs function socially in packs—a very interdependent style of living. They have a social order within the pack that assists them in their ability to pull down prey, fight off predators, and determine who will mate. Bears have no need for pack functioning, since they are capable of meeting basic needs without social assistance. Thus lower animals engage in social behavior because their basic survival depends upon it.

Human beings are also social animals; and we, too, depend upon one another for basic survival. But because of our more advanced thinking abilities, our social needs have progressed far beyond simply finding food and mating. Our society continues to become more complex as we attempt to satisfy needs through our relationships with others.

Abraham Maslow (1970) provides a listing of human needs. He proposes that we have lower needs that must be satisfied before we go on to address higher needs. He therefore arranges them in a hierarchy, according to lowest and highest needs:

• *Physiological needs*. Physiological needs are those involving basic survival: having enough food to eat, water to drink, air to breathe, ability to sleep, and so on; these are similar to the needs of lower animals.

- *Safety and security needs.* These needs concern knowing that we are safe from immediate harm. Having a stable living situation, knowing we have a roof over our heads and a steady source of income, and feeling free from imminent attack or some other danger are all part of feeling safe and secure.
- *Love and belongingness needs.* Human beings need to share affection and companionship with one another, have a place in society, and have meaningful roles that define how they can interrelate with others.
- *Self-esteem needs.* We need to feel good about ourselves, to have a sense of self-worth and self-confidence. Such needs involve self-acceptance—the ability to look at ourselves positively, no matter how we might occasionally err.
- *Self-actualization needs.* Self-actualization, as you may recall, involves a striving for activity that is congruent with our sense of self. We feel personally fulfilled when we take on activity and challenges that enhance our sense of identity. We enjoy being creative, and revel in finding ways to express ourselves as unique individuals. The striving in and of itself is satisfying, even if we never meet some of the more ambitious goals we might set.

According to Maslow, we do not even consider our higher needs until our lower needs are met. For example, we would not be likely to start thinking about the state of our self-images if we were in the middle of an air raid. Likewise, a person may engage in prostitution, drug trafficking, and other self-denigrating behavior because putting food on the table has become a more pressing need than experiencing good self-esteem.

All of the needs described by Maslow are met at least in part through the relationships we establish with others. In our society, we depend on one another to produce the consumables necessary for our basic physiological survival. When was the last time you met any individuals who bake their own bread, made with flour ground from wheat they have grown themselves? We are much more likely to depend on the local supermarket than on the gleanings of solitary hunting and gathering behavior. If we were stranded on a desert island we might be able to survive, but would have a much better chance of making it if we were stranded with 10 others who brought along a variety of skills to contribute toward the provision of basic physiological needs.

The saying "there is safety in numbers" well describes the role of relationships in satisfying safety and security needs. An army of warriors certainly provides better protection from intruders than a single person carrying a dart-blower. We also depend on society for a steady source of income, so we can purchase food and shelter. We work for others, or others pay us directly for goods or services we provide.

Love and belongingness needs are obviously satisfied through having others with whom to form relationships. Likewise, self-esteem and the capacity to feel self-accepting develop largely through observing significant others act acceptingly toward us. Even self-actualization requires a medium—the social environment—within which we can work out a sense of congruence between who we are and the lifestyle we choose. Thus the ability to form relationships with others is important on many need levels for a variety of reasons.

A simpler way to look at how we benefit from relationships is to condense them into two broad social need areas: **social ties** and **emotional attachments**. Social ties involve our sense of connectedness with the world. We seek a particular "niche," a social source for satisfying material needs, and an identity as part of a group. Emotional attachments involve the availability of support and nurturance as we need them, knowing that someone is going to be there for us. When we lack social ties and emotional attachments, we experience loneliness (Weiss, 1974). Through relationships, we escape loneliness and meet our needs for having social ties and emotional attachments.

There are several basic characteristics that apply to all healthy relationships, whether the relationship involves friends, neighbors, employees/employers, spouses, or relatives:

- *Awareness of one's own rights.* What rights do we have as we enter into relationships with others? Grasha (1983) lists a number of interpersonal rights. First, we have the right to express ourselves to those with whom we have relationships. We have the right to let others know how we feel, to request that they listen to our point of view, to ask if they will address problems that affect us, to persist in asking that problems not responded to the first time be addressed, to ask others to compromise when we are in conflict with them, and to ask others for reasonable favors.

Second, we have the right to our separateness. We have the right to say "no" to a request, to change our minds, to be alone when that is our desire, to maintain our dignity in relationships, to avoid manipulation by others, to make mistakes and accept responsibility for them, and to evaluate ourselves on our own rather than accept someone else's evaluation of us.

- *Respect for one another's rights.* The same interpersonal rights that apply to us apply to those who relate with us as well. While we have the right to make a request, the other person has the right to say "No." While we have the right to express our feelings and opinions on various topics, others have the right to reject them. Successful relationships thrive on equal rights such as these.

- *Effective communication.* Healthy relationships use direct communication–free of game-playing, clear, and assertive. Communication will be covered in greater depth in the next chapter.

- *Supportiveness and caring in the degree appropriate for the particular relationship.* In healthy relationships, individuals neither neglect one another nor smother one another. The degree of supportiveness and caring depends on the amount of **intimacy**, **passion**, and **decision and commitment** the two individuals share, characteristics that will be discussed later in this chapter.

If we do not keep healthy relating in mind as we strive toward forming relationships, our efforts can go awry. This is well-illustrated by the processes involved in the concept of **brainwashing** (Sadock, 1985). When most people think of brainwashing they think of extreme cases, such as those involving cults and political kidnappings–where people have been actively coerced to behave in ways that previously would have been considered uncharacteristic of them. However, the same sorts of social influences can affect anybody, even in seemingly innocent situations: the dorm group you live with, your employment setting, a sports team, or any club or organized group. A more appropriate term to describe these phenomena would be situations of **excessive social influence**. Such social effects interfere with personal growth and adjustment, since they create incongruencies between who we see ourselves to be and how we are actually behaving.

The four factors that follow are typically present when we are being excessively socially influenced according to the principles of brainwashing:

1. *Lowered sense of ego strength.* **Ego strength** refers to the inner resources we have that enable us to take care of ourselves as well as to an essential belief that we are competent enough to do so. Many different circumstances can lower our sense of ego strength:
    a. A sudden change in our living conditions, such as losing a job or moving to a new area, can cause some temporary loss of inner balance as we adjust and set down new roots within the new living situation.
    b. A serious problem in a current important interpersonal relationship can leave us questioning our inner competence or desirability. Being rejected by or cut off from our family of origin, being

divorced or widowed, or breaking off other significant long-term relationships can cause a sense of vulnerability. It brings to the forefront the question, Can I take care of myself on my own?

c. Sudden crises can also throw us off balance. Serious physical illnesses or injuries can have this effect. Natural disasters such as floods, earthquakes, forest fires, tidal waves, and volcanoes can put us in touch with how vulnerable we really are. Likewise, social disasters such as wars, riots, and economic depressions can leave us feeling helpless and uncertain about our ability to take care of ourselves.

d. **Culture shock** occurs when we move from one culture to another. In any new setting, it takes a while to learn the rules of the social group. This results in some delays in our ability to interact effectively with the environment. If a foreign language is involved, we may not even be able to communicate well with others. Thus we truly are temporarily impaired in our ability to take care of ourselves, which affects self-esteem accordingly. The new setting does not need to be a foreign country. It could be brought about by something like moving from one segment of society to another, such as entering the workplace after leaving a college setting.

e. Some people, for many reasons, are chronically lacking in self-esteem and self-acceptance. Their lowered ego strength is an ever-present reality.

2. *Isolation or alienation from others*. Sometimes physical isolation from others interferes with how well we can find emotional attachments and social ties. For example, people often feel temporarily isolated right after changing to a new social situation, such as a new job setting. When individuals have moved to different parts of the country and not yet had the opportunity to make new social connections, they feel isolated. Sometimes we are blocked from spending time with friends and family when we feel pressured to spend more time at work or at school. When physical isolation occurs, we can develop feelings of being socially unsupported.

Interpersonal alienation occurs when something intangible interferes with a person's feeling connected with others. Feelings of alienation are common during adolescence (e.g., Keniston, 1960). As adolescents experiment with their emerging formal operational reasoning ability, they become more and more able to develop their own ideologies, which they soon recognize as being different from those of others. This is a drastically different state of being than what is experienced by the concrete operational child, who sees the world in terms of absolute rights and wrongs. Awareness of subjectivity increases awareness of our separateness. Thus adolescents experience a temporary state of alienation as they adjust to their recognition of their aloneness of perspective.

New changes in our lives can also alter our perceptions of how close we are to others. Getting married when all of your friends are single, quitting drinking when your social circle's favorite pastime is hanging around in bars, or going back to work or to school when your young mother cohorts are still staying at home are all life changes that can alter your feelings of closeness to your significant others.

Depression is well-known to include the symptom of alienation (APA, 1994). But on the other hand, positive personal growth can also lead to a sense of alienation. We all grow and change as we get older, and may grow in a direction that produces new needs that cannot be met through our current circle of friends.

3. *There is no hope of release from the situation of vulnerability.* Sometimes there is indeed little hope of escape, such as when a person is being held prisoner. But most of the time when you feel there is no way out, you just haven't stumbled across that exit, or the available alternatives seem as bad or worse than the ongoing situation, so you haven't considered them options.

   For example, school becomes frustrating. You think you would like to quit but do not see that as an option, because should you quit you would not have completed your goal, would owe money and have no better means of paying it back, might not have any other career in mind, might be concerned about what others will think, and so on. In spite of these drawbacks, quitting is still an option. Your task is to decide which alternative is the "lesser of two evils" or to look for ways to minimize the drawbacks of the options. Perhaps you could take a temporary hiatus from school.

   While being affected by excessive social influence, we often do not see options as being truly available. We tend to focus only on their drawbacks, since our lowered ego strength and feelings of isolation make the challenge of dealing with potential adversities seem overwhelming.

4. *Emotional support and social ties are offered by the brainwashing or excessively influential agent.* Emotional support and social ties can come in

many forms. In cults, they can be manifest in a party line of "adopt our beliefs and join our group and you will have an identity, as well as friends who will always be there for you." The highly publicized kidnapping of Patty Hearst, who eventually joined the cause of her terrorist kidnappers, illustrates how vulnerable individuals can be swayed from their usual behavior.

Emotional support and social ties can also come in the form of an **ultimate rescuer**—some person who seems or presents him- or herself as almost godlike: all-knowing and all-powerful, protecting you and helping you along in all things (Yalom, 1980). Unfortunately, the support is usually only given as long as you go along with the ultimate rescuer's agenda. The tragedy of David Koresh and the Branch Davidians is a good example of how excessively influenced individuals might give in to the agenda of an ultimate rescuer.

Why do cult recruiters tend to hang out on college campuses? Most likely because college freshmen meet so many of the criteria for being susceptible to excessive social influence. The sudden changes in lifestyle and new expectations thrust upon them can be both isolating and challenging to their self-esteem. Freshmen may find themselves initially isolated and alienated from others, as for the first time they are substantially separated from family and childhood friends. Also, most 18-year-olds are still resolving some lingering inner conflicts of adolescence, which can lead to further feelings of isolation and confused identity and self-esteem. The pressures of college life are very real, and students often feel there is no escape from these pressures. The support, identity, and social ties offered by a cult may indeed seem enticing.

Once you become involved in a situation of excessive social influence, leaving can be difficult. You learn to depend on the group for your relationship needs, and the idea of leaving this support seems frightening. While the group does provide an escape from feelings of vulnerability and alienation, unfortunately it also has the tendency to encourage those feelings. You learn to depend on group competence rather than on self-competence to meet needs, further lowering your ego strength. Relating to one isolated group of individuals further isolates you from the rest of the world. This is especially true if the group functions around some extreme position, such as a cultlike religious or political agenda. It can foster an attitude of "you're either with us or against us," such that leaving the group becomes unthinkable.

Even if you do change your beliefs, peer pressure can keep you from changing your behavior. In Solomon Asch's (1955) classic studies on compliance, he found that people often go along with behavior they understand to be expected, even when it is not behavior they would have chosen on their own.

Another factor that can keep us from leaving a situation of excessive social influence is our tendency to conform to the dictates of leaders. Leaders can draw a larger following if they demonstrate a high level of competence or credibility, are charismatic, or at least likable, and show they can be trusted to meet the needs of their followers. Stanley Milgram

(1974) demonstrated the strong influence a leader can have if he or she is perceived as highly competent and willing to take responsibility for the consequences of the group members' actions. Milgram was able to get most "experimenters" to continue to give electrical shocks to "learners" even after the learners—who were actually audiotaped confederates of the researcher—complained of severe pain. If we have this kind of confidence in the leader of our group, leaving against his or her wishes can be very difficult.

As groups become more and more extreme and isolated, a process called **groupthink** develops. These groups are usually very cohesive, are isolated from views other than their own, and endorse the agenda of the group leader. Janis (1972) describes several characteristics of the process of groupthink:

- *Feelings of invulnerability.* The group feels that it cannot go wrong, and may take unreasonable risks.
- *Rationalization.* Any evidence going against the group leader's beliefs are rationalized away, no matter how obvious the gaps in logic might be.
- *Inerrant morality.* The group sees itself as being aligned with a cause that is bigger than the group itself. Perhaps they believe "God is on our side," so moral considerations of what the group proposes can be rationalized away in an "ends justifies the means" manner.
- *Downgrading of opponents.* Those who oppose the group's position are judged in terms of some stereotypical representation of inferiority, terms like stupid, evil, immoral, and weak.
- *Pressure to conform.* Group members put a lot of pressure on one another to stick to the party line.
- *Self-censorship.* The group itself seeks ways to keep opposing ideas from surfacing.
- *Illusion of unanimity.* Group members perceive themselves as being in 100% agreement, which of course is rarely the case.
- *Self-appointed "mindguards."* These individuals take on the role of "protecting" other members from information that might sway them from the party line, generally through suppressing other viewpoints and encouraging the illusion of unanimity.

A recent example of how groupthink can interfere with group effectiveness involved a measure that recently appeared on the Oregon state ballot. Measure 9 was drawn up by a group known as the Oregon

Citizens' Alliance (OCA), which sought to keep homosexuals from receiving civil rights protection status as a minority. The measure included a paragraph describing homosexuality as "abnormal" and "perverse" and stating that passage of the measure would ensure state government would not be supportive of such a lifestyle. During their campaign OCA distributed videotapes of militant and unquestionably deviant gays from San Francisco and implied that they represented a typical homosexual lifestyle. They also quoted "experts" on homosexuality, who actually had been discredited by the scientific community. Various mental health and medical organizations pointed out the claims of OCA were not consistent with research, and many major religious groups pointed out the measure's inconsistencies with mainstream religious moral teachings. However, the response of OCA leaders was to ignore the content of the criticisms and point out that these groups had obviously been subverted by homosexuals (*Oregonian,* October 28, 1992). Voters in Oregon chose not to pass Measure 9. But had the OCA not been so affected by groupthink, had they drawn up a measure that simply objected to the protected minority status classification, they might have had a better chance at passing their measure.

Historically, there are many examples of groupthink having had a major impact on society: Janis's work developed out of interest in the decision-making processes behind the 1961 Bay of Pigs incident, the Kennedy administration's ill-fated attempt to invade Cuba; during the Watergate scandal of the 1970s, the Nixon administration might not have engaged in such damaging cover-up activities had it not been for groupthink processing among his limited number of advisors; in 1985, the space shuttle *Challenger* might not have blown up after takeoff had the decision-making group listened to the engineers who knew of its flawed parts. As you can see, not only political extremists and cult members fall victim to these influences.

Likewise, you need not have a cultist, kidnapper, or someone else actively trying to brainwash you for you to be affected by excessive social influence. The effects of brainwashing can be produced purely by accident.

Let's say you are working as a dental assistant in a clinic run by two dentist partners, Dr. Jones and Dr. Smith. They get into an ongoing conflict over how to handle some important clinic policies and procedures. This causes stress and tension throughout the clinic, and employees worry about whose heads might roll. Dr. Jones works toward enlisting your support for his side in their squabbles, telling you how bad Dr. Smith is (and implying how wonderful you must be since he is confiding in you). You feel protected from getting the ax because of this relationship you have developed with Dr. Jones, and go along with his agenda concerning Dr. Smith.

This situation is an ideal set-up for the effects of excessive social influence. Your ego strength is affected by the clinic turmoil, as well as the potential for some kind of shake-up resulting in your losing your job. Interpersonal alienation occurs because of all the tension and divided factions in your work setting. Escape is not easily seen, since you cannot realistically expect to solve Dr. Jones's and Dr. Smith's conflict for them, and quitting your job would leave you without an income. Dr. Jones then provides you with emotional support and a social tie by taking you in as a confidant.

Unfortunately, your going along with this unholy alliance can be expected to increase your insecurity. The more you attribute your job security to Dr. Jones's protection, the less you attribute it to your competence as a dental assistant. Your ego strength is thus further weakened. Alienation increases, as Dr. Smith and other employees see the special relationship you have with Dr. Jones and become concerned about the influence you have over him and, ultimately, their interests. Your job security feels even less certain, since you know that holding onto your job may depend on which dentist comes out on top of the squabbles. The longer the conflict continues, the more insecure you become, the more suggestible you become to input from Dr. Jones, and the more fearful you become of the eventual outcome. As a result, you find yourself acting in ways you never would have considered before the conflict.

This is a microcosm of brainwashing. In all likelihood, Dr. Jones was not purposely trying to exert excessive social influence over you. It may well have been that he was simply looking for "any port in a storm," as the saying goes. Although there are indeed some people who try to use these principles to manipulate others, most of the time when we find ourselves behaving uncharacteristically due to social influences, the factors behind brainwashing have popped up in the form of random life circumstances.

Fortunately, a little preventive medicine can help us guard against meeting relationship needs in these destructive ways:

1. *Don't carry all of your eggs in one basket.* In other words, have a support network that extends beyond one tight group. If you had a support system that extended beyond your dental clinic work setting you might not have been so easily drawn into the conflict, or at least not have been as significantly influenced. You would have been more able to back off from Dr. Jones's invitations to confidences, since you would have the

option of satisfying your needs for emotional support and social ties elsewhere.

2. *Be wary of extreme positions.* In the case of Drs. Smith and Jones, the party line was that one dentist was all right and one was all wrong. Cults and extreme political groups also tend to present themselves as all right, morally correct, and your best buddies; and they encourage a conceptualization of all competition as being all wrong, morally incorrect, and your worst enemies. If the leader or high-profile individuals of a group take an extreme position and refuse to discuss any other, you might consider whether these individuals are appropriate for leadership status within the group.

3. *Whenever possible, look at both sides of the story.* When forming your opinions, ask dissenting questions. During group decision making, make sure someone is playing "devil's advocate." Meichenbaum (1977) talks about the importance of looking for such **disconfirming data**. He points out that most of the time we make note of that which agrees with our current perspective. As was mentioned in the chapter on development, our cognitive development proceeds in part through the creation of schemas that can serve as representations of our understanding of the world. Assimilation of new material to old and trusted schemas is a much easier task than accommodating and changing our schemas as we sort through disconfirming information. As a result, we can conveniently ignore disconfirming data that could help us form more adaptive beliefs. Remember to think like a scientist: What alternative hypotheses could explain my observations?

4. *Rely on traditional support systems.* When you find yourself feeling lonely and vulnerable, look for traditional means of support. Means of support become traditional because they work. Clubs, churches, volunteer jobs, neighbors, family members, old friends you've temporarily lost track of—all these potential support sources are avenues to consider as you develop your support network. Or if your difficulties are becoming severe, seek the assistance of legitimate professionals, rather than individuals who are working at selling themselves to you.

5. *Utilize outside information.* If you find yourself living a lifestyle that results in contact with only a small group of people, seek outside input. Again, limited input over an extended period of time can direct you toward a groupthink mentality of making up reality as you go along. Respect the need for a reality check every now and then. Licensed professionals of many fields are required to get continuing education and encouraged to seek peer consultation for the purpose of staying in touch with their field's greater reality.

Biases: How Do I See Thee? Let Me Count the Ways

As we get to know people, a number of internal reasoning processes can encourage us to see others in certain ways. These personal biases often lead to inaccurate assessments of others and can affect how we react to them.

Many of our biases stem from using various forms of "mental shorthand." We think in terms of generalizations as a means of speeding up the reasoning process, since analyzing and integrating every conceivable detail is time-consuming and, in most cases, counterproductive. **Prejudice** is one of the most well-known results of this mental shorthand. Prejudice involves a predisposition to judge groups or persons before we have observed them well enough for our judgments to be accurate. Instead, we make assumptions on the basis of our shorthand analysis of a group's or person's characteristics. Racism, sexism, ageism, and heterosexism are well-known forms of prejudice in today's society.

We are also prone to think in terms of **stereotypes**, where we assume people have a rigid set of characteristics because of the groups they belong to or the social roles they occupy. The well-known **halo effect** can result in our attributing all good characteristics to someone because we are aware of one of their good characteristics, or attributing all bad characteristics because we have become aware of one undesirable characteristic. A person's **reputation** also involves limited information, yet it may bias us in our decision of whether to get to know that person. First impressions, also known as the **primacy effect**, can lead us to believe our initial impressions of a person based on a brief period of exposure and give less weight to information learned later (Hayden & Mischel, 1976).

Other biases are a product of the strategies we often use for attributing characteristics to others. **Fundamental attribution error** (Ross, 1977) results when we assume people have certain characteristics on the basis of a behavior we observe, when in fact anyone–including ourselves–might act the same way if placed in the same situation. On the other hand, the **leniency effect** results in our giving people the benefit of the doubt during questionable behavior if it is important to us to view them positively, such as when our friends or relatives are being judged. The **false consensus effect** (Ross et al., 1977) leads us to assume that everyone else thinks and acts the same way we do. The **false uniqueness effect** (Marks, 1984) can lead us to believe others do not have the same desirable characteristics that we ourselves possess.

As we begin to collect information about those we observe, other biases can affect our predictions of their behavior. **Availability** theory suggests that we judge how others will act on the basis of how easy it is for us to retrieve memories of how they have behaved in the past (Tversky & Kahneman, 1973). Thus we might expect a person who once performed a tremendous act of heroism to behave altruistically because of the outstanding nature of such an act, and his or her more usual but less noticeable self-centered behavior will not enter into how we make our predictions. As we use the availability heuristic, over time we can develop **illusory correlations** (Hamilton & Gifford, 1976). We have illusory correlations when we overestimate the number of times we have seen one outcome, underestimate how often we have seen its opposite, and make our predictions accordingly. This process often involves **confirmation bias**—we look for data that affirms our previous assumptions (Levine, 1966). Thus biases may start as primacy effects, be reinforced by the availability heuristic, and then be strengthened over time by means of illusory correlations and confirmation bias!

Here is an example of how these various biases might play in a budding relationship. Let's say a young woman, Jane, feels attracted to one of her college classmates, Tom, who happens to play lineman on the school's football team. She is delighted when he asks her out. They decide to take in the movie playing on campus that week, *Terminator II*, which actually does not fit in with Jane's movie preferences. When Tom goes to get refreshments, he comes back with a soft drink she does not like. As he sits down he accidently drops it on her coat. By the end of the evening, Jane is questioning whether or not Tom is her type after all. Here are some of the biases she might be experiencing that would encourage such judgment:

- "As a first date, this one's a bust. I'm not so sure this guy's for me." *Primacy effect:* Jane is making her assumption on the basis of a single date.
- "I'm not surprised he dropped the soda—linemen are known for letting balls bounce off of them." *Stereotype:* She is assuming that Tom has certain characteristics on the basis of the role he plays on the football team. Actually, he dropped the drink because the container was slippery.
- "Nobody else likes that kind of soda—what's wrong with him?" *False consensus effect:* She figures that everyone sees things the same as she does and therefore judges Tom as being out of touch.
- "He never would have asked me to such a violent movie if he weren't such a jerk." *Fundamental attribution error:* She is blaming the choice on Tom, rather than attributing the circumstances to the fact that a violent movie happened to be playing on campus that week.

- "This happened with Harry only when he didn't know ahead of time how violent the movie would be." *Leniency effect:* If someone Jane already cared about made the same errors in judgment, she would judge him much more leniently.
- "I knew ahead of time he would enjoy violence, considering the sport he plays." *Prejudice:* She was primed to see Tom a certain way on the basis of her preconceptions concerning football players.
- "This guy's a klutz. He probably doesn't have much to offer in the boyfriend department either." *Halo effect:* Since he blew it in his choice of movie and soft drink, she is assuming that he will also be inept at intimacy.

Jane may not be thinking these actual thoughts as she comes to a decision about her future with Tom. However, we do not need to have conscious awareness of such biases for them to have a significant effect on our judgment.

Finding Friends

Certain parameters influence us regarding which people we are likely to befriend. Suppose you're new on campus, or have just moved to a new area. Let's look at the factors that may affect your choice of new friends.

Proximity

The most obvious requirement for finding friends is finding yourself in the same place as other people. Proximity refers to physical closeness, or existing in the same general location as others. We are much more likely to form friendships with those who are physically near, such as those who live next door to us in an apartment complex (Festinger et al., 1950). When we are exposed to anything over a long period of time it becomes familiar and we begin to develop positive feelings about it (Zajonc, 1968). As we get used to our new setting, we will probably form more friendships among our dormitory roommates or next door neighbors than those who live down the hall, on a different floor, or in the building across the street. Also, tenants whose rooms are near the mail area, elevators, work rooms, and other frequently visited areas are more likely to be counted by us as friends than those whose rooms are more isolated (Worchel et al., 1988).

Similarity

After we meet people and get to know them, we are more likely to seek them out as friends if their beliefs and attitudes are similar to our own (Byrne, 1971). We also tend to seek out those whom we judge to be equivalent to ourselves in attractiveness (Cash & Derlega, 1978). We keep our relationships going by finding enough in common to be able to hold one another's interest. On a recent dating game show, a couple came back from their "dream date" having discovered that the only thing they had in common was a dislike for cauliflower. They had nothing bad to say about one another as individuals. They simply did not find enough common ground for their relationship to progress.

This seems to lend some believability to the old saying "birds of a feather flock together." But what about the contrasting saying that "opposites attract?" This second adage refers to the **complementarity** often found in successful relationships. An introverted person may have a richer social life because of his or her association with a more extroverted friend. Or, a person who prefers to take a passive role in life may hook up with a friend who prefers to dominate in relationships. Likewise, the introverted person may encourage the extroverted friend to tone down unnecessarily risky behavior. The passive person can help provide insight when the domineering person finds himself or herself in frustrating situations. In this manner, they can complement one another's individual differences. In spite of the phenomenon of complementarity, however, our new friends will most likely share the majority of our own values, beliefs, and attitudes.

Reciprocity

We tend to like people who show that they like us. We feel good when others say good things about us, which we experience as positive reinforcement. However, reciprocity does not occur if we do not view the flattery as being sincere. If people tell us they like us on the basis of factors that do not fit in with our own self-concepts, we are not so likely to be affected by their attentions (Shrauger, 1975). But what about "playing hard to get?" That suggests the opposite—that we would be more interested in a person of the opposite sex whose attention is nonreciprocal. Research suggests that, in fact, we tend to be interested in those who play hard to get only if they are hard for others to get but show some interest in us (Walster et al., 1973). Thus as we make new friends, they will no doubt be those who have indicated they like us in return or are interested in spending time with us, rather than those who have been aloof and avoidant.

Starting Conversations

After we meet people and decide we would like to get to know them a little better, the next step is to get a conversation going. Think back to when you have enjoyed conversing with new acquaintances. Also think back to when you have found new acquaintances to be so boring you could hardly wait for an excuse to leave the room. You might recall a number of conversational errors made by the boring person as he or she drifted out of your range of interest.

Generic Comments

The person opened the conversation with a hugely general comment such as "Nice party," "How do you like the weather?" or "How about those Blazers?", which might have been fine for an opener. However, if nothing more specific follows, you are left with the task of coming up with something to talk about. A comment such as "Tell me all about yourself" is also too all-encompassing and overwhelming, perhaps resulting in a person feeling put off and asking "So what is it you want to know?"

Negativistic Attitude

Some people seem to have something critical to say about everything. When we are around someone like this for long the atmosphere becomes depressing, so we tend to avoid them. If you open conversations with lines such as "This party sure is a dud," "Our representative in the school congress sure turned out to be a loser," or "I just hate that kind of music, don't you?" others can get the impression you are one of these negativistic people. It does not matter if the party really is a dud, the representative is lackluster, or the music could have been better selected. We form impressions of negativity of others because the negative is what they choose to focus on when initiating conversations. Because of the primacy effect, we are likely to flavor any additional observations with this initial impression.

Self-Absorption

Boring people constantly change the subject to themselves. Naturally, we all talk about ourselves as we share information with one another in conversation. But some people do not listen as you share your ideas and experience, beyond listening for an excuse to change the subject to their own lives and perceptions. After speaking with a self-absorbed person, you may wonder if he or she remembers anything at all about you, or even cares. Such a person may bring up an extremely boring topic, which he or she finds interesting, talk about it endlessly, and not even notice that your interest in the conversation or the person ended quite some time ago.

Know-It-All Attitude

Related to the self-absorbed conversationalist is the self-appointed expert on everything. No matter what topic comes up, your conversation partner speaks as if he or she has the inside track and will kindly educate you. People feel condescended to when others act this way in a social setting. It is one thing to be spoken to with such a tone when you are consulting with a physician, financial advisor, instructor, or spiritual leader. But when this stance is introduced into a simple acquaintanceship conversation, we often perceive the speaker as pompous and conceited, not at all someone we would like to hang around with for very long.

Rigidity

Some people inform you there is only one opinion to be had on a topic, it is the correct opinion, and of course it is their opinion. They seem to live in a black-and-white world where everything is either all good or all bad, absolutely right or absolutely wrong. They show little interest in or acceptance of the opinions of others. They have a tendency to shut down a conversation, since we are not likely to have much enthusiasm for sharing thoughts with those who constantly reject input.

Silence

Silence often does settle over the early stages of a conversation when someone can't think of anything to say, as often happens with shy people, or any of us when we are in a setting where we feel like a fish out of water. We don't necessarily leave a negative impression with others when we struggle with the search for conversational ground, but we certainly don't give them much reason to stay interested in us.

Interesting people, on the other hand, become interesting because they have the ability to hold our attention. They succeed in this task by using a number of techniques:

- *They invite people to talk about themselves.* We all enjoy talking about ourselves. Recognizing this and that we all tend to be interested in people who show interest in us can help us become successful conversationalists through finding ways to help others talk about themselves. Uncovering and examining common ground can be useful. You can ask how the person knows the host who invited you both to the gathering, what led the person to join the group of which you are both a part, how the person likes the apartment dwelling in which you both live. You can also initiate conversation by mentioning something you have heard or noticed about the person:

"I hear you're on the debate team."

"So you're a football fan?" (having noticed the team shirt the person is wearing)

"How's the salsa?" (as you notice the person's apparent favorite choice of refreshment)

"What do you think of Dr. Jackson's thesis?" (as you prepare to leave the seminar you had been attending)

"I was admiring your hairstyle. Do you mind telling me where you have it done?"

Once you get a conversation started, you can keep a person talking by probing whatever information they do share:

"Yes, I've been on the debate team since I transferred here last year." Possible probes: "You're a transfer student? Where did you transfer from? What led to your decision to transfer? What did you like about your old school? What do you like about this school? Do you ever miss your old school?"

"The salsa's actually pretty good. It reminds me of when I went to Mexico." Possible probes: "Really? Tell me about Mexico." "What is it about the salsa that reminds you of the authentic stuff?" "What led to a trip to Mexico?" "Have you been there often?"

- *They capitalize upon open-ended questions.* Open questions take a fair amount of explanation to answer. Closed questions are those that can be answered with only one or a few words. Yes-or-no questions are closed questions:

"Do you like living in Smithstone Hall?"

"Do you have any homework?"

"Are you going to the beach this weekend?"

Once you answer yes or no the conversation may be over, unless you have something else you are dying to add. However, similar questions can be asked that would require a person to do much more talking:

"What's it like living in Smithstone Hall?"

"How do you go about organizing your homework?"

"What do you like to do at the beach?"

There are other types of closed questions that usually involve very short answers:

"Where are you from?"

"What do you do for a living?"

"What time is it?"

Closed questions are good for when you are trying to get at specific information. In a developing conversation, these closed questions can then be probed with more open or progressive ones:

"I'm from New York." Probe: "Really? What's it like living on the East Coast?"

"I'm a stenographer." Probe: "What kind of company do you work for?"

"It's 10:30." Probe: "I still have half an hour before class. Would you care to join me for a cup of coffee?"

- *They use open body language.* Each culture recognizes some kinds of posturing as friendly, and others as distancing or closed off. In our Western culture, we interpret a number of nonverbal cues as evidence of interest or disinterest:

   1. *Eye contact.* People who are interested in us use a lot of eye contact. Those who do not use much eye contact may just be shy or lack self-confidence, but they can also be perceived as being disinterested, evasive, or shifty.

   2. *Body posture.* When people face us and aim their entire bodies toward us as they speak, it delivers the message that our presence is important enough for them to devote their entire body attention toward our direction. Interesting people may also lean forward slightly at times to show when they are especially interested in what we have to say. And rather than folding their arms across their chest, their arms are usually hanging relaxed and open-palmed at their sides or in their laps.

   3. *Voice intonation.* Tone of voice also can sound interested or disinterested. Volume, pitch, and rate of speech vary when people are interested or excited, and these changes in intonation also tend to keep us interested in what they have to say. Speaking with a dull monotone, portraying an under-your-breath sarcastic commentary, or making long-winded speeches that take off like a house afire do not sound quite so appealing or interesting to fellow conversationalists.

- *They use appropriate levels of self-disclosure.* **Self-disclosure** involves telling others about yourself: your feelings, thoughts, plans for your life, personal experiences, and other personal information. The amount of information we disclose to others depends upon the nature of the relationship. We reveal much about ourselves to our spouses, physicians, therapists, spiritual leaders, and close friends and relatives. We reveal less to our classmates, co-workers, neighbors, and other acquaintances, and relatively little or nothing to those we consider complete strangers.

We human beings seem to be inherently nosy. We like to know things about other people. Just look at the success of the tabloid newspapers, success in spite of the fact that most people recognize what they print as fiction! Sharing personal information with others often will hold their interest. We usually perceive the self-disclosures of others as evidence that they like us, which in fact is consistent with research findings (Derlega et al., 1987). Self-disclosure is also useful as we try to find common ground when we are trying to get to know one another.

However, how disclosure is handled can also contribute toward others viewing you in either a positive or a negative light. If one person shares something personal about himself or herself and the other person still avoids any self-disclosure, the second person is usually viewed as being unfriendly. On the other hand, if a low-disclosure conversation is occurring and one person starts revealing very intimate, personal information about himself or herself, often we will judge that person to be in some way maladjusted (Derlega & Chaikin, 1975). Gender also plays a role in how we view the disclosures of others. Women typically disclose more about themselves than men do (Cozby, 1973), and we appear to expect men and women to fall into gender stereotypes. When men self-disclose to the same degree that women do, we may perceive them to be maladjusted, even though we would not make such a judgment about a woman making the same disclosure (Kleinke & Kahn, 1980). Yet there is opposing evidence that in some situations, such as while speaking with strangers, men are actually more self-disclosing than women (Rosenfeld et al., 1979). A general rule of thumb, therefore, appears to be that those who disclose in a manner similar to that of their conversation partner and do not disclose too much too quickly will be the most successful at building the new relationship.

Building Blocks of Liking and Loving

As relationships progress, they can follow many different pathways toward attachment. Sternberg (1988) conceptualizes the different types of liking and loving in terms of three components: intimacy, passion, and decision and commitment.

Intimacy

Intimacy refers to the degree of emotional investment a person has placed in the relationship. Many factors contribute to how much intimacy we feel toward one another: ability to give and receive emotional support, mutual understanding and appreciation, desire to enhance one another's well-being, successful intimate communication, ability to rely on one another in times of need.

Passion

Passion involves the need investment of the relationship. We are most familiar with the relationship between romance and sexual needs. However, there are other types of passion, which are not sexual in nature, such as the strong attachment between parent and child and the mutual investment toward learning between a student and a mentor.

Decision and Commitment

Decision and commitment are directed by our sense of will, rather than our needs or emotional states. This aspect of love is the one we actively choose. We decide to show love toward our significant other and commit ourselves to continue to do so.

Different Types of Love

The different types of love are based on the absence or presence of these three components. The absence of all three components indicates **nonlove**. We experience nonlove toward those we do not know, or with whom we may have only a fleeting acquaintanceship. **Liking** occurs when intimacy alone is involved. We enjoy spending time with the person and care about his or her well-being, but there is no passion or decision and commitment. When such individuals are no longer a part of our lives, we miss them but are not likely to become grief-stricken or preoccupied by their absence.

They glanced across the crowded room . . . their eyes met . . . flames of passion melted their hearts as they each suspected they had encountered the one true love of their lives. . . . This narrative, the stuff we frequently find in paperback romantic novels, describes **infatuated love**. Passion is present, but little else. When the passion is sexually linked, such individuals feel sexually drawn toward one another. Infatuated love can also come in the form of idolizing a mentor or role model. In spite of its intense nature, infatuated love is generally short-lived.

A relationship consisting only of commitment is called **empty love**. For whatever reasons, the person has decided to be committed toward making the relationship work even though passion and intimacy are absent. Often this stems from convenience. Perhaps passion and/or intimacy were present at one time and are now absent, but for the sake of finances, the children, or lifestyle choices the two parties decide to keep the relationship going. Empty love can also mark the beginning of a relationship, such as taking on a foster child about whom you know nothing, or when you live in a culture where arranged marriages are the norm.

Romantic love involves both intimacy and passion. It may begin with that "glance across the crowded room," and then as the two begin to get to know one another, intimacy develops as well. Or, two people may begin as casual friends, and over time develop the passionate feelings we associate with romantic relationships. Decision and commitment toward the relationship are not yet a part of these romantic feelings.

The combination of passion and decision and commitment produces a relationship called **fatuous love**. The commitment stems from reasons of passion only, usually of a sexual nature between lovers. The two may be very committed to one another in the pursuit of this passion, but there is no intimacy in the relationship. Thus as the passion dies down, the decision and commitment usually go as well.

Companionate love is made up of intimacy and decision and commitment. This is a friendship-based love and can occur between members of the same or opposite sex. The two people care about each other, enjoy each other, and are committed toward keeping their friendship going indefinitely. A child was once asked about his relationship with a long-term opposite sex playmate, and he explained the relationship as being "in like"—a fair assessment of the underpinnings of companionate love.

When intimacy, passion, and decision and commitment are all present, the two people are experiencing **consummate love**. Most of us dream of experiencing this kind of love with our lifetime mates. While consummate love can exist, a lot of energy must be expended to be able to simultaneously prolong the states of passion, intimacy, and decision and commitment.

There are some intense relationships that are often mistaken for love but are in fact obsessions. Many of us have seen or heard of the film *Fatal Attraction,* concerning a woman who stalks a man with whom she had a one-night-stand relationship and then terrorizes him and his family in her attempts to convince him to return her "love." Obviously, this sort of behavior does not represent a caring feeling, but is instead an obsession with the stalker's own need to extract something from his or her victim.

Robin Norwood's *Women Who Love Too Much* (1985) describes another type of obsessed "lover," involving individuals who remain in destructive relationships and design their lives around rescuing or trying to win the affection of their significant others. Sometimes, such a relationship becomes codependent, similar to relationships involving substance abusers. Thus the relationship revolves around the partner's dysfunction, rather than intimacy, passion, or decision and commitment.

Susan Forward and Joan Torres describe a complementary pair of obsessed partners in *Men Who Hate Women and the Women Who Love Them* (1986). One partner acts in a hostile manner toward the other—highly critical, controlling, emotionally and perhaps even physically abusive. The motivation for this behavior has little to do with love, and much more to do with a need to "get even" with the other partner for the past perceived punitiveness or other shortcomings the abusive partner experienced with his or her primary caretaker. In other words, the abusive partner experiences his or her mate in the same way that a small child experiences a parent figure. This magical mommy or daddy is obligated to see that all needs, whims, and desires are gratified. If they fail, they are justifiably punished in order to promote future compliance. An abused partner who chooses to remain in the relationship typically has bought into the batterer's agenda. He or she sees that whatever the batterer is demanding at a given moment is actually not such a big deal, and eventually believes that as a truly caring partner, he or she could provide for it. The battered partner becomes obsessed with trying to win the affection and approval of the batterer—as well as avoiding being punished—by constantly trying to second-guess what the batterer wants, just as a mother or father tries to anticipate the needs of a small child. Intimacy, passion, and decision and commitment do not play much of a role in this relationship; nor do other aspects of healthy relationships, such as self-respect, mutual respect, and concern for one another's rights and well-being. Instead, the relationship is driven by fear. The battered partner fears the batterer's wrath, and the batterer fears that once again he or she will be shown unworthy of the primary caretaker's "love."

Stanton Peele and Archie Brodsky (1976) describe ways of evaluating whether or not we are experiencing healthy love or destructive love. We can ask ourselves the following questions:

- *Can your true love do no wrong?* If so, since there are no perfect people, you are probably idealizing your partner. Healthy love is sustained by ongoing cooperation through awareness of each partner's strengths, weaknesses, and desirable or undesirable idiosyncracies. These sorts of negotiations cannot occur if ignoring one another's shortcomings is a premise of the relationship.

- *Does this relationship provide a refuge from the harsh realities of life?* Healthy love adds to the ongoing enjoyment of life. While we all turn to our loved ones for comfort during times of stress, destructive love relationships can be based on an attempt to escape life. The concept of "me and you against the world" can feel very romantic at first. But over time, the initial passion of novelty begins to wear down and the relationship becomes your reality rather than your escape from it. Eventually, the unstable grounds for the relationship, as well as the social withdrawal it has promoted, remove the luster from your partner's glow.

- *Do you lose yourself in your relationship with your partner?* In a healthy relationship, both individuals grow and their daily experiences are enhanced. In destructive love, one partner's life, or both lives, may become absorbed by the other and no growth occurs. This can come in the form of two people hurting one another and fighting more often than they build up one another. Destructive love disables, while healthy love enables us to both maintain ourselves and personally grow even further.

• *Did this relationship develop out of an unexpected whirlwind of volatile passion?* Healthy love involves getting to know someone, seeing one another realistically, intelligently believing in one another's goodness and common values, and planning the relationship in ways that are constructive for both individuals' lives. Destructive love depends on a rush of strong feeling, which is neither planful, controllable, nor reliable. Peele refers to destructive love as being "addicted to love," since one who relates to others in this manner becomes dependent upon that rush of feeling, just as a drug addict depends on his or her next "fix." The relationship therefore lasts only as long as it can provide the rush.

Expanding Your Experience

Graduate training often produces friendships of intense intimacy, especially in programs of clinical psychology. My own graduate school experience led to my discovery that the social ties and emotional attachments involved with doctoral training contain all the elements necessary for producing excessive social influence.

Ego strength was definitely lowered. Our personal capacities for learning were being challenged to the max, often leaving us questioning our capabilities and our chances for success. Most of us were feeling off-balance due to the sudden changes in living conditions and lifestyle that go along with returning to school. The quality of interpersonal relationships that had previously made up our support systems suffered, as we directed almost all of our time and energies into our studies. A certain amount of culture shock applied, as we immersed ourselves in the rules, beliefs, and behaviors of a yet-to-become-familiar professional society.

Isolation and alienation coincided. The intensity of training restricted the amount of time we could spend with others, outside of our fellow graduate students. We needed to constantly click ourselves into "intellectual mode" in order to integrate huge amounts of material, which left precious little opportunity for staying in touch with our emotional responding.

The only releases from stress and intensity occurred between terms. Other than that, we felt no hope of escape other than to finish the program and graduate. Of course, we all had the choice of quitting any time we wanted. However, none of us wanted to give up the dream of becoming a clinical psychologist. We had worked too long and hard toward attaining that goal. Furthermore, most of us had borrowed substantial amounts of money to pay for our studies. If we quit, we would not only be faced with our massive debts, but also would not have any greater earning capacity for paying them back. So we continued with this intense life pursuit, wishing away the days of our lives that preceded the next break.

Emotional support and social ties came easily among our fellow classmates. It was as if we were all drifting along in the same lifeboat, feeling vulnerable, isolated, and temporarily(?) trapped. We had little difficulty identifying with one another's feelings. We worked together diligently in study groups, and were almost as invested in the grades of our study partners as we were in our own. In many ways we began to think and behave as one, moving along in a herdlike manner, looking out for one another's interests, yet ever-guarding against becoming like lemmings running over a cliff (nature's ultimate example of excessive social influence!).

One of my early professors of psychology pointed out to me that I could not become involved with psychology without also becoming a politician. I suppose intuitively it made sense. After all, psychologists hold public welfare as their highest priority, and politicians tend to exert control over the conditions within which the "public" attempts to live. However, with my introverted tendencies I did not visualize myself ever playing too great a role of this nature.

My attachments with and emotional reliance upon my fellow doctoral students changed all that. In order to keep moving with the others as one, I needed to be as assertive as everyone else just to keep up. School politics abounded, and I always seemed to be finding myself in the middle of them. Even trying to be invisible didn't help; they would find me. As I was inevitably swept along, I took on more and more personal responsibility for our group. I became highly involved with the student union, eventually holding office. My knack and penchant for writing had a way of frequently getting me assigned the task of composing formal communications when they were needed. Later, as a resident, I became an informal leader as newer trainees came to me for guidance and shared their tales of woe, confusion, and triumph.

It took about 2 years for me to recover from my graduate training. I have heard that 2 years is about average. However, I suspect that I was left reeling from the experience especially because it resulted in my behaving in so many ways that were not characteristic of my nature. In the process of healing, many of the effects of feeling excessive social influence have passed by the wayside. I choose my battles a lot more carefully than I did back then. My professional direction has become more molded by personal interest and opportunity, rather than by what my cohorts thought might be the fashionable way to go.

Yet this period of excessive social influence was not entirely ego dystonic (meaning *not like myself*). I learned to assert myself in ways I had at one time believed would emotionally annihilate me. I desensitized myself to my overactive stress reaction neurochemistry, to the point where now I even feel comfortable doing crisis mental health work in the midst of natural disasters. Furthermore, among my classmates I developed some of the closest and most rewarding relationships I have ever known.

The first exercise for this chapter will give you an opportunity to evaluate the possibility of excessive social influence having played a role in your life. There is also an exercise that will help you evaluate what is most important to you as you select a significant other. Another exercise looks at the role of prejudice in our attitudes and interpersonal relating. The last exercise gives you a chance to get brainstorming assistance from your small group members concerning social situations where you feel at a loss for words.

Study Questions

1. Describe Maslow's hierarchy of human needs. How is it relevant to interpersonal relationships?
2. Describe the rights we all have as we enter into interpersonal relationships.
3. Think of a couple or pair of friends you know who you believe have a good relationship. How is their relationship consistent with the characteristics of good relationships as described in this chapter?
4. What four variables are typically in place when "brainwashing," or excessive social influence, is in place?
5. Does someone have to be trying to brainwash you when the effects of excessive social influence occur? Explain your answer.
6. "Hazing" still occurs on some college campuses, even where it has been banned and results in severe consequences. How might the components of "groupthink" be affecting the decision making of those involved?

7. How might you guard against falling victim to the effects of excessive social influence?
8. Describe the different biases that can adversely affect our judgment.
9. You have just moved into new student housing. What factors are likely to affect who you choose to befriend?
10. When meeting people for the first time, what characteristics are likely to turn a person off?
11. How can you help others enjoy your company and want to get to know you better?
12. What role does self-disclosure play in the early stages of getting to know someone?
13. Describe the "building blocks" of liking and loving.
14. What kind of love is typically portrayed by the media? What kind of love would you prefer to have within your own intimate relationships? Why?
15. Describe how obsessive relationships are different from love-based relationships.
16. How might you assess whether your own relationships are healthy or obsessed?

CHAPTER ELEVEN

Marriage and Alternative Relationship Lifestyles

First comes love then comes marriage then comes (playmate of choice) and a baby carriage

We've done it twice now—can we call it a tradition?

Past generations have viewed love, marriage, and family as an inevitable sequence, spawning skip-rope chants such as the one on the preceding page. Most people do in fact marry. A successful, happy marriage can enrich and enhance every aspect of our lives.

For instance, let's look at the history of Fred and Denise. They met and began their courtship while attending college classes. After they decided to marry, Denise temporarily dropped out of school in order to support them while Fred earned his master's degree in business education. After Fred became situated in his work, she returned to school and completed her degree in nursing. She was offered a prestigious position in a neighboring state; after much discussion, they decided Fred would leave his current position and find a new job near the one Denise had been offered.

There they built their lives together. They picked out a home, made friends, and found activities to do together in their spare time. They began developing traditions that would eventually cement the structure and connectedness of their family for generations. When they decided to have children, Denise wanted to stay home with them until they reached school age. Fred supported her decision, taking some consulting work on the side in order to make ends meet. Once the children were school-aged, Denise returned to work. She and Fred continued to enjoy one another's company and found additional pastimes in which they could include the children. They had a few tumultuous times as they dealt with their children's adolescence, but cared about one another and respected one another enough not to let parenting difficulties interfere with their commitment of working together on joint goals.

Now their children are gone, and they are well on their way to becoming senior citizens. They've had their relationship ups and downs, but they have been content thus far with their journey as life companions. They have supported one another through various illnesses and injuries, and have rejoiced with one another through many delights and triumphs. Marriage has been very fulfilling for Denise and Fred.

But while many people find marriage to be a satisfying way of life, it is not for everybody. For some, these individual differences can result in going through painful experiences such as divorce. For others, it may mean choosing an alternative relationship lifestyle. But first, let's look at the stages of marital adjustment and the factors that contribute toward its success.

Stages of Marriage

Marriages are rarely static. They continually evolve as the partners experience and adjust to their own personal growth issues and changing life tasks. Many of these tasks are products of the evolution of the marital relationship itself. Marriages progress through several stages, with each stage presenting its own set of relationship issues (Carter & McGoldrick, 1988).

THE NEW COUPLE

New couples are faced with sorting out more tasks than those participating in any other stage of marriage. Aggressively tackling this job is essential. Many marriages fail during the first year, in part because the partners do not resolve the many conflicts and other important relationship issues that emerge as the two partners learn to "do" marriage. Often young couples carry on under the illusion that "love conquers all" and that, if two people truly love each other, all problems will automatically sort themselves out to their mutual satisfaction. This is a myth: Many couples split up still loving one another but unable to live together because they have not effectively organized the task.

Becoming both "one" and "two."   Within the community, each new couple takes on an identity. They tend to become referred to as a couple, such as "the Taylors," rather than as "John" and "Jane." They are more likely to be included in social gatherings as a couple and less likely to be included in activities of single individuals. Many personal goals become joint goals as the two individuals' lives become intertwined. Their opinions and attitudes may move closer to one another's than they had been before the relationship. Resources such as time, money, material possessions, and personal power or status become mutual resources. Likewise, many responsibilities and liabilities become jointly owned.

Thus in many ways, the "two" become "one." Many a marriage has failed because one or both members had expected to continue living their lives as they had while they were single. Defining the parameters of the couple's "one-ness" is therefore an important relationship task.

However, as elaborated on in the last chapter, healthy relationships encourage enhancement of each partner's individual life as well. No one person should become lost in the identity of the other. Healthy self-esteem and feelings of self-worth emerge from who we are, not whom we chose to marry. Another common mistake of young couples is going into the relationship thinking they can change their partner into the person they want them to be. While it is possible and in fact desirable to negotiate behavioral changes in ways that take into account the two partners' individual rights and needs, you cannot change who your partners are as individuals.

Thus the couple's "two-ness" is also important to recognize. In what ways will each partner continue to satisfy his or her own personal striving? A good deal of communication, acceptance, and compromise goes into creating a "one" and still maintaining the personal boundaries of the "two."

Rules of the relationship. Each partner comes to the relationship having internalized his or her own set of rules for guiding marital and family behavior. Many of these rules are unspoken, but we nevertheless expect others—especially our partners—to behave in ways that correspond with those rules. Here are some typical "rules" that have governed family behavior:

- Any money left over at the end of the month goes to leisure spending.
- Mom has primary responsibility for child care and housekeeping; Dad has primary responsibility for bringing home an income.
- We always go out to breakfast on Easter.
- The last can of soda in the refrigerator belongs to Dad.
- Everyone picks up after himself or herself at the end of the day.

- Nobody borrows Mom's sewing scissors.
- Family or couple activities take precedence over any individual activities a member might have.
- The toothpaste is always squeezed from the bottom end of the tube.

Suppose John and Jane are getting ready to celebrate the winter holidays. John has always spent the holidays with his family; Jane has always spent them with hers. How do they divide their time between the two families? Furthermore, each family has its own set of traditions for *how* to celebrate. Does John or Jane expect to participate in certain activities? Are there rituals involved? What religious activities does each member expect to observe? Even if both John and Jane are church-involved Christians, they may have dramatically different expectations for Christmas merrymaking. Even something so simple as whether to open gifts on Christmas Eve or Christmas morning can go against the grain of John's or Jane's holiday expectations and result in significant conflict and disappointments.

Although the fact that John and Jane love one another will not automatically resolve their conflict, love is still an asset for their capacity for conflict resolution. When you truly care about a person, you are more willing to work toward breaking down any roadblocks to intimacy or enhancing one another's personal feelings of well-being. Many rules are both formally and informally negotiated as couples willingly compromise for their loved one's benefit. Thus love plays the role of being a motivator, but it is not in itself a conflict resolution strategy.

However, other conflicts are not so easy to sort out. Even trivial rules can conflict and in spite of their relative unimportance may be held tightly by both partners. We are creatures of habit and can feel uncomfortable making some changes even when they objectively do not seem like that big of a deal. Which way do you place the toilet paper on the holder, with the end on the outside or the inside? Are beverages at dinner poured and then placed on the table, or do you place the beverage pitcher on the table and let people help themselves?

One strategy that many couples find useful while sorting out conflicting family rules and traditions is **exchange contracting**. Suppose Jane and John conflict on the toilet paper and dinner beverage rules just mentioned. They both feel very strongly about doing things their way. Through exchange contracting, John might get the toilet paper set up his way and Jane might get the dinner beverages handled her way, or vice versa. They both give in on something, but they also both get to keep something they want.

As you enter into or explore your own marital relationship, here are some questions that might be useful for you as you organize your lives:

- How are our responsibilities divided?
- What does our budget look like, and how are money decisions made?
- How do we spend our free time?
- How do we decide important issues such as where to live, how many children to have, and career moves to make?
- What are the acceptable and unacceptable ways of expressing ourselves to one another?
- In which areas are we considered accountable or not accountable to one another?
- How will we go about resolving conflict?
- Which aspects of our relationship are private, and which aspects can we feel free to discuss with others? Which others?
- What role will extended family play in our lives?

Most likely, you will probably readdress these questions throughout your relationship, as your lives change and you address new stages of marital and family living.

Having Babies

Most married couples eventually produce children. During the early parenthood stage, young couples adjust to a drastically different lifestyle. They move away from being just "two" and go on to become "three," "four," "five," or more. Their identity as a couple changes, as they find they have more in common with other young parents than they do with childless couples. They have numerous new tasks and rules to set up and address.

How will they handle child care responsibilities? Will one person stay home and take primary responsibility for the children, or will they use day care? Or will they rotate work schedules so that one parent is always home? And what about specific responsibilities, such as staying home when the child is sick, getting up when the child wakes up in the middle of the night, getting children out of bed mornings and ready for their day, or chauffeuring them to their various activities? Also, which child-rearing techniques will they use, and what style of discipline do they agree upon?

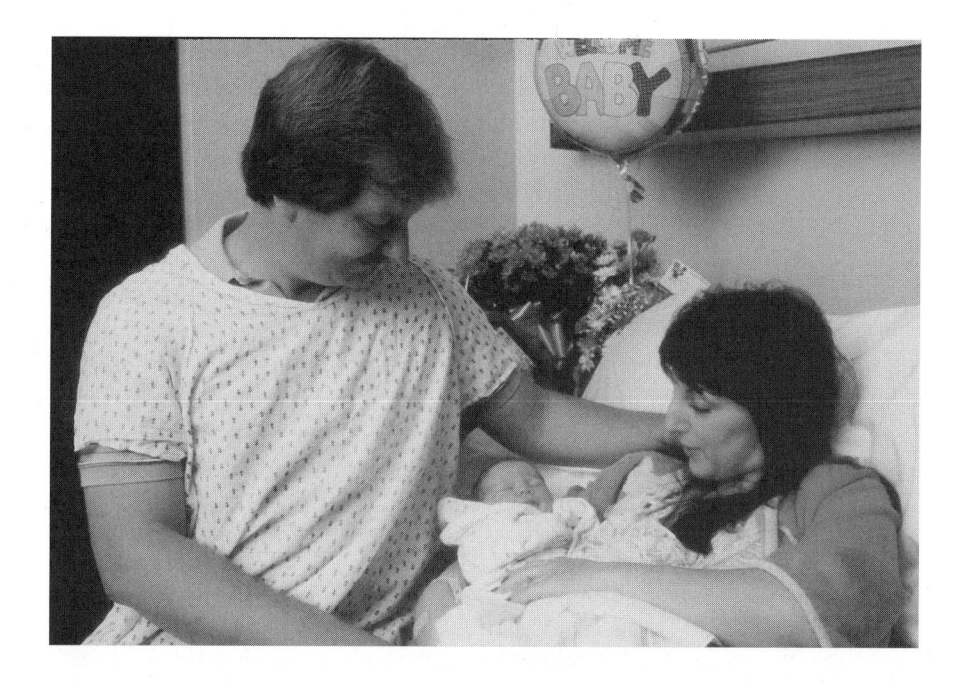

Another necessary adjustment concerns division of resources. Children are very expensive. The amount of money available for fun, games, and impulse spending may no longer be available, especially if one parent has quit working in order to take care of children. Free time is also harder to come by, since child-rearing is a 24-hour-a-day job. New parents find that they cannot do anything without first considering what they are going to do with the children. Energy becomes a more limited commodity, since taking care of young children can be both physically and emotionally draining.

Spontaneous living temporarily becomes a thing of the past as young parents adjust to more extensive planning before they can do anything. They cannot simply get up and go on the spur of the moment if a baby is coming along. First of all, any major outing immediately turns into "moving day," as they pull together all the equipment and feeding and diaper-changing supplies. Also, they must keep in mind the baby's schedule. If they try to go somewhere when the baby normally sleeps, eats, or tends to be crabby, it may interfere with enjoying much of their outing.

With so many changes and new tasks, couples need to actively make time for their marital relationship. Thus a new task for young parents is figuring out how to preserve time for one another, in spite of the intrusion into the relationship caused by the presence of young children. Such time no longer automatically presents itself. And continuing to have such time is important. Occasionally finding ways to get away from family responsibilities allows couples to touch base with one another as individuals and as marital partners, rather than as "Mommy" and "Daddy." Father's ability to participate in care-giving and desire for affiliation within the new family also appears to play a major role in the continued marital satisfaction of both spouses (Levy-Shiff, 1994).

Organization and planning helps new parents surmount all of these new tasks and conflicts. Babies are so cute and cuddly. Watching them react, learn, grow, and reveal who they are is fascinating. They can be a source of great joy and satisfaction. However, loving and enjoying your children is not going to automatically result in an effective family lifestyle. So as you plan to become a family, be sure to discuss openly the many issues involved with the addition of children, so that you can experience your child-rearing years as rewarding and enhancing of your marital relationship.

In Come the Adolescents

As parents make the necessary adjustments for child-rearing, they fall into a groove of family living. Everyone learns the routine and rules and generally agrees to live by them. As the children enter adolescence, however, new adjustments must be made. Adolescence is a period of moving toward adulthood. In order for children to do this successfully, the parents must foster more independence in them by letting them do more of their own decision making, giving them more adult responsibilities, and letting them make a few of their own rules. Typically, adolescents will find ways to do this all on their own, regardless of how their parents react to them! Thus many structural changes take place within the family.

Likewise, parents find that they need to converse with their children differently during adolescence. Having become formal operational, adolescents understand issues on a more abstract level. They begin to question the "status quo" more effectively and become more persistent in challenging the views and desires of parents. This leads to a significantly higher degree of conflict within the family.

Conflicts presented by the addition of adolescents can become either a help or a hindrance to the marital relationship. First, both parents must accept that the rules of the game of family living have changed. As they do so, they can address conflict directly and successfully work through it, thus strengthening their relationship as a couple. On the other hand, if parents try to hold adolescents to childhood rules, or handle conflict by working around it, ignoring it, or using it as grounds for competition, the relationship can become strained.

The Empty Nest

Eventually, children grow up and leave home. Parents find themselves back to being "two" and learn to redefine their relationship in the absence of children. If children have become all the parents had in common and they did not work to preserve their relationship as a couple, this can be a difficult period for them. It can also be especially trying if one parent had chosen to stay at home and devote his or her life to child-rearing and is now suddenly without a job.

However, if the partners have kept their relationship going, it can be a great time of life. There are fewer financial worries, fewer household responsibilities, more privacy, and much more time for partners to spend with each other. They have more freedom to make career moves, and are probably at a stage in their careers where they are making more money than they had in the past. They can also share in the pleasure of relating to their children as adults and watching them grow into their own futures, without feeling so much the weight of responsibility. Again, active planning helps empty nest parents adjust to their newfound resources and changes in family structure.

Retirement

During retirement, couples generally quit or drastically cut back on working outside the home. They have more time for each other, hobbies, volunteer work, or just doing what they feel like doing. They can do the things they have always wanted to do but which they have not had time or energy for.

Retired couples are faced with a new set of adjustments. First, what is it like to no longer be working? Some people—especially men—tend to define themselves in terms of their work or career. Thus retirement can result in a major identity crisis, as a person seeks answers to the question "Who am I without my work role?" This can put significant stress on the marital relationship.

Take the example of a wife who had primary responsibility for running the household and a husband who worked primarily outside the home. During retirement, the wife continues to have a significant work life; self-care does not go away with retirement. However, how does the husband spend his time? He may spend it driving his wife up the wall, following her around through her routine and getting in the middle of activities she previously participated in independently.

Another set of adjustments involves health and financial security. Retired couples need to adapt to growing older physically, to the limitations that can result from growing older. If one partner becomes more limited–losing eyesight, for example–the other may need to assume more responsibility, such as taking over all the driving. Too, most retired couples are on a fixed income and may need to monitor their spending more carefully than they have been accustomed to. They may again turn to exchange contracting as they decide what they will need to give up and which pastimes and luxuries they will be able to keep.

Success at Marital Relationships

Social science researchers have uncovered many correlates of the success or failure of marital relationships. However, different researchers have different opinions of how to define "success." Is it whether or not the couple stays married? Is it a certain set of behavioral criteria, such as the ability to have a conversation without getting into an argument? Or is it a function of the level of satisfaction each partner experiences within his or her marital relationship?

Everybody answers this question differently, depending on whatever each individual values most. Therefore, let's look at "successful" marriage from three different standpoints: longevity, relationship qualities, and level of satisfaction.

SUCCESS AS LONGEVITY

Success defined as **longevity** simply means that the marriage hangs in there no matter what. Research has uncovered a number of factors that appear to be associated with marital longevity. These include absence of premarital pregnancy (Furstenberg, 1976), marrying while in the late twenties or later (Booth & Edwards, 1985), coming from a family of origin without an extensive history of divorce (Mueller & Pope, 1977), and higher income (L'Abate et al., 1986).

The reasons for these statistical relationships are not always particularly clear. For example, couples with higher incomes may stay together because so many disagreements in marriages concern finances; thus the higher the income, the fewer the arguments. However, the statistical finding could also be due to the fact that people with higher incomes have more to lose by dividing their households. Therefore, they decide to stick it out in order to maintain the lifestyle to which they have become accustomed.

In addition to individual predictors, there are certain styles of marriages occurring in relationships that are able to endure (Cuber & Haroff, 1980). Actually, enduring marital relationships may take on all of the following forms during the various stages of a marriage. While some appear to be more desirable than others, they all have their advantages and disadvantages.

Conflict-habituated marriage.

These couples are constantly at odds with one another. They rarely resolve conflict unless there is a major crisis. Most of their actual fighting takes place in private, but family and close friends are usually aware of their continual state of conflict.

Why would a marriage of this nature endure? Actually, aggression is very personal; it is a form of detached intimacy. For some people, conflict is the only kind of intimacy they know, especially if they came from tumultuous backgrounds. There are also individuals who have been so badly burned in relationships that they actually prefer conflictual intimacy. For them, the interpersonal distance and detachment feels safer.

Devitalized marriage.

Sometimes the fire dies down in a marital relationship. In devitalized marriages, couples still genuinely care about one another but have become less intimate. They may spend less time with each other, do less personal sharing, and have less sexual intimacy. Usually this occurs because the partners are heavily invested in some other aspect of their lives, such as taking care of children, career demands, or individual interests. They are not necessarily fighting more; in fact, they may be fighting less, as they deal with marital conflicts by sticking them on the back burner while they focus on other aspects of their lives.

Marriages commonly become devitalized for almost every couple. Often devitalization takes place as couples are shifting from one stage of marital or personal development to another and are temporarily parceling out their energy toward adjustment issues. Fortunately, devitalized marriages are usually easily revitalized through patience, understanding, and increased communication.

Marriage encounter groups are especially useful for devitalized marriages. Such groups are offered by many churches, as well as by many secular organizations. At marriage encounters couples meet in large groups, usually over a weekend. Speakers give talks on a variety of marital topics. The talks are interspersed with periods of time for everyone to write about the topics in journals. Later they get together with their partners to share what they have written. In the process, they share a number of good feelings they have for one another that never really went away but which they just have not had time or opportunity to express.

Passive-congenial marriage. Sometimes couples grow so far apart during their individual growth that emotional involvement leaves their marital relationship. In passive-congenial relationships, couples are often comfortable with the reduced emotional involvement. They experience little or no intimacy and do not have much involvement in one another's lives, but they still have platonic feelings toward one another—sort of like being roommates.

Usually each individual's emotional energy is focused in some other direction, such as work, raising children, or personal adjustment issues. There is little open conflict in the relationship, most likely because they are each expecting so little from the relationship. They still feel love and appreciation toward one another; they just are not very involved with one another. Like the devitalized marriage, a passive-congenial relationship may occur as a temporary solution to limited time and energy.

Vital marriage. Vital marriages are common during the honeymoon phase. The two partners truly enjoy being with one another. They try to spend as much time together as possible. They have certain activities they do together that they tend not to enjoy as much without their partner. They play the role of "Number One" in each other's lives, even when it means making personal sacrifices.

This style of marriage can be either an advantage or disadvantage for conflict resolution. The couples are highly motivated to resolve conflict so they can get back to the good feelings of their intense relationship. However, because of their haste this style can lead to superficial solutions or ways to avoid conflict that result in difficulties never being adequately addressed.

Total marriage. The total marriage is the relationship most of us dream of having with our significant others. It is like the vital marriage, but involves more than being obsessed with having each other's company. The partners enjoy all aspects of life with each other. They are not only marital partners, but also friends and lovers. They have common goals in all aspects of life: what they truly want for themselves, as well as for each other.

Having a total marriage involves hard work. Often couples with such marriages have become this strong because they have found ways to successfully work through the serious problems that often come up during marital relationships. Thus they typically handle conflict well, rather than becoming avoidant of the temporary uncomfortable feelings involved with exploring a problem to its fullest. They have put the strength of their commitment to the test and have passed the test.

SUCCESS AS RELATIONSHIP QUALITIES

Social perspective often plays a role in how we define the **relationship qualities** of a successful marriage. If you ask the average person on the street what they would expect to see in a successful marriage, you will most likely hear certain general themes among their responses: They get along with each other. They have a good attitude. They can communicate with one another. Let's look at these themes individually.

They get along with each other.

We usually think of a couple as having a successful marriage if they look happy with one another. They seem to respect one another, and they do not abuse one another's individual rights. When they disagree, they resolve conflict effectively and fairly.

What is "fair fighting"? Why do some couples deal with conflict in ways that seem to enhance the relationship, while others appear to approach conflict as an opportunity for a search and destroy mission? Ineffective arguers often make the following mistakes:

• They participate in a competition sometimes known as "sandbagging." Partner 1 voices a complaint about Partner 2. Partner 2 counters with a different complaint about Partner 1. Partner 1 accuses Partner 2 of yet something else. Partner 2 points out that it's not as bad as another behavior of Partner 1's. They continue to parry back and forth, as if the winner will be the one who has thought up the most criticisms of the other. Unfortunately, none of the complaints ever gets addressed fully enough to be resolved.

• They become defensive. They make excuses for their behavior, rather than acknowledge that it has caused a difficulty for their partner. They react to each other's concerns as personal attacks, rather than as issues their partners want to resolve.

• They resort to put-downs and name-calling. Personally attacking one another only leads to more bad feelings and less desire by the "insultee" to work with the "insulter" on the problem at hand.

- They are rigid in their views and demands and are intolerant of the fact that all partners have individual differences.

- They tell their partners what they believe their partners think or feel, and then chastise them for having these imagined thoughts or feelings. In this manner couples can direct their energies toward arguing about issues that do not even exist.

Couples who effectively argue are effectively focused. One way to be effectively focused is to use a problem-solving technique similar to the one described in Chapter 4. Define the problem and separate out all of the subproblems, so you are not sidetracked by them. Explore the possible causes of the problem and describe the feelings each of you has about it. List potential solutions and their advantages and disadvantages. For each partner, list a hierarchy of preferences for which solution to use, then choose the solution that appears closest to the top on both hierarchies. As with individual problem solving, also decide how you will set up the chosen solution and follow through on it.

In addition to using problem solving, successful couples agree to follow many other rules of arguing:

- They use "I" statements rather than "you" statements. They state how they themselves feel. They let it be known what they want. They take responsibility for their own feelings by saying "I feel…when you…," rather than "you make me feel…" These strategies help partners avoid the temptations of blaming and name-calling behaviors or putting their partners on the defensive.

- They acknowledge their partner's point of view or feelings. They may repeat back what they have heard their partner say, in order to be sure that they have heard and understood. They do not assume they know their partner's thoughts and feelings better than their partner does. They may even modify their own point of view, based on what they have learned from their partner.

- When necessary, they can "agree to disagree." They can acknowledge the validity of each partner's point of view. They recognize that as individuals, they will always have differing opinions and desires, and that nobody has yet cornered the market on reality. In spite of their differences, they are able to compromise and negotiate solutions that may not be what any individual partner thinks is best but is the most effective middle ground between the two partners' viewpoints.

They have a good attitude. As has been described in several of the previous chapters, your beliefs affect both your feelings and your behaviors. Beliefs about one another's roles in the marital relationship are not an exception. Here are some irrational beliefs that are likely to fuel dissatisfaction in a marital relationship:

> "When my spouse upsets me I have little control over my feelings."
>
> "My spouse is responsible if I am unhappy with him/her; he/she must change before I can feel better."
>
> "If my spouse really cared about me he/she wouldn't act this way."
>
> "My spouse only does that in order to get on my nerves."
>
> "If my spouse really loved me, he/she would know what I want."
>
> "My spouse's behavior shows that he/she is bad and deserves to be punished."
>
> "It's horrible, terrible, and awful if my spouse and I have an angry disagreement."
>
> "When unpleasant events occur within my marriage, I must get upset."

As with other irrational beliefs, these thoughts can be challenged. We *do* have some control over our feelings; we *can* feel better even if our partners do not change; our partners generally do not organize their lives around irritating us; they cannot read our minds and know our needs or know what we dislike; and so on. Marital partners are more likely to experience quality relating if they are not affected by such irrational beliefs.

They can communicate with one another.

The phrase "good communication" so easily and frequently rolls off the tongue as individuals describe successful relationships that it has become almost trite. However, if you ask your interviewees to elaborate on what "good communication" actually means, they might not be so quick to respond.

Communication is a complicated process. Take the example of Tim wanting to ask Mary for a date. Actually communicating this desire involves several steps. The process can break down due to errors or inaccuracies during any of these steps.

The first step is formulating his idea: I want to take Mary to the new Kevin Costner movie. If he speaks to her before he has such a concrete plan, he may call her up and find himself babbling. This is not only ineffective communication but also is not likely to impress Mary.

Second, he needs to put his thoughts into words; in this case, in the form of a question. What specifically will he say when he talks to her? Only knowing what he wants will not automatically result in verbalizing it effectively.

Third, he actually delivers the message. Having decided to say "How would you like to go see the new Kevin Costner movie Friday night?" he calls Mary and asks. Interference at this level generally involves physical factors: Did he speak directly into the receiver? Did he stutter? Did he speak slowly enough and with sufficient volume to be heard?

Fourth, Mary receives the message, hearing the actual sound of Tim's voice. Interference at this level is also physical, such as Mary being distracted by the television as Tim asked, or having a hearing problem.

Fifth, Mary processes the sound of Tim's voice into meaningful words and is able to recreate the mental picture represented by what Tim was asking. Misinterpretations can occur at this point. Perhaps Mary only speaks Spanish. Or, not being a moviegoer, she does not know who Kevin Costner is.

Sixth, Mary recognizes what Tim is asking based on her own understanding of the interaction. Here is where her biases can play a role. Suppose she thinks guys only ask women out because they are "interested in one thing." She will thus interpret Tim's request in a manner other than what he had originally intended. Or perhaps Mary's peers consider Kevin Costner to be a "geek," in which case Mary may feel that Tim is insulting her.

And last but most importantly, Mary gives Tim feedback letting him know that a message has been received. Feedback helps Tim know if his question has been received in the manner it was intended. Thus it is important that Tim not have the stereo turned up while he is asking so that he has difficulty hearing her response, or call Mary when he knows she is about to leave for a class and does not have time to fully respond. Feedback also marks a new beginning, as Mary formulates an idea, puts it into words, and so forth.

Here is an example of how the communication process can go awry in a marital relationship. Mr. Taylor is in charge of taking out the garbage. He usually takes it out in the morning as he is leaving for work. However, Mrs. Taylor would like him to take it out in the evening instead. She has noticed that sometimes it begins to smell when left inside, and on other occasions the dog has gotten into it during the night and spread it around. As time goes on, she becomes more and more upset by the inconvenience caused by this habit of his. She decides to say something to him about it.

First, she needs to formulate her idea. What is she really upset about? What does she want her husband to do? Unrealistic expectations can play a role here. Does she expect Mr. Taylor to read her mind and know what is bothering her? If she does, she will most likely tack on some additional resentment, as she perceives her husband as purposely ignoring her needs and doing something to upset her. Egocentrism can become a problem as well. Perhaps Mr. Taylor doesn't notice the smell or isn't as bothered by the occasional mess the dog has made out of the garbage. If Mrs. Taylor believes her husband should feel the same way she does, she may become even more indignant. The more misperceptions on her part, the further away she will get from simply asking if he would mind taking out the garbage at night instead of in the morning.

As she puts her request into words, the message will be most clearly understood if she says something along the lines of "I would appreciate it if you would take out the garbage at night instead of in the morning. Sometimes I notice a smell in the morning, and occasionally the dog gets into it. Would you be willing to do this for me?" Such an approach is direct, does not beat around the bush, and follows the basic rules of assertive behavior. She is expressing her need without attacking Mr. Taylor, sandbagging on a collection of other issues, trying to get even for his "inconsiderate behavior," or disregarding his right to choose whether or not he will comply with her preference.

As Mrs. Taylor physically expresses her request she speaks clearly and assertively, as if she means what she says, but without becoming hostile or sarcastic. In order to make sure Mr. Taylor physically receives her message, she makes sure she has his attention before speaking. She does not verbalize her request while he is half-asleep, watching TV, or otherwise preoccupied. Nor does she catch his attention, turn on the dishwasher or some other noisemaker, and make her request as he struggles to hear.

The more directly and clearly Mrs. Taylor delivers the message, the more likely Mr. Taylor's understanding of it will be accurate. However, he may read things into it based on his own faulty assumptions and other sorts of overreactions. If he is being oversensitive, he may become defensive or start listing off things Mrs. Taylor does that he doesn't like in order to get even. This reaction is not likely to lead to effective problem solving. Also, if Mrs. Taylor has been critical of a number of his behaviors lately, he may see this request as just one more criticism and not take it seriously enough to be willing to comply.

This example shows how communicating successfully involves not only avoiding breakdowns at the various stages but also having strategies for being able to successfully deal with miscommunication. Communicative efforts are easily foiled if one partner not only misinterprets what the other is saying, but also refuses to address or acknowledge the miscommunication. The following guidelines can enhance the communication process:

- Exercise care in when and where you choose to communicate something important, so your partner has a better chance of hearing you and you have a better chance of receiving useful feedback.
- Think before you speak, so you do not blurt out the first thing that comes to mind.
- Truly listen to what your partner has to say; do not jump to conclusions before complete explanations have been shared. Paraphrase back what you have heard so you can verify its accuracy.
- When unsure about what your partner is actually saying, give him or her the benefit of the doubt and ask for clarifications.
- Do not assume that your partner knows what you think or how you feel. Your partner may be able to guess, but he or she may also guess incorrectly. If you want your partner to know something, tell him or her!

Success as Satisfaction

Surveys have turned up a number of **level of satisfaction** factors that appear to predict whether or not a couple will be satisfied with their marriage (e.g., Grover et al., 1984; Lauer & Lauer, 1986). Happy couples often come from families where the parents had happy marriages, or the partners were happy as children themselves. They marry after they have a certain amount of independent life experience, rather than rushing into marriage when they are still relatively young. They usually know their future spouse for a long period of time before deciding to marry, and their choice of spouse tends to have their parents' approval. Their reasons for marrying are based on love and commitment, rather than unexpected pregnancies, uncertain personal goals, or attempts to escape from family of origin or other life circumstances.

But what specifically provides the basis of the couples' feelings of satisfaction? Overwhelmingly, partners in happy marriages view one another positively, both as individuals and as friends. They also view marriage as an institution positively and are committed toward making their marriages last. They genuinely work toward finding agreement on their goals, philosophy of life, and styles of affection and sexual intimacy.

We all vary in the degree of happiness we are willing to settle for in our marriages. Furthermore, we require more or less from our marriages at different times in our lives. Suppose the quality of a marital relationship were presented on a continuum, with a fantastically perfect, total marriage at one end, and the worst marriage on the face of the earth at the other end, as represented by the illustration in Figure 11.1. Where along that continuum would you place your own desires? In other words, at this point in your life, how good would your marriage have to be for you to feel satisfied?

Some individuals are satisfied with relatively little. Perhaps their marital relationships exist purely for the sake of convenience. Or perhaps their relationships are distant, quarrelsome at best. However, they are satisfied with the current quality of interrelatedness. They may be finding intimacy and outlets for emotional energy elsewhere at this point in their lives, such as through work, friends, children, or pastimes. They look to their marital relationship for reasons other than intimacy, such as having a co-parent or fellow wage earner, or structuring their lives around social or religious expectations.

Other individuals require a lot before they can feel satisfied with their marital relationships. They insist on working toward having a total marriage at all times, and are disappointed by the usual fluctuations away from that end of the continuum. While these individuals are more likely to be motivated to work on their relationships, they also have a more difficult time feeling satisfied.

Dissatisfaction erupts when partners find themselves with significant differences between what each partner requires of the relationship. The partner who wants more intimacy is likely to feel ignored or unloved, and the partner who wants more distance is likely to feel pressured or smothered. However, if a couple is committed toward making the relationship work, they can communicate their needs and make compromises that bring their level of relatedness to a negotiated middle ground. Their ability to communicate, problem-solve, and adjust to one another thus contributes to their ability to feel satisfied.

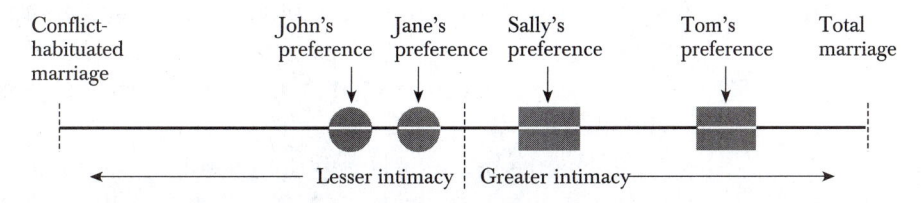

FIGURE 11.1 Preferred marital intimacy continuum
Even though Sally and Tom prefer more intimacy in their relationship than John and Jane, the greater difference between their two preferences may result in their experiencing more marital dissatisfaction than John and Jane.

Another variable that affects level of satisfaction is the role of expectations. Actively discussing and organizing family rules early in the relationship increases the likelihood that the partners will be satisfied. Expectations must also be realistic. This chapter, as well as Chapter 10, has already hinted at a number of unrealistic relationship expectations that can derail marital satisfaction:

- In stable relationships, partners' feelings toward one another never change.
- If two people truly love one another, conflict and arguments do not occur.
- Another person can meet all of my needs. Or, I can meet all of my spouse's needs.
- I can change my spouse into the person I want him or her to be. Or, I can turn into the person my spouse wants me to be.
- Becoming a couple means giving up your individual identity in order to become part of the other person.
- Appropriate marital roles are more or less etched in granite.
- Having a baby will provide the basis for a happy relationship.
- Love conquers all.

Obviously, those who ascribe to such myths of relationships are going to have difficulty experiencing satisfaction within their marriages.

Divorce

About half of all marriages end in divorce (Cherlin, 1981). However, this statistic should not be interpreted to mean that if you get married your marriage only has a 50-50 chance of making it. Many divorces are accounted for by individuals who marry, divorce, and remarry several times; thus pumping up the statistic. Most people fervently avoid divorce. It is a painful process.

Ending a marital relationship is a process of tearing down the lifestyle so carefully set up when the couple married. Bohannon (1975) categorizes the changes during divorce according to six different levels: emotional, legal, economic, co-parental, community, and psychic. Emotional divorce is one of the most difficult, as a couple's previous emotional intersupportiveness is replaced by conflict and disengagement. Legal divorce is the lawyers' arena: filing various documents and getting specific arrangements down on paper. Economic divorce involves the rearrangement of finances, as a couple divides up their belongings, arranges for any support payments, and relearns financial coping individually. Co-parental divorce determines the custodial arrangements of children. Community divorce involves the rearrangement of the individuals' social lives, such as losing relationships with friends and relatives who may take sides and making new connections as part of the singles scene. Psychic divorce is the dissolution of the sense of being "two" and going back to the sole identity of being "one."

Thus losses abound during divorce. In some ways, divorce is even worse than the death of the spouse, since the former spouse is still around to remind you of your losses and the failure of your marriage. Little wonder that divorced individuals experience an increased likelihood of stress, physical illness, depression, and suicidal ideations (Bloom et al., 1978; Stack, 1980).

In recent years, therapists have sought out ways to minimize the destructive effects occurring during the aftermath of divorce. Divorce mediation and divorce counseling have proven useful in this respect, as they help couples sort out the many changes they must address. One arrangement that appears to help couples heal and move on is creating distance between one another right after the divorce, yet maintaining close ties with the children, often by involving third parties who help with custody transfers (Abelsohn, 1992). Divorce counseling also helps individuals understand what went wrong, so they will be less likely to repeat the same patterns in future relationships (Peck & Manocherian, 1988).

Alternative Lifestyles

Entering the state of matrimony is the most commonly used solution to the problem of establishing partnership intimacy. However, in recent years other solutions have become more popular and are being met with increasing levels of social acceptance. Three such solutions are staying single, cohabiting, and forming committed homosexual relationships.

Staying Single

Individuals who choose to remain single have more freedom and more control over their lives and enjoy more feelings of independence. They can enjoy a variety of intimate relationships with others without feeling like they are betraying somebody. They do not have to worry about sharing responsibilities and personal resources. Their life goals are not limited by the constraints presented by their partners' needs and rights. Single individuals have more opportunities for education, career moves, and pursuing individual interests, as well as for altruistic pastimes.

On the other hand, single individuals are more subject to loneliness. When they become ill or financially strapped, they often lack a support system to help them through their difficult moments. Governmental policies discriminate against singles, since tax breaks are given to those who are married and/or have children.

Child-rearing may not be an option for singles, and when it is, single parenthood can be extremely difficult. Children are expensive, and you typically would find yourself trying to support them *and* pay for day care with only one income, unless you are successful in collecting child support. Finding time to spend by yourself or with other adults is difficult without a live-in partner to provide adult company or help share the load of child care. And if you become sick, unemployed, or injured, who will take care of the children's needs?

In spite of the disadvantages, singlehood may be the best option for some people. Some of us are "loners," valuing our time and privacy. Others of us have had so many unfortunate experiences with previous relationships that we feel too "burnt" to enter any serious interpersonal commitments. Yet others may not have found the "Mr." or "Ms. Right" they believe will measure up to their expectations of a marital partner. Given the painful consequences of an ill-advised marriage or possibility of going through the divorce process, forestalling committed relationships temporarily or indefinitely may be the most viable choice for some individuals. Remember that life is not static; you can always change your marital status if your needs and values change.

Living Together

Cohabiting, better known as "living together," provides an alternative to the loneliness of singlehood. You have someone to share expenses and household responsibilities, someone to help support you in times of vulnerability. And, of course, you have a built-in conversational companion and sex partner.

However, living together is not without its disadvantages. Live-in partners face many of the same issues to sort out as newly marrieds, such as who has which household responsibilities and how finances will be handled. Establishing the rules of the relationship is harder, because there are no traditional guidelines. How much commitment is expected in the relationship? What are the criteria for breaking up? To what extent should I organize my life around this person, knowing that he or she could be gone tomorrow? And if the couple does break up, the partners also lack traditional means for figuring out how to divide up the possessions accumulated during the relationship.

Some couples choose to live together as a "trial marriage," hoping that practicing ahead of time will help a future marriage succeed. Unfortunately, it does not appear that living together helps couples avoid divorce; in fact, it may even predict a higher likelihood of divorce (Teachman & Polonko, 1990). This finding is probably because the same factors that contribute to the couple's hesitancy to marry also affect the success of their marriage, such factors as poor communication ability, discomfort with intimacy or commitment, and indecisiveness in personal goals. Also, living together rather than marrying sometimes represents a lack of respect for the institution of marriage, which as mentioned earlier runs contrary to research on predictors of marital success.

Homosexual Couples

When gay and lesbian couples enter committed relationships, they deal with many of the same issues as heterosexual couples. However, there are other issues as well (McGoldrick, 1988). There are no usual societal rituals to mark the beginnings and endings of the relationships. The usual sorting out of partner tasks by gender does not apply. Since both individuals are of the same gender, there may be a greater likelihood of forgetting their "two-ness" and losing themselves within each other. Also, many people in society view homosexuality as a choice—an "immoral" one at that—and look down on such couples. The homosexual couple is thus faced with the decision of whom they will allow to know of the true nature of their relationship and how they will deal with its aftermath.

A number of commonly held myths have led to prejudices against the viability of committed homosexual relationships. Most of these myths have been refuted by psychological and sociological research.

Homosexuals are mentally ill. Homosexual individuals show no higher incidence of anxiety, depression, and other ailments than heterosexual individuals (Saghir & Robins, 1973).

Homosexual relationships are short term. Actually, committed homosexual relationships last as long as those of heterosexual couples who have chosen to live together. In fact, committed lesbian relationships tend to last even longer than those of married heterosexual couples (Blumstein & Schwarz, 1983). In recent years, fear of AIDS has encouraged more-exclusive sexual relationships among gay men as well.

Homosexuals cannot be trusted to raise children. Two arguments typically surround the appropriateness of homosexual parenthood: the concern that providing a homosexual relationship as a role model will cause children to have confused gender identities and the belief that homosexuals typically seduce young children. Neither is true (Bozett, 1988; Gelles & Cornell, 1990). In fact, 90% of child molesters are actually heterosexual men.

Expanding Your Experience

The more things change, the more they seem to stay the same. Forming couples has taken many twists in the past few decades that were not so acceptable in centuries past. Weddings take place in the middle of fields, on beaches, in nudist colonies, and so on. Wedding garb can be traditional or highly individualized deviations from the norm. Partners may even decide to enter a committed relationship without the benefit of marriage vows. Even when vows are exchanged, they are now frequently written by the partners themselves rather than dictated by whoever presides over the ceremony. I recall frequent *Laugh-In* entertainer "Tiny

Tim" getting married to his "Miss Vicky" on the Johnny Carson show and that one of the vows they took was to "not get fluffed up." I never did figure out what not being "fluffed up" was, but seeing as the marriage did not last long, it apparently was not an essential part of the relationship.

But despite the differences between how various generations have celebrated the creation of couples, the elements that keep them going have remained constant. Caring, mutual respect, a positive attitude, and the desire to keep the relationship healthy all continue to be the most important factors for solid relationships.

I have included two exercises in the activity book for this chapter. The first can be used to assess the current status of your own relationship with a significant other. The second is designed to help you hypothesize why certain conditions seem to contribute to marital success.

Study Questions

1. What is meant by becoming both "one" and "two" after marriage?
2. List reasons why new marriages often break up during the first year. What can new couples do to smooth out their early relationship and increase their chances of success?
3. Describe "exchange contracting."
4. In addition to the presence of an infant, what other changes will a couple experience with the addition of children?
5. Describe how a couple might avoid experiencing discomfort during the "empty nest" stage.
6. Which factors appear to contribute to a happy relationship during retirement?
7. Describe five marital relationships that seem to last, and explain why you think they tend to endure.
8. Create a list of rules for "fair fighting."
9. If you had something important and complicated to explain to someone, what measures would you take to make sure you communicated your ideas successfully? Use an example.
10. Are people who are satisfied with their marriages always also experiencing "total marriage"? Explain your answer.
11. Describe the six different levels of divorce, as explained by Bohannon.

12. What can divorcing couples do to help minimize the negative impact of divorce?
13. List the advantages and disadvantages of staying single.
14. What reasons can you give for the fact that living together first doesn't seem to help couples succeed at marriage?
15. Describe the difficulties homosexual couples are more likely to encounter than heterosexual couples.

CHAPTER TWELVE

Parenting and Family Life

Personal Growth: The Next Generation

Mommy, Daddy, watch me. Watch me. Watch this. Keep watching. No, wait. Now watch me. Watch me, Daddy. Mommy, you're not watching. Watch me. Keep watching.

One of the most challenging life stages is the adventure of becoming a family. Almost anyone can produce a family; it takes no special training to find yourself in a biological state of parenthood. Unfortunately, the biology of parenting does not come with a built-in instruction manual. Living successfully as a parent and family member is learned, and the task has become more and more complex with each new generation.

Parenthood occurs for many reasons other than careful planning. Couples become parents by accident. A woman becomes pregnant because she feels her biological clock ticking away and worries that if she does not start having children soon, the option will no longer be available for her. Some teenagers become pregnant for manipulative purposes. The urge to produce that can emerge between two people in love can feel overpowering, outshining any regards for practical concerns.

The decision to have children is a big step and should be made for reasons other than the impulsive ones. As with any life decision, there are both advantages and disadvantages to this venture. Following is a discussion of issues you may want to consider as you decide whether or not you are ready for parenthood.

Do I Want to Have Children?

No other human experience compares with having and rearing children. As you are considering whether you are ready to take that step from being two to being three, four, or five, the many pleasures of child-rearing may come to mind:

- The closeness of the relationship is unique and satisfying. The child will be devoted to you, loving you and being emotionally attached to you as to no other.

- Having children of your own gives you the ability to replay certain aspects of your own childhood. In the role of parent, you can repeat childhood activities and experiences you enjoyed and change aspects you wish had been different. You may look forward to giving the child the experiences and advantages you wanted as a child but were denied.

- A child in some ways is an extension of yourself. Your children will probably outlive you, taking a piece of you into the future after you are gone. They will carry along your heritage and similar values, and you may hope they will stand on your shoulders and go even further than you did in important life pursuits.

- Child-rearing is an opportunity to give something of value to the community. Becoming a parent gives you maximum influence on a new member of society. You can help your child shape his or her unique characteristics and abilities toward contributing to a better world.

- Parenthood itself is valued by our society. Not long after couples marry, friends and family begin asking "When are you going to start having children?" The continuation of our species depends upon having children, and by producing them you join an ancient tradition as well as enjoy the status our society places upon that role.

- Most people enjoy a good challenge. Parenting is one of the most challenging enterprises you can ever experience. The responsibility of the task is immense. It gives you the opportunity to show what you can do, and to succeed at an important societal role. You will have the opportunity to exercise power as you structure and guide your child's life.

- Having children is pleasurable. Watching your children grow and develop, discovering who they are as their personalities emerge, seeing things from a child's standpoint again, and participating in children's activities are all both enjoyable and nostalgic.

While all of these returns have their merits, each also produces its own set of difficulties. When sorting out various considerations, you may want to keep the down-side in mind:

- The intimacy of the relationship is demanding. The love and supportiveness required of you cannot be substituted for by others. At times, you will suffer the frustration of not being able to figure out what your child wants or needs, or you will not be there to provide it. Giving love as a parent is also mostly one-way. The love of a child toward a parent is a needy love; the love of a parent toward a child is a selfless love. And as you become enveloped in the intimacy needs of your child, you are going to have less time and opportunity for meeting your own intimacy needs through your spouse, extended family, and close friends.

• While you may want to give your children everything you appreciated or wanted as a child, your children will most likely have their own ideas about how their lives should progress. What if your child despises the sports or other activities and pastimes you enjoyed as a child? Also, what if you do not have the resources to give your child what you always wanted? Finances, time, and energy will be just as limited for you as they were for your parents. And chances are, you will occasionally find yourself making the same parenting "mistakes" you experienced in your relationship with your own parents.

• While the possibility of extending your role in society beyond your own pursuits may feel gratifying, it can also result in trying to live your life through your children. This is a half-known life for you, depending on the behavior and accomplishments of your children for feelings of self-worth and self-acceptance rather than feeling whole and valuable as yourself. And what about genetic concerns? More and more personality traits and psychological abilities have been discovered as shared among blood relatives. Is there a possibility that your child might carry one of the less desirable sets of genes into society?

• While wanting to contribute to the well-being of society is commendable, you may also want to consider society's shortcomings. The world is becoming less safe and secure with each new generation and more plagued by conditions such as violence and crime, world conflict, overcrowding, and pollution of the environment. Are you up to the challenge of bringing a child into such a world? Also, the time you devote to child-rearing is going to substantially subtract from time available for applying your own unique talents and making your own contributions toward a better world.

• While being a part of the parenting tradition can be satisfying, parenthood should be a personal choice. You should not feel compelled to have children just because your culture expects it. You may come to resent your children if you feel that parenting was foisted on you. And in terms of practical concerns, you may have much to give your society that would be squelched if you took on such a time-consuming role. Also, this is your life. Unless you believe in reincarnation, it is the only one you will have. Choosing to have a child is an irrevocable decision; you will have a hard time backing out of it if you change your mind about your level of dedication to the task. As with all life choices, be sure that your decision to have children is consistent with your own life goals and desires.

• The challenge of parenthood can result in major frustration. You only have so much influence over how your children develop, and much is determined by outside forces over which you have little if any control. Genetics, culture, and world conditions all play a role. What if you perceive your efforts as having "failed"? Or what if you discover that you really aren't very proficient at parenting? As with any other skill, some people are good at it and others are not.

• While there are pleasurable aspects of parenting, this brand of good times will end as children eventually grow up and leave. And since they have the perspective of youth, they may not be grateful for all you have done with them and for them. In fact, they may resent you for the unpopular choices you made in their best interests. After all, you are the one responsible for introducing the "real world" into your children's ideas of what might be fun or appropriate to do. Rather than joining in on their fun, you may often be cast in the role of "wet blanket."

Considering the following questions may be helpful as you decide whether or not you are ready to become a family:

• Do you like children?

• Are you financially ready to take this step?

• Can your careers be interfaced with the introduction of children? Do you have the flexibility to make predictable and unpredictable adjustments as needed?

• Is your house/apartment big enough for an expansion of the number of occupants? Is it designed in a way that considers children's play and safety needs?

• Are you located in a community and neighborhood that is conducive to raising children? Are the schools good? Is safety adequate? Are playgrounds and other childhood amenities available?

• Are you willing to sacrifice a good-sized chunk of your own time and energy, as well as temporarily set aside or limit involvement in a number of your own personal goals and pastimes?

• How is your physical health? Do you have any reason to believe physical limitations will interfere with meeting at least 18 years of child-rearing needs? And if you are a woman, you will need to take especially good care of yourself during the child-producing years. Are you willing to make the necessary sacrifices?

• How is your emotional health? Is your self-esteem sturdy enough to deal with the demands and frustrations of child-rearing in an adaptive manner?

Family Structure

Well-adjusted families function as a unit. When families become dysfunctional it is generally not due to the content of the problems they are dealing with. Instead, the process of how they interact with one another as problems arise creates the dysfunction. Three constructs come into play as we look at the makeup of the functioning family: structure, subsystems, and boundaries.

Structure

Family **structure** is made up by the rules of the family. These rules are recognized by all those involved, even if everyone does not agree with their validity. Some rules involve tasks or roles:

- Mother is the housekeeper, and father is the breadwinner.
- Father is responsible for waking everybody up on time.
- Mother is in charge of driving the children where they need to go.
- Father keeps track of the yard work.

Other rules are more concerned with how people interact with one another or what they require of one another. These rules are sometimes verbally acknowledged, but many times they are not:

- Nobody openly disagrees with father.
- If something goes wrong, it is probably Junior's fault.
- Johnny usually gets his way, unless Suzie is home.
- On holidays, meal time nutrition goes out the window.

Subsystems

Three family **subsystems** exist within the family structure: marital, parenting, child. Each subsystem has its own responsibilities and functions. The marital subsystem usually consists of husband and wife. Their responsibilities involve providing emotional support for its members, as well as sexual gratification.

The parenting subsystem also often comprises the husband and wife. But it might also consist of a single parent, a parent and stepparent, grandparents, or even a mother and an aunt. The parenting subsystem has the responsibility of providing for the children, caring for them, disciplining them, and educating them. The parenting subsystem wields most of the legitimate power in the family.

The child subsystem is usually made up of the children in the family but in some circumstances can include other dependent family members, such as the frail elderly and mentally handicapped. The members of the child subsystem have little responsibility, other than that assigned by parents or society. Their main task is usually just growing up.

BOUNDARIES

Boundaries exist around all family structures. Boundaries protect the integrity of the family structure, its subsystems, and its members. For example, a family structure boundary might be a rule banning phone calls during the dinner hour, or not talking about Donny's bed-wetting problem with people outside the family. Such rules protect the family's privacy.

Subsystem boundaries reinforce the tasks of the subsystem, such as when children are not allowed to interrupt while parents are discussing something important. Parents are not so likely to succeed at problem solving and decision making if constant interruptions are allowed.

Boundaries also exist around individuals. As was mentioned in Chapter 10, we all have a number of personal rights, such as the right not to be abused and the right to be treated fairly. These individual rights apply among family members as well.

Family Dysfunction

As long as everybody sticks to their roles as defined within the systems, the family will run relatively smoothly. Everyone knows what is expected of them; they know what to expect from others; and they feel secure within the clear boundaries of the family, subsystems, and individual rights.

Problems erupt when these boundaries are violated, or when boundaries are not clearly defined. For example, if a son bullies his mother into letting him do or have most anything he wants, he has been allowed to enter the parenting subsystem, since he is accessing the power of the parental system. If the husband thinks his daughter is "Daddy's Miss Perfect" who can do no wrong, turns to her for affection and emotional support, and sides with her when conflict arises between this daughter and his wife, he has allowed his daughter to enter the marital subsystem. If the husband makes all the decisions for the family, controls the money, and tells everyone else what to do—in other words, has kept all the power in the family to himself—he has put his wife in the child subsystem.

All of these scenarios inevitably lead to family dysfunction. The boy who has bullied his way into the parenting subsystem is going to feel extremely insecure. Children recognize that they depend on parents for guidance and resources and that they cannot make it on their own. Children often act out in hopes of finding the boundaries of living by getting others to expose them through enforcement. Thus the young bully is going to feel more and more insecure and push harder and harder as he continues to search for guidance. The mother is going to feel helpless and bad about herself for not being able to control her acting-out child. The father may become fed up with both of them and become overcontrolling. In the worst case scenario, the father might even become overpunitive and abusive, as the mother becomes even more lenient in order to "make up" for Daddy's "meanness."

The "Daddy's Miss Perfect" scenario becomes an incest situation in more cases than we like to think about and causes severe damage to a child's emotional development. Even if the problem does not become this severe, the marriage between the parents will be strained, as the wife is not getting her emotional support from anywhere in the system. Bad feelings are likely to develop between mother and daughter as they see each other as competition. Other siblings will most likely become rejecting of their sister because of the special treatment she gets, thus alienating her from her own subsystem.

One spouse taking all the power causes tremendous resentment by the spouse who is left with no more power than a child. If the children see that Dad has the power and Mom has none, they no longer respect the guidance and support the mother tries to offer and ignore her, causing even more frustration and resentment.

So as you become a family, prepare yourself for the necessary structuring. Develop agreements with your co-parent concerning what your family structure will look like. Make note of the differences between how each of you were raised, and come to a decision on which aspects of each pattern will work best for your new family. Sorting out your own understanding of the family structure before the children arrive will be much easier than trying to come to an agreement when you are in the middle of a family conflict.

Parenting

What do we want our children to be like? How satisfying it would be if we could simply find all the right ingredients, throw them together, and have that perfect child. Unfortunately, much of who our children become is outside of our control. Inborn temperament, birth order, significant traumas, the era of the child's birth, the size of the child's community, and the child's culture and social class all affect child development. However, the one thing we can exercise significant control over is how we parent.

Parents in the United States value certain personal attributes. We want our children to be intelligent, cognitively skilled, and able to master academic skills as needed. We want them to develop a sense of autonomy, so they can handle problems on their own. We want them to feel happy with themselves and be able to express their feelings. Socialization is important, as we hope that our children are able to get along with others, make friends, and form lasting relationships. We want our children to have a strong sense of conscience—a personal set of values and a deeply believed sense of right and wrong. Good self-esteem and self-acceptance are yet other attributes we would like to see in our children.

Sometimes parents try too hard to produce these characteristics. As with any task, we can become perfectionistic and idealistic and get pushy about how our children behave while they are still young. Some parents assume that coercion of desired behavior should occur at all costs, as we tell ourselves we are guiding them toward the goals of good socialization and adjustment. Unfortunately, going along with this parental perfectionism and idealism has the potential to teach children a number of maladaptive beliefs and perspectives on life (Napoli et al., 1992):

- You should not cry when you feel the need.
- You should never get angry and always be kind and loving.
- Parents are always right, even when they contradict themselves.
- Obedience should be absolute, even when it is unreasonable or violates our own values, self-esteem, and safety.
- You should avoid saying what you think, so you do not inadvertently embarrass or upset your parents.
- You should give in to the desires of others at the expense of yourself.
- You should automatically know what your parents want, even if they do not say what that might be.
- Getting all A's is the only acceptable report card.

Obviously, these perspectives are not the ones we would like our children to carry into adulthood. So how do we parent, then? How do we help our children become who they are as well as fit in with society adaptively?

Parenting Styles

Library and bookstore shelves abound with different approaches to child-rearing. Over the years, theorists have proposed a variety of parenting stances, each supposedly guiding the way toward producing a well-adjusted child. Emerging from all the hypothesizing are two extreme styles, representing opposite ends of the child-rearing spectrum. These two approaches have come to be known as "permissive" and "authoritarian."

Permissive and Authoritarian Parenting Styles

Permissive parents typically give in to whatever their child wants. In fact, few if any demands are made on the child. The parents rarely use punishment. They may even try to protect the child from experiencing any negative consequences provided by the environment as a result of the child's misbehavior. Such parents usually choose this style because they believe the child needs maximum freedom and absence of external structuring in order to find and experience their true selves. Children may also receive permissive parenting by default when parents take an uninvolved stance, sometimes known as "laissez-faire." Usually these parents are too busy with other life problems to take a more active role in parenting; and in some unfortunate situations, the parents really don't care about their children.

Authoritarian parents believe obedience is a virtue that must be maintained absolutely or punishment will follow. They attempt to shape and control a child's behavior according to some absolute standard they believe must be met. They make all of their child's decisions for him or her and believe their own will is absolute. Their directives must be accepted, and never questioned. These parents are typically big fans of the behavioral approach, since it teaches that we learn a lot from external controls and the consequences of our actions. The parents also recognize that by providing examples of appropriate choices and behaviors, children can learn through the effects of modeling.

Both of these extreme parenting styles are problematic, and in spite of their being opposites, they tend to produce the same problems. For example, more child rebellion occurs when either of these two styles is used, since neither style teaches a child how to go about moderating his or her sense of will. Those raised by a permissive style learn that self-will rules. The only form of interaction with the will encouraged by the authoritarian style is to ignore it in order to avoid punishment. So if no punishment is visible, self-will rules. Self-control itself is poorly shaped. Children raised by authoritarian parents learn that control comes from others, rather than from themselves, while those raised in a permissive environment learn to be a slave to their whims or whatever feels good at the moment. Thus neither of these groups of children are trained to make sound decisions.

Both styles tend to produce insecurity. The children of authoritarian parents are often overcontrolled, have their own will and ideas squelched, and live with heavy criticism. As a result, they have difficulty feeling confident in their ability to succeed on their own. Those raised by permissive parents suffer similarly, but for different reasons. Children intuitively know that they need guidance. That is why they so persistently test boundaries. Permissive parents do not provide boundaries to test, and children feel insecure when they do not feel the containment of the social boundaries enveloping them. Likewise, neither group of children feels loved. Children with authoritarian backgrounds learn that love is conditional, something to be earned through obedience and self-denial. The nonexistence of direction or containment felt by children of the permissive style also feels like an absence of love.

Interpersonal functioning is also likely to suffer. Neither group of children is taught how to go about healthy conflict resolution. Permissive parents typically avoid conflict—indulging their child, shielding the child from the consequences of his or her actions, or by giving in to tantrums, whining, and yelling. Thus they avoid any opportunities for teaching rational give-and-take and healthy negotiation and compromise. Authoritarian parents nip all conflict in the bud by insisting that the child go along with their mandates, another form of avoiding conflict. They also teach by way of example that conflict is resolved by demanding your own way; unless of course the other person has more power, in which case you resolve conflict by giving in to the other person's demands.

Individually, the two styles in extreme forms present their own sets of problems. The permissive style does not provide a means of developing a healthy philosophy of morality. The permissive environment gets no further than reinforcing the lowest level of Kohlberg's hierarchy, "If it feels good, it must be right" (see Chapter 2). Basic structures for living and self-care may be underdeveloped, as the parents avoid any child-rearing interventions that might result in containment of the child's spontaneous self.

The authoritarian style's extensive use of controls and punishments produces an immense set of difficulties. When we set up punishments, our intention is that the recipient will cease an undesired behavior in order to avoid being punished again. The problem is that the recipient's motivation is avoidance of unpleasant consequences, not necessarily that of changing the undesired behavior. There are many methods for avoiding unpleasant consequences that have nothing to do with changing the undesired behavior.

Suppose you have a child who is not doing her homework. You take away her SuperNintendo whenever she procrastinates. Possibly she will stop procrastinating in order to get her electronic games back. However, there are many other ways she might go about avoiding the unpleasantness of going without her SuperNintendo:

- She could lie, saying that her homework is already done.
- She could copy someone else's work after she gets to school the next day.
- She could go play SuperNintendo at someone else's house.

- She could play SuperNintendo when you are not around.
- She could go play video games at the local arcade instead.
- She could give up on playing electronic games and find something else to do that is stimulating, like join a street gang, start taking drugs, become sexually active, etc.
- She could break into the school and alter the teacher's records.

All these new behaviors would help her avoid having to feel punished, yet they do not get the parents what they want. In fact, the unpleasant consequences result in a variety of new undesirable behaviors that parents prefer to avoid. A basic shortcoming of punishers is that they do not teach the child correct behavior. All the child learns is that if a certain behavior occurs, punishment will follow. And any changes in behavior may be only temporary. Another problem with punishers is that they only change behaviors for as long as the punisher is present. When the punisher is removed, unless some other motivation exists, children will go back to engaging in the undesired behavior.

Punishments are often used because the parents believe they are giving their children "an offer they can't refuse"–either comply or be punished. Unfortunately, that is not the case. They are being given a choice, and they can choose to take the punisher rather than do what is required of them.

Punishment also destroys intrinsic motivation. Since parental punishers come from the outside, children learn to look outside of themselves for direction, rather than develop and consult with personal beliefs about what is right or wrong. Thus when parents are not available to provide direction, they are left looking for external direction. What is everybody else doing? Will anything happen to me if I do it? Will I get caught if I do it? As is the case with permissive parenting, the reasoning encouraged by authoritarian parenting represents a primitive level of moral development.

The effects of modeling are also a concern. Punishment models that if you do not like something people are doing, or you are angry at people, you punish them. Obviously, this is a poor conflict resolution skill. And since punishers do not guarantee that the desired behavior change will occur, it may not even get you what you want.

The classical conditioning that can occur during punishment presents another set of concerns. If you recall, during classical conditioning when a feeling and some environmental factor are experienced simultaneously, the presentation of the external variable alone produces the feeling. Children feel rage, fear, helplessness, and other unpleasant emotions when they are punished. Generally speaking, the parents are present when punishers are being delivered. Thus, over time, children can learn to feel rage, fear, and helplessness whenever in the presence of their parents, regardless of their parents' current behavior. It is difficult for children to feel loved under these circumstances.

Some parenting manuals based on the authoritarian style address the problem of feeling unloved after being punished by suggesting that parents follow punishment with affection (e.g., Dobson, 1970). For example, first you spank the child, then hug the child to let him know that you love him: the old "I spank you because I love you" routine. Unfortunately, such an approach may not get the desired message across. Very young children are cognitively unable to effectively sort out conflicting emotions (Bennett & Hiscock, 1993). Children will mainly feel confused. There are additional concerns, such as teaching children to ignore the real feelings they have when someone hits them, showing them that they can ultimately receive affection when they misbehave, and classically conditioning them to connect love with violence (Hughes, 1988).

Research has examined how raising children using these extreme styles affects their school behavior (Baumrod, 1973; Dornbusch et al., 1987). Children raised by the authoritarian style are more aggressive with the other children, are less able to engage in cooperative play, and use fighting as their main strategy for dealing with conflict. They tend to withdraw from the adults in the environment, which is unfortunate since this restricts the amount of learning that can occur. Those who are growing up with permissive parenting have difficulty knowing what to do with the rules in the classroom and tend to be even less well-adapted to the classroom than those raised by authoritarian parents. Children raised by either of the two extreme styles tend to get the lowest grades.

While the two extreme parenting styles have problems, they nevertheless point out some important components of parenting. The authoritarian style recognizes that children need guidance, while the permissive style capitalizes on children's needs to feel love and supportiveness. Effective parenting includes both of these components, rather than one of the two extremes.

For healthy development, children need something called an **average expectable environment** (Hartmann, 1958). As the label suggests, the middle-of-the-road environment typically gives a child both the support and the guidance the child needs. You need not be a certain type of "superparent" in order to encourage healthy development of your offspring. All of us have our own unique styles of interacting with others, including how we interact with children. As long as our individual styles provide a healthy combination of both support and guidance, we are giving our children what they need to be able to flourish.

Authoritative Parenting

The **authoritative** parenting style, also sometimes called "democratic," is the middle-of-the-road approach. It seeks out a balance between giving guidance and providing love and support. Under the authoritative style, there are still rules that children are required to follow. However, the parents explain rules and give the reasoning behind them, so that the children can better apply rules and develop their own when clear-cut guidelines are absent. Rules are also allowed to be questioned. In fact, questioning is encouraged, since the reasoning behind rules can then be better understood. Questioning may also result in a parent deciding to change a rule, if the child has discovered some faulty reasoning that has not previously come to the parent's attention.

Rules are consistently enforced with the authoritative style, but extreme consequences for breaking rules are generally avoided. Corporal punishment is rare, usually only used with very young children in safety-threatening situations. In other circumstances requiring consequences, the punishment typically fits the crime. If the child is abusing phone privileges, phone use is restricted for a period of time. Or, consequences are designed to fit what would happen to the child in the real world since, after all, parenting is intended to help the child fit in with real-world circumstances. For example, if children spend all of their allowance and do not have enough money for planned activities at the end of the week, it means going without the planned activities. Or if they lose their belongings due to carelessness, they must take as much responsibility as possible for replacing the items.

Authoritative parents encourage children to make their own decisions. However, important decisions are made only after much discussion with parents concerning all relevant considerations. The parents also hold the right to veto if decisions could have disastrous consequences for which the child is not prepared. However, parents might let a child go ahead with an ill-advised decision when they can't talk the child out of it, if they think the child is capable of handling the potential fallout. After all, we learn as much or more from our mistakes as we do from our successes.

Authoritative parents also demonstrate love and acceptance toward their children. Unlike authoritarian parents, their love, acceptance, and support are provided unconditionally, regardless of the child's current behavior. However, unlike permissive parents, they do not let their love for their children interfere with giving them appropriate instruction and discipline when necessary.

The drawbacks of the permissive and authoritarian styles are less likely to be reflected in children raised by an authoritative style. The rebellion is not as severe or problematic, since the child is given an arena for debate. Children develop a sense of self-control, because they practice self-control during daily decision making. Adaptive decision making itself is developed as a basic part of childhood training. Children feel more secure than is possible with the extreme styles, since they experience the unconditional support of their parents, as well as the security of the internal skills their parents are helping them build. They learn ample conflict resolution skills through reasoning, negotiating, and compromising as the reasoning behind rules, and in's and out's of potential choices are explored and questioned. And since there are no strings attached to the expression of love and acceptance, they receive the unconditional positive regard that all children need as they learn to love and accept themselves.

Research suggests that children from authoritative homes are the most well-adjusted. In school, they are more at ease than children raised by the extreme styles and conform easily to new rules and social situations. They tend to be more self-controlled and socially responsible. Furthermore, their grades tend to be better (Dornbusch et al., 1987).

As we examine outcome research, however, we need to be careful about our inferences. The groups studied are not randomly assigned, with parents of each group of children being told which parenting style to use. Possibly, parents choose certain parenting styles because they are the ones with which their particular children seem to progress. Some children need a lot of structure. For example, hyperactive children need much more guidance and direction as they are encouraged toward self-control (Hunt, 1988). Likewise, some temperamentally sensitive children may only need to be looked at sideways for them to crumble emotionally. Their parents may choose to place more emphasis on showing acceptance and supportiveness than on ensuring stern consequences for misbehavior. Thus the results of parenting outcome research could in part represent the fact that parents choose certain types of parenting because of the type of child they have, rather than that certain types of parenting produce a certain type of child.

Current Child-Rearing Issues

Our culture has come to recognize the importance of parenting and how it can affect both child development and an individual's eventual place in society. When you factor in the emotional attachment and protectiveness parents experience toward their children, any debate over child-rearing practices tends to become volatile and obsessively picked over. We do not skimp when it comes to our children! Over the years many different debates have come and gone. Following are some of the child-rearing issues that currently fill our plates.

When Both Parents Work

Over the last couple of decades, parents have been expressing concern over the effects of children growing up in day care, rather than at home with a primary caretaker. The stay-at-home mother is actually a fairly recent phenomenon. Before the Industrial Revolution, both mother and father typically worked within the family business. Childcare assistance came from other members of the family, unless children were old enough to work side by side with their parents. When family businesses became a minority, most homes were made up of a father who left home to work, and a mother who took care of the children. And since workers frequently moved away from extended family as they followed the dictates of their companies, women did not have the benefit of extended family to help out. Thus women were initially left with little choice but to build their lives around child-rearing.

Today, because of the feminist movement and economic necessity, women have been moving back into the work force. Yet the tradition of extended family shouldering the child care load is often no longer an option. So who takes care of the children? And what effect do our child care choices have on our children's development? Generations accustomed to stay-at-home motherhood have seriously questioned leaving children in day care, partly in defense of how they chose to dedicate their lives and the meaning it had for them (Hughes, 1991). How can you expect a baby to learn to attach if the attachment figure is constantly changing? How can you expect children to learn your values if you limit the time you are there to help them guide their choices?

Some families address this difficulty by having staggered work schedules, so that while one parent is gone, the other can be home with the children. While children may benefit from this arrangement, if both parents are working full time they see so little of each other their marriage typically suffers (Bradt, 1988).

Outcome studies have not supported most parental concerns about putting children in day care. Infants placed in day care do not necessarily show evidence of impairment in their ability to attach (Kagan et al., 1980). Later, in preschool, some children raised in day care show more attention-getting behavior such as impulsiveness and aggressiveness (Schwartz et al., 1974). However, you would expect to see this in any setting where the caregiver's attention is divided among several children. On the positive side, however, children who grow up in day care show a higher level of social cooperation with their peers than those who are raised exclusively at home (Moore, 1975). Furthermore, when a parent's work environment provides the experiences of challenge, stimulation, and complex working with people, there appears to be an increase in the quality of parenting (Greenberger et al., 1994).

Thus it appears that our concerns need not be directed so much toward the institution of day care itself but more toward the quality of care the child receives in any individual day care setting:

- What is the child/caregiver ratio? The younger your child, the fewer children the caregiver should be keeping. Look for a ratio of no more than 3:1 for infants and young toddlers, 5:1 for preschoolers, and 7 or 8:1 for grade-school children.
- What is the caregiving environment like? Is it sensitive to the needs

of children of that particular age group? Are there adequate toys, equipment, and play and rest areas?
- Are day care personnel the same individuals from day to day, or is the staffing constantly changing?
- Observe the caregiver with the children. Is the caregiver warm and sensitive, or cold and abrupt? Does the caregiver give structure and guidance without jumping on the children over every little thing?
- Is the day organized around a set routine? Children feel more secure in an environment that provides an expectable structure.

Some parents are not so concerned with the effects of day care as they are with missing out on some of their children's development. They want to be there for that first smile, the first step, the first word, or even that first home run. During my experiences observing and working with parents, I have noticed that although parents of children in day care may miss a few of those firsts, the second or third ones are just as thrilling and special the first time the parents observe them. However, we all have our individual differences. Depending on how important it is to you to be there for those moments, you might prefer to make the necessary sacrifices of your time for career, marital, and other personal endeavors. This is an individual choice, and one to be made carefully.

Children and Television

Chapter 5 described a relationship between viewing violent television and behaving aggressively. This relationship is especially evident among children (Liebert & Sprafkin, 1988). There is also evidence that the more television children watch, the less active they are, as well as the more poorly developed their reading skills appear to be (Williams, 1986).

Another difficulty with children's television-watching concerns attention span. In the late 1960s, a television show called *Sesame Street* created a revolution in children's programming. The program was originally created in hopes of making academics more interesting to children living in intellectually understimulating environments. It accomplished this end by presenting ideas within fast-moving collections of very brief learning capsules. Because of its stimulating nature, children from all backgrounds found it to be both entertaining and educational. It became highly successful, and in the tradition of American marketing, other children's television programming incorporated its fast-moving, high-stimulation format.

The drawback of *Sesame Street* formatting is that it accustoms children who do not need such a learning format to high-stimulation presentation of material. Later, when children enter the classroom, such presentation is not possible. Thus children become easily bored. My own observations and those of some of my colleagues has been that today even college students who grew up with the *Sesame Street* format have a more difficult time listening to an hour of straight lecture than students of previous generations. Keeping the class stimulating enough to hold student attention has become a much more difficult task for the instructor, since students have been trained toward expecting externally based stimulation, rather than comingling the process with pauses for personal reflection on what is being presented.

In spite of the drawbacks of television, it can also be valuable as a learning tool. It exposes children to whole new worlds, experiences they may never be able to see firsthand. It provides entertainment when children become bored and you are too busy, ill, or otherwise preoccupied to meet their immediate needs, although it is best not to rely on the television extensively as a babysitter. As you develop your game plan for child-rearing, establish television-viewing policies that capitalize upon its benefits and avoid its drawbacks:

• Consider the age of the child. How much television a day is reasonable? Which programs are acceptable viewing for which age groups?

• Balance television-watching with other pastimes, perhaps by requiring that equivalent amounts of time be spent reading or engaging in physical activity.

• Be aware of the effects of modeling. Do you spend all of your free time glued to the boob-tube? Or does your free time balance television-viewing with reading, hobbies, and physical activities?

• Discuss issues that arise in television programs. How could the television character resolve his difficulty without resorting to violence or aggression? If it were you, what would you do? What kinds of attitudes and beliefs are represented by the characters' choices? Are your beliefs the same or different from those presented? Is the outcome presented likely to happen in the real world? What did you like about the program? Why? This line of discussion helps you teach your children to use their own introspection as a form of stimulation, rather than rely solely on what passes across the television screen.

• Explain the reasoning behind your television-viewing policies. In this manner, you can help your children develop their own criteria for what they prefer to watch.

- Decide how you want to enforce your policies. At times this will become difficult, since the older your children get the more time they will spend in other environments. However, you can be selective about which places you will allow your children to spend large amounts of time. At home, you can buy physical controls that allow you to shut out certain stations if you find them not to be of your liking.

Effects of Divorce on Children

Divorce is hard on children. Hart (1982) lists a number of reasons why:

- It signals the end of life as they have known it. The children can no longer feel as secure, since the bedrock of their environment has crumbled. They worry about who will take care of them and question the custodial parent's ability or desire to do so, since the noncustodial parent has already seen fit to "abandon" them.

- The parents, temporarily preoccupied with their own emotional and pragmatic difficulties, are less available for parenting. Thus the children have less support for dealing with one of the most distressing emotional experiences they can endure as children.

- Divorce usually involves parents tossing back and forth a lot of extreme unpleasant emotions. The children become confused about their loyalties. Is Daddy right and Mommy is all bad? Or is Mommy right and Daddy is all bad? Young children will make such assumptions, even if they do not accurately represent what the parents are saying. Whichever way the children decide to go, it means losing one parent. The parents' expression of strong emotions in itself is very frightening to the young child.

- Children become very anxious for their parents, as they see their parents' vulnerability and worry about their parents' well-being during the ordeal.

- Divorce often means a number of tangible losses, such as having to move, change schools, lose long-time friends, and try to live within a more limited income. The primary caretaker may need to return to the workplace in order to make ends meet financially, resulting in the children losing a stay-at-home parent and being placed in day care. Since grief reactions follow significant losses, children whose parents are divorcing can be expected to become depressed.

Many studies have examined these negative effects on children and the types of psychopathology that can appear during times of divorce.

Implied is a belief that the impact is permanent, that irreparable damage is being done to children when their parents divorce. One often-heard myth of child-rearing has been that parents should stay together even in an extremely troubled marriage, since divorce is so traumatic to children.

However, more recent work focuses on divorce as a transitional crisis to be worked through and observes distress as a normal reaction that will eventually pass (Ahrons, 1980). Research has indicated that while children have significant emotional and behavioral difficulties after their parents divorce they tend to regain their equilibrium after two years (Hetherington et al., 1982). It is certainly less traumatic than spending the rest of their childhood with two people who are constantly fighting.

As with any transition, there are ways we can facilitate rather than hamper its passage. Divorcing parents can help their children deal with the turmoil by using the following guidelines:

• Try to maintain as much of the children's routine as possible. Do not change their place of residence unless it is inevitable. If you must move, endeavor to keep the children in the same school and near enough to the old neighborhood so they can continue ongoing friendships. Continue to structure the children's home life similarly, and avoid drastic changes in discipline.

• Let the children know that they are not at fault for their parents' breakup. Since children occasionally hear parents arguing over the children's behavior, they need to hear that parents break up because of failure to get along with each other, rather than failure to get along with the children.

• Let children talk about their losses and acknowledge their sadness, anger, worries about the future, and other grief reactions. Let them know these feelings are normal, you know that they hurt, but they will eventually pass. Your children are going to need extra attention during the divorce process, and if you are one of the divorcing parents, you may need to find a way to keep your own distress from interfering with your ability to provide it.

• Assure children that there will always be someone to take care of them, since a major part of the divorce proceedings is designed around making sure that the children are cared for. If at all possible, make sure the noncustodial parent still plays an active role in their lives.

• Do not use the children as pawns for expressing your anger toward your ex-spouse. Certainly you will be experiencing a significant amount of anger and hurt. But regardless of the perceived wrongdoing, the ex-spouse is still your children's parent. Children find security in whatever image of their parents they carry with them. If you unnecessarily tarnish that image, the children's security suffers.

- Assure the children you will be all right. It is best to avoid letting children observe extreme expressions of unpleasant emotions, as it is scary. But at the very least, they will notice some differences in moodiness. Let them know that the emotionality they may observe will not destroy you and that you will still be able to care for and provide for them. If you have difficulty doing so, seek professional help so that your own emotional neediness does not diminish your ability to parent.

Child Abuse: What It Is and How to Avoid It

Child abuse is currently a hot issue. Punitive behaviors toward children once considered the sovereign rights of parents and other authority figures are now seen as horrific and sadistic. Other more serious incidents of abuse—leading to significant injury or even the death of a child—make us all shake our heads and wonder how these things can happen.

Defining child abuse can be difficult. A permissive parent might say that anything causing discomfort to a child is abusive. On the other hand, an authoritarian parent might be expected to say that extreme punitiveness is justifiable if the child has done something to "deserve" it. Even child protection agencies have difficulty defining abuse. Most agencies say that anything leaving a mark on the child is considered abusive. However, some authoritarian parenting manuals teach methods for inflicting excruciating pain upon children without leaving a mark (e.g., Dobson, 1970). Is such pain then not abusive?

While we might argue about exactly where discipline ends and abuse begins, most everyone seems to agree that at some point methods of discipline can become unreasonable. Drawing this line becomes somewhat easier if we go back and look at the principles behind using punishers in the first place. We use them in an effort to change behavior. If a method such as spanking is used to try to get a child to stop doing something, but it has no effect, it cannot be called a punisher. Continuing to spank over that offense would then be considered abusive, since it meets no disciplinary end, not to mention that a more natural consequence could prove to be more effective.

Abused children show characteristics similar to those who are raised by an authoritarian style, only with the volume turned up a few notches.

They tend to score lower on tests of cognitive and intellectual ability and have difficulty forming relationships with others, often reacting to new situations with fear and apprehension. Aggressive and destructive behavior is common, self-esteem is poor, and abused children are usually sad and dejected. In the minds of the abused children they are bad people, otherwise they would not deserve such harsh treatment. Self-destructive behavior and suicide attempts are not unusual. Even basic neurological functioning of abused children is different from those who are not abused (Green, 1988).

Why do parents abuse their children? A number of factors appear to be involved. Often it is a result of frustration, as parents deal with stressors by taking them out on their children. Unemployment appears to be especially prone to precede child abuse (National Center on Child Abuse and Neglect, 1982). The frustrations may stem from parenting itself, as the parent "loses it" with a distressed infant or small child who cannot be soothed.

Child abuse is also a phenomenon that tends to run in families. Abusive fathers almost always come from homes where abusiveness occurred, or where at least a very rigid, punitive, parenting style was used. This background is not necessarily found among abusive mothers (Fisher, 1984). It is important to note, however, that most abused children do not grow up to become abusers themselves. Thus other variables must play into the equation.

You can avoid letting abusiveness enter into your parenting by developing your strategies ahead of time. What are your current perspectives and expectations concerning parenting? Have you checked out these perspectives against medical and psychological research findings or the opinions of professionals within those fields? Is the manner in which you were raised more violent than what you observed in other individuals' homes? Did you come away from childhood with little more than aggressive behavior as the model for dealing with stressors? How will you deal with stressors so that you do not become abusive when you are frustrated? What do parents of well-behaved children seem to use for discipline? Most of all, be aware of what you want from your children. Are the child-rearing strategies you have decided upon likely to get you what you want?

Expanding Your Experience

I entered the parenting arena armed with Bandura and the tenets of social learning theory. I vowed to shield my children as much as possible from any influences that might have the potential for modeling undesirable behavior. For example, when my sons were preschoolers I carefully monitored their television-viewing habits in order to make sure they were not exposed to excessive violence. I did not even let them see *Bugs Bunny* cartoons, let alone *He-Man* and *Skeletor*. And I certainly refused to let them own toy guns.

To my dismay, my protective practices did not seem to have much impact on my sons' interest in aggressive or violent play. Within their active and creative imaginations, any stick or toy block could become a "gun." As they grew older and more coordinated, they created toy guns out of lego bricks. "War," "cops and robbers," "cowboys and Indians," and other good guy/bad guy trysts were as popular for them as they were for their other male playmates, who had not been protected from the evils of maladaptive modeling.

Several years later, my daughter entered the scene. By then I had given up trying to restrict my sons' cartoon viewing, especially since they had reached the age when they could see violent cartooning at friends' houses anyway. However, I still refused to let them own the "action figure" toys that depicted these violent cartoon characters. At any rate, my daughter watched violent cartooning from a very early age. She was especially enthralled with *She-Ra*, a feminine version of *He-Man*.

It was only a matter of time before someone gave my children action figures as gifts. As it turned out, my daughter was the first lucky recipient. She was delighted with her new She-Ra figures, and I didn't have the heart to tell her she couldn't keep them. At this point I threw my hands in the air and gave up. My daughter had spent her formative years on a diet of violent cartooning and now would be playing with toys representing violence. Obviously, this child was now a lost cause.

However, as I watched her play with these toys I did not witness reruns of the violence that had been modeled before her. She-Ra and her friends might have arguments, but they always made up. They often traded clothes and styled their hair differently—as much as was possible on toys so small. But most of the time, She-Ra and her friends "flew" from one part of the house to the other, rescuing each other from "cliffs" and other precarious situations and otherwise helping one another as they found themselves in need.

What I learned from this experience is that no one parenting practice or intervention creates the entire child. In this instance, gender differences—whether innate or learned—appear to have played a greater role in my children's choices of behavior than the effects of playing with violent toys or watching cartoon depictions of violence.

So whatever parenting plan you put together for your own children, consider the many known effects of child development, rather than get wrapped up in one cure-all approach. Usually, a lot of what we start out with is made up of how we were parented ourselves. I have included one exercise that can help you explore how you were parented, as well as the effect you would like to see it have on your own parenting choices. Another exercise gives you practice at choosing different styles of discipline for hypothetical situations. There is also a checklist that can help you explore your own readiness for becoming a parent.

Study Questions

1. List issues you might want to consider as you decide whether or not to have children.
2. Describe family structure, subsystems, and boundaries. How well do they play a role in the level of the family's functioning on *Married... With Children*, and *Doogie Howser, M.D.*? Explain.
3. Describe the authoritarian, permissive, and authoritative parenting styles.
4. What do parents typically want their children to be like? Which parenting style is most likely to encourage such a result, and why?
5. List the advantages and disadvantages of using punishers as a means of child discipline. How might you maximize their effectiveness and limit their drawbacks?
6. What is an "average expectable environment"?
7. What difficulties do you see with presenting both discipline and supportiveness by saying "I spank you because I love you"?
8. What effect do authoritarian, permissive, and authoritative styles appear to have on school performance?
9. Is putting a child in day care detrimental to his or her development? Explain your answer.
10. What sorts of effects do you think television-watching had on you as a child? What effects do you remember seeing it have on your friends? How might you avoid or encourage such effects as you raise your own children?
11. Why is parental divorce so traumatic to children?

12. In view of the trauma of divorce, should you stay together no matter how bad the marriage for the sake of the children's well-being? Why or why not?
13. How would you define "child abuse"?
14. How does child abuse appear to affect children?
15. Describe the steps you plan to take in order to ensure that you will not become abusive as a parent.

Chapter Thirteen

Work and Play
In All Things Be Joyous

If you can't stand the heat, apply for a job on Pluto.

The previous three chapters explored the structures of our interpersonal lives: friendship, partners, and family. Our interpersonal lives represent one corner of the triangle of living and being. The other two corners, work and play, are equally important for healthy personal adjustment. The investment of time and energy into a healthy lifestyle is balanced in all three corners.

Overinvestment into any single corner hinders our growth and impairs our adjustment. Those who are preoccupied with their interpersonal lives are distracted from their work and have difficulty experiencing the spontaneity of play. Those who live for the moment of play have difficulty becoming focused enough to adequately develop their interpersonal and work lives. And we have all most likely heard some form of the expression "All work and no play make Jack and Jill pretty dull people." The phenomenon called "workaholism" will be discussed in greater detail later in this chapter.

Work

What is work? Generally speaking, it is doing or producing something meant either for your own benefit or for the benefit of others. It could be the job you perform to earn money and satisfy the conditions of your employer. Or, it could be something you do to care for others, care for your belongings, or pursue forms of self-maintenance and personal growth.

Work is usually pursued out of necessity. You may or may not feel motivated for the chore. Many mundane tasks, such as retyping a paper or packing a lunch, involve forcing ourselves to "go through the motions." Other tasks, such as writing an outstanding newspaper article or creatively helping a struggling student to master a difficult concept, can be highly meaningful and enjoyable. Most of us prefer the more meaningful and enjoyable tasks. Rather than having just a job, we want a career. We take pride in our work. We want our work to be meaningful. We want it to make a difference, to contribute toward our feelings of social striving as we apply our own unique talents and elbow grease. The type of work we prefer is one piece of our identity, and we like to see ourselves reflected in the work we choose.

In addition to contributing to our personal identity, work provides a structure for our lives. A regular work schedule gives our lives a sense of predictability and security. It also provides a structure within which we usually have social contacts with others, which satisfies some of our needs for affiliation. Being able to see what we have accomplished with our work frequently leads to increased feelings of self-worth.

Since we are constantly growing and changing, the type of work we find to be meaningful and consistent with our identity and other work motivators also changes. Changing careers midstream is becoming more and more commonplace. Chances are, you are currently preparing for your first career, and you cannot fathom how someone could make themselves return for even more intensive, long-term training. Fortunately, the second time around is usually not so intensive. Many work skills are transferable from one job to the next. Being mechanically minded, having good communication skills, being able to recognize inconsistencies, and having language art skills are examples of personal capacities that can prove useful for any number of different occupations.

Thus the most important issue to explore as you organize your career pursuits is, "What kind of work will be meaningful for *me*?"

Job Satisfaction

Many people begin their career investigations with the question "Which jobs pay the most money?" Money is, of course, one of the main reasons we seek employment. However, money alone is not going to result in your being satisfied with your career choice. Witness the common expression "You couldn't pay me enough to do that." For all of us there are drawbacks to some things that having a lot of money simply will not overcome.

You will probably invest around 40 hours a week, 50 weeks a year, for around 40 years of your life into working at your job. That's a big investment! Since so much of your life will involve working, you will be much more likely to experience healthy personal adjustment if you feel satisfied with your job. So what leads people to feel satisfied?

Herzberg explored this issue according to what he called **motivation-hygiene theory** (Herzberg, 1975). He says certain factors are likely to create worker satisfaction, while others are likely to create dissatisfaction. If the factors that create dissatisfaction—what Herzberg calls **hygiene**—are remedied, a worker is not necessarily satisfied. He or she is simply not dissatisfied. Other factors—what Herzberg calls **motivators**—must be present before the worker will feel truly satisfied.

It is a little like a football play where all that the players accomplish is making it back to the line of scrimmage. They are glad they did not lose yardage; but they are not satisfied, because they did not gain anything positive. Likewise, if workers have all hygiene factors taken care of, they are not going to be as likely to sit around moaning and groaning about their jobs. However, they will not be actually satisfied until motivator factors are present.

So what are motivator and hygiene factors? Table 13.1 is a chart illustrating how these satisfiers and dissatisfiers tend to fall out. Workers were asked to mark which out of a list of factors were likely to lead to extreme job satisfaction and which were likely to lead to extreme job dissatisfaction. Naturally, given our individual differences, all factors fell into both categories.

TABLE 13.1

Herzberg's Motivator and Hygiene Factors

Motivators (satisfiers)	*Hygiene Factors (dissatisfiers)*
Achievement	Company policy and administration
Recognition	Supervision quality and quantity
The work itself	Relationship with supervisor
Responsibility	Work conditions
Advancement	Salary
Personal growth	Relationship with peers
	Effect on personal life
	Relationship with subordinates
	Status
	Job security

However, most of the workers loaded more factors into one category than the other. Satisfiers tended to include those factors that enhanced the worker as a person: opportunities for achievement, recognition for what the worker accomplished, work that felt enjoyable or interesting, being given individual responsibility, and having opportunities for advancement and personal growth. Factors leading to dissatisfaction tended to be part of the concrete work setting: unfair or oppressive company policies and administration, inadequate supervision, poor relationships with bosses, unpleasant work conditions, skimpy salaries, and poor co-worker relationships.

Another way of looking at these factors is that the satisfiers tend to be *intrinsic* and the dissatisfiers *extrinsic.* Factors such as accomplishment, recognition, advancement, and the like help us feel that our jobs are a part of who we are. Thus we feel a reward value that is delivered by our inner selves. Factors such as bosses, company policies, and work conditions are more part of the external environment. When these factors are in good shape we may be appreciative, but we associate the factors with the work environment rather than with who we are as individuals.

Further evidence of this lack of a relationship between extrinsic factors and job satisfaction is the effect of satisfaction on productivity or job performance. Increased satisfaction does not necessarily lead to improved job performance (Steers & Porter, 1975). Workers occasionally report feeling more satisfied when they produce more, either because of an internal sense of accomplishment or because they earned incentives that were provided for improved performance; however, this is a matter of personal productivity leading to feelings of satisfaction, rather than satisfaction leading to productivity. Productivity may also occasionally be higher when workers are satisfied because there is less absenteeism and turnover when the workers are satisfied, thus there are more people around to get things done. But again, productivity improves due to the external factors of less absenteeism and turnover, rather than as a direct result of satisfaction.

Ironically, when people apply for jobs, the first questions they ask tend to be about issues of pay, benefits, job security, hours, and other extrinsic factors. While these are important questions to ask, they are not the questions that will necessarily help applicants choose jobs that are satisfying. So when you go on job interviews, be certain to also ask questions that will give you an idea of how the job might fit you, rather than solely trying to make yourself fit the constraints of the job.

Choosing a Career

As you decide what you would like to pursue as a vocation, you have three basic tasks (Isaacson, 1985). First, you have to evaluate your individual interests and abilities. Second, you need to figure out which occupations are consistent with your interests and abilities. And third, you need to evaluate and prioritize the various options. Your campus career counseling center is likely to assist you with each of these tasks and is probably the first place to look for help if you are in the process of deciding upon a career. Following is a discussion of the elements of consideration relevant to making such an important decision.

Surveying individual interests and abilities. You are probably already aware of most of the activities that either interest you or appear to fall within the bounds of your personal competence. You know which classes you have taken, which ones you liked, in which subjects you did well, which work experiences have worked out for you in the past, and the characteristics of any other training you might have received. The amount of time you spend reading about various topics, watching presentations on them, or even actively engaging in certain activities can sometimes act as an objective gauge of that which interests you. However, most people have not exhaustively and systematically listed and analyzed their interests and abilities. Tests are available that can help you with this task. To be thorough, you can evaluate yourself according to three dimensions: achievement, aptitude, and individual interests.

Achievement refers to skills you have already demonstrated, or those for which you have received effective training. The tests you take during finals week are almost always achievement tests. The most widely used generalized test of achievement within both school and work settings is the Wide-Range Achievement Test (WRAT). It measures academic skills such as reading comprehension, spelling ability, and prowess with various mathematical calculations. There are also many specialized achievement tests measuring competencies within specific fields, such as those related to individual job tasks or those required as part of various licensing and certification procedures.

Aptitude refers to abilities you do indeed have but have not necessarily had the opportunity to put to use. Individual aptitudes tend to be inborn, rather than created through training. Aptitude tests measure such skills as reasoning abilities, ability to mentally rearrange objects in space, and physical coordination such as manual dexterity. Two widely used generalized tests of aptitude are the Differential Aptitude Test (DAT) and the General Aptitude Test Battery (GATB). You are probably also well aware of one of the more specialized aptitude tests, the Scholastic Aptitude Test (SAT). It is used to help figure out the likelihood of an individual's succeeding in college, although many feel that this particular aptitude test is also a measure of individual achievement.

Interest tests systematically explore what you like to do, the fields of information or activities that hold your interest. You may have informally assessed your interests when you chose your academic major. Tests of interest help you assess interests you may not yet have considered. The Strong-Campbell Interest Inventory not only points out which fields appear to appeal to you, but also compares your overall interests with those who are satisfied with various kinds of work, even when the interests seem to have little relationship to the job itself. Another interest test, the Kuder General Interest Survey, uses a "forced choice" format. This format helps you prioritize your interests. Since you will probably find you are interested in many things, the Kuder presents and re-presents interests and requires you to choose which ones are the *most* interesting as you go along.

Matching abilities and interests with occupations. There are a variety of materials that can help you survey jobs that are consistent with your abilities and interests. One is the *Dictionary of Occupational Titles* published by the Department of Labor, which lists 20,000 different jobs, coded so that you can figure out the various personal skills, traits, and interests relevant to each job. The *Occupational Outlook Handbook,* also published by the Department of Labor, zeros in on a few hundred of the most popular careers and gives more extensive details about them, including how to go about getting more information about specific careers.

One way to help figure out which job is right for you is to invest in career-planning guides such as Bolles's *What Color Is Your Parachute?* (1993) Such manuals describe processes for selecting vocational fields that capitalize on your strengths and interests. Another useful resource is the computer. There are programs such as SIGI, DISCOVER, and CHOICES available that can help you match up your interests and abilities with potential career choices. Many campus career counseling centers offer students resources such as these.

Evaluating and prioritizing career choices. As you match up your interests and abilities with potential careers, numerous nontangibles also apply to whether or not your career choice will be successful. Some may be pleasant surprises; others may be enough to send you running. Here are some questions you will want to consider:

• What is the job actually like? In other words, how does the average person so employed actually end up spending most of his or her time? For example, most police officers enter their profession because, at least in part, they want to go out and stop criminals and help victims. Once they enter the profession, however, they find that they spend much of their time dealing with paperwork and other red tape, rather than catching villains. If you enjoy paperwork, this is a plus; if you despise it, it is a minus.

• How much training is involved, and what is it like? If there is a lot of training, it may take exceptional dedication and personal resources to be able to get yourself through the program. Financial considerations may become relevant. If there is little training involved, you may be faced with on-the-job training, which causes some people to feel self-conscious or even threatened.

• What sorts of physical demands does the job present? With many jobs, it is obvious. Dock workers expect to do a lot of heavy lifting; secretaries expect to spend a lot of time sitting and typing. But often there are unexpected twists. Suppose you are fond of animals and would like to become a veterinary technician. Are you aware that you will spend most of your day standing? Since you have to wash your hands between animals, how are you going to handle the effect on your skin of constant washing and drying? Are you physically able to help lift an overweight German shephard onto an examination or surgery table?

• What are your chances of success at actually getting a position within your chosen career? You might be the best high school level Russian and Italian language teacher in the state. But how many positions for teaching those languages actually exist? You also want to be sure to check how much competition you will run up against in the field, no matter how many positions are available. Physical therapy and occupational therapy are two hot fields, but schools for professional training are so limited in number that you might finish your undergraduate work only to find your training at a dead end.

• Are job requirements consistent with your personal values and morals? What if your employer requires you to interact with the public in ways you feel consist of "lying by omission"? Or what about the field of law, where you speak to another person's legal interests rather than to whatever your own personal feelings about the case might be? Or being required as an insurance adjuster to limit disbursements to claimants as much as possible, even though you think the guidelines sometimes result in unfairness?

- Will the job pay enough for you to get by? There are many fascinating and rewarding jobs that pay very little, such as pastoring and missionary work. Some jobs—American Red Cross disaster work, for instance—are available almost solely as volunteer positions. Positions as adjunct faculty members on most college campuses pay only a fraction per credit hour of what full-time faculty are paid; thus if teaching half-time or teaching parttime on numerous campuses sounds interesting, you may need to arrange for additional means of financial support.

- How will the job affect your personal life? Suppose you are considering becoming a psychotherapist. If you pursue this career track, your life will never be the same, for both positive and negative reasons (Guy, 1987). On the positive side, your capacity to experience intimacy is likely to improve. As you become more psychologically minded, you are likely to become more self-aware and self-assured and to feel less easily threatened during conflict with others. You may experience increases in assertiveness, self-reliance, introspection, self-reflection, sensitivity, and comfort with self-disclosure. These positive effects can be useful in your personal life, in addition to your practice as a psychotherapist.

However, there are also negative effects. You may feel emotionally "used up" at the end of the day, wanting to just withdraw into solitude rather than become engaged with your significant others and their trials and tribulations. The need to keep the content of your work life confidential means you will not be able to discuss much of your work life with friends and family, which can result in additional feelings of isolation. You may lose some of your spontaneity, since what you say and do as a therapist is tightly controlled and organized around the needs of your clients, rather than what you really feel like saying or doing. You may find yourself analyzing others, or looking for hidden meanings behind what others say or do, rather than just letting yourself be a part of the moment.

If you discover some limitations to your potential career choices, use these evaluative points to create a hierarchy according to which have the fewest disadvantages and most advantages. You can also take the approach of looking for ways of dealing with any disadvantages so that they need not be so negative. For example, you could research and maximize the variables that are likely to get you into your chosen training program. Or, you can be sure to simultaneously prepare for plan 2, in the event you do not succeed in being accepted into training for your first preference.

Life as an Employee

The American dream typically includes fondly contemplating owning your own business, or at least working your way up to the top of the corporate ladder so you can be your own boss. That scenario now tends to be the exception rather than the rule. Currently, most people work for someone else, and very few of those make it to the pinnacles of their fields or upper management. Even those who eventually run businesses of their own usually begin under the tutelage of somebody else.

So no matter what field you choose, you will most likely at some point in your career be an employee. Competence in your field is only one of the important elements to consider as you apply for positions. There are other elements that are common to success as an employee no matter what your field. Drucker (1952) describes a number of considerations.

Choose a work environment that is right for you. There are four basic decisions you will need to make. First, are you more interested in a stable routine, company loyalty, and security than in having constantly changing tasks and a good challenge—with the inherent risk of failure? Your temperament is important when making this choice. If you are high strung you may not enjoy the tumultuousness of constantly trying to impose structure onto chaotic task presentation. And if you require a great deal of stimulation before a task holds your attention, you may fall asleep in a more routine setting. On the other hand, you can always kick up your heels during your leisure hours if you enjoy stimulating challenges but also need the stability and security of a routine job.

Second, would you rather be part of a large or a small organization work setting? Each has its advantages, depending on what is most important to you. A small organization gives you a greater opportunity to become the proverbial "big fish in a small pond," since there are fewer people competing for the role. You get to wear many hats, since fewer people to spread around means a greater variety of tasks being assigned to each individual. A small work setting allows you to get to know your co-workers—as well as the entire work environment—fairly well. When wrinkles need to be ironed out, you can usually communicate with others directly and informally. This allows for more flexibility, since there are fewer people and systems with which to coordinate efforts.

However, a large organization allows you to have the privacy and anonymity of being the "small fish in the big pond." When difficulties arise they are typically handled through "channels," working around any need for direct confrontations. There is the security of established policies to fall back on, as well as the greater job security typically offered by a major organization. You gain the status of being associated with a large, established company. You can be more of a specialist in your field, since large companies hire specific individuals to take care of all the administrative and pragmatic details that you might get stuck with in a smaller organization.

Third, do you want to start at the bottom and work your way up within the job specialties, or do you want to begin your career as a management trainee? Consider whether you better function when you can concentrate on your own tree and ignore the rest of the forest or feel more comfortable working with an overview of the entire terrain. Starting at the management level does mean needing to learn a great deal all at once. Management, and being a visible part of the whole, also leaves you more exposed, as more of the organization is going to be aware of your mistakes and perhaps be affected by them. However, others will also be more likely to be aware of your successes, and you will be in a better position to right any problems you find.

Beginning your career by diligently focusing on your single tree at the base of the valley allows you to maintain more privacy and more control over your individual tasks. As you become so specifically focused, you are in a better position to train yourself thoroughly in practicing and applying your profession. Also, you can feel more comfortable with any risks or challenges you take, since they will more likely affect only your corner of the woods, rather than burning down the whole forest.

Fourth, do you want to be a specialist or a generalist? Everybody needs to be trained in his or her own specific field. However, some prefer to perform the more administratively oriented duties of their fields, while others prefer to zero in on the meat of their applied field of choice. Administrators must be skilled at seeing how things fit together, providing leadership, coordinating, planning, and giving direction. Specialists are more likely to focus on continued development of their personal competence in the field, and for exploring, expanding, and applying their creativity to their work endeavors.

Care for your character. Employers do indeed want to hire someone who is good at what he or she does. However, they also want someone they can trust, someone who will show up on time, follow through on things, be honest about how things are going so problems can be addressed, get along with the other employees and not create interpersonal tension, and generally reflect well upon the organization. If your work life takes place in an isolated closet or you need relate to little more than a computer, your character may not be as important to your ability to be hired and/or promoted. But if your job involves working with others—either co-workers or clientele and customers—character becomes crucial. Character flaws have kept many competent employees from rising to their highest potential within an organization.

Develop your thinking skills and learn to communicate effectively.
These last areas are provided as two of the greatest advantages of having a four-year college or university education. Maybe required courses such as philosophy, economics, creative writing, and others seem completely irrelevant to you and your chosen career. However, they do teach you how to look at a thing both as whole and in its parts, and at how things fit together. These courses teach you to discern and weed out the irrelevant and zero in on what is germane to the task at hand. They give you practice incorporating new variables into old structures. And through writing papers and giving oral presentations, you learn to organize your unique thoughts and present them in ways that are useful and that others can digest.

Thinking skills and the ability to effectively communicate your thoughts demonstrate your value to an organization. They expose your strengths, your creativity, and your interest in the functioning of your firm. Even if you start your own business and become the employer, the ability to think analytically and to express yourself well to others will help sell you to the public, as well as make life easier for your employees. These abilities are two of the most valuable transferable skills you can develop as you prepare to climb to the heights of your field.

How to Become a Workaholic

This heading is offered tongue-in-cheek. "Workaholic" is a label sometimes pasted onto those who are overinvested in their work lives and underinvested in their interpersonal and play lives. Unfortunately, they may suffer greatly as a result of their lifestyle imbalance. If you wrote up 10 basic rules describing how such individuals manage to have a workaholic lifestyle, they would look something like this:

1. *Your achievements and acquisitions always come first.* After all, you prove your worth as a person through what you can accomplish and what you own, as well as who you know and how much status you can achieve.

2. *Don't let friends and family get in the way of your accomplishments.* Those you are close to should be there to cheer you on, agree with whatever you say or do, and tell you how wonderful you are. You are doing enough for them just by providing them with an income and vicarious status. Don't get suckered into adjusting your life to meet their needs.

3. *If others get in your way, blow up at them.* They're diminishing your

worth as a person. Who cares if you hurt their feelings? They're only looking out for themselves, anyway.

4. *If you are not on top of the pile, you may as well be on the bottom.* If anyone else has done something better than you, redouble your efforts. Claw your way up to the top, or else you are worthless.

5. *Never put yourself in a position of looking like you can't do something or don't know something.* Avoid taking on new challenges or putting yourself in a learning position, unless you're pretty sure you can either excel at it immediately or hide your incompetence as you learn.

6. *Make sure you win every argument.* Keep on arguing until the other person gives in. It doesn't matter how absurd you begin to sound. As long as the other person eventually backs down and you never admit being wrong, you are vindicated.

7. *Never waste time.* Play is for wimps. It's okay to get involved with a sport like golf or tennis or something if it helps get you in good with your boss or clientele. And it's also okay if it gives you the opportunity to beat the socks off the other players. Otherwise, you are better off scheduling your time by cramming as many achievement-related activities into your lifestyle as you can.

8. *Avoid change.* If anything changes in your life structure—even ideas—you risk losing your ability to excel or your appearance of competence or status.

9. *Don't make decisions unless you have to.* You might make a mistake. That would be disastrous.

10. *Don't get sidetracked by health issues.* As long as you are not six feet under, you can keep going. If you begin to feel uptight, you can always escape the unpleasantness with a drink or two.

These rules sound ridiculous. Yet as you read them, you probably recognized someone you know. You may even have recognized certain aspects of your own life. If you actually followed these rules, you might do a fair amount of achieving. However, you probably would not be very happy or well-adjusted. You would also not be particularly healthy, either physically or emotionally.

Not all workaholics think this dysfunctionally. Many people place a hefty investment of time and energy into their work because they find it to be meaningful and rewarding. These individuals are usually well adjusted. However, their families' lives often suffer because of their preoccupied lifestyle.

The Type A Behavior Pattern

Physicians and mental health professionals have extensively studied the dysfunctional characterization of a large group of workaholics as the **type A behavior pattern**. This behavior pattern was originally identified by a couple of cardiologists. They discovered that the front edges of the chairs in their waiting room wore out more quickly than was the case when the doctors had a more general medical practice. In other words, their heart patients were literally "on the edge of their seats" (Friedman & Rosenman, 1974). Because of this early correlation, the syndrome was originally called the "coronary-prone personality." It became a hot topic because it showed the significant effect that our behavior can have on our physical health.

You might recall having heard that some later longitudinal studies failed to find a relationship between the type A behavior pattern and heart disease (Miller et al., 1991). This can be attributed in part to some inadequately managed experimental variables, as well as some early definitional problems. For example, the type A individual was originally defined as being highly competitive and achievement oriented. While this finding has in fact held up over time, you need not be type A in order to be competitive and achievement oriented. There are plenty of well-adjusted individuals who enjoy competing and achieving. Thus other factors are at play, two of which have been revealed by subsequent studies.

The two main variables behind the type A behavior pattern are **free-floating hostility** and **time urgency** (Friedman & Ulmer, 1984). Free-floating hostility is an ongoing feeling of anger or irritation. It is free-floating because it cannot be accurately attached to any current stressors. It is instead a poltergeist from the past. Somewhere along the line, these individuals developed the feeling of being emotionally slighted, of not getting what they felt they needed or deserved. They may in fact have been deprived of nurturance as a child, or perhaps they were just born with needy temperaments. Either way, they release the safety valve on this anger as they regularly and inappropriately blow up over day-to-day trivia.

Time urgency is the practice of cramming more and more activity into less and less time. It is a product of low self-esteem. Rather than looking inward for a sense of worth, the type A behavior pattern involves looking outside to everyone and everything else in order to establish a sense of worth. Thus the more you do and the better you can make yourself look to others, the more self-worth you have. The ways in which we can develop low self-esteem are too numerous to mention here. The practice of time urgency, however, is one way to emotionally cope with low self-esteem, no matter how the low self-esteem found its way into the person's self-evaluation. As long as you keep yourself busy, focus on the next goal, and do whatever you can to avoid being in touch with the here-and-now experience, you can avoid the unpleasant feelings of low self-esteem and free-floating hostility.

Physically, individuals who follow the type A behavior pattern suffer the effects of excess stress. Friedman and Ulmer (1984) believe that coronary problems erupt in these individuals because of the excess norepinephrine that is secreted during times of stress. For those with type A characteristics, this happens when goals are somehow being blocked or something is upsetting them. The constant injections of norepinephrine contribute to the breakdown of the plaque that lines the inside of the coronary arteries. When the damaged plaque eventually ruptures, blood clots form. As these become lodged within the coronary arteries, they block the flow of blood to the heart muscle itself. The lack of nourishment causes parts of the heart muscle to die, eventually leading to a heart attack.

These individuals further complicate their coronary problems with the types of exercise they often choose. They usually select some activity that shows they can "take it," such as handball, running, racquetball—anything that forces them to push themselves to their outer limits. Their already-damaged heart muscles have difficulty keeping up with such high-pressure workouts. Also, since individuals who dedicate their time disproportionately to work and achievement-oriented activity tend to exercise inconsistently, they are exponentially increasing their chances of causing themselves physical harm when they do exercise, as described in Chapter 8.

Healthy achievers engage themselves with their lives in less destructive ways (Hughes, 1991). Their competitiveness and achievement orientation do not exist for the sole purpose of coming out on top. They enjoy participation in the activity itself, regardless of how well they do. They enjoy the excitement of competition, even when it involves seeing someone else win. They enjoy the process of achieving, and can stop and enjoy their accomplishments as they occur, rather than hurrying on toward the next goal. When they share their achievements with others, it is for the purpose of sharing the good feeling, rather than saying "see how much better I am than you are."

The differences between relatively laid-back healthy achievers and hard-driving, stress-ridden type A achievers can be attributed to their differing inner philosophies. Their philosophies of the world, self, and others are markedly different from one another. Healthy achievers see themselves as inherently valuable and worthwhile, no matter what their level of achievement. They also see others as valuable and enjoyable, as fellow travelers in the journey of living. They view the world as exciting and inviting, presenting challenges as opportunities for growth and enjoyment.

Type A achievers are not so optimistic. They see themselves as having worth only if they can achieve or look good to the outside world. Others are competition, rather than kindred spirits. And the world is a frightening place, threatening their security at every turn.

As previously discussed in other chapters, your beliefs and life philosophy are your choice. Nobody can select them for you. Why choose beliefs about yourself, others, and the world that can impair your physical and emotional health, interfere with your interpersonal relationships, do away with your ability to enjoy leisure time, and destroy the inherent enjoyment to be found in being while working?

Job Burnout

No matter how much we may like our jobs, we are all susceptible to **job burnout**. Burnout typically occurs when we have had excessive stress on the job over a long period of time. As happens with any other type of chronic stress, we eventually arrive at the exhaustion phase of the general adaptation syndrome (see Chapter 4).

Often people suffering from job burnout try to cope by emotionally or psychologically distancing themselves from their work. They stop caring so much about how well they do, and as might be expected, their level of performance drops. They start feeling cynical toward customers or clients and become more rigid in how they go about dealing with them. They might start spending more time socializing on the job.

Some people seem more likely to burn out than others. Those who already have a tendency to worry a lot, become depressed, or experience social phobias are prime candidates. Low self-esteem and feelings of inadequacy can place limits on how long such individuals can successfully cope with excessive job stress. Those who cope with stress by withdrawing or becoming passive and inactive are less likely to effectively remove the stressors that lead to burnout, and are therefore more likely to eventually experience burnout symptoms.

Many burnout victims think of quitting as a solution. In most cases, such a reaction is drastic and unnecessary. Chapter 4 describes numerous stress management techniques that can be useful for overcoming the stressors that lead to job burnout. Community centers, hospitals, and churches often have support groups for dealing with job stress. In addition, many employers recognize the importance of addressing job burnout and provide in-house support groups and self-help groups for guiding their employees back toward effectively dealing with on-the-job stressors.

Play

Play is becoming a lost art. As our work hours become longer and our time for leisure less abundant, we seem to be tossing play to the wayside. Leisure certainly doesn't get the press that work does. When you are standing around at a party and someone asks you what you do, you typically mention your career life, rather than your play life. Different from earlier generations, when individuals invested more effort and less mechanization into entertaining themselves, play is now often considered to be a pastime of childhood. Work is much more valued by our society: It usually results in collecting money and acquisitions, defines much of our status, and as we climb the ladder of success provides us with more power and control over our lives. With all of these rewards, little wonder that our work lives are so heavily emphasized!

The rewards of play are more subtle. While there are no concrete goals, other than the enjoyment of the moment, the benefits of play are nonetheless many.

What Is Play?

What sets play apart from our other life experiences? Garvey (1990) describes several components of play:

1. *Play is fun.* We enjoy doing it. It holds our attention and our interest. Even if we don't actually look happy while we are taking part in play activities, we are still valuing the experiences positively.
2. *Play has no extrinsic purpose.* Play may result in the construction of some concrete object, but constructing the object is not the main purpose of the activity. We engage in play for *intrinsic* reasons, the joy of experiencing as we are doing. If a project begins to feel pressured, it is no longer play.
3. *Play occurs by choice.* While you can be pressured to take part in an activity, nobody can actually force you to play.

4. *Play involves participation.* Perhaps you remember as a child trying to include some of your nearby playground chums in a game, only to be told "I'm not playing." Simply being present at a play activity does not mean you are playing. You must be in some way actively engaged, even if only as an interested spectator.

5. *Play activities are in some ways related to real-world activity.* During play we experiment with many of the "transferable skills" of the working world, only the stakes are much lower. Play also lets us try out inappropriate or aggressive interpersonal behaviors without the risk of alienating others. However, play may also feel like play because it is so different from what we do in our work and interpersonal lives.

Why Is Play Important?

Karl Groos, an early pioneer in the research of play, pointed out that in spite of its seeming purposelessness play appears to serve many purposes (Groos, 1908). Although his work predates recognition of the current perspectives of psychology, his observations appear to touch bases with almost all of them. The value of play becomes clear as we examine the intertwined nature of its relationship with what makes us "tick."

Biological perspective. The earliest theory focused on the biological aspects, viewing the role of play in terms of a release of energy. This release was believed to stem from seemingly instinctual impulses, such as a kitten chasing a "dust bunny" much as it might one day chase a mouse. Currently also, the role of play in physical well-being appears to involve its release value. It provides a distraction from the everyday world. It often includes some repetitive playful movement that feels almost intoxicating as it captures our interest and provides a reward unto itself, and we may continue it until we are in a state of exhaustion. However, taking a break to play can also invigorate us back into working condition after we think we have "burnt out."

Behavioral perspective. Play provides many benefits for our behavioral adjustment. It lets us imitate behaviors that we would like to try out but which have no place in our everyday worlds. We can practice skills we would like to be able to perform more efficiently. Just learning to enjoy play increases our self-efficacy, as we discover that we can succeed in giving ourselves pleasure and enjoyment.

Cognitive perspective. Similar to our biological needs, play can function as a release in our cognitive lives. Releasing ourselves from the constraints of logic is fun. This is one of the reasons why we enjoy jokes, as the boundaries of reality are bashed by the conflicting paradigm of the punch line. Also, the nonserious nature of many games and play activities allows us to play out and test morals, values, and beliefs in ways that may not be possible in the real world.

Psychodynamic perspective. The psychodynamic perspective explains the role of play in dealing with inner conflict. Sometimes we act out things that are bothering us, and afterward do not feel so bad about them. Perhaps we act out what we wish would happen. Play allows for many types of self-expression, through action and/or fantasy.

Existential perspective. However, the most tightly engaged perspective of play is that represented by the existential standpoint. Play is a smorgasbord of the senses, tied in with the spontaneity of the here-and-now moment and heightening our sense of immediate reality. Play lets us feel as one with our fellow players, as well as joined with the cause of action involved with our play.

How Do We Learn to Play?

Nobody needs to teach children to play. Play happens spontaneously during infancy. Through play, children learn to plan, try out various communication styles, practice conflict and negotiation skills, explore the boundaries of real/pretend and appropriate/inappropriate, and rehearse expression of thoughts and feelings. Play has few rules, yet rules can be made up as the children go along. Play prepares children for real life.

For adults, though, play is more complex and in many ways has become somewhat institutionalized. We seem to have developed socially accepted guidelines for how adult play activities may be done, when and where they are permissible, and who is allowed to play them.

For example, a group of children with a badminton set could actually play badminton. On the other hand, they might improvise some other play activities: badminton without the net, "golfing" the shuttlecock up off the lawn when serving, ignoring boundaries, or even using the racquets for playing air guitar as they have Metallica imitation competitions. Adult play with a badminton set is typically much more structured. Certain rules are followed, it can only be played where there is enough room to set up a net and boundaries, and you can only play if you know how or are willing to be taught.

This institutionalization of adult play has resulted in less and less true play among adults. The joy of playing a sport may be replaced by working toward winning league competitions. People may be excluded altogether from some forms of play because their skill level is not high enough to be competitive. Others engage in play activities because they believe social obligations are involved, but the activity does not really feel like play to them. The elaborate paraphernalia associated with many forms of play put many socially acceptable activities out of reach of the average person on the street.

The Characteristics of Play

If you are going to ensure that you have true play in your life, you must remember these five characteristics of play:

- Play is fun or interesting.
- Play has no extrinsic purpose.
- Play occurs by choice.
- Play involves participation.
- Play may mimic real-world activity, but it takes place for the benefit of the first four points.

If any of these points are violated, the activity is no longer play. If you no longer enjoy the activity, for whatever reason, it is not play. If you only involve yourself with an activity because you "need to keep in shape," want to make good on your investment in equipment, or indulge solely for the purpose of producing some final product, it is not play. If you do it only because your friends do it, or you keep doing it even though you would rather not, it is not play. If you only show up and go through the motions, not involving yourself either directly or vicariously, it is not play.

There are many different types of play. Some play can be competitive in addition to being enjoyable, but other types do not involve competition. One way to classify play is by means of categories that describe the primary characteristic that provides the enjoyment. Six possible categories are hunting, curiosity, roving, creativity, vicarious enjoyment, acquisition, social benefit, and aesthetics (Mitchell & Mason, 1948).

Hunting. Hunting is a form of play that may involve actually looking for and killing prey. It can also involve preparation for hunting prey, such as caring for weapons, shooting trap, or taking archery lessons. On the other hand, hunting is also involved in such activities as watching and identifying birds, gathering mushrooms, collecting shells, hunting bargains/treasures at garage sales, searching for words in a crossword puzzle, or even tracking down facts to include in a personal growth textbook.

Curiosity. Some forms of play involve curiosity. Why do things work the way they do? What will happen if I interact with an object in a particular way? What does the world look like from the top of a mountain? What is it like to come barreling down a roller-coaster ride? Horseback ride across a dusty plain? Snorkel in a shallow bay? Scuba dive on the sea floor? Most forms of play are fueled at least in part by curiosity.

Roving. Roving is a form of wandering aimlessly, purely for the enjoyment of wandering. It can involve hopping in the car to go for a drive, going for a nature walk, walking the dog, bicycling, hiking, sailing, canoeing, rollerblading, or even hang-gliding.

Creativity. Creative play is very popular. Creative efforts can be channeled into actually producing artistic or functional products, or may be nonmaterial as in the case of making up stories or drawing lines in the sand.

Vicarious play. Some play is enjoyed passively. In other words, we can have fun by watching the activities of someone else. Spectator sports, reading, watching plays or movies, listening to live or recorded music, and even being around friends as they joke around with one another are all vicarious play.

Acquisition. Acquisitive play occurs when we collect things. Many hobbies take the form of collections. Virtually anything can be collected: stamps, coins, baseball cards, butterflies, rocks, antiques, Agatha Christie novels, or even various molds, spores, and fungi.

Socializing. Social play can occur almost anywhere and at any time. Being the social animals that we are, we enjoy simply being around other people. We often gather informally just for the fun of it. Games, clubs, contests, dances, volunteer groups, and church activities are some of the more-structured ways by which we place ourselves around others.

Aesthetics. Human beings find joy in beauty. Becoming entranced with a beautiful painting, appreciating the intricacies of a fugue performed by a symphony orchestra, lingering over the softness of a labrador's ears, or even just stopping to smell the roses are a few of the many forms of play that involve appreciation of beauty.

Finding Play

What kind of play do you enjoy most? We all have our own styles and preferences, but it is a good idea to give some thought to the way you spend your leisure time. Is it all in front of the boob-tube? Consider what you might be missing by limiting yourself to passive, isolated play. If there is an activity you enjoy and you find a way to make money at it, all the better, but make sure you also have a fun activity that is not work. Turning your fun activity into a job can take away its voluntary nature and thus minimize its play value. In any event, find the forms of play that feel right for you. Then make them a priority: not as replacements for work, but as companionable alternatives during balanced living.

Expanding Your Experience

When I was an undergraduate, I complied with the usual tradition of taking on weird menial jobs in order to help pay my way through school. One position required that I spend a lot of time preparing mass mailings.

Keep in mind that this was before easy access to machines that collate and staple as they reproduce, not to mention machines that stuff, seal, address, and stamp envelopes. We had to do almost all of the work manually. However, I was taught specific techniques for accomplishing these steps. After a while, I actually began to enjoy the job. By arranging materials optimally and using certain repetitive, efficient motions, the task almost became a game.

Many years later, I found myself performing survey research involving mass mailings and wowed my colleagues with my whiz-bang mail preparation skills. I continue to use these old-time strategies when I mail out Christmas cards. And I still enjoy using them! My enjoyment stems from many things: the joy of doing, having found a transferable skill that has followed me through many life phases, maintaining a skill that is becoming lost in our high-tech culture, and my personal play preference for repetitive creation such as knitting, digging weeds, compulsive editing, etc.

I have included activities that I hope you will find useful as you pursue your own career and play lives. The first exercise gives you an opportunity to share past work experiences with your classmates and explore what you liked and did not like about them. Next, there is an exercise that allows you to evaluate your job search skills. The third exercise is an assessment and discussion of possible "workaholism." The last exercise is directed toward helping you discover and capitalize upon your preferred style of play.

Study Questions

1. Define "work." What are the differences between a "job" and a "career"?

2. According to Herzberg, what is the difference between "motivators" and "hygiene"? Which are more likely to result in job satisfaction, and why?

3. What effect would you expect job satisfaction to have on your productivity? Explain.

4. Describe the three tasks involved with choosing a career, according to Isaacson.

5. What are the differences between what can be measured by achievement tests, aptitude tests, and interest tests?

6. Jerry is considering a career as a test pilot. Using the questions provided for evaluating and prioritizing career choices, what positives and negatives can you think of that Jerry might want to keep in mind?
7. Describe the four decision points suggested by Drucker that can help you become an effective and successful employee.
8. Suppose you plan to work for a large organization. What advantages and disadvantages do you see? How about advantages and disadvantages of working for a smaller organization?
9. Jane is planning on applying for a job as a data processor at a large, conservative company. She is very good at data processing. However, she coiffures herself like a rock star and spends time with companions that many individuals might describe as "questionable." She tends to be opinionated and interacts with others in ways that some find to be offensive. Jane points out that her personal style has no effect on her data processing ability, and thus it should not affect her employability. What would you say to her?
10. What sorts of "transferable skills" are developed as you take college courses that seem irrelevant to your major?
11. Are competitive and achievement-oriented individuals necessarily unhealthy? Explain your answer.
12. Describe the two variables that provide the basis of the type A behavior pattern. How do they result in heart disease?
13. Describe the life philosophies of the healthy and unhealthy achiever.
14. Describe the main characteristics of "play."
15. According to the various perspectives of psychology, what benefits do we reap by taking time to play?
16. Why do you think children find it easier to play than adults do?

Chapter Fourteen

Middle Adulthood, Aging, and Dying

Ultimate Lessons in Existentiality

Are we having fun yet?

For a young person, it is hard to imagine reaching middle or late adulthood, let alone facing impending death. It may be equally difficult to imagine actually enjoying these life phases, let alone find any meaning in them. Those of you who are still young adults may indeed wonder what your future phases of living may bring. Since our culture worships youth, the media typically play up the benefits of early adulthood alone, ignoring the freedoms and delights that await us in our later years. Thus it is difficult also for those of you who have already reached these phases to sort out the "normality" of your experience. This chapter should leave you with an understanding of the shifting nature of experiencing our existence, as well as the knowledge that graduation from youth is not just a collection of painful endings but also the introduction of invigorating new beginnings.

Midlife

As I researched this topic, I was struck by how the verbiage contrasted from the way theorists and scientists usually write their articles. As you have probably discovered by now, academically oriented pieces tend to be written in a yawningly cut-and-dried manner. But these articles concerning middle adulthood had an undeniable spark to them. The feelings of the writers were not merely evident but unabashedly undisguised. The writers seemed more comfortable with taking poetic license, and they wandered off onto existential tangents just as naturally as they cited the masters.

What occurred to me was that the vast majority of theory writers are passing through midlife themselves. I suspect that as they wrote on the topic of midlife, their compositions actually became gently woven combinations of scientific research and profound personal experience, so profound they could not contain themselves within the scientifically accepted dust-bowl empirical style. Contrary to popular belief, there is more to midlife than "crisis" and the first clangings of death knells. Midlife brings with it new ways of evaluating and experiencing. As these authors' writing styles reflected, midlife is a transitional period its sojourners come to cherish rather than curse.

Midlife as a Stage

Erikson (1963) was one of the first to identify middle adulthood as a stage. He described it as a time of **generativity** versus **stagnation**. Generativity is an outpouring of our social striving, as we find ways of putting our knowledge and expertise to use, as well as passing them on to the younger generation. Passing the torch can be accomplished through child-rearing, mentoring, teaching, writing, or any other activity that allows us to pass along our unique knowledge and abilities.

Stagnation occurs if we react to midlife with withdrawal, continuing a more self-centered focus. Perhaps we continue to build ourselves toward some ongoing illusion of perfection or personal accomplishment, just as we did during younger adulthood. Or we might wallow in a shallow lifestyle of superficiality: knowing the right people, giving the right party, belonging to the right profession, owning the right car, wearing the right clothes.

Levinson expanded the conceptualization of middle adulthood into phases (Levinson et al., 1978). He proposed that during middle adulthood we question how we have structured our lives about every 10 years. The questioning transforms into life restructuring, as we find new niches that allow us to incorporate our new structures. This might include actual external changes, such as finding a new career or moving to a different neighborhood. But it could also be a matter of changing inner belief structures or values, thus keeping the previous lifestyle but looking at it with a fresher viewpoint.

Levinson's work popularized the concept of **mid-life crisis**. A person suffering from midlife crisis is described as being somewhere between 35 and 45, a person drastically disillusioned with his or her life who frequently makes sudden sweeping changes in lifestyle.

As these ideas first got rolling in the late 1970s, a stereotype emerged that identified men who were going through a midlife crisis. The first thing these men did was frizz their hair. They sold their sedans and drove convertibles instead. They forced themselves to like disco. They started wearing brightly patterned sport shirts, which they left unbuttoned at the top so chest hair would be sure to stick out, and topped it all off with a gold chain around their necks. Little wonder that the mid-life crisis was sometimes referred to as a "second adolescence"! These middle-aged adults were conforming to a "self"-defined, like-dressing peer group similar to those of teenage generations.

Currently, we recognize that most people do not have full-blown midlife crises. Instead, most of us will experience a **midlife transition**: a period of reappraisal and restructuring, similar to other middle-adulthood transitions. Crises tend to occur when our reappraisals expose huge chasms between who we are and what we have chosen to do with our lives. Thus those who will be most vulnerable are those who structured their lives around the wishes of others, pursued unrealistically high or limited life goals, or made their life choices based on misperceptions or misinformation concerning what the world is all about.

Carl Jung noticed that we are especially susceptible to difficulties with our spiritual lives during middle adulthood. As we get caught up in the young adult tasks of acquiring possessions and building a niche in society, we may neglect or ignore our spiritual selves. Having accomplished our more concrete adult tasks, we may be suddenly confronted with realization that we have also arrived at **spiritual bankruptcy**.

Midlife as an Experience

What is it like to experience middle adulthood? Cognitive restructuring seems to play the biggest role. We come to the realization that much of life is built on illusions and stereotypes. The "shoulds" and "oughts" that carried us up to middle adulthood suddenly seem a little murky or hard to swallow. Throughout young adulthood we worked with goals in mind: setting up a home, establishing a career, deciding whether or not to get married and have children, finding a place in society. By midlife, these goals typically have been reached. So what is left to aim for? Death? What kind of a goal is that?

We also begin to recognize that some of our dreams will probably never be realized. Perhaps the dreams were unrealistic, or certain of our life choices did away with any chance for fulfilling them. Our desire to eventually mold ourselves into some preconceived perfect person, or to achieve our "ideal" life, loses its grounding as we question some of the hard and fast structures we had so depended upon. Thus we begin to relearn many things: how to focus, to cope, and to find meaning and purpose in our lives.

While these aspects of midlife at times can feel uncomfortable, they also result in new freedoms. We are no longer emotionally tied to old rigid structures we may never have understood anyway. We experience more personal plasticity, as we feel less judgmental and more at ease with modifying our beliefs and perceptions. We reevaluate and reorganize our life commitments so they are more consistent with our inner experience. It is not that we finally find ourselves; we simply become comfortable with continually rediscovering who we are. Successful resolution results in increased feelings of purpose, competence, and productivity. We are likely to address any spiritual bankruptcy and begin feeling spiritually whole. Research has found that we actually feel better about ourselves during middle adulthood than at any other time in our lives (McGrath, 1992).

Working through Midlife Transition

Successfully resolving the issues of midlife begins with acceptance. Fox (1983) describes this form of acceptance as "befriending" darkness and pain. We accept the unpleasant realities of life that we intuitively try to avoid or defend against experiencing. This pain often involves losses, such as losing a loved one to death or divorce, losing a dream, or becoming limited by severe illness or physical disabilities. There is the pain of the transition itself, as we leave behind a previous way of being. It could be the pain of injustice—being discriminated against, being victimized by crime, discovering good guys don't finish first, being unjustly persecuted in some way. And there is the pain of human suffering in general.

To the outsider, this may seem masochistic. It certainly doesn't fit in with the pleasure principle. Why make yourself experience the pains of living? The answer is that by avoiding pain you cut yourself off from a major part of the human experience. And since we each react to life experiences in our own unique way, continuing emotional avoidance of the disasters of living also results in avoidance of significant parts of ourselves.

When you embrace your pain you find personal meaning, rather than overwhelming discomfort. You do not wallow around in pain as though you enjoy it, you face it in order to find renewed purpose in living and then let the pain go. Fox organizes the process into four main phases:

1. *Let pain be pain.* Do not continue to deny its presence, numb yourself against it, rationalize it away, or rebel against it. Acknowledge it for what it is.

2. *Develop an understanding of the pain.* What does it feel like? Not all pain feels the same. What kind is uniquely yours? Where did it come from? Did it generalize from the overall human condition, or is it specific to some life experience of your own? How do you see it affecting you?

3. *Let go of the pain.* Letting go is also unique for each of us, since we all let go of something a little different. Letting go may be an abstraction, such as ceasing to judge others or forgiving someone from the past for having wronged you. You might adopt a new life philosophy, viewing the world through a different set of glasses. Letting go can also involve concrete changes. You might alter behaviors you acknowledge as having developed from your pain. You might manage your anger more effectively, or use less alcohol. You might take on new challenges to help sublimate the strivings of the pain, such as changing to a different career, working on an interpersonal relationship, or finding ways to help the needy. You

can even symbolically let go of your pain by creating your own rite of passage, perhaps by putting a symbol of the pain in a jar and burying it in the back yard.

4. *Reap the benefits.* Having worked through the pain and let it go, new strengths and more genuine experiencing emerge. You are more "you" at this point than you are likely to have been at any time in your life.

Gender Differences at Midlife

At midlife, both men and women tend to reevaluate gender roles (O'Neil & Egan, 1992). They may emerge from the other side of transition with less rigid expectations based on gender, or perhaps come up with new or even more rigid expectations. However, given the biological and cultural role differences between men and women and their lives, some of the issues they face at midlife fall into differing patterns.

Women at midlife. One of the most significant midlife experiences for women is menopause. Women stop menstruating, and their likelihood of bearing children more or less ends. In the past, women were rumored as naturally experiencing severe depression stemming from this milestone change in their lives, but the rumor has proved unfounded. Even though menopause does represent a loss, most women report feeling relieved (McGrath et al., 1990) that they no longer have to worry about pregnancy, contraception, and dealing with the inconvenience of menstrual periods. Women who chose not to have children or were unable to conceive, however, may experience a more profound form of mourning.

Women who chose to be stay-at-home mothers are likely to have significant transitional experiences due to the empty nest. A woman who had no life outside that involving her children may struggle, as she perceives the absence of children as an end to her life purpose. However, most women report that they are glad to have the house to themselves. They appreciate having to feed and clean up after fewer people. They enjoy the increased privacy, free time, time alone with their spouse, and new possibilities.

During middle adulthood, women begin getting their first tastes of ageism. Our culture prescribes that, until a certain point, men are more valued and respected as they grow older. Women tend to become devalued with age, since they no longer look so "young and attractive." Thus women often begin to experience a new form of discrimination during their middle adulthood. As they learn to identify less with cultural standards, women work through this form of pain and loss.

Financial considerations can result in women having fewer options for dealing with some transitional material. As it is, working women are paid about 75% of what men are paid, even when they have the same training and experience (Reis & Stone, 1992). When you factor in the imbalance in salaries offered for jobs typically held by men and jobs typically held by women, a woman's ability to financially support her preferred lifestyle on her own is especially limited.

Thus divorce is often not as viable an option for women as for men. Statistically, women become much more financially vulnerable after divorce: A woman's standard of living falls by an average of 73% within a year after the divorce, while a man's increases an average of 42% (U.S. Bureau of the Census, 1981). With this in mind, many women choose to stay in unsatisfying marital relationships. Many women resolve transitional conflicts concerning their spouses by learning to adjust to the limitations of the relationship, viewing it from a less judgmental perspective, or remedying the marriage by learning to interact differently.

Men at midlife. Gender issues concerning men at midlife have not been studied as extensively as those for women. Past tendencies for male psychology to be equated with "normal" psychology and that of women to be studied as something outside the norm have worked against men in this respect. However, in recent years the men's movement has been making up for this deficit, as men are becoming more comfortable with exploring the meaning of manhood and defining the male experience.

Generativity versus stagnation is an especially relevant issue for men at midlife. Our culture often places value on men according to their profession and how much money they make. Men who arrive at midlife with a low-paying or low-status job may begin having difficulties with low self-esteem. On the other hand, those who attained high status may find, like Richard Corey in Chapter 1, that money and status are relatively meaningless when compared to having an inner purpose for living. Resolution of this transitional issue becomes less traumatic as men learn to let go of some of the stereotypical images of manhood presented by our culture.

As men let go of stereotypes, they allow themselves to become more nurturing and interested in intimacy (Kovacs, 1992). Unfortunately, this change often occurs just as the wife and kids are going through developmental tasks that do not allow a man to practice these newly discovered attributes. Children of middle-aged men have typically reached adolescence and are trying to move away from emotional dependence on their parents. And if the man's wife is also passing through midlife, she is most likely becoming more assertive and independent and focusing more on goals away from home and her marital relationship. Men can resolve the transition by demonstrating types of intimacy acceptable to their significant others, such as being supportive of their efforts to increase their integration with life outside the family. They can also find intimacy by sharing more genuinely with their male friends.

Some men deal with their struggling intimacy needs by running off with a younger woman. Kovacs (1992) suggests that some middle-aged men's preoccupation with younger women may in fact be neurobiological, programmed in as a safety valve for the survival of the species. Just as women's menstrual cycles may go through a phase of occurring more closely together just before menopause, men may feel a physiologically based urge to "pollinate" before their bodies begin their physical demise.

Another hypothesis explaining why middle-aged men are so attracted to younger women concerns death anxiety. Kovacs proposes that men are more afraid of dying than women are. Women feel more connected to the ongoing stream of life, since they become pregnant, give birth, nurse babies, and spend much of their young and middle adulthood nurturing the new generation. Men play a more vicarious role in producing the next generation and do not feel so strong a connection. They may deal with the resulting feelings of death anxiety through the youth of a younger wife and/or having a second family. Or, they might try to seek immortality through their accomplishments, or by returning to the perceived immortality characterizing an adolescent lifestyle.

Healthy resolution of midlife death anxiety issues evolves from creating something of *personal* meaning and purpose, rather than pursuing something society might prescribe for creating personal worth. And as Erikson pointed out, accepting the role of mentor of the younger generation, rather than trying to rejoin it, can become an asset while seeking such meaning.

In a discussion of counseling and teaching, Buscaglia (1982) quotes Saint Exupery as saying "perhaps love is the process of my leading you gently back to yourself." Midlife is a time of self-teaching. We return to recognizing our uniqueness and inner beauty, having become sidetracked by the tasks and goals of young adulthood. Thus successful midlife transitioning is not just a period of generativity. It is also an enhancement of identity and intimacy, a return to and reworking of these previous life tasks, as well as a time of learning to nest within the comfort zone of "becoming."

Becoming a Senior Citizen

To the young, the term "senior citizen" can sound like a euphemism for hopelessly over the hill, ancient, and decrepit, perhaps not even able to handle more excitement than a rocking chair and pablum. This is an inaccurate stereotype. Thanks to modern health care, most people in their sixties and even older are still in pretty good shape. For some, late adulthood is a time of freedom and adventure, as they hop into their Winnebagos, drive off into the sunset, and enjoy a number of active yet carefree years.

However, our culture tends to characterize late adulthood more by its deficiencies (Prado, 1986). While describing an older person we might say something like "seventy years old and as spry as ever," in order to negate any immediate assumptions we expect the listener to make about the person's physical state. Like any other stage of life, late adulthood has disadvantages, but it has its advantages as well.

B. F. Skinner points out that sitting around and catastrophizing over the downside of old age does not lead to an enjoyable late adulthood. Instead, he suggests that old age be viewed as a problem to be solved, rather than something to be feared (Skinner & Vaughan, 1983). Furthermore, he suggests we younger folks will have more enjoyable and productive later years if we plan for old age, rather than wait around for it to overtake us.

CHANGES DURING LATE ADULTHOOD

The most obvious changes of late adulthood are the physical ones. Our skin spends many years fighting gravity, weather, and any other abuse we may selectively inflict upon it. By old age it becomes wrinkled and sagging. Our senses are not what they used to be, either. Eyesight, hearing, taste, smell, and even our sense of balance become less sensitive than they once were. Our hands may begin to shake, creating difficulty with fine motor tasks. Arthritis is common, as the lubrication in our joints starts to dry up. Our bones become more brittle and susceptible to breakage.

During old age we also experience changes in our ability to process memories. Most difficulties occur as a result of short-term memory impairment. We do more forgetting because information is more likely to fail transfer from short-term to long-term memory. We have more difficulty thinking clearly, since the short-term memory deficit interferes with simultaneously hanging on to all of the relevant details. We need more time to be able to make decisions and process information accurately (Salthouse, 1994).

In concert with the combination of slower physical and mental processing, our reaction times become slower. We may have difficulty joining in conversations, since the appropriate moment to make our comments may pass before we make them—or else we forget what we were about to say by the time the appropriate moment arrives!

Depression is a significant problem during old age. In fact, the elderly have the highest suicide rate of any age group (Stillion et al., 1989). This may be in part because depression is so underdiagnosed among the elderly. The social withdrawal, memory problems, and muddled thinking that correspond with depression are traits we come to expect in older people. Thus we just accept such symptoms as being a product of the sufferer's age rather than evidence of depression.

Older people also have a reputation for being "set in their ways." This assumption may be a misinterpretation of our observations of older adult behavior (Prado, 1986). Suppose you have two different routes you might take to get to town. You want to determine the fastest route. You drive each route 30 times, and find that route A gets you there an average of 5 minutes faster than route B. So you usually take route A. However, one day a highway construction project results in your deciding to take route B. On this occasion, you happen to get there 2 minutes faster than your average time on route A. On the basis of this information, do you change over to using route B regularly? Probably not. Unless there has been some sort of concrete change on route B that suggests it would now be faster most of the time, you still know from experience that, on the average, you will save more time by taking route A.

By the time we reach old age, we have traveled a number of routes A and B. Based on our experiences, we choose the routes we have found to be most likely to meet with success. So when some newfangled idea or way of doing something comes across our paths we meet it with skepticism, even if we see it work once or twice. We know what has worked before and is likely to hold up in the long run, and unless we see a consistent pattern of greater success with the new system, change may not be pragmatic.

Our greater life experience at old age may also make us seem "set in our ways" as a result of the huge amount of data we are processing. The human brain can make sense out of only so much information. Thus the more information we have to process, the more likely we are to use generalized shorthand statements to explain our conceptualizations.

Societal expectations also play a role in how the elderly are perceived. If a younger friend of yours should refuse to change over to a newer and seemingly better way of doing things, you might say he or she is stubborn or foolish or some other similar pejorative. Older people behaving the same way are more likely to be called "set in their ways," since that is a characteristic expected of them. Society may even *create* stereotypical behavior in senior citizens, as seniors mold themselves to societal expectations of their role. We forgive a lot of crotchetiness, forgetfulness, and stubbornness in the elderly because we have come to expect such behavior. Likewise, the elderly may engage in more of it because they believe it is expected of their assigned role.

During old age we become less productive, usually retiring from full-time employment, and become more reflective. Erikson (1963) refers to this phase of living as ego **integrity versus despair**. We find meaning and purpose by looking back on our lives and finding satisfaction in how we have contributed to the world through our social striving. Or, we become bitter as we refuse to accept our lost dreams, failings, and other pitfalls of living. In other words, we either enjoy a "life review" or hopelessly demand a "life re-do." The process of reminiscing itself encourages a sense of wholeness and completion (Sherman, 1991). Thus the elderly tend to become known as great storytellers, often repeating the same stories without appearing to recognize they have already told them. This is part of their life review process, and the gracious listener is willing to sit through the reruns.

Adjusting to Old Age

Skinner and Vaughan (1983) point out that a life review is all well and good, but what are you going to do with the rest of your time during old age? We put a lot of energy and resources into preparing for the physical aspects of being old, making sure we have money and the other concrete necessities for retirement and taking care of our health. However, we are not so likely to plan for *enjoyment* of our golden years.

Under what conditions will you enjoy your senior citizenship? As with any other life pursuit, you will want to maximize the pleasant aspects and find ways to minimize or overcome the disadvantages and obstacles. Many of the following suggestions will seem like obvious common sense. But as Skinner and Vaughan point out, it is amazing how many people do not take advantage of them.

Dealing with physical limitations. By middle adulthood many people have already begun losing some of their eyesight. Glasses are the obvious solution. Those who have been visually impaired from birth have learned to use a number of other strategies to help them find things. For example, you can get rid of a lot of the junk laying around that might camouflage what you are really looking for. Having specific places to keep specific items (especially your glasses!) also increases the likelihood that you will find what you are looking for. You can get telephones and some other equipment with large print on the buttons, so they are easier to operate. Even something as simple as getting heavy-based drinking glasses that are harder to knock over can help make life more hassle-free.

Most cases of hearing loss can be helped with hearing aids. Many of the newer models are small and inconspicuous, some even designed as a part of your glasses. You can also get amplifiers for your phone, television, stereo, or just about anything else you would like to be a little louder. However, if you are living with people who are not hearing impaired, you might also want to get a headset. Accessorizing your doorbell and telephone with a flashing red light can also help you resolve the problem of missed communications.

You can avoid some frustration by accepting some of the limitations of your hearing and working around them. If you cannot hear a conversation or broadcast no matter what you do, stop listening. You do yourself no favors by fighting a lost cause. You might also learn to spend more of your conversational time talking, so that you need to spend less time straining to hear. If what you say does not fit in very well or you begin to sound like you are rambling, you can always plead old age.

Less sensitive taste buds are easily remedied by the addition of a little extra seasoning to your food. If you prepare food for others, remember to add the extra seasonings to your portion only, rather than the whole batch. You might also want to make sure you always have a glass of water handy as you eat, since your saliva glands may not work as well as they used to.

A lowered capacity for smell can at times be a blessing. However, there are other times when the sense of smell is a crucial commodity, such as when smoke is in the environment. Make sure you have a functioning smoke alarm. Establishing a routine for taking care of health and hygiene practices can also help if you are not able to smell that you need a shower or clean clothes, or that the garbage needs to be taken out.

The problem of losing balance can be minimized by your moving more slowly. This not only gives your vestibular system more time to catch up with you, but also gives your eyes a chance to fix onto visual balance cues. You might also consider carrying a cane or walking stick to help you catch your balance, even if you do not have difficulties with lameness.

Create an enjoyable environment. Get rid of the minor annoyances that can ruin your day. If you have a bad mattress, it will be even more uncomfortable as you get older because your skin thins as you age. Replace that mattress, as well as any chairs that have become uncomfortable and lighting that is either inadequate or glaring. Fix sticking doors and drawers, and place items that you use frequently within easy reach.

If you plan to change residences when you enter old age, consider choosing a home that consists of a one-story building. Numerous conditions of old age can impair your ability to negotiate stairs. Or, if you can, restructure your own multiple-story home so it is possible to live on a single floor.

Do what you can to make your environment hazard-free. Take care of loose carpets; recover slippery ceramic tile floors; get electrical cords off the floor; and install railing fixtures on your bed, bathtub, and stairways. Install switchplates that visibly stand out from the rest of the wall, so you do not need to struggle to find a light switch. Having good solid locks on your doors and windows will help you feel more secure from break-ins. You may even consider getting a burglar alarm, either mechanical or canine.

Handling forgetfulness and confusion. I recently heard a joke about an older person who disagreed with new research suggesting that older people do not think much about the hereafter. He claimed that every time he walked into a room he wondered what he was here after.

We all experience forgetfulness. Old age is a great time to capitalize on the strategies we have developed for dealing with it. Use a calendar to keep track of appointments, and make a habit of looking at it every morning. Be sure to write down any time commitment the moment you make the appointment. If there is a pastime you might like to pursue on a certain day, write that down as well. You can also make sure you do not forget to do something by taking care of it the moment you think of it, writing it down on a note pad, or leaving sticky-yellows around as cues to remind you. Some routine tasks, like remembering to take medicine, can be paired with other activities you know you will always do—try leaving a pill container on top of your pillow.

Having specific storage places for specific items helps with the problem of remembering where you left something. If you are in a habit of hiding things, make sure you draw yourself maps of where you hid them. You can help yourself remember to turn appliances on or off by becoming accustomed to setting up brightly colored signs saying "on" or "off" in the work vicinity.

Forgetting is the biggest nuisance during conversation. You forget people's names. You forget what you were going to say. You wander off on a tangent and forget where you were originally headed. You become confused as you forget pieces of information that were a part of your reasoning.

Conversation becomes easier if you use shorter sentences. That way you do not lose the first part of the sentence before you get to the end. You can practice mental rehearsal or make notes to yourself as you listen to others so you do not forget any comments you wanted to add. Or, go ahead and apologetically interrupt so you can make your comment. You're old. People will forgive it.

The confusion resulting from short-term memory loss can be aided by organizing complex thoughts on paper. Allow yourself more time to think things through. As a retired person, you probably have a lot more time on your hands anyway. Why rush? You might also want to save important thinking and decision making for when you are well rested. Lowering your standard for reading material and other intellectually oriented pastimes can also help such activities remain enjoyable rather than become frustrating.

Having a life. The stereotype of the retirement years is of having a "time of rest." However, all our lives we have practiced taking time out for the purpose of vacations and then eventually returned to work. Many people enjoy a long period of relaxation after retirement but then start getting restless, looking around for something to do. Retirement can leave a lot of extra time on your hands. And even if you were not particularly fond of your job, retiring from it will result in many losses: built-in social contacts, a regular and habitual schedule, the status of your profession, and the sense of purpose and contributing that comes with working.

There are plenty of things for retired people to do. In fact, many retired people stay just as busy as when they were working. The difference is that they can do what they *want* to do, rather than what they *have* to do. Do not take on any task just for the sake of keeping busy. Find something you really like to do. Consider volunteerism in your community, such as tutoring at the local grade school; or even contributing to the world at large, as is possible with organizations such as the Red Cross. Old age is a great time to find ways of sublimating parts of yourself that had no outlets during earlier years. You can even become an old-age activist: Join the Gray Panthers; become involved with the American Association of Retired Persons; or lobby for politicians who advocate for the needs of the elderly.

Of course, you can always choose more low-key retirement activities, such as more deeply pursuing an activity you have always enjoyed. Then again, you might decide to learn something new. Perhaps you are a senior citizen reading this textbook as a requirement for a class you had always wanted to take. You are never too old to learn; you just might have to go about it a little more slowly than you used to.

Most important, don't let the standards of society tell you how active you can be, including how much you can do for yourself. Don't depend on others for routine needs any more than is necessary. Self-care is one way of filling hours that may otherwise be empty. Also, the more you depend on others, the less you do for yourself. "Use it or lose it" is not based on an old wives' tale. Any bodily function that remains active is likely to hold up longer; whatever lies stagnant will more quickly wither away.

Keep a good sense of humor. As described in Chapter 5, humor is one of the most sophisticated coping mechanisms we can use. If you have not yet learned to laugh at yourself, you may have a difficult time with aging. The changes of later adulthood result in a number of circumstances where the expected norm is bashed about by the limitations of age. If while conversing with a friend in a dimly lit restaurant you suddenly discover she left for the salad bar some time ago, do not allow your gaffe to humiliate you. Enjoy the humor.

Returning to Dependency

Most senior citizens are able to live independently until the end of their days. However, everybody's body eventually wears out. Unless you die before you reach this stage, your physical condition will eventually change to the point where you need to depend on others for some of your basic needs. This is often referred to as the "frail elderly" stage. Perhaps your vision no longer allows you to drive, and you need to count on others for transportation. Maybe your hands develop such a tremor that you can no longer write legibly, and others need to write your checks and correspondence. If you suffer some of the illnesses and injuries of old age, you may even depend on others for being fed and going to the bathroom.

Potential horrors of the frail elderly stage abound. You cannot do anything physical—not even take a walk—without worrying about falling, breaking a bone, and ending up in a nursing home. As your physical capacities decline, you may not be able to pursue the pastimes you previously enjoyed during retirement. Thus you may end up with even more time with nothing to do. Constantly trying to think up something to do can be exhausting. Your dependency on others can result in your spending a lot of time waiting around. None of us likes to wait. Not only is it frustrating, but it emphasizes the lack of control and inferior status we hold as we wait upon someone else.

Emotionally, you experience a number of contradictions. Desiring help for needs you previously took care of yourself feels like a loss of selfhood; so you may deny needing help even when doing without results in life no longer being meaningful or enjoyable. You may appreciate the help that others give but resent them because of your dependency on them. You may worry about losing the help of others or whether it is really worth others' time to keep you going.

Some question whether anything happens during the frail elderly stage of life that could make living worthwhile. Wendy Lustbader (1991) disagrees with such a pessimistic outlook. Successfully living through a phase of inability to "do" occurs if we have learned the lesson that life is being, not doing. Rabbi Kushner eloquently describes this lesson:

> When we stop searching for the Great Answer, the Immortal Deed which will give our lives ongoing meaning, and instead concentrate on filling our individual days with moments that gratify us, then we will find the only possible answer to the question, "What is life about?"... It is about loving and being loved. It is about enjoying your food and sitting in the sun rather than rushing through lunch and hurrying back to the office. It is about savoring the beauty of moments that don't last, the sunsets, the leaves turning color, the rare moments of true human communication.... There is no Answer, but there are answers: love and the joy of working, the simple pleasures of food and fresh clothes, the little things that get lost and trampled in the search for the Grand Solution to the Problem of Life and emerge... only when we have stopped searching. (Kushner, 1986, pp. 142–143)

You do not have to "do" to be of value, or to appreciate living. As Rabbi Kushner instructs, true living occurs when we learn to fully experience and enjoy the existential nuances: fresh clothes, the change of seasons, a joke with a close friend, or the sound of a child's laughter.

If you have already developed a number of interests or a routine for living during late adulthood, the frail elderly stage will be much less boring. Cease yearning and striving for those things that are clearly no longer possible; it is painful and pointless. If you were too active to pursue life review activities during late adulthood, now you have plenty of time for it. Tell your stories to others. It helps you make sense out of your life, as well as pass on learning and history to the next generation. If you can, write your stories down or tape them for others. You may also want to start investigating your genealogy and the life stories of your ancestors, helping yourself realize your part in the continuum of humankind.

Remember that everybody has the need to strive in ways that satisfy their social interest. You are doing others a favor when you let them take care of the needs you can no longer meet for yourself. Remember also that your dependence on others does not signify the end of your selfhood. They know your needs and wants because you assert yourself by telling them, and compliance with the instructions of caregivers is also a choice. Most important, keep in mind that independence is at best a self-created illusion. As described in Chapter 10, we are all interdependent. Why grieve for a condition that never really existed?

Dying

As the saying goes, the one certainty of life is death. As a general rule, we go through our lives not knowing when death will come. However, many of us end our lives with foreknowledge of impending death because we have been told we have fatal conditions. When faced with such knowledge, we appear to go through three phases (Pattison, 1977):

1. *The acute phase.* We feel overwhelmed by the significance of the knowledge. We experience shock, strong anxiety, and other powerful feelings.
2. *Living-dying cycles.* After recovering from our initial reaction, we begin to sort out the implications of our impending death. We deal with failing bodily functions, fear of the unknown beyond death, feeling isolated, and the impending loss of our previous way of being. Resolution may involve making final contributions to the world of the living in ways that are much more meaningful to the dying person than they were before.
3. *The terminal phase.* We accept the inevitable and emotionally withdraw from the world of the living.

Dying a Good Death

What is a "good death"? How do we die with dignity and a sense of life resolution? There appear to be several factors that contribute to a good death (Weisman, 1985):

- The support and care of loved ones are present.
- The terminally ill person has been kept aware of the progress of his

or her condition and has participated in the planning of his or her care as much as is possible.
- Physical and emotional pain are managed.
- The person has ample opportunity to communicate with others.
- The person feels his or her continuity with the past, present, and future, in spite of his or her passing, and no longer dwells on those things that cannot be changed.
- A sense of closure occurs as the person has made peace with those things that can yet be impacted and those that cannot, and the person falls within an existential niche that he or she has personally designed.

Hospice

In centuries past, people died at home. As medical practices began to offer more and more ways to keep people alive longer, they were more likely to die in hospitals. Dying in a hospital eventually became a tradition in our culture. Over time, however, we have recognized the limitations of hospital deaths. Being shut away in a controlled, sterile environment and being given minimal, impersonal care by strangers is not particularly conducive to dying a good death.

The **hospice movement** came about as a reaction to these limitations. Hospice environments allow a terminally ill person to die with dignity (Kubler-Ross & Magno, 1983). Hospices are set up more like home environments than hospital rooms. The patient is given as much control over his or her final days as is possible. Visiting hours are unlimited and, when possible, loved ones are given the opportunity to provide care for the patient. Efforts are made to minimize the dying person's physical and emotional pain.

A hospice environment can be pursued in a number of ways. In addition to freestanding hospice facilities, many hospitals now offer hospice environments in addition to more traditional hospital settings. A person can even arrange to die at home by arranging a hospice environment through the use of visiting nurses.

Euthanasia

Modern medicine has indeed increased our potential for having a long life. Unfortunately, it has also created a situation where our bodies can be kept alive even though quality of life, or even consciousness itself, is dramatically impaired or absent. Many question the ethics of dumping so much of our finite (not to mention expensive) health care resources into last-ditch efforts toward gaining a few more days of mindless bodily functioning. The alternative, however, is **euthanasia**, or "mercy killing": purposely "pulling the plug" on a person who is terminally suffering and not expected to recover. The ethics of allowing someone to die when you have the ability to keep their bodies going creates additional debate.

We like to think of ourselves as the first culture that has had to deal with these issues. Actually, we are not (Glassock, 1990). Elder killing and death hastening through neglect are both commonplace and accepted in many nonindustrialized nations. Three situational characteristics seem common to all these cultures: (1) the senior has significantly declined in mental or physical well-being, (2) the person has become burdensome to himself or herself, to others, and to the community, and (3) the decision to do something so drastic and final is very difficult and involves family members and usually the terminally ill person as well. Like Western culture, these less sophisticated cultures have recognized that quality of living is essential to continued existence, as well as acknowledged the drain that the terminally declining population can put on a community. The only difference between us and them is that we have not yet reached a consensus on what to do about it.

The Living Will

Many people attempt to avoid putting their loved ones through the agony of such a decision by making their wishes known ahead of time. The **living will** is a legal document that leaves instructions in the event of a terminal illness or injury where the person is no longer in any shape to address such a decision. It expresses the person's desire not to have his or her body's life extended by artificial means when there is no hope of revival.

While living wills have become increasingly more popular in recent years, they are not always enforced. The ill person still depends heavily upon loved ones to make certain the attending physician knows of and remembers his or her wishes. And even when hospital personnel are informed, they may not comply because of their perceived diagnostic and ethical considerations. Until the legalities and medical ethics of these decisions are officially sorted out, the terminally ill, their loved ones, and hospital staff will most likely continue to struggle and play it by ear.

Mourning and Bereavement

After losing a loved one, we proceed through a period of grieving. In recent decades, our culture has tried to ignore the emotional impact of loss. We convinced ourselves we could control such reactions with a "stiff upper lip" and other efforts of the will. Extended periods of mourning were viewed as a form of weakness, and well-meaning friends and relatives encouraged the bereaved to "snap out of it." Some dying individuals even request that there be no memorial services for them, thinking that they are doing the living a favor by not encouraging them to mourn. In reality, funerals are meant for the living, as they assist the bereaved in going through the grief process.

Kubler-Ross (1969) was one of the first to bring us back to the realization that grief is a natural and necessary process. She perceived it as occurring in five stages:

1. *Denial.* The reality of the loss has not yet set in. We may refuse to believe it, perhaps even making plans as if the loss had not occurred.
2. *Anger.* Having realized the loss, we resent it. We look for someone to blame, perhaps even being angry at the lost loved one for having left.
3. *Bargaining.* We "make deals" with God or other perceived powers in an attempt to negate the loss. For example, a mother might pray that God take her instead of her already-deceased child.
4. *Depression.* We realize the finality of the loss, experiencing hopelessness and emptiness.
5. *Acceptance.* We accept the loss and develop a sense of inner peace. We might continue to have a lingering feeling of sadness as we remember the loss, but we are no longer overpowered by it.

While other researchers agree that such phases are common to the grieving process, we now recognize that everyone grieves in his or her own way (Shneidman, 1984). We might actually grieve in the order suggested by Kubler-Ross, or we might experience the same emotions but in a different order. A common experience of mourning is to be rereminded of the lost loved one by various life circumstances, such as anniversaries, and to reexperience the grieving process from yet another perspective. Thus the more life connections we had with the loved one, the longer the grieving process will take.

Grieving is not only normal, but necessary. We are designed at birth to attach to others. Furthermore, it is not realistic to expect to experience a significant loss and not react to the many different impacts it can have on our lives. Buried feelings eventually have their "out," whether they express themselves through unexplained depression, physical symptoms, aggressiveness, or anxiety. Grief is to be worked through, not ignored. Come to an understanding of your losses and their significance to your own life, and allow your feelings the freedom to express themselves.

Expanding Your Experience

Middle age has even allowed me to forgive B. F. Skinner.

My undergraduate training in psychology was heavily influenced by behaviorism. My master's degree program, however, was hard-core psychodynamic in flavor. By hard-core, I mean that anything even hinting of the other perspectives of psychology was systematically picked apart. Meanwhile, Skinner continued to expound that virtually every aspect of human functioning could be explained by the principles of behaviorism.

I became impatient with the lot of them. One of my pet projects during undergraduate training had been research concerning how people used logic. The whole psychodynamic-behavioral conflict seemed to me like one big illicit conversion. Each side was taking evidence of some human functioning that had been empirically demonstrated to support their thesis, and then erroneously expanded that to mean that all human functioning is a result of their thesis. So as I proceeded through my doctoral training, I made a point of internalizing and developing my own personalized perspective—which is eclectic, as you have probably guessed by now.

However, as my career proceeded, I continued to carry along baggage of resentment from my early exposure to academic intolerance. As I taught introductory psychology, I would pass around a copy of the *APA Monitor* showing a picture of Skinner as he was delivering a speech 2 weeks before he died. I would point out that up until his dying days, he clung to a black-and-white interpretation of his thesis.

In recent years, however, I have come to appreciate the mental shorthand represented by theoretical extremism. While it may not take into account all of the relevant variables, it does allow the researcher to become more focused on what he or she is attempting to explore. Witness the proliferation of old-age behavioral strategies I have included from the writings of Skinner! Chances are, if he were not so behaviorally focused, he would have been distracted by components of other philosophies.

Maybe during late adulthood, I will also be able to forgive Sigmund Freud.

The first activity is a competition of sorts between small groups, for the purpose of helping you understand the physical experience of being elderly. The second exercise is more concrete. It is a life expectancy scale, as well as an exercise in hypothesizing causation. The third exercise will help you assess your own current level of existential contentedness.

Study Questions

1. Describe Erikson's conceptualization of midlife.
2. What are the three phases of Levinson's middle-adulthood cycles?

3. Should we all expect to have a midlife crisis? Explain your answer.
4. What freedoms occur during midlife?
5. How would Fox suggest you go about dealing with transition through midlife?
6. Describe issues that are more likely to confront women at midlife.
7. Describe issues that are more likely to confront men at midlife.
8. Describe the physical and mental changes of old age.
9. Are older people really set in their ways? Why do we perceive them as being so?
10. Describe Erikson's conceptualization of old age.
11. What does Skinner mean by "planning to enjoy old age"? Think of an older person you know. How might the person help himself or herself in this respect?
12. What is it like to become dependent again during the frail elderly stage?
13. How can you experience the frail elderly stage as meaningful?
14. How does Pattison describe the process of acknowledging impending death?
15. What factors appear to contribute to "dying a good death"?
16. Define the hospice movement, euthanasia, and the living will.
17. Is grieving a sign of weakness, or a necessary process? Explain your answer.
18. List Kubler-Ross's five stages of grieving. Do we all grieve this way? Explain your answer.

Chapter Fifteen

Perspectives and Objectives

Where do I take it from here?

If you don't know where you're going, you will wind up somewhere else.
—Yogi Berra

When you make plans for living, you inevitably take into account a number of challenges. Some challenges can be planned for ahead of time; others must be met head-on as they present themselves. This book has described numerous challenges that are likely to occur in the course of your life span. Knowing what you do now, have you given some thought to how you will meet them? With success? With failure? With determination? With confusion? With a sense of purpose? Or with a sense of meaninglessness?

Human beings in general tend to aspire toward meaningful, manageable goals (Brim 1992), a characteristic that can be an asset when it comes to meeting our life challenges. Often, even after we have mastered an activity, we add our own little twists to performing the task in order to keep it interesting. Assembly line workers relieve the boredom of routine, repetitive tasks by trying to surpass their previous output. A video game enthusiast can continue to enjoy a game he or she has conquered by attempting to win in spite of new self-imposed restrictions, or by redefining what winning consists of.

We generate our own conditions for wins and losses depending on what we have to work with. An infant makes a challenge out of trying to coordinate movements to make a toy rattle or jingle. A billionaire may become challenged by looking for new and creative ways to see how much more money he or she can scrape into a pile. An elderly person might create a challenge out of getting to the mailbox and back.

Even the time period in which we came of age plays a role in how we generate challenges. Back in the 1950s and 1960s, when the expected norm for women was maintaining a house and home, one way housewives kept their lives interesting and challenging was by constantly refining their household skills. Newspaper columns such as "Hints from Heloise" and those that addressed etiquette abounded during that era, as housewives enthusiastically gobbled up new goals that helped them feel challenged.

Some people have moral misgivings about ambitious striving. Often they equate it with selfishness or competitiveness. Brim (1992) points out this is not an accurate perception. Challenges can be either cooperative or competitive: Compare the goals for winning in "King of the Mountain" with seeing how many fraternity brothers can fit into a Volkswagen bug. Likewise, ambitious striving need not be selfish. Chapter 1 described Adler's social striving, the need to contribute toward and feel connected with our social groups. Ambition need not be "against" someone else, either. Ambitious goals strive to overcome the challenge, rather than overcome someone else. What we actually seek as we set our goals may involve morals or values, as will be discussed later in this chapter. However, the striving of the drive itself is not a moral issue.

Some of you may see goal-seeking and the pursuit of personal growth work as activities to take up once you are through some current crisis. Perhaps you are waiting until after you have found solutions to certain problems in living. Or maybe you feel like you will be satisfied if you can just "survive" and feel secure from immediate harm. After all, most college educations are not structured around helping a person find a high-quality life. They attempt to help us become intellectually skilled, prepare for a vocation, and in the process find a secure and productive niche in society. But there is more to living than surviving. In reality, some of the most rewarding goal-setting and seeking behaviors are those that occur regardless of current limitations.

Brodie (1993) put it this way: "It is difficult to have real change, improvement or growth in your life while you are resisting or fighting the reality of who you are and how your life stands right now." You will always face problems in living. Those aspects of the world that fall short of perfection will always be apparent. You will probably always be aware of your own shortcomings, as well. However, you can still pursue the esoteric, the simple and pleasurable, and that which you find challenging no matter what dissatisfactions you may have in your current state of being. *You* have the ultimate choice of which goals you will seek, and they need not be limited to just surviving.

Thus we all set challenges or goals for ourselves based on who we are, what we value, what we know, and the internal and external resources available. As you have explored various personal growth issues this term, you have probably run across a number of personal goals that you would like to implement. The rest of this chapter provides guidelines for choosing and pursuing goal-directed behavior you can apply now or at any other point in living.

Accomplishing Your Goals

You are more likely to get what you want out of living if you set your goals actively rather than wait for them to passively set themselves. Porter and Lawler (1967) describe three determinants for whether or not you might set and follow through on your goals:

1. *How intense is your motivation?* How badly do you want to achieve your goal? You must have a sufficient level of desire to succeed before you are likely to accomplish anything. Otherwise, you will find yourself making a half-baked effort, or not even trying at all. You also need to expect that your efforts will in fact result in the desired outcome. If you want to do a better job of handling your anger but believe that stress inoculation training is just a bunch of hocus-pocus, the training loses its potency for helping you toward your goal.

2. *Are your personal traits and abilities consistent with your goals?* Goals can be set too high or too low, based on our individual differences. If you want to be a rocket scientist but could never get better than a "C" in physics, you are not likely to succeed. On the other hand, if you have superior intellectual skills and aim no higher than routine office work, you will probably become so bored your goals will not hold your interest long enough to be achieved.

Your personal traits may also be inconsistent with a goal choice. If you have an introverted personality, you are likely to experience considerable discomfort if your goals include a career in politics. If your temperament falls more into the extroverted domain, your goal of having a farming lifestyle will probably fall flat long before you get there.

Personal skills must also be consistent with goals. If you like to write and can do it well, a goal of writing letters to family members every week has a high chance of succeeding. However, if you are a person who has always been "all thumbs" and make a goal of being able to type 85 words a minute, you are destined for frustration.

Sometimes education and training act as a step toward developing the competencies necessary to meet a goal. For example, you can take natural childbirth classes before you actually go into labor; or you can have the gym attendant show you how to use the appropriate equipment before attempting a body-building program. In this manner you become more likely to meet your goals, as you maximize your personal chances of success while goal-setting.

3. *How clear or accurate is your goal?* Do you have an accurate perception of what your goal is all about? Suppose you want to improve your ability to communicate within close personal relationships. What qualifies a relationship as being "close" or "intimate"? And what do you think communication within intimate relationships is supposed to be like? Are these expectations accurate? Also, what specific behaviors would you expect to see in such a relationship, and which ones do you see yourself performing deficiently?

One theorist described striving toward goals as **targeting** (Tec, 1980), defining targeting as an "ability to direct behavior to recognized, predetermined objectives." In other words, in addition to deciding what you are aiming toward, you need to organize yourself around taking appropriate steps. For example, suppose during a game of golf you find yourself in the position of needing to chip in 70 feet to reach the putting green. Successful golfers have learned they use fewer strokes if they first aim for the general vicinity of the hole and then finish it off with a short putt, rather than aiming for the hole itself. The goal, of course, is to actually get the ball into the hole; but by breaking down the goal into steps that are more likely to be attained, golfers increase their chances of succeeding.

Many goals are better dealt with through targeting because you do not really expect to meet them. As a writer, you may aim toward a goal of never making a spelling error. You might move closer toward this goal by improving your spelling ability, developing your proofreading skills, and learning to use a spell-check program. However, even if your spelling errors do decrease and you are satisfied with this improvement, you are still going to make occasional spelling errors. So even though you are pursuing something very concrete and specific, you are really hoping for a less than perfect outcome.

Career strivings also tend to fit in with the constructs of targeting. You may dream of being the head of pediatric nursing in a major teaching hospital; however, you might still be satisfied with your career even if you get no further than practicing pediatric nursing in a small community hospital. You might also dream of an ideal mate. But you will no doubt find happiness with someone who meets just a number of your preferred criteria, rather than waiting around for some perfect person who probably doesn't even exist.

So how can you use a targeting approach to pursue your goals? Let's break it down into steps.

Defining and Analyzing Your Goals

What do you hope to accomplish, either in the immediate future or at some point in your lifetime? Following is a list one person might brainstorm as potential goals:

- Learning to hang glide
- Being a good parent
- Using more eye contact
- Becoming a better listener
- Visiting Australia
- Getting along better with Cousin Albert
- Stop being late for work
- Being a good citizen and productive member of society
- Having a happy marriage

Some of these goals are fairly clear-cut. We know what hang gliding is, where we have to go to visit Australia, what time we have to arrive at work in order to be punctual, and that eye contact consists of looking someone in the eyes. Other goals are less clear. What is a better listener, good citizen, or productive member of society? How do we judge whether we are good parents, have happy marriages, or get along better with Cousin Albert? These murkier goals are abstractions. Abstractions by themselves cannot be met as goals because there is no way to tell if you have met them. So before you can proceed with them, you need to make them more concrete. How will you know that such an abstract goal has been met? Here are some questions you might ask yourself as you analyze abstract goals (Mager, 1984):

1. *What do I need to see happen in order to know that my goal has been achieved?* What would you observe in someone else that would lead you to conclude that the person had met the desired goal? For example, you might say a person is a good citizen if you see that he or she does volunteer work, helps a lost child, pays taxes on time, disposes of litter appropriately, or any number of other "good citizen"-type behaviors.

2. *If I had to separate a room full of people into two groups—those who have met the goal and those who have not—what would I consider?* If you were at a party and were trying to decide who were the good listeners and who were not, what would you look for? The good listeners might be using body language that suggests interest, such as facing the speaker directly, leaning slightly forward, nodding occasionally, and using a lot of eye contact. They might also occasionally probe for more information, and ask questions indicating that they must have been listening.

3. *What would someone who had achieved this goal be doing or look like?* What does your idea of a good parent look like? Would they be talking with their children instead of yelling at them? Spending time with them? Coaching their Little League teams? Helping them with their homework? Providing consistent and fair discipline?

4. *What would someone who had achieved this goal not be doing or look like?* You might figure out what you want on the basis of what you do *not* want to see happen. A happy marriage might be one that doesn't include a lot of arguments, conflicting goals, mutual dissatisfaction, broken china, or eventual divorce.

5. *Who do I know who I believe has met this goal?* Once you think of such a person, you can analyze just what it is that the person does that led you to make such a judgment. Perhaps Uncle Joe is good at getting along with Cousin Albert. As you observe him, you notice that he doesn't try to cheer Cousin Albert out of his constant complaining but instead just

smiles and sympathetically nods until the conversation ends. When Cousin Albert says something insulting to Uncle Joe, rather than reacting defensively Uncle Joe paraphrases Cousin Albert's criticisms and expresses understanding of his concern. You also notice that Uncle Joe avoids bringing up certain topics whenever Cousin Albert is around.

Once you have a solid definition and description of your goal, you can begin breaking it down into the specific behaviors you would like to see changed. Suppose you choose to work on the goal of getting to work on time. What seems to be contributing to your late arrivals? As you think back on the times you have been late, you notice several recurring themes:

- Your alarm didn't go off.
- Traffic was heavy.
- Your car pool didn't show up on time.
- You were hung-over.
- You were playing video games and lost track of the time.

Your specific goal-directed behaviors will be based on addressing these themes:

- Develop a strategy to make sure the alarm gets set.
- Leave earlier in order to allow for heavy traffic.
- Confront your car pool members, or find a different car pool.
- Don't drink the night before you go to work.
- Don't play video games before leaving for work, or set a timer to go off when you need to leave.

Your goal-seeking behavior is analyzed and ready to apply once you have made it completely concrete and formed a specific plan of action: the what, when, how, and under what circumstances. It is helpful to write these out as a specific statement. For example, for a goal of increasing eye contact you might write "I will look my advisor in the eye (what) when she is speaking (under what circumstances) for at least ten seconds (how) when I go see her tomorrow (when)." When a goal is this concrete, there can be no doubt as to whether or not you have reached your goal.

Many goals require multiple steps. Visiting Australia is a goal that usually takes a lot of planning. Do you have the time off? Is your passport up to date? Do you have enough money? Do you need any shots? What do you pack? Who will pick up your mail and newspapers? Can you get a flight at the time you desire to leave? What about hotel reservations?

When many steps are involved, they are best arranged in their most optimal sequence. In other words, they follow some logical order. Consider arranging the steps toward visiting Australia temporally:

1. Saving up enough money: "I will put $25 into savings each week until I have saved up enough for the trip."
2. Getting time off: "I will see my supervisor tomorrow at 9:00 A.M. and ask her if I can use my vacation time the last two weeks of next June."
3. Making travel arrangements: "I will call my travel agent during my lunch hour and have him make flight and hotel reservations. I will also ask about passport and inoculation needs."
4. What to pack: "Two weeks before the trip I will call my travel agent and ask what the weather is like and whether there is anything unusual I might need."
5. Who picks up the mail and newspaper: "Two days before the trip I will call Aunt Sarah and remind her that she agreed to pick up the mail and papers while I am away."

Prioritizing Your Goals

As you design your goal-seeking behaviors, values play an important role. For example, suppose you value both honesty and material wealth and are considering cheating on your income tax return. The concrete behaviors you choose and negative consequences that may occur as a result will differ according to which value is more important to you. If you value honesty more, you will probably not cheat on your income taxes and make do with less money. If you value money more, you might go ahead and cheat but live with the inevitable guilt feelings.

Values play a role in just about all personal growth goals. Whether or not you take steps to increase your ability to be assertive will depend on where you see your rights to assertion ending and others' rights beginning, which is a value judgment. How you go about more carefully managing your sexual behavior and relationships will differ depending upon how you interpret the moral responsibilities regarding the consequences of sexual behavior. Whether or not you choose to work on your relationship with your spouse or significant other is going to depend on how you view and value commitment. Even the type of job you choose to train for will depend on which career characteristics you value more: being able to control your own schedule? the security of routine? having a dependable income? or having a social life in conjunction with the work environment?

Thus how we arrange our goals will be strongly affected by what we value. Actually, most of us have a number of high values. If you completed the value scale in Chapter 1, you may have noticed a sort of halo effect: either you value many things highly, many things moderately, or have little dedication to values in general. However, placing an equal personal value on a number of goals creates difficulty when you try to sort out which one will take priority in any given circumstance.

Many value conflicts are more well known than others in today's society: the conflict between dedication to excellence in your career versus spending time at home with your family, having a comfortable home and a number of belongings versus practicing altruistic giving, developing a sense of status versus maintaining humility, and so on.

Value conflicts eventually translate into behavioral conflicts. Suppose you become both a parent and a psychotherapist. Just as you are getting ready to head out to Janie's piano recital, you get a frantic call from your answering service, informing you that one of your patients is threatening suicide. Which event takes priority?

Defining and evaluating your values and priorities ahead of time can help you avoid collisions. In this manner you can assess their potential for conflict as you set them. You begin by making a list for yourself, and rank order them according to which one is most important, second most important, and so on. Let's use Alice's priorities as an example. She generates the following priorities and rank orders them in the following manner:

1. Owning a successful catering business
2. Having a happy marriage
3. Traveling to many strange and exotic places
4. Entertaining friends
5 Becoming an accomplished accordion player

Next, she creates a grid that will allow her to assess the effect each priority-driven goal might have on the other. Table 15.1 shows how this grid would appear. Now she is ready to start looking for conflict. Column by column, she explores how the goals across the top of the column are likely to impact the goals listed below them. Do they have a positive impact? A negative impact? Or no impact at all?

For example, let's look at goal 1. What impact will having a successful catering business have on having a happy marriage? It could work either way. If Alice becomes so busy that she does not spend much time with her husband, it could have a negative effect. If she is burnt out on

Table 15.1
Alice's Goal-Setting Gridwork

	Goal 1 Owning a successful catering business	Goal 2 Having a happy marriage	Goal 3 Traveling to exotic places	Goal 4 Entertaining friends	Goal 5 Playing the accordian
Goal 1 Owning a successful catering business	X	Positive effect: husband's support helpful	Negative effect: time away slows business growth	Positive effect: opportunity for practice	No effect
Goal 2 Having a happy marriage	Negative effect: time and energy conflict	X	Positive effect: creates time away together	Positive effect: husband likes to entertain	Negative effect: husband hates the accordian
Goal 3 Traveling to exotic places	Positive effect: provides traveling money	Positive effect: automatic traveling partner	X	No effect	No effect
Goal 4 Entertaining friends	Positive effect: can do it in style	Positive effect: comfortable with sharing home	Positive effect: something to talk about	X	Positive effect: friends like the accordian
Goal 5 Playing the accordian	Negative effect: time constraint	No effect	No effect	No effect	X

food preparation she is probably also going to feel less than enthusiastic about doing her share of the cooking at home, which could also become a source of conflict. However, if the catering business provides a healthy income, she can hire others to do the grunt work. Having a lot of money also helps address one of the main problems over which married couples tend to get into arguments.

Next, what impact will the catering business have on her ability to travel? It will depend a lot on how she sets up her business. If her clientele require her to provide food on a regular basis, she is not going to be able to get away unless she has adequate staff to cover her end of the responsibilities. On the other hand, travel takes money. If her business provides a good income, it will pay for her travels.

As you can see, priority conflicts often occur as a result of life commodities that are finite. In other words, we only have so much time, so much money, so much energy, and so many personal resources to divide among our chosen priorities.

Another important aspect of priority organization is recognizing that each prioritized goal is actually a collection of smaller goals and behaviors. For example, becoming an accordion player involves signing up for lessons, getting access to an accordion, buying sheet music, and making time to practice. Being able to entertain friends means choosing whom to have over, inviting them, making various preparations, and implementing the event. As you may recall, Alice places a higher value on being able to entertain friends than she does on becoming an accordion player. However, that does not mean that all of the second-level priorities for entertaining friends take precedence over all of the second-level priorities for becoming an accordion player. If the only way she can sign up for lessons at her desired institute is to show up at a certain time on a certain day, that is going to take priority over calling around to find someone to invite for dinner the following Friday evening. The guest search can always be done before or after lesson sign-up.

While this may seem obvious, we often neglect to stop and think this way when we are in the heat of doing. Clearly it is more important for a psychotherapist to take steps to manage a suicidal patient than it is to show up for one piano recital. However, if the therapist values parenting more highly than his or her career demands, the choice can be agonizing.

Overcoming Obstacles

At some point in your goal-seeking you may be going along, following your steps, generally minding your own business when suddenly something gets in your way. You find yourself getting derailed or going off on some track that is completely different from what you had intended. You only discover your lost focus after it is too late.

Here is an example. You approach your car pool members, intending to confront them about their tardiness:

You You know, we've been late to work on three out of the last four mornings. I wonder if we could find a way to....

Member 1 Well I hope you're not blaming me.

You I'm not trying to blame anyone, I just want to....

Member 2 Well being late isn't anywhere near as irritating as sitting in here and gagging over the smell of your hair spray every morning.

Member 1 You're a fine one to talk! I don't see how you can smell anything anyway—you always come in here reeking of cigarette smoke.

Member 2 You don't want me smoking in the car, do you? What other choice do I have than to have a few puffs before we take off? My smoking habits are my business, anyway. End of subject.

As you all head off fuming into the sunrise, you realize that the problem of the car pool getting a late start was never completely addressed, unless you have decided it has been caused by Member 2's smoking habits. This form of obstacle is well-handled with refocusing:

You Let's leave the smoking out of it for now. What can we do to see that we get to work on time?

Sometimes goals become blocked because you yourself feel blocked. Perhaps you are fatigued and have not yet realized it. You may temporarily have lost interest in your goal. Maybe the task has become too complex to handle at the level at which you designed it. You might be experiencing the manifestations of some thorn-in-the-paw-type personality trait, such as lack of self-confidence, pessimism over achieving your desired outcome, fear of failure, or exaggerating how difficult or unpleasant the tasks might be.

Whatever the cause, there are several ways you might overcome the feeling of being blocked (Tec, 1980):

- Take yourself away from the task for awhile, so you can come back feeling refreshed.
- Shift over to some other phase of your goal that seems more interesting or less difficult.
- Visualize the completed task, so you can mentally rehearse the reward value you will receive.
- Break down the task into smaller units, ones that can more easily be attained.

Another obstacle to following through on goal-directed behavior is immediate conflict with other goals, as was described earlier. Suppose you are working on the goal of using more eye contact. Unfortunately, Cousin Albert has stopped by for an extended visit. You find that the more eye contact you use with him, the more irritated and impatient you become, which interferes with your goal of getting along better with Cousin Albert. By second-level prioritizing, you could set aside your goal of increasing eye contact until after Cousin Albert's visit is over. Or, depending on what is more important to you, you could decide to continue using a lot of eye contact but not expect your relationship with Cousin Albert to improve.

However, if you seem to have so many goal-directed behavior conflicts that you rarely come close to meeting your goals, you may need to reevaluate how you have structured them. Three elements that are helpful for ensuring follow-through are routine, compartmentalization, and flexibility (Tec, 1980). Through the use of routine, you can increase the likelihood that the steps toward meeting your goal actually take place. Suppose your goal is to avoid having any cavities at your next dental checkup. One step in meeting this goal is to brush your teeth regularly. If you plan certain times each day during which you will perform all your routine tasks, and include teeth-brushing among them, you are more likely to follow through than if you just wait for it to come to mind.

Compartmentalization is another focusing technique. You assign specific blocks of time that are to be devoted solely to specific goal-directed behaviors. For example, you and your significant other might resolve a conflict by choosing a specific time and place when you will discuss that particular problem. You minimize contamination by other goals as you arrange the pragmatics, as by having the discussion after the children are asleep so that your discussion does not interfere with getting them to bed on time. The time-scheduling material in Chapter 3 can also be used while implementing compartmentalization as you work on your goals.

Flexibility refers to leaving some room for movement in your goal-setting and scheduling. If a certain goal-directed behavior is time consuming, as is writing a paper, allow yourself a little more time than you really think you will need. If your goal is finance-consumptive, as is visiting Australia, save a little extra money. If you are concerned about becoming stressed out as you prepare for a big presentation, allow yourself extra leisure time and pampering during the period preceding the event and avoid piling on any unnecessary stressors.

Goal-Striving or Goal Obsession?

Folklore sometimes implies that you should continue to fight toward achieving your goals no matter what:

- Anything worth having is worth working hard for.
- Quitters never win.
- No pain, no gain.
- If at first you don't succeed, try, try again.

However, is this really the case? At what point do our goal-seeking behaviors cease as personal growth strivings and continue on as obsessions?

Overinvolvement

One form of goal obsession occurs when you become overinvolved with a single target. For example, a trial lawyer may be highly invested in honing his skills at debate. He may work diligently toward achieving this goal. But if his need to win every argument at all costs follows him into his personal life, he is going to have a hard time keeping many friends.

Goal obsession is thus defined by the consequences of your goal-directed behavior, rather than the intensity of your drive and efforts. As you become highly involved in an important goal, becoming a little absentminded or preoccupied with your strivings is not unusual. In fact, it can indicate that you are successful in staying focused. However, this is not the same as becoming irrationally persistent. Your goal-seeking has become overinvolved if:

- Other important goals in your life begin to suffer.
- You routinely neglect to follow through on responsibilities.
- You can't seem to talk about anything else.
- Your efforts are causing you to feel uncomfortably isolated from others.
- You are constantly fearful or apprehensive concerning the current status of your goal or goal-directed behavior.

Here is an example of goal-seeking that has become obsessively overinvolved. Louise wants to be as good a parent as she can possibly become. However, she builds her entire life around her son, Johnny. Her goal of having a happy marriage suffers as she ignores her husband in order to spend more time with Johnny. She cancels her interior design business appointments and stays home with Johnny if he has even so much as a sniffle. Her conversations with friends always seem to come back around to the topic of Johnny and his antics. At Christmas she prints and mails out long, boring newsletters that consist solely of Johnny's accomplishments and positive attributes. She worries excessively about Johnny's well-being, often restricting him from participating in potentially "dangerous" childhood activities. Or if she does actually let him leave the house, she can't get her mind off all the potential disasters awaiting him. When he returns, she insists on hearing every detail of his day and searches for other ways to become more involved. She tries to join in with Johnny's friendships and becomes jealous of any closeness he might develop with others.

The "Staying Syndrome"

Another form of goal obsession involves sticking with goals that would be better revised or left behind. Barranger (1988) refers to such obsessed behavior as **the staying syndrome**. He notes the following symptoms in afflicted individuals:

1. An intense desire for security. Change is scary, and thus the afflicted individuals do not want to change life goals or circumstances no matter what the cost.

2. Excessive concern about the possibility of hurting or inconveniencing others. Usually such individuals have difficulty taking into account how their "caring" behavior might be damaging to themselves.

3. A sense of hope that is missing the underpinnings of reality.

4. Excessive need for comfort. Ironically, they may endure incredible pain as they maintain their obsessive behavior in order to avoid some other feared pain that might not be anywhere near as severe.

5. Out of touch with feelings. They do not recognize the pain their situation is causing them because they tune out unpleasant feelings. They seek happiness by remembering and trying to reproduce past pleasant experiences, not recognizing that these are probably no longer possible.

6. Fear of being seen as selfish. These individuals perceive looking out for one's own best interests as being "selfish." The undesirability of such a label is excessively and irrationally feared.

7. The belief that quitting is always a copout and staying is always noble. Even as their mental and physical health deteriorates, they will continue to defend and expound upon the virtues of not giving up.

The behavior of battered spouses illustrates the elements of the staying syndrome. Often they stay in horrendously unpleasant and even dangerous relationships. They refuse to stop working toward their goal of having a successful marriage because:

- They are afraid of changing to a new, unknown lifestyle.
- They do not wish to hurt the feelings of their spouses or children, or are concerned with meeting others' expectations of the sanctity of marriage.
- They erroneously believe that if they can just find the right formula for their behavior, their abusive spouses will become transformed.
- They do not want the pain of admitting to a failed marriage and dealing with the pain of loss.
- They do not recognize how destructive their relationships have been to their emotional well-being.
- They are concerned that others will see abandoning the relationship as a form of selfishness, not thinking about the children, reneging on their vows, and so on.
- They manage to salvage at least a little bit of self-esteem by perceiving themselves as not being "quitters."

Avoiding Goal Obsession

Tec (1980) offers three ways you can help minimize obsessive goal-seeking:

1. *Recognize the possibility that goal obsession may occasionally occur in your own behavior.* We all fall victim to it from time to time. It has a tendency to sneak up on us, hiding behind our blind spots as we enthusiastically visualize a completed dream. If you can admit that you might occasionally lose your overall perspective, you are ahead of the game.

2. *Make a habit of evaluating your goal-directed behavior in terms of both the short- and long-run.* Teach yourself to occasionally step back and take an objective look at what you are doing. What are the long- and short-term benefits of your goal-directed behavior? On the other hand, what are the long- and short-term disadvantages?

3. *Take regular breaks away from intense goal-directed behavior.* When you are involved with an intensive project, be sure you have scheduled in times when you can leave it behind completely. Plan to take part in an activity that is entirely different from the goal-directed behavior. Not only will you come back to your project feeling mentally refreshed, but you will also have created some emotional distance, allowing for greater objectivity.

Do You Believe in Yourself?

Just before a big game, coaches give their teams a pep talk. They tell the players how good they looked in practice, how much better they are than the other team, how they will decimate their opponents on the playing field, how they know they can do nothing but win, and now they're going to go, go, go, do it! Coaches know that if players go into a game with a positive attitude, they are more likely to win. If you visualize success, you get success. If you visualize failure, you get failure.

There is much about the human mind that we do not yet understand. Neither do we understand many mysteries of how other animals seem to succeed at phenomenal tasks. Salmon spend a number of years at sea and then return to the stream of their birth in order to spawn. Birds flock together and migrate with concise regularity. Some species travel many miles during mating season in order to find a member of the opposite sex. How did certain whales manage to find mates scattered throughout entire oceans successfully enough to get off the endangered species list? There are stories of family pets that became lost many miles from home and traveled great distances to find their way back. How did they do this?

While I was pregnant with my first child, Frank, I was working as a secretary at the Washington State University library administrative office, while my husband, Bill, was finishing his last year of veterinary medical school. Since Bill was rarely near a phone during his heavily scheduled days, we normally did not get to speak with one another until he picked me up after work. Two months before Frank was due to arrive, I suddenly went into premature labor. I called the main office at the vet school and asked that an urgent message be delivered to my husband. As soon as I hung up the phone, another secretary walked over and handed me a message, saying my husband had called while I was on the other line. He had started his large animal rotation, noticed a pay phone in the barn, and decided to call.

Was this telepathy, or some other form of extrasensory perception? Or was it just a coincidence? This type of mind power may never be understood. Scientific method, practically by definition, cannot study extrasensory perception. Scientific method is the study of that which can be measured by our known senses. Something that is defined as being outside the senses thus cannot be scientifically studied, other than disproving it with evidence of known sensory perceptions that explain the observed phenomena. Yet most all of us have had experiences of this nature for which we could find no explanation. What can our minds do that we have not yet found ways to tap?

Believing in ourselves may be one of the greatest untapped skills of this nature. We can break down our mental strategies into their component parts and study how our positive or negative attitude affects our goal-seeking and goal-directed behaviors. If we did so, much of what we would find consists of the content of this book. However, my experience as a clinician has shown me that there is more to developing a positive attitude than examining and manipulating its component parts. At some point, successful people *choose* to believe in themselves. They do it when they are ready.

Are you?

Expanding Your Experience

I never dreamed I would write a textbook. What a gargantuan task—the research, the organization, the planning, the flow and integration of material, exploring applications, and the endless hours of trying to find just the right way to get a point across. This creation illustrates that virtually anything can be accomplished if you break it down into small enough steps.

The first exercise for this chapter is designed to help you assess how well you already set goals for yourself. The second exercise gives you a chance to scan various values and consider which ones are most important to you. The third exercise is a rating scale that you can apply to any current value conflict in order to assess how comfortable you feel with potential solutions. The fourth exercise is an expansion of the goal-setting grid that I applied to Alice's life goals earlier in this chapter.

The last exercise gives you a chance to reflect upon your sum-total experience of taking a course on personal adjustment. I call it the "final" entry, with the word *final* in quotation marks. As you have probably surmised by now, the personal work represented by your personal activity log is never really final. We are all constantly growing and changing.

Awareness of where you currently stand can help you with your growth process. However, recognition of a conflict or weakness does not necessarily mean you must resolve it in order to move forward. Accept yourself as you are. Make concerted efforts for desired changes only when they fit in with your own needs and timetable.

As for me, I am going to step back and admire this creation of mine for a while before I take on any new major projects. I have a few more years left during which I still have the opportunity to devote myself to being mainly a stay-at-home mom. I think I'll try that again while I still have the chance. By the time my children have fully emancipated, I'll be rested up and ready for my next challenge.

Study Questions

1. Is ambition morally wrong? Explain your answer.
2. According to Porter and Lawler, what determines the likelihood of whether or not you will set up and follow through on your goals?
3. What is meant by "targeting"?

4. Suppose you have a goal that is actually an abstraction. What questions might you ask yourself in order to help turn it into a more attainable goal?
5. What role do values play in our goal-setting?
6. Which life commodities tend to create value and priority conflicts, and why?
7. List several reasons why people sometimes feel "blocked" and thus fail to follow through on their goals.
8. How might you overcome feelings of being "blocked"?
9. What is "second-level prioritizing," and how can it be helpful?
10. List and describe the three elements Tec describes that help ensure follow-through on goals.
11. What cues might you use to alert you to the possibility that you have become overinvolved with a goal?
12. What are the symptoms of "the staying syndrome"?
13. Describe three steps you might take in order to minimize the possibility of becoming involved in obsessive goal-directed behavior.

References

Abelsohn, D. (1992). A "good enough" separation: Some characteristic operations and tasks. *Family Processes, 31,* 61–83.

Adler, A. (1927). *The practice and theory of individual psychology.* New York: Harcourt Brace Jovanovich.

Adler, C., & Adler, S. (1984). Biofeedback. In T. Karasu (Ed.), *The psychiatric therapies.* Washington, DC: American Psychiatric Association.

Ahrons, C. (1980). Divorce: A crisis of family transition and change. *Family Relations, 29.*

Alberti, R., & Emmons, M. (1978). *Your perfect right: A guide to assertive behavior.* San Luis Obispo, CA: Impact Publishers.

Alloy, L., & Abramson, L. (1979). Judgments of contingency in depressed and nondepressed students: Sadder but wiser? *Journal of Experimental Psychology: General, 108,* 1441–1485.

Allport, G. (1961). *Patterns and growth in personality.* New York: Holt, Rinehart & Winston.

American Psychiatric Association (1994). *Diagnostic and statistical manual of mental disorders,* 4th ed. Washington, DC: APA.

American Red Cross (1993). American Red Cross Disaster Mental Health Training Program. Presented at Oregon Psychological Association, Portland, OR.

Anderson, C. (1987). Temperature and aggression: Effects on quarterly, yearly, and city rates of violent and nonviolent crime. *Journal of Personality and Social Psychology, 52,* 1161–1173.

Antoni, M. (1990). Psychoneuroimmunology and HIV-1. *Journal of Consulting and Clinical Psychology, 58,* 38–49.

Asch, S. (1955). Opinions and social pressures. *Scientific American, 193,* 31–35.

Averill, J. R. (1982). *Anger and aggression: An essay on emotion.* New York: Springer-Verlag.

Bandura, A. (1973). *Aggression: A social learning analysis.* Englewood Cliffs, NJ: Prentice-Hall.

Barlow, D. (1986). Causes of sexual dysfunction: The role of anxiety and cognitive interference. *Journal of Consulting and Clinical Psychology, 54,* 140–148.

Baron, R. A. (1977). *Human aggression*. New York: Plenum.

Barranger, J. (1988). *Knowing when to quit*. San Luis Obispo, CA: Impact Publishers.

Baumrod, D. (1973). Childcare practices anteceding three patterns of preschool behavior. *Genetic Psychological Monographs, 75,* 43–88.

Beal, G., & Muehlenhard, C. (1987). Getting sexually aggressive men to stop their advances: Information for rape prevention programs. Paper presented at the Annual Meeting of the Association for Advancement of Behavior Therapy, November, Boston.

Beck, A. (1976). *Cognitive therapy and the emotional disorders*. New York: International Universities Press.

Beck, A., & Emery, G. (1985). *Anxiety disorders and phobias*. New York: Basic Books.

Beck, A., Rush, A., Shaw, B., & Emery, G. (1979). *Cognitive therapy of depression*. New York: Guilford Press.

Beck, A., Wright, F., Newman, C., & Liese, B. (1993). *Cognitive therapy of substance abuse*. New York: Guilford Press.

Becker, E. (1973). *The denial of death*. New York: Free Press.

Beckham, E., & Leber, W. (1985). The comparative efficacy of psychotherapy and pharmacotherapy for depression. In E. Beckham and W. Leber (Eds.), *Handbook of depression: Treatment, assessment, and research*. Pacific Grove, CA: Brooks/Cole.

Bem, S. (1981). Gender schema theory: A cognitive account of sex typing. *Psychological Review, 88,* 354–364.

Bem, S. (1985). Androgyny and gender schema theory: A conceptual and empirical integration. In T. Sonderegger (Ed.), *Nebraska symposium on motivation 1984: Psychology and gender,* Vol. 32. Lincoln, NE: University of Nebraska Press.

Benbow, C., & Stanley, J. (1980). Sex differences in mathematical ability: Fact or artifact? *Science, 216,* 1029–1031.

Bennett, M., & Hiscock, J. (1993). Children's understanding of conflicting emotions: A training study. *Journal of Genetic Psychology, 154,* 515–524.

Benson, H. (1975). *The relaxation response*. New York: Avon.

Bernstein, A. (1993). Dinosaur brains: The seminar. Presentation at Oregon Psychological Association, June 26, Portland, OR.

Beyth-Marom, R., Austin, L., Fischhoff, B., Palmgren, C., & Jacobs-Quadrel, M. (1993). Perceived consequences of risky behaviors: Adults and adolescents. *Developmental Psychology, 29,* 549–563.

Bezchlibnyk-Butler, K., Jeffries, J., & Martin, B. (1994). *Clinical handbook of psychotropic drugs*. Seattle: Hogrefe & Huber.

Bieri, J. (1955). Cognitive complexity-simplicity and predictive behavior. *Journal of Abnormal and Social Psychology, 51,* 61–66.

Black, C. (1981). *"It will never happen to me!" Children of alcoholics as youngsters–adolescents–adults*. New York: Ballantine.

Bloom, B., Asher, S., & White, S. (1978). Marital disruption as a stressor: A review and analysis. *Psychological Bulletin, 85,* 867–894.

Blumstein, P., & Schwarz, P. (1983). *American couples*. New York: William Morrow.

Bly, R. (1990). *Iron John: A book about men*. New York: Addison-Wesley.

Bogardus, C., Lillioja, S., Ravussin, E., Abbott, W., Zawadzki, J., Young, A., Knowles, W., Jacobowitz, R., & Moll, P. (1986). Familial dependence of resting metabolic rate. *New England Journal of Medicine, 315,* 96–100.

Bohannon, P. (1975). The six stations of divorce. In R. Albrecht & W. Bock (Eds.), *Encounter: Love, marriage, and family.* Boston: Holbrook Press.

Bolles, R. (1993). *The 1993 what color is your parachute: A practical manual for job hunters and career changers.* Berkeley: Ten-Speed Press.

Booth, A., & Edwards, J. (1985). Age at marriage and marital instability. *Journal of Marriage and the Family, 47,* 67–75.

Borysenko, J. (1987). *Minding the body, mending the mind.* Reading, MA: Addison-Wesley.

Bowlby, J. (1969). *Attachment and loss. Vol. I: Attachment.* New York: Basic Books.

Bozett, F. (1988). Gay fatherhood. In P. Bronstein & C. Cowan (Eds.), *Fatherhood today: Men's changing role in the family.* New York: Wiley.

Bradt, J. (1988). Becoming parents: Families with young children. In B. Carter and M. McGoldrick (Eds.), *The changing family life cycle: A framework for family therapy.* New York: Gardner Press.

Breier, A., Albus, M., Pickar, D., Zahn, T., Wolkowitz, O., & Paul, S. (1987). Controllable and uncontrollable stress in humans: Alterations in mood and neuroendocrine and psychophysiological function. *American Journal of Psychiatry, 144,* 1419–1425.

Brigham, J. (1986). *Social psychology.* Boston: Little, Brown.

Brim, G. (1992). *Ambition: How we manage success and failure throughout our lives.* New York: Basic Books.

Brodie, R. (1993). *Getting past OK: A straightforward guide to having a fantastic life.* Seattle: Integral Press.

Brown, L., & Gilligan, C. (1992). *Meeting at the crossroads: Women's psychology and girls' development.* Cambridge: Harvard University Press.

Brownell, K. (1988). Yo-yo dieting. *Psychology Today, 22* (1), 20–23.

Brownell, K., & Rodin, J. (1994). The dieting maelstrom: Is it possible and advisable to lose weight? *American Psychologist, 49,* 781–791.

Burt, M. (1980). Cultural myths and supports for rape. *Journal of Personality and Social Psychology, 38,* 217–230.

Buscaglia, L. (1982). *Living, loving, and learning.* New York: Holt, Rinehart & Winston.

Buss, A., & Plomin, R. (1975). *A temperament theory of personality development.* New York: Wiley.

Byrne, D. (1971). *The attraction paradigm.* New York: Academic Press.

Byrnes, J., & Takahira, S. (1993). Explaining gender differences on SAT-math items. *Developmental Psychology, 29,* 805–810.

Campbell, R. (1985). Miscellaneous organic therapies. In H. Kaplan and B. Sadock (Eds.), *Comprehensive textbook of psychiatry/IV,* 4th ed. Baltimore: Williams & Wilkins.

Cannon, W. (1929). *Bodily changes in pain, hunger, fear, and rage.* New York: Appleton.

Carter B., & McGoldrick, M. (1988). *The changing family life cycle: A framework for family therapy,* 2nd ed. New York: Gardner Press.

Cash, T., & Derlega, V. (1978). The matching hypothesis: Physical attractiveness among same-sexed friends. *Personality and Social Psychology Bulletin, 4,* 240–243.

Casler, L. (1965). The effects of extra tactile stimulation on a group of institutionalized infants. *Genetic Psychology Monographs, 71,* 137–75.

Cassell, C. (1984). *Swept away: Why women fear their own sexuality.* New York: Simon & Schuster.

Centers for Disease Control (1991). Cigarette smoking among adults: United States, 1988. *Morbidity and Mortality Weekly Report, 40,* 757–765.

Check, J., & Malamuth, N. (1983). Sex-role stereotyping and reactions to depictions of stranger versus acquaintance rape. *Journal of Personality and Social Psychology, 45,* 344–356.

Cherlin, A. (1981). *Marriage, divorce, remarriage.* Cambridge: Harvard University Press.

Cohen, J., Evans, G., Krantz, D., Stokols, D., & Kelly, S. (1981). Aircraft noise in children: Longitudinal cross-sectional evidence on adaptation to noise and the effectiveness of noise abatement. *Journal of Personality and Social Psychology, 40,* 331–345.

Conner, R., Levine, S. (1969). Hormonal influences on aggressive behavior. In S. Garattini & E. Sigg (Eds.), *Aggressive behavior.* New York: Wiley.

Cozby, P. (1973). Self disclosure: A literature review. *Psychological Bulletin, 79,* 73-91.

Cuber, J., & Haroff, P. (1980). Five types of marriage. In J. Henslin (Ed.), *Marriage and family in a changing world.* New York: Free Press.

Danish, S., & D'Augeli, A. (1980). Promoting competence and enhancing development through life development intervention. In L. Bond & J. Rosen (Eds.), *Competence and coping during adulthood.* Hanover, NY: University Press of New England.

Debold, J., & Miczek, K. (1981). Sexual dimorphism in the hormonal control of aggressive behavior of rats. *Pharmocological and Biochemical Behavior, 14,* 89–93.

Department of Health and Human Services (1986). The health consequences of involuntary smoking: A report of the surgeon general. (Publication no. DHHS [CDC] 87-8398). Washington, DC: U. S. Government Printing Office.

Derlega, V., & Chaikin, A. (1975). *Sharing intimacy: What we reveal to others and why.* Englewood Cliffs, NJ: Prentice Hall.

Derlega, V., Winstead, B., Wong, P., & Greenspan, M. (1987). Self-disclosure and relationship development: An attributional analysis. In M. Roloff & G. Miller (Eds.), *Interpersonal processes: New directions in communication research.* Newbury Park, CA: Sage Publications.

Diener, E. (1984). Subjective well-being. *Psychological Bulletin, 95,* 542–575.

Dobson, J. (1970). *Dare to discipline.* Wheaton, IL: Tyndale House.

Dollard, J., Doob, L., Miller, N., Mowrer, O., & Sears, R. (1939). *Frustration and aggression.* New Haven, CT: Yale University Press.

Donnerstein, E. (1983). Erotica and human aggression. In R. Geen & E. Donnerstein (Eds.), *Aggression: Theoretical and empirical reviews.* New York: Academic Press.

Dornbusch, S., Ritter, P., Leiderman, P., Roberts, D., & Fraligh, M. (1987). The relationship of parenting style to adolescent school performance. *Child Development, 58,* 1244–1257.

Drabman, R., & Thomas, M. (1974). Does media violence increase children's toleration of real life aggression? *Developmental Psychology, 10,* 61–68.

Drucker, P. (1952). How to be an employee. *Fortune Magazine, 45,* 126–127, 168–174.

Edwards, D. (1968). Mice: Fighting by neonatally and androgenized females. *Science, 161,* 1027–1028.

Egeland, J., Gerhard, D., Pauls, D., Sussex, J., Kidd, K., Allen, C., Hostetter, A., & Housman, D. (1987). Bipolar affective disorders linked to DNA markers on chromosome 11. *Nature, 325,* 783–787.

Elkind, D. (1967). Egocentrism in adolescence. *Child Development, 38,* 1025–1034.

Ellis, A. (1962). *Reason and emotion in psychotherapy.* New York: Lyle Stuart.

Ellis, A. (1971). *Growth through reason: Verbatim cases in rational-emotive therapy.* No. Hollywood, CA: Melvin Powers/Wilshire Book Company.

Ellis, A., & Harper, R. (1961). *A guide to rational living.* Englewood Cliffs, NJ: Prentice-Hall.
Erikson, E. (1963). *Childhood and society,* 2nd ed. New York: Holt, Rinehart & Winston.
Eysenck, H. (1952). The effects of psychotherapy: An evaluation. *Journal of Consulting Psychology, 16,* 319–324.
Festinger, L. (1957). *A theory of cognitive dissonance.* Evanston, IL: Row, Peterson.
Festinger, L., Schacter, S., & Back, K. (1950). *Social pressures in informal groups: A study of a housing community.* New York: Harper.
Field, T., Woodson, R., Greenberg, R., & Cohen, D. (1982). Discrimination and imitation of facial expressions by neonates. *Science, 231,* 179–181.
Fisher, K. (1984). Family violence cycle questioned. *APA Monitor, 15* (12), 30.
Fleming, I., Baum, A., Davidson, L., Rectanus, E., & McArdel, S. (1987). Chronic stress as a factor in physiologic reactivity to challenge. *Health Psychology, 6,* 221–237.
Forward, S., & Torres, J. (1986). *Men who hate women and the women who love them: When loving hurts and you don't know why.* New York: Bantam Books.
Fox, M. (1983). *Original blessing.* Santa Fe, NM: Bear and Company.
Freedman, D. (1974). *Human infancy: An evolutionary perspective.* New York: Halstead Press.
Freud, S. (1911/1958). Formulation on the two principles of mental functioning. In J. Strachey et al. (Eds.), *The standard edition of the complete psychological works of Sigmund Freud,* Vol. XII. London: Hogarth Press.
Freud, S. (1914). *The psychopathology of everyday life.* New York: MacMillan.
Freud, S. (1920/1935). *A general introduction to psychoanalysis.* New York: Liveright.
Freud, S. (1926/1948). *Inhibitions, symptoms, and anxiety.* London: Hogarth Press.
Frey, W., Hoffman-Ahern, C., Johnson, R., Lydden, D., & Tuason, V. (1983). *Integrative Psychiatry,* September issue. Elsevier, 94–98.
Friedman, M., & Rosenman, R. (1974). *Type A behavior and your heart.* New York: Knopf.
Friedman, M., & Ulmer, D. (1984). *Treating type A behavior–and your heart.* New York: Fawcett Crest.
Furstenberg, F. (1976). Premarital pregnancy and marital instability. *Journal of Social Issues, 32.*
Gagnon, J. (1977). *Human sexualities.* Glenview, IL: Scott, Foresman.
Garvey, C. (1990). *Play: Enlarged edition.* Cambridge: Harvard University Press.
Geen, R. (1990). *Human aggression.* Pacific Grove, CA: Brooks/Cole.
Gelles, R., & Cornell, C. (1990). *Intimate violence in families,* 2nd ed. Newbury Park, CA: Sage Publications.
Gendlin, E. (1981). *Focusing.* New York: Bantam Books.
Giles, T. (1983). Probable superiority of behavioral interventions–I: Traditional comparative outcome. *Journal of Behavior Therapy and Experimental Psychiatry, 14,* 29–32.
Gillespie, W. (1971). Aggression and instinct theory. *International Journal of Psychoanalysis, 52,* 155–160.
Gilligan, C. (1982). *In a different voice.* Cambridge: Harvard University Press.
Glassock, A. (1990). By any other name, it is still killing: A comparison of the treatment of the elderly in America and in other societies. In J. Sokolovsky (Ed.), *The cultural context of aging: Worldwide perspectives.* New York: Bergin & Garvey.
Goodwin, D. (1985). Alcoholism and alcoholic psychoses. In H. Kaplan and B. Sadock (Eds.), *Comprehensive textbook of psychiatry/IV,* 4th ed. Baltimore: Williams & Wilkins.
Gould, R. (1978). *Transformations: Growth and change in adult life.* New York: Simon & Schuster.

Goulding, M., & Goulding, R. (1979). *Changing lives through redecision therapy.* New York: Brunner/Mazel.

Graden, J. (1985). Caffeine and tobacco dependence. In H. Kaplan & B. Sadock (Eds.), *Comprehensive textbook of psychiatry/IV,* 4th ed. Boston: Williams & Wilkins.

Grasha, A. (1983). *Practical applications of psychology.* Boston: Little, Brown.

Green, A. (1988). The abused child and adolescent. In C. Kestenbaum and D. Williams (Eds.), *Handbook of clinical assessment of children and adolescents,* Vol. II. New York: New York University Press.

Greenberger, E., O'Neil, R., & Nagel, S. (1994). Linking workplace and homeplace: Relations between the nature of adults' work and their parenting behaviors. *Developmental Psychology, 30,* 990–1002.

Groos, K. (1908). *The play of man.* New York: D. Appleton.

Grover, K., Paff-Bergen, L., Russell, C., & Schumm, W. (1984). The Kansas City Marital Satisfaction Scale: A further brief report. *Psychological Reports, 54,* 629–630.

Guy, R. (1987). *The personal life of the psychotherapist.* New York: Wiley.

Halmi, K. (1985). Eating disorders. In H. Kaplan and B. Sadock (Eds.), *Comprehensive textbook of psychiatry/IV,* 4th ed. Baltimore: Williams & Wilkins.

Hamilton, D., & Gifford, R. (1976). Illusory correlation in interpersonal perception: A cognitive basis of stereotypic judgments. *Journal of Experimental Social Psychology, 12,* 392–407.

Hart, A. (1982). *Children and divorce: What to expect and how to help.* Waco, TX: Word Publishers.

Hartmann, H. (1958). *Ego psychology and the problem of adaptation.* New York: International Universities Press.

Havighurst, R. (1972). *Developmental tasks and education,* 3rd ed. New York: McKay.

Hayden, R., & Mischel, W. (1976). Maintaining trait consistency in the resolution of behavioral inconsistency: The wolf in sheep's clothing? *Journal of Personality, 44,* 109–133.

Heath, A., & Stanton, M., (1991). Family therapy. In R. Frances & S. Miller (Eds.), *Clinical textbook of addictive disorders.* New York: Guilford Press.

Hebb, D. (1955). Drives and the C.N.S. (conceptual nervous system). *Psychological Review, 62,* 243–254.

Heiman, J. (1977). A psychophysiological exploration of sexual arousal patterns in females and males. *Psychophysiology, 14,* 266–274.

Herzberg, F. (1975). One more time: How do you motivate employees? In R. Steers & L. Porter (Eds.), *Motivation and work behavior.* New York: McGraw Hill.

Hetherington, E., Cox, M., & Cox, R. (1982). Effects of divorce on parents and children. In M. Lamb (Ed.), *Nontraditional families: Parenting and child development.* Hillsdale, NJ: Erlbaum.

Higgins, E. (1987). Self-discrepancy: A theory relating self & affect. *Psychological Review, 94,* 319–340.

Hoffman, M. (1977). Sex differences in empathy and related behaviors. *Psychological Bulletin, 89,* 712–729.

Hogan, J. (1989). Personality correlates of physical fitness. *Journal of Personality and Social Psychology, 56,* 284–288.

Holinger, P., & Luke, K. (1984). The epidemiological patterns of self-destructiveness in childhood, adolescence, and young adulthood. In H. Sudak et al. (Eds.), *Suicide in the young.* Boston: John Wright/PSG.

Holmes, D. (1984). Meditation and somatic arousal reduction: A review of the experimental evidence. *American Psychologist, 39,* 1–10.

Holmes, T., & Rahe, R. (1967). The social readjustment rating scale. *Journal of Psychosomatic Research, 11,* 213–218.

Hopson, J. (1988). A pleasurable chemistry. *Psychology Today,* July/August, 29–33.

Huesmann, L., Eron, L., Klein, R., Brice, P., & Fischer, P. (1983). Mitigating the imitation of aggressive behaviors by changing children's attitudes about media violence. *Journal of Personality and Social Psychology, 44,* 899–910.

Hughes, L. (1988). *How to raise good children: Encouraging moral growth.* Nashville: Abingdon Press.

Hughes, L. (1991). *How to raise a healthy achiever: Escaping the type A treadmill.* Nashville: Abingdon Press.

Hunt, M. (1974). *Sexual behavior in the 1970's.* Chicago: Playboy Press.

Hunt, R. (1988). Attention deficit disorder and hyperactivity. In C. Kestenbaum & D. Williams (Eds.), *Handbook of clinical assessment of children and adolescents,* Vol. II. New York: New York University Press.

Hyde, J. (1981). How large are cognitive gender differences? *American Psychologist, 36,* 892–901.

Hyde, J. (1990). *Understanding human sexuality,* 4th ed. New York: McGraw Hill.

Institute of Medicine (1987). *Causes and consequences of alcohol problems.* Washington, DC: National Academy Press.

Isaacson, L. (1985). *Basics of career counseling.* Boston: Allyn & Bacon.

Jacobson, E. (1938). *Progressive relaxation.* Chicago: University of Chicago Press.

Jacobson, E. (1964). *The self and the object world.* New York: International Universities Press.

Jaffe, J. (1985). Opioid dependence. In H. Kaplan & B. Sadock (Eds.), *Comprehensive textbook of psychiatry/IV.* Baltimore: Williams & Wilkins.

Janis, I. (1972). *Victims of groupthink.* Boston: Houghton Mifflin.

Jung, C. (1955). *Modern man in search of a soul.* New York: Harcourt Brace Jovanovich.

Kagan, J. (1989). *Unstable ideas: Temperament, cognition, and self.* Cambridge: Harvard University Press.

Kagan, J., Kearsley, R., & Zelazo, P. (1980). *Infancy: Its place in human development.* Cambridge: Harvard University Press.

Kandel, E., & Schwartz, J. (1985). *Principles of neural science,* 2nd ed. New York: Elsevier.

Kanin, E., & Parcell, S. (1977). Sexual aggression: A second look at the offended female. *Archives of Sexual Behavior, 6,* 67–76.

Keeshan, B. (1989). *Growing up happy: Captain Kangaroo tells yesterday's children how to nurture their own.* New York: Doubleday.

Kelly, G. (1955). *The psychology of personal constructs.* New York: Norton.

Keniston, K. (1960). *The uncommitted: Alienated youth in American society.* New York: Dell.

Kinsey, A., Pomeroy, W., & Martin, C. (1948). *Sexual behavior in the human male.* Philadelphia: Saunders.

Kleinke, C., & Kahn, M. (1980). Perception of self-disclosures: Effects of sex and physical attractiveness. *Journal of Personality, 48,* 190–205.

Klerman, G. (1986). Drugs and psychotherapy. In S. Garfield and A. Bergin (Eds.), *Handbook of psychotherapy and behavior change,* 3rd ed. New York: Wiley.

Knoth, R., Boyd, K., & Singer, B. (1988). Empirical tests of sexual selection theory: Predictions of sex differences in onset, intensity, and time course of sexual arousal. *Journal of Sex Research, 24,* 73–89.

Kohlberg, L. (1976). Moral stages and moralization. In T. Lickona (ed.), *Moral development and behavior: Theory, research, and social issues*. New York: Holt, Rinehart & Winston.

Kovacs, A. (1992). Helping men at midlife: Can the blind ever see? in B. Wainrib (Ed.), *Gender issues across the life cycle*. New York: Springer.

Kraemer, D., & Halstrup, J. (1986). Crying in natural settings: Global estimates, self-monitored frequencies, depression and sex differences in an undergraduate population. *Journal of American College Health, 34,* 24–32.

Krantz, D., Contrada, R., Hill, D., & Friedler, E. (1988). Environmental stress and biobehavioral antecedents of coronary heart disease. *Journal of Consulting and Clinical Psychology, 56,* 333–341.

Kubler-Ross, E. (1969). *On death and dying*. New York: Macmillan.

Kubler-Ross, E., & Magno, J. (1983). *Hospice*. Santa Fe, NM: Bear and Company.

Kupers, T. (1993). *Revisioning men's lives: Gender, intimacy, and power*. New York: Guilford Press.

Kurdek, L. (1991). Sexuality in homosexual and heterosexual couples. In K. McKinney & S. Sprecher (Eds.), *Sexuality in close relationships*. Hillsdale, NJ: Erlbaum.

Kushner, H. (1986). *When all you've ever wanted isn't enough: The search for a life that matters*. New York: Pocket Books.

L'Abate, L., Ganahl, G., & Hansen, J. (1986). *Methods of family therapy*. Englewood Cliffs, NJ: Prentice-Hall.

Lauer J., & Lauer, R. (1986). *'Til death do us part: How couples stay together*. New York: Haworth Press.

Lazarus, R., & Averill, J. (1972). Emotion and cognition: With special reference to anxiety. In C. Spielberger (Ed.), *Anxiety: Current trends in theory and research*, Vol. 2. New York: Academic Press.

Levin, J. (1990). *Alcoholism: A bio-psycho-social approach*. New York: Hemisphere.

Levine, M. (1966). Hypothesis behavior by humans during discrimination learning. *Journal of Experimental Psychology, 71,* 331–338.

Levinson, D. (1990). Seasons of a woman's life. Symposium presented at APA, Boston.

Levinson, D., Darrow, C., Klein, E., Levinson, M., & McKee, B. (1978). *Seasons of a man's life*. New York: Knopf.

Levy-Shiff, R. (1994). Individual and contextual correlates of marital change across the transition to parenthood. *Developmental Psychology, 30,* 591–601.

Liebert, R., & Sprafkin, J. (1988). *The early window: Effects of television on children and youth*, 3rd ed. New York: Permagon Press.

Linn, M., & Peterson, A. (1986). A meta-analysis of gender differences in spatial ability: Implications for mathematics and science achievement. In J. Hyde & M. Linn (Eds.), *The psychology of gender: Advances through meta-analysis*. Baltimore: Johns Hopkins University Press.

Linville, P. (1982). The complexity-extremity effect and age-based stereotyping. *Journal of Personality and Social Psychology, 42,* 293–311.

Linz, D., Donnerstein, E., & Penrod, S. (1988). Effects of long-term exposure to violent and sexually degrading depictions of women. *Journal of Personality and Social Psychology, 55,* 788–798.

Lipsey, M., & Wilson, D. (1993). The efficacy of psychological, education, and behavioral treatment: Confirmation from meta-analysis. *American Psychologist, 48,* 1181–1209.

Long, B. (1984). Aerobic conditioning and stress inoculation: A comparison of stress-management interventions. *Cognitive Therapy and Research, 8,* 517–542.

Lorenz, K. (1966). *On aggression*. New York: Harcourt Brace Jovanovich.
Lustbader, W. (1991). *Counting on kindness: The dilemmas of dependency*. New York: Free Press.
Mager, R. (1984). *Goal analysis*, 2nd ed. Belmont, CA: Pitman Learning.
Maier, S., Watkins, L., & Fleshner, M. (1994). Psychoneuroimmunology: The interface between behavior, brain, and immunity. *American Psychologist, 49,* 1004–1017.
Marks, G. (1984). Thinking one's abilities are unique and one's opinions are common. *Personality and Social Psychology Bulletin, 10,* 203–208.
Mash, E., & Barkley, R. (1989). *Treatment of childhood disorders*. New York: Guilford Press.
Maslow, A. (1970). *Motivation and personality,* 2nd ed. New York: Harper & Row.
Masters, W., & Johnson, V. (1966). *Human sexual response*. Boston: Little, Brown.
Maxwell, M. (1984). *The Alcoholics Anonymous experience: A close-up view for professionals*. New York: McGraw Hill.
May, R. (1951). *The meaning of anxiety*. New York: Ronald Press.
McCann, I., & Holmes, D. (1984). Influence of aerobic exercise on depression. *Journal of Personality and Social Psychology, 46,* 1142–1147.
McCord, J. (1992). Another time, another drug. In M. Glantz & R. Pickens (Eds.), *Vulnerability to drug abuse*. Washington, DC: American Psychological Association.
McGoldrick, M. (1988). The joining of families through marriage: The new couple. In B. Carter & M. McGoldrick (Eds.), *The changing family life cycle: A framework for family therapy,* 2nd ed. New York: Gardner Press.
McGrath, E. (1992). New treatment strategies for women in midlife. In B. Wainrib (ed.), *Gender issues across the life cycle*. New York: Springer.
McGrath, E., Keita, G., Strickland, B., & Russo, N. (1990). *Report of the American Psychological Association National Task Force on Women and Depression*. Washington, DC: American Psychological Association.
McNeal, E., & Cimbolic, P. (1986). Antidepressants and biochemical theories of depression. *Psychological Bulletin, 99,* 361–374.
Meichenbaum, D. (1977). *Cognitive-behavior modification: An integrative approach*. New York: Plenum.
Meichenbaum, D., & Novaco, R. (1978). Stress inoculation: A preventative approach. In C. Spielberger & I. Sarason (Eds.), *Stress and anxiety,* Vol. 5. New York: Halstead Press.
Mellody, P., & Miller, A. (1989). *Breaking free: A recovery workbook for facing codependence*. San Francisco: Harper & Row.
Milgram, S. (1974). *Obedience to authority: An experimental view*. New York: Harper & Row.
Miller, T., Turner, C., Tindale, R., Posovac, E., & Dugoni, B. (1991). Reasons for the trend toward null findings in research on type A behavior. *Psychological Bulletin, 110,* 469–485.
Miller, W., & Munoz, R. (1976). *How to control your drinking*. Englewood Cliffs, NJ: Prentice-Hall.
Mitchell, E., & Mason, B. (1948). *The theory of play*. New York: Ronald Press.
Money, J. (1988). *Gay, straight and in-between*. New York: Oxford University Press.
Moore, T. (1975). Exclusive early mothering and its alternatives: The outcome to adolescents. *Scandinavian Journal of Psychology, 16,* 255–272.
Mueller, C., & Pope, H. (1977). Transmission between generations. *Journal of Marriage and the Family, 39*.
Murstein, B., Case, D., & Gunn, S. (1985). Personality correlates of ex-swingers. *Lifestyles, 8,* 21–34.

Myers, M., Templer, D., & Brown, R. (1985). Reply to Wieder on rape victims: Vulnerability does not imply responsibility. *Journal of Consulting and Clinical Psychology, 53,* 431.

Napoli, V., Kilbride, J., & Tebbs, D. (1992). *Adjustment and growth in a changing world,* 4th ed. St. Paul, MN: West.

National Center on Child Abuse and Neglect Report (1982). *Children Today,* January/February, 27–28.

National Institute of Alcohol Abuse and Alcoholism (1990). *Seventh special report to the U. S. Congress on alcohol and health.* Rockville, MD: Author.

Newcomer, J., & Urdry, J. (1984). Mothers' influence on the sexual behavior of their teenage children. *Journal of Marriage and the Family, 46,* 477–485.

Norwood, R. (1985). *Women who love too much: When you keep wishing and hoping he'll change.* New York: Pocket Books.

Novaco, R. (1979). The cognitive regulation of anger and stress. In P. Kendall & S. Hollon (Eds.), *Cognitive behavioral interventions: Theory, research and procedures.* New York: Academic Press.

O'Connell, A., & O'Connell, V. (1992). *Choice and change: The psychology of holistic growth, adjustment, and creativity.* Englewood Cliffs, NJ: Prentice-Hall.

Olson, S., & Gerstein, D. (1985). *Alcohol in America: Taking action to prevent abuse.* Washington, DC: National Academy Press.

O'Neil, J., & Egan, J. (1992). Men's and women's gender role journeys: A metaphor for healing, transition, and transformation. In B. Wainrib (Ed.), *Gender issues across the life cycle.* New York: Springer.

Pattison, E. (1977). *The experience of dying.* Englewood Cliffs, NJ: Prentice-Hall.

Pavlov, I. (1928). *Lectures on conditioned reflexes.* New York: Liveright.

Peck, J., & Manocherian, J. (1988). Divorce in the changing family life cycle. In B. Carter & M. McGoldrick (Eds.), *The changing family life cycle: A framework for family therapy,* 2nd ed. New York: Gardner Press.

Peele, S., & Brodsky, A. (1976). *Love and addiction.* New York: New American Library.

Phoenix, C., Goy, G., Gerall, A., & Young, W. (1959). Organizing action of prenatally administered testosterone propionate on the tissues mediating mating behavior in the female guinea pig. *Endocrinology, 65,* 369–382.

Piaget, J. (1936). *The origins of intelligence in children* (M. Cook, trans.). New York: International Universities Press, 1974.

Pierce, J., Fiore, M., & Novotny, T. (1989). Trends in cigarette smoking in the U.S.A.: Projections to the year 2000. *Journal of the American Medical Association, 261,* 61–65.

Piet, S. (1987). What motivates stunt men? *Motivation and Emotion, 11,* 195–213.

Pietropinto, A., & Siminauer, J. (1977). *Beyond the male myth.* New York: Signet.

Porter, L., & Lawler, E. (1967). What job attitudes tell us about motivation. *Harvard Business Review, 46,* 118–126.

Prado, C. (1986). *Rethinking how we age: A new view of the aging mind.* Westport, CT: Greenwood Press.

Quadrel, M., Fischhoff, B., & Davis, W. (1993). Adolescent (in)vulnerability. *American Psychologist, 48,* 102–116.

Raskin, R., Bali, L., & Peeke, H. (1981). Muscle biofeedback and transcendental meditation: A controlled evaluation of efficacy in the treatment of chronic anxiety. In D. Shapiro, Jr., et al. (Eds.), *Biofeedback and behavioral medicine 1979/1980: Therapeutic applications and experimental foundations.* Chicago: Aldine.

Rebok, G. (1987). *Life-span cognitive development.* New York: Holt, Rinehart & Winston.

Reinke, B., Ellicott, A., Harris, R., & Hancock, E. (1983). Timing of psychosocial changes in women's lives. *Human Development, 28,* 259–280.

Reinsch, J., & Saunders, S. (1986). A test of sex differences in aggressive response to hypothetical conflict situations. *Journal of Personality and Social Psychology, 50,* 1045–1049.

Reis, H., Lin, Y., Bennett, M., & Nezlek, J. (1993). Change and consistency in social participation during early adulthood. *Developmental Psychology, 29,* 633–645.

Reis, P., & Stone, A. (1992). *The American woman 1992–93: A status report.* New York: Norton.

Reiss, I. (1989). Society and sexuality: A sociological theory. In K. McKinney & S. Sprecher (Eds.), *Human sexuality: The societal and interpersonal context.* Norwood, NJ: Ablex.

Reynolds, C., Frank, E., Thase, M., Houck, P., Jennings, J., Howell, J., Lilienfeld, S., & Kupfer, D. (1988). Assessment of sexual function in depressed, impotent, and healthy men: Factor analysis of a brief sexual function questionnaire for men. *Psychiatry Research, 24,* 231–250.

Riccio, D., Rabinowitz, V., & Axelrod, S. (1994). Memory: When less is more. *American Psychologist, 49,* 917–926.

Robins, C. (1988). Attributions and depression: Why is the literature so inconsistent? *Journal of Personality and Social Psychology, 54,* 880–889.

Robinson, E. (1950). Richard Corey. In L. Untermeyer (ed.), *Modern American poetry.* New York: Harcourt, Brace.

Robinson, F. (1970). *Effective study.* New York: Harper & Row.

Rogan, H. (1984). Executive women find it difficult to balance demands of job, home. *The Wall Street Journal, 35,* October 30, 55.

Rogers, C. (1951). *Client-centered therapy.* Boston: Houghton Mifflin.

Rogers, C. (1959). A theory of therapy, personality, and interpersonal relationships as developed in the client-centered framework. In S. Koch (Ed.), *Psychology: A study of a science,* vol. 3. New York: McGraw-Hill.

Rogers, C. (1961). *On becoming a person: A therapist's view of psychotherapy.* Boston: Houghton Mifflin.

Rogers, C. (1980). *A way of being.* Boston: Houghton Mifflin.

Rokeach, M. (1968). *Beliefs, attitudes, and values.* San Francisco: Jossey-Bass.

Rosenfeld, L., Civikly, J., & Herron, J. (1979). Anatomical and psychological sex differences. In G. Chelune et al. (Eds.), *Self-disclosure: Origins, patterns, and implications of openness in interpersonal relationships.* San Francisco: Jossey-Bass.

Roskies, E., Seraganian, P., Oseasohn, R., Hanley, J., Collu, R., Martin, N., & Smilga, C. (1986). The Montreal type A intervention project: Major findings. *Health Psychology, 5,* 45–69.

Ross, L. (1977). The intuitive psychologist and his shortcomings: Distortions in the attribution process. In L. Berkowitz (Ed.), *Advances in experimental social psychology,* Vol. 10. New York: Academic Press.

Ross, L., Greene, D., & House, P. (1977). The "false consensus effect": An egocentric bias in social perception and attribution processes. *Journal of Experimental Social Psychology, 13,* 279–301.

Rothballer, A. (1967). Aggression, defense, and neurohumors. In C. Clemente & D. Lindsey (Eds.), *Aggression and defense.* Berkeley, CA: University of California Press, 135–150.

Rothenberg, A. (1990). *Creativity and madness.* Baltimore: Johns Hopkins University Press.

Rotter, J. (1966). Generalized expectancies for internal versus external control of reinforcement. *Psychological monographs: General and applied, 80* (1, Whole No. 609), 1–28.

Rotton, J., Barry, T., Frey, J., & Soler, E. (1978). Air pollution and interpersonal attraction. *Journal of Applied Social Psychology, 8,* 57–71.

Rotton, J., Frey, J., Barry, T., & Fitzpatrick, M. (1979). The air pollution experience and interpersonal aggression. *Journal of Personality and Social Psychology, 16,* 265–273.

Ryckman, R., Robbins, M., Thornton, B., & Cantrell, P. (1982). Development and validation of a physical self-efficacy scale. *Journal of Personality and Social Psychology, 42,* 891–900.

Sadker, M., & Sadker, D. (1985). Sexism in the schoolroom of the '80's. *Psychology Today,* March issue, 54–57.

Sadock, V. (1985). Other conditions not attributable to a mental disorder. In H. Kaplan and B. Sadock (Eds.), *Comprehensive textbook of psychiatry/IV,* 4th ed. Baltimore: Williams & Wilkins.

Saghir, M., & Robins, E. (1973). *Male and female homosexuality: A comprehensive investigation.* Baltimore: Williams & Wilkins.

Salthouse, T. (1994). The nature of the influence of speed on adult age differences in cognition. *Developmental Psychology, 30,* 240–259.

Sandbek, T. (1986). *The deadly diet: Recovering from anorexia and bulimia.* Oakland, CA: New Harbinger.

Schwartz, D., Dodge, K., & Coie, J. (1993). The emergence of chronic peer victimization in boys' play groups. *Child Development, 81,* 1755–1772.

Schwartz, J. (1987). *Review and evaluation of smoking cessation methods: The United States and Canada, 1978–1985* (NIG Publication No. 87-2940). Washington, DC: Government Printing Office.

Schwartz, J., Strockland, R., & Krolick, G. (1974). Infant daycare: Behavioral effects at preschool age. *Developmental Psychology, 10,* 502–506.

Scribner, S. (1977). Modes of thinking and ways of speaking: Culture and logic reconsidered. In P. Johnson-Laird & P. Wason (Eds.), *Thinking: Readings in cognitive science.* New York: Cambridge University Press.

Seligman, M. (1974). Depression and learned helplessness. In R. Friedman & M. Katz (Eds.), *The psychology of depression: Contemporary theory and research.* New York: Wiley.

Selye, H. (1976). *The stress of life,* rev. ed. New York: McGraw Hill.

Shapiro, D., & Shapiro, D. (1982). Meta-analysis of comparative therapy outcome studies: A replication and refinement. *Psychological Bulletin, 92,* 581–594.

Sherman, E. (1991). *Reminiscence and the self in old age.* New York: Springer.

Shneidman, E. (Ed.) (1984). *Death: Current perspectives,* 3rd ed. Palo Alto, CA: Mayfield.

Shrauger, J. (1975). Responses to evaluation as a function of initial self-perception. *Psychological Bulletin, 82,* 581–596.

Singer, J., & Singer, D. (1986). Family experiences and television viewing as predictors of children's imagination, restlessness, and aggression. *Journal of Social Issues, 42,* 107–124.

Skinner, B. F. (1938). *The behavior of organisms.* Englewood Cliffs, NJ: Prentice-Hall.

Skinner, B., & Vaughan, M. (1983). *Enjoy old age: A program of self-management.* New York: Norton.

Sonstroem, R. (1984). Exercise and self-esteem. *Exercise and Sport Sciences Reviews, 12,* 123–155.

Spethman, M. (1992). *How to get into and graduate from college in 4 years with good grades, a useful major, a lot of knowledge, a little debt, great friends, happy parents, maximum party attendance, minimal weight gain, decent habits, fewer hassles, a career goal, and a super attitude, all while remaining extremely cool!* Miami: Westgate Publishing.

Spitz, R. (1957). *A genetic field theory of ego formation: Its implications for pathology.* New York: International Universities Press.

Sprecher, S. (1989). Influences on a choice of a partner and on sexual decision making in the relationship. In K. McKinney & S. Sprecher (Eds.), *Human sexuality: The societal and interpersonal context.* Norwood, NJ: Ablex.

Stack, S. (1980). The effects of marital dissolution on suicide. *Journal of Marriage and the Family, 42,* 83–92.

Stanislaw, H., & Rice, F. (1988). Correlation between sexual desire and menstrual cycle characteristics. *Archives of Sexual Behavior, 17,* 499–508.

Steers, R., & Porter, L. (1975). *Motivation and work behavior.* New York: McGraw Hill.

Steinberg, R., & Shapiro, S. (1982). Sex differences in personality traits of female and male Master of Business Administration students. *Journal of Applied Psychology, 67,* 306–310.

Stern, D. (1985). *The interpersonal world of the infant.* New York: Basic Books.

Sternberg, R. (1988). *The triangle of love: Intimacy, passion, commitment.* New York: Basic Books.

Stillion, J., McDowell, E., & May, J. (1989). *Suicide across the life span.* New York: Hemisphere.

Stunkard, A., Sorenson, T., Hanis, C., Teasdale, T., Chakraborty, R., Schall, W., & Schuslinger, F. (1986). An adoption study of obesity. *New England Journal of Medicine, 314,* 193–198.

Sue, D. (1979). Erotic fantasies of college students during coitus. *Journal of Sex Research, 15,* 299–305.

Szasz, T. (1974). *The myth of mental illness: Foundations of a theory of personal conduct.* New York: Harper & Row.

Tavris, C. (1982). *Anger, the misunderstood emotion.* New York: Simon & Schuster.

Tavris, C., & Sadd, S. (1978). *The Redbook report on female sexuality.* New York: Dell.

Taylor, M., & Hall, J. (1982). Psychological androgyny: Theories, methods, and conclusions. *Psychological Bulletin, 103,* 193–210.

Teachman, J., & Polonko, K. (1990). Cohabitation and marital stability in the United States. *Social Forces, 69,* 207–220.

Tec, L. (1980). *Targets: How to set goals for yourself and reach them.* New York: Harper & Row.

Thoits, P. (1983). Dimensions of life events as influences upon the genesis of psychological distress and associated conditions: An evaluation and synthesis of the literature. In H. Kaplan (Ed.), *Psychosocial stress: Trends in theory and research.* New York: Academic Press.

Thomas, A., Chess, S., & Birch, H. (1970). The origins of personality. *Scientific American, 223,* 102.

Tversky, A., & Kahneman, A. (1973). Availability: A heuristic for judging frequency and probability. *Cognitive Psychology, 5,* 207–232.

U. S. Bureau of the Census (1981). *Money, income, and poverty status of families and persons in the United States: 1980.* (Current Population Reports, Series P-60, No. 127). Washington DC: U. S. Government Printing Office.

U. S. Bureau of the Census (1992). *The statistical abstract of the United States, 1992,* 12th ed. Washington, DC: U. S. Government Printing Office, 81.

Urdry, J., & Billy, J. (1987). Initiation of coitus in early adolescence. *American Sociological Review, 52,* 841–855.

van Gennep, A. (1908, 1960). *The rites of passage.* Chicago: University of Chicago Press.

Walster, E., Walster, G., Piliavin, J., & Schmidt, L. (1973). Playing hard-to-get: Understanding an elusive phenomenon. *Journal of Personality and Social Psychology, 26,* 113–121.

Watson, J., & Rayner, R. (1920). Conditioned emotional reactions. *Journal of Experimental Psychology, 3,* 1–14.

Weisman, A. (1985). Thanatology. In H. Kaplan and B. Sadock (Eds.), *Comprehensive textbook of psychiatry/IV,* 4th ed. Baltimore: Williams & Wilkins.

Weiss, B., & Laties, V. (1962). Enhancement of human performance by caffeine and the amphetamines. *Pharmacological Review, 14,* 1.

Weiss, R. (1974). The provisions of relationships. In Z. Rubin (Ed.), *Doing unto others: Joining, molding, conforming, helping, loving.* Englewood Cliffs, NJ: Prentice-Hall.

Weiten, W. (1988). Pressure as a form of stress and its relationship to psychological symptomatology. *Journal of Social and Clinical Psychology, 6,* 127–139.

Wells, C. (1985). Organic syndromes: Delirium. In H. Kaplan and B. Sadock (eds.), *Comprehensive textbook of psychiatry.* Baltimore: Williams & Wilkins.

Wickelgren, W. (1981). Human learning and memory. *Annual Review of Psychology, 32,* 21–52.

Williams, T. (1986). *The impact of television: A natural experiment in three communities,* New York: Academic Press.

Worchel, S., Cooper, J., & Goethals, G. (1988). *Understanding social psychology,* 4th ed. Pacific Grove, CA: Brooks/Cole.

Yalom, I. (1980). *Existential psychotherapy.* New York: Basic Books.

Yates, J. (Ed.) (1992). *Risk taking.* New York: Wiley.

Youngren, M., & Lewinsohn, P. (1980). The functional relation between depression and problematic interpersonal behavior. *Journal of Abnormal Psychology, 89,* 333–341.

Zajonc, R. (1968). Attitudinal effects of mere exposure. *Journal of Personality and Social Psychology, 9,* 1–27.

Zgourides, G. (1995). *Human sexuality: Contemporary perspectives.* New York: Harper Collins.

Zimbardo, P., & Formica, R. (1963). Emotional comparison and self-esteem as determinants of affiliation. *Journal of Personality, 31,* 141–162.

Zuckerman, M., Eysenck, S., & Eysenck, H. (1978). Sensation-seeking in England and America: Cross cultural, age, and sex comparisons. *Journal of Consulting and Clinical Psychology, 46,* 139–149.

Zuelke, W. (1995). Presentation on substance abuse, February 7, 1995. Portland, OR: University of Portland.

Name Index

Abelsohn, D., 293
Adler, A., 39, 43
Adler, C., 94
Ahrons, C., 320
Alberti, R., 124
Alloy, L., 131
Allport, G., 42–43
Anderson, C., 81
Antoni, M., 84
Asch, S., 250–251
Averill, J., 114, 117

Bandura, A., 9, 41, 118, 322
Barlow, D., 222
Baron, R., 117
Baumrod, D., 312
Beal, G., 121
Beck, A., 10–11, 115, 123, 131, 208, 210
Becker, E., 87
Beckham, E., 163
Bem, S., 63–66
Benbow, C., 49
Bennett, M., 312
Benson, H., 95
Bernstein, A., 125–128
Beyth-Marom, R., 184
Bezchlibnyk-Butler, K., 192, 194
Bieri, J., 10
Black, C., 211–213
Bloom, B., 293
Blumstein, P., 296
Bly, R., 57
Bogardus, C., 174
Bohanon, P., 293
Bolles, R., 332

Booth, A., 282
Borysenko, J., 95
Bowlby, J., 35
Bozett, F., 296
Bradt, J., 316
Brigham, J., 49
Brown, L., 51
Brownell, K., 176
Burt, M., 120
Buscaglia, L., 359
Buss, A., 86
Byrne, D., 259
Byrnes, J., 50

Campbell, R., 174
Cannon, W., 82
Carter, B., 275–282
Cash, T., 259
Casler, L., 35
Cassell, C., 227
Check, J., 120
Cherlin, A., 293
Cohen, J., 81
Congreve, W., 105
Conner, R., 117
Cozby, P., 264
Cuber, J., 283–285

Danish, S., 107
Debold, J., 117
Derlega, V., 264
Diener, E., 63
Dobson, J., 312, 321
Dollard, J., 117
Donnerstein, E., 120

410

Name Index

Dornbusch, S., 312, 314–315
Drabman, R., 119
Drucker, P., 335

Egeland, J., 129
Elkind, D., 184
Ellis, A., 11, 102, 115, 123, 186
Erikson, E., 38–39, 43, 61–62, 353, 362
Eysenck, H., 157

Festinger, L., 28–29, 258
Field, T., 41
Fisher, K., 322
Fleming, I., 81
Forward, S., 267
Fox, M., 356–357
Freedman, D., 28
Freud, S., 7–8, 36–37, 59, 86, 93, 117, 226
Frey, W., 105
Friedman, M., 340, 341
Furstenberg, F., 282

Gagnon, J., 220
Garvey, C., 343–344
Geen, R., 119
Gelles, R., 296
Gendlin, E., 95
Giles, T., 162
Gillespie, W., 117
Gilligan, C., 35, 61–62
Glassock, A., 370
Gould, R., 62
Goulding, M., 62
Gradin, J., 205, 206
Grasha, A., 246–247
Green, A., 322
Greenberger, E., 316
Groos, K., 344
Grover, K., 290
Guy, R., 334

Halmi, K., 179
Hamilton, D., 257
Hart, A., 319
Hartmann, H., 312
Havighurst, R., 59–61
Hayden, R., 256
Heath, A., 197
Hebb, D., 82
Heiman, J., 222
Herzberg, F., 329–330
Hetherington, E., 320
Hoffman, M., 35
Hogan, J., 103
Holinger, P., 185
Holmes, D., 94
Holmes, T., 84, 85
Hopson, J., 132

Huesmann, L., 119
Hughes, L., 312, 316, 341
Hunt, M., 228
Hunt, R., 315
Hyde, J. 49, 230

Isaacson, L., 331

Jacobson, E., 94, 116
Jaffe, J., 209
Janis, I., 252–253
Jung, C., 59, 355

Kagan, J., 27–28, 316
Kandel, E., 182, 183
Kanin, E., 120
Keeshan, B., 45
Kelly, G., 10
Keniston, K., 248–249
Kinsey, A., 228
Kleinke, C., 264
Klerman, G., 163
Knoth, R., 222
Kohlberg, L., 33–34, 35, 310
Kovacs, A., 358, 359
Kraemer, D., 105
Krantz, D., 84
Kubler-Ross, E., 369, 371
Kupers, T., 51
Kurdeck, L., 230
Kushner, H., 367

L'Abate, L., 282
Lauer, J., 290
Lazarus, R., 88
Levin, J., 198
Levinson, D., 59, 60, 353–354
Levy-Shiff, R., 280
Liebert, R., 317
Linn, M., 49
Linville, P., 10
Linz, D., 120
Lipsey, M., 158
Long, B., 103
Lorenz, K., 117
Lustbader, W., 367

Maier, S., 84
Marks, G., 256
Maslow, A., 12, 244–246
Masters, W., 223
Maxwell, M., 202
May, R., 93
McCann, I., 103, 132
McCord, J., 198
McGoldrick, M., 295–296
McGrath, E., 355, 357
McNeal, E., 129
Meichenbaum, D., 11, 101, 122–124, 255

Mellody, P., 213
Milgram, S., 251–252
Miller, T., 340
Miller, W., 195
Mitchell, E., 347
Money, J., 230, 231
Moore, T., 316
Moustakas, C., 88
Mueller, C., 282
Murstein, B., 227
Myers, M., 120

Napoli, V., 308
Newcomer, J., 220
Norwood, R., 267
Novaco, R., 122

O'Connell, A., 46–47
Olson, S., 199
O'Neil, J., 357

Pattison, E., 368
Pavlov, I., 8
Peck, J., 294
Peele, S., 268–269
Phoenix, C., 117
Piaget, J., 28, 29–32
Pierce, J., 206
Piet, S., 186
Pietropinto, A., 228
Prado, C., 360, 361

Quadrel, M., 184

Raskin, R., 94
Rebok, G., 58
Reinke, B., 61
Reinsch, J., 117
Reis, H., 62
Reis, P., 358
Reiss, I., 220
Reynolds, C., 223
Ricco, D., 100
Robins, C., 131
Robinson, F., 71
Rogan, H., 60
Rogers, C., 12, 43, 87, 132
Rokeach, M., 21
Roosevelt, E., 108
Rosenfeld, L., 264
Roskies, E., 103
Ross, L., 256
Rothballer, A., 117
Rothenberg, A., 104
Rotter, J., 62–63
Rotton, J., 81
Ryckman, R., 103

Sadker, M., 49
Sadock, V., 247
Saghir, M., 296
Salthouse, T., 361
Sandbek, T., 178
Schwartz, D., 125
Schwartz, J., 207, 316
Seligman, M., 131
Selye, H., 82, 114
Shapiro, D., 133
Sherman, E., 362
Shneidman, E., 371
Shrauger, J., 259
Singer, J., 118
Skinner, B. F., 9, 360, 362–365, 372–373
Sonstroem, R., 103, 172
Spethman, M., 72–73
Spitz, R., 116
Sprecher, S., 222
Stack, S., 293
Stanislaw, H., 220
Steers, R., 330
Steinberg, R., 50–51
Stern, D., 36
Sternberg, R., 264–267
Stillion, J., 361
Stunkard, A., 174
Sue, D., 221
Szasz, T., 141

Tavris, C., 114, 239
Taylor, M., 66
Teachman, J., 295
Thoits, P., 84
Thomas, A., 28
Tversky, A., 256–257

Urdry, J., 220

van Gennep, A., 57

Walster, E., 259
Watson, J., 8
Weisman, A., 368
Weiss, B., 206
Weiss, R., 246
Wickelgren, W., 71
Williams, T., 317
Worchel, S., 248

Yalom, I., 250
Yates, J., 184
Youngren, M., 131

Zajonc, R., 258
Zgourides, G., 219
Zimbardo, P., 108
Zuckerman, M., 184
Zuelke, W., 198

Subject Index

Boldface page numbers indicate page on which entry is defined.

Accommodation, **28**
   group decision making and, 255
   scientific inquiry and, 29, 255
Achievement tests, **331**
ACOA (adult children of alcoholics), 214
Acquisition of possessions and young adulthood, 59
Acronyms, **71**
Actualization anxiety, **88**
Actualizing tendency, **12**
Addiction. *See* Drug dependence
Adolescence
   alienation and, 248–249
   conflict and, 280–281
   gender developmental differences, 62
   gender role expectations and, 50
   identity and, 61
   midlife crisis and, 61, 354, 359
   parenting during, 280–281
   physical development and, 58
   psychosexual development and, 37–38
   risk-taking and, 184, 185
   self-concept development and, 43
   smoking and, 206
   substance abuse and, 211
   weight and, 177
   Western culture and, 55–57
Adrenalin. *See* Epinephrine
Adulthood
   defining, 55
   frail elderly, 366–368
   Havighurst's tasks of, 59–60
   late, 360–368
   middle, 352–359

Adulthood *(continued)*
   stages of, 61, 353, 362
   young, 55–65
Advice-giving, 109
Ageism, 256, 357
Aggression, **113**, **117**–121
   authoritarian parenting and, 312
   behavioral perspective of, 117–118
   biology and, 117
   child abuse and, 322
   coping and, 117
   daycare and child's, 316
   environmental stressors and, 118
   gender and, 117–118
   grief reactions and, 372
   managing, 125
   play and, 344
   pornography and, 222
   psychodynamic perspective of, 117
   rape as, 120
   social learning theory and, 118, 119
   television and, 118–119, 317
   testosterone and, 117
AIDS, 235, 236, 237–239
   dating and, 56
   drug use and, 208
   homosexuality and, 230, 237, 296
Air pollution, 81, 118
Al-Anon, 214
Albert and the white rat, 8
Alcohol, 192, 194–204. *See also* Substance use and abuse
   barbiturates and, 192
   blood alcohol level, 198–199, 200

413

Alcohol *(continued)*
  composition of, 194–195
  digestion of, 196, 199
  effect on brain of, 195–196
  treating addiction to, 202–204
  vomiting response and, 196–197, 199
Alcoholics Anonymous (AA), 203–204
Alcoholism, 198, 201–202
  codependency and, 213–214
  family relationships and, 211–213
  treating, 202–204
Alienation, 248–249, 250, 254, 269
Altruism, **106**
  coping and, 106–107
  spirituality and, 12
Ambition, 377
Amnesia, **151**
Amphetamines, **192**, 209
Anal stage, **36–37**
Androgens, 220
Androgyny, **65**–66
Anger, 113–116
  cognitive perspective of, 115–116
  depression and, 129
  diary, 123
  divorce and, 320–321
  grief reactions and, 371
  managing, 122–125
  managing others', 125–128
  physiology and, 113–114, 123–124
  type A behavior pattern and, 340, 341
Anhedonia, **153**
Anorexia, **177**–179, 180
Antabuse, 161, 202
Antisocial personality disorder, **155**
Anxiety, **78**, **86–89**
  anorexia and, 178
  behavioral perspective of, 88
  biological perspective of, 86
  children of alcoholics and, 212
  cognitive perspective of, 88–89
  cognitive therapy and, 161–162
  death, **87**, 359
  defense mechanisms and, 7–8
  depression and, 129, 149
  drugs and, 192
  grief reactions and, 372
  impending death and, 368
  insomnia and, 181
  moral, 86, **87**
  neurotic, **86–87**
  psychodynamic perspective of, 86–87, 92, 93
  reality, **86**, 87
  sexual arousal and, 222–223
  state, **86**, 87, 89
  systematic desensitization and, 160–161
  trait, **86**, 87, 88, 89
Anxiety disorders, **147**–149

Aptitude tests, **331–332**
Arousal
  anger and, 113–114, 123–124, 126
  sexual, 220–223
  stress-related, 81, 82–86
Assertive behavior, **124**–125
  becoming a psychotherapist and, 334
  healthy relationships and, 247
  marriage and, 289
  role-playing and, 161
Assimilation, **28**
  group decision making and, 255
  scientific inquiry and, 29, 255
Attachment
  day care and, 316
  depression and, 130
  grief reactions and, 372
  infants and, 35
Attention deficit hyperactivity disorder
  diet and, 164
  heritability and, 28
  parenting and, 315
  stimulants and, 192
Attunement, infant, **36**
  gender development and, 50
Authoritarian parenting, 309–312, 321
Authoritative parenting, 313–315
Autism, 29
Automatic thoughts, 123
Autonomy vs. shame and doubt, **38**
Availability theory, **256–257**
Average expectable environment, **312–313**
Aversion therapy, **161**
Avoidance, as coping mechanism, 91

Barbiturates, **192**
Baseline, **160**
Battered partners
  learned helplessness and, 131
  obsessive love and, 267–269
  psychopathological categorizations and, 146
  staying syndrome and, 391
Batterers, 146, 267–269
Bed-wetting, 161
Behavioral perspective
  anxiety and, 88
  child development and, 40–42
  cognitive distortions and, 116
  depression and, 130
  homosexuality and, 229
  personal adjustment and, 8–10
  play and, 345
  psychotherapy and, 160–161
  sex therapy and, 232–233
Behavior modification, **160**
Bereavement. *See* Grief reactions
Biases, interpersonal, 256–258
Bibliotherapy, 164–165

Bingeing and purging, **179**
Biofeedback, **94**
Biological perspective
   adulthood and, 58
   anger and, 113–114
   anxiety and, 86
   coping and, 89
   depression and, 129, 174
   development and, 27–28
   personal adjustment and, 13
   play and, 345
   self-esteem and, 45
   sexual arousal and, 220
Biopsychosocial approach, 219–220
Bipolar disorder, **150**
Birth control pills, 226, 234, 235
Blackouts, 196, 199, 201
Blind experimentation, **17**
Body fat, 174–176
Body language, 263–264
Borderline personality disorder, **155**
Boundaries, interpersonal
   children of alcoholics and, 214
   family, 305–306
   parenting and, 309
Brainwashing, 247–255
Brooding
   coping by, 99
   depression and, 129, 134
Bulimia, **179**–180

Caffeine, 192–193, 204–206
Cannabis, **193**–194
Cardiovascular system
   aerobic exercise and, 172–173
   alcohol abuse and, 198
   anorexia and, 178–179
   birth control pills and, 234
   bulimia and, 180
   caffeine and, 205
   sexual-response cycle and, 223, 225
   stress and, 82, 84
   syphilis and, 236
   type A behavior pattern and, 340, 341
Careers
   choosing, 331–338
   goal-setting and, 380
Castration anxiety, **37**
Cervical caps, **234**
Child abuse, 306–307, 321–322
Child-rearing. *See* Parenting
Chlamydia, **236**
Classical conditioning, **8**
   anxiety and, 88
   fears and, 8
   Pavlov's dogs and, 8
   punishing children and, 311–312
   sexual deviancies and, 231

Clitoris, **225**, 226
Cocaine, 192, 208, 209
Codependency, **213**
   battered partners and, 267
   families of alcoholics and, 213–214
Cognitive dissonance, **28–29**, 238–239
Cognitive distortions, 115–116, 131, 133
Cognitive perspective
   anger and, 115
   anxiety and, 88–89
   childhood development and, 28–35
   coping and, 99–103
   depression and, 131–132
   managing anger and aggression and, 122–125
   personal adjustment and, 10–11
   play and, 345
   psychotherapy and, 161–162
   sex therapy and, 233
Cognitive rehearsal, **100**
Cohabiting, 295
Communication
   conversation and, 260–264
   dying a good death and, 369
   levels of, 287–290
   marriage and, 276, 283, 287–290, 291
   sexual satisfaction and, 233, 239, 240
   successful relationships and, 247
Compensation, **39**
Competitiveness
   conditions of worth and, 44
   goal-setting and, 377
   low self-esteem and, 44
   play and, 346, 347
   sexual behavior and, 228
   stress and, 78
   type A behavior pattern and, 340, 341, 342
Complaining, 98, 106
Complementarity, developing relationships and, **259**
Compulsion, **141**
Concrete operations, **31**, 249
Conditions of worth, **44**
   depression and, 132
   self-esteem and, 44
Condoms, 234, 235, 237
Confirmation bias, **257**
Conflict
   decision making and, 80–81
   fair fighting and, 285–286
   inner, 7–8, 159, 345
   marital, 277, 278, 283, 284, 285, 288–289
   parenting adolescents and, 280–281
   resolution, 106, 277, 289
   resolution by children, 310, 311, 312, 314
Conflict-habituated marriage, **283**, 291
Confrontation
   problem-solving and, 98
   social support and, 108–109

Congruence, **12**, 13
Conscience, **7**
  goal-setting and, 383
  parenting and development of, 307
Constructs, **10**
Contraception, 233–235
  discussion of, 121
  midlife and, 357
  sexual revolution and, 226
Contraceptive sponge, 234
Control group, **16**
  psychotherapy vs., 157–158
Controls, experimental **16**–18
  in psychotherapy research, 157
Conventional moral reasoning, **33**–34
Conversations
  late adulthood and, 361, 363, 365
  starting, 260–264
Conversion disorder, **154**–155
Coping, **78**, **89**–110
  aggression and, 117, 122–125
  alcoholism and, 202–203
  altruism and, 106–107
  anger and, 122–125
  behavioral, 103–105
  brooding and, 99
  cognitive perspective and, 99–103
  cognitive rehearsal and, 100
  complaining and, 106
  creativity and, 104
  crying and, 105
  daydreaming and, 99–100
  distractions and, 91, 204
  environment and, 91
  exercise and, 103
  existential/humanistic perspective and, 93–99
  forgetting and, 100
  increasing self-efficacy and, 101
  job burnout and, 342–343
  manipulative behavior and, 106
  midlife and, 355
  music and, 105
  nervous habits and, 103
  perseverence and, 100
  play and, 104
  pleasant events and, 136
  positive reappraisal and, 101
  prayer and, 100–101
  problem-solving and, 95–99
  psychodynamic perspective and, 92–93
  relaxation techniques and, 94–95
  risk-taking and, 104–105
  social support and, 107–110
  substance use and, 104
  time management and, 91
  vacations and, 91
  withdrawal and, 91
  work and, 104

Corticosteroids, **83**
Counseling, 156–157, 163
Creativity
  coping and, 104
  daydreaming and, 99–100
  individuality and, 46
  play and, 347
  work and, 337
Crowding, 81, 118
Crying
  coping and, 105
  degree of, 141
  depression and, 129
Cults, 250, 255
Culture shock, **248**
Cycling, bipolar, **150**
Cyclothymia, 150–**151**

Date rape, 121–122
Day care, 315–317
Daydreaming, 99–100, 151
Decision and commitment
  cohabiting and, 295
  healthy relationships and, 247
  homosexual couples and, 296
  love and, 265–269
Decision making
  children and, 309, 314
  conflict and, 80–81
  workaholism and, 339
Defense mechanisms, **7**
  coping and, 92–93
  listed, 92–93
Delusions, **150**
  cocaine and, 192
  distress and, 143
  hallucinogens and, 193
  sleep deprivation and, 180
Denial, **92**
  adaptiveness of, 93
  alcoholism and, 203, 212
  grief reactions and, 371
  problem-solving and, 98
Depo-Provera, **231**
Depressants, **191**–192
Depression, **113**, **128–129**, 128–135
  alienation and, 249
  anorexia and, 178
  anxiety and, 134, 149
  behavioral perspective of, 131
  biological perspective of, 129
  bulimia and, 179
  caffeine and, 205, 206
  child abuse and, 322
  clinical, 149–151
  cognitive perspective of, 131
  cognitive therapy and, 161–162
  divorce and, 293
  drug therapy and, 163

Subject Index

Depression *(continued)*
  exercise and, 103
  grief reactions and, 371, 372
  hopelessness and, 133
  humanistic perspective of, 132
  job burnout and, 342
  late adulthood and, 361
  lethargy and, 132–133
  managing, 132–135
  menopause and, 357
  nutrition and, 174
  psychodynamic perspective of, 130
  risk-taking and, 187
  self-criticism and, 133
  sexual arousal and, 223
  stimulants and, 192
  substance use and, 136
  suicide and, 134–135, 149
  withdrawal and, 361
Depressive disorders, **149**–151
Descriptive statistics, **18**–20
Devitalized marriage, **283**–284
Diagnostic and Statistical Manual of Mental Disorders (DSM), 144–147
Diaphragms, 234, 235
Dieting, 174–177
  anorexia and, 178
  bulimia and, 179–180
  exercise and, 175–176, 177
  yo-yo, 176
Differential Aptitude Test (DAT), 331
Dinosaur brain, 125–128
Disconfirming data, **255**
Discriminative stimuli, **41**
Displacement, **92**
Dissociation, **151**
Dissociative disorders, **151**–152
Divorce, 293–294
  children and, 319
  cohabiting and, 295
  family of origin and, 282
  midlife and, 358
Dizygotic (fraternal) twins, **27**, 174, 229–230
Double standard, 226, 227, 240
Drinking games, 201
Drug dependence, **191**
  alcohol and, 203
  caffeine and, 192
  cocaine and, 192, 208
  depressants and, 192
  hallucinogens and, 193
  heroin and, 209
  nicotine and, 192, 206, 207–208
  prescription medications and, 209
Drug therapy, 163
Drug tolerance, **191**, 192
Drug withdrawal, **191**
  alcohol and, 202, 203
  caffeine and, 193, 206

Drug withdrawal *(continued)*
  depressants and, 182
  nicotine and, 207, 208
  sharing needles and, 208
Dualism, **171**
Dying, 368–370
Dyspareunia, **232**
Dysthymia, **150–151**

Eating behavior, 174–180
  depression and, 129, 130, 149
  sleep and, 182
Ego, **7**–8
  development, 116, 117
  transactional analysis and, 62
Egocentrism, **31**, 289
Ego complex, **59**
Ego dystonic, **271**
Ego-ideal, **7**
Ego strength, **247**
  and excessive social influence, 247–248, 249, 250, 254, 269
Electra complex, **37**
Employee, life as, 335–338
Empty nest, 281, 357
Endorphins, **132**
  depression and, 132
  exercise and, 172
  opiates and, 192
Environment
  coping and, 91
  late adulthood and, 363, 364
  stress and, 81–82
  work, 335–337
Epinephrine, **82**
  addiction to, 269
  anger and, 114, 115
  excitement and, 114, 115
  gender development and, 50
  perceptions and, 114
  risk-taking and, 104
  stress and, 82, 83
Erogenous zones, **223**
Ethanol, **194**
Euthanasia, 369–**370**
Exchange contracting, **277**, 282
Exercise, 171–172
  aerobic, 172
  alcohol avoidance and, 204
  anorexia and, 177
  college life and, 72
  coping and, 103
  depression and, 132
  dieting and, 175–176, 177
  sleep and, 182
  type A behavior pattern and, 341
Exhaustion
  anorexia and, 178
  general adaptation syndrome and, 83–84

Exhibitionism, **231**
Existentialist/humanistic perspective
  anxiety and, 87–88
  choice and, 47
  coping and, 93–99
  depression and, 132
  development and, 39
  personal adjustment and, 11–13
  play and, 345
  psychotherapy and, 162
  spontaneity and, 185
  stressors and, 87
Experimental group, **16**
Experimenter bias, **16**
Extrasensory perception, 392–393
Eye contact, 263

Fair fighting, 285–286
False consensus effect, **256**, 257
False uniqueness effect, **256**
Family
  abusiveness, 306
  boundaries, 305–306
  dysfunction, 306–307
  incest, 306–307
  structure, 304
  subsystems, 304–305
Fantasy reflex, **227**
Female orgasmic disorder, **232**
Female sexual arousal disorder, **232**
Fetishism, **231**
Fight-or-flight, **82**, 83, 89, 114, 125, 126
Fixation, **36**
  adulthood, 37
  development of, 36
Flashbacks, **149**, 193, 194
Flat affect, **153**
Flooding, **161**
Focusing, **95**
Forgetting
  coping by, 100
  late adulthood and, 364–365
Formal operations, **32**
  alienation and, 248–249
  college education and, 32
  parenting adolescents and, 280
Frail elderly stage of adulthood, 366–368
Free association, **159**
Free-floating hostility, **340**
Free will, 12, 45–46
Friends, finding, 258–260
Fundamental attribution error, **256**, 257
Funerals, 371

Gender development, 47–51
Gender differences
  aggression and, 117–118
  cognitive development and, 49
  crying and, 105

Gender differences *(continued)*
  gender expectations and, 64–66
  gender roles and, 48
  identity development and, 61–62
  infant attunement and, 50
  insurance and, 183
  intimacy and, 227–228
  mentors and, 61
  midlife and, 357–359
  moral reasoning and, 35
  parent behavior and, 49
  peer behavior and, 50
  personality disorders and, 155
  phallic stage and, 37
  reinforcers and, 49
  self-concept and, 51
  self-disclosure and, 264
  sexual arousal correlates and, 222
  sexual behavior and, 226–227
  sexual dysfunctions and, 232–233
  sexual satisfaction and, 239–240
  smoking and, 206
  social learning and, 41
  suicide and, 135
  Western culture and, 37
  young adulthood and, 60–61
Gender identity, **47**
  confusion, 57
  development, 48
  homosexual parents and, 296
  sexual identity and, 218
Gender roles, **47–48**
  anorexia and, 178
  child development of, 48
  cultural expectations of, 63–66
  date rape and, 120
  homosexual couples and, 295–296
  psychopathology categorizations and, 146
  sexual revolution and, 226–227
Gender-splitting, **60**
Gender transcendence, **66**
General adaptation syndrome, **82**
  anxiety and, 86, 87
  coping and, 89
  job burnout and, 342
  stress and, 82–86
General Aptitude Test Battery (GATB), 332
Generalized anxiety disorder, **149**
Generativity vs. stagnation, **353**, 358
Genetics. *See* Heritability
Genital stage, **37–38**
Genital warts, **236**
Global Assessment of Functioning Scale, 5, 6
Goal achievement
  goal-setting and, 378–386
  obstacles to, 386–388
  personal adjustment and, 10
  time management and, 66–67
Goal conflicts, 383–386, 388

Goal obsession, **389**–392
Goal orientation
  ambition and, 377
  anxiety and, 94
  personal adjustment and, 3
  sexual behavior and, 228
  superego and, 7
  time management and, 66
  type A behavior pattern and, 341
Goal-setting, 376–386
  attitude and, 393
  cohabiting and, 295
  marriage and, 276, 290
  midlife and, 354, 355, 359
  positive feelings and, 172
  self-esteem and, 245
  single living and, 294
  values and, 383–386
  women and, 60
  young adulthood and, 355
Gonorrhea, **235–236**
Good feelings, promoting, 135–136
Grief reactions, **130**
  children of divorce and, 319, 320
  death and, 371–372
  midlife and, 356
Group therapy, 163–164
Groupthink, **252**–253
Growth psychology, 46–47
Guilt feelings
  anorexia and, 178
  conscience and, 7
  depression and, 129, 149, 150
  moral anxiety and, 87
  values and, 383

Hallucinations, **150**, 180, 193
Hallucinogens, **193**–194
Halo effect, **256**, 258
Hashish, **193**
Heart. *See* Cardiovascular system
Heritability, **13**
  alcohol absorption and, 199
  alcoholism and, 202, 213
  anxiety and, 86
  body fat and, 174
  depression and, 129, 150, 151
  mental illness and, 28
  parenting and, 302
  personal adjustment and, 13
  temperament and, 27–28
Heroin, **192**, 208
Herpes, **236**
History, in experimentation, **16**
Holistic approach, 47
Homosexuality, **229**–230
  AIDS and, 237
  committed relationships and, 295–296
  masturbation and, 228

Homosexuality *(continued)*
  mental illness and, 296
  Oregon Citizens Alliance and, 252–253
  parenting and, 296
Hormone implants, 234, 235
Hospice, **369**
Humanistic perspective. *See* Existentialist/humanistic perspective
Humor
  coping and, 93
  late adulthood and, 365
Hypoactive sexual desire disorder, **232**
Hypochondriasis, **154**
Hysteria. *See* Conversion disorder

Id, 7–8
  anxiety and, 86, 87
Ideal self, **12**
  depression and, 132
  sexual identity and, 218
Identification, psychosexual development and, 37
Identity
  existential anxiety and, 87
  frail elderly stage and, 367
  vs. identity confusion, **39**, 61–62, 211, 359
  marital, 275–276, 278
  risk-taking and, 184
  sexual, 218–219
  social ties and, 246
  work and, 328, 330
  young adulthood and, 59, 74
Illusory correlations, **257**
Imaging, **161**
Immune system, **84**
Implosion, **161**
Impulses
  alcohol use and, 197, 204
  anxiety and, 86–87
  borderline personality disorder and, 155
  bulimia and, 179
  choices and, 46
  daycare and child's, 316
  drug use and, 210
  free will and, 12
  id, 7–8
  parenting and, 279
  risk-taking and, 185
  sexual, 121, 219, 241
  time management and, 66
Individuality theory, **39**
Individuation, **59**, 62
  gender differences and, 61–62
Industry vs. inferiority, **38–39**
Inferiority-superiority complex, **39**, 43, 211
Initiative vs. guilt, **38**
Insanity, **140**
Insomnia, **181**, 182, 183
Integrity vs. despair, **362**

Intellectualization, **92**
Intentional drinking, **186**, 198–202
Interest tests, **332**
Interpretations, psychodynamic, **160**
Intimacy
  conflict resolution and, 277
  healthy relationships and, 247
  vs. isolation, **61**, 210, 359
  love and, 265–268
  marital, 290–291
  midlife, 358–359
  parenting, 301–302
Intrauterine devices (IUDs), **234**
In vivo, **161**
Irrational beliefs, **89**
  anger and, 115
  challenging, 90, 102–103
  cognitive therapy and, 161
  drug addicts and, 210
  listed, 90
  managing anger and aggression and, 123
  marriage and, 287
  sexual attitudes and, 233
  sublimation of, 136–137
Isolation
  becoming a psychotherapist and, 334
  college living and, 250
  excessive social influence and, 248–249, 269
  impending death and, 368
  play and, 348

Job burnout, **342**–343
Job satisfaction, 328–330

"Know-it-all" attitude, and developing relationships, 261
Kuder General Interest Survey, 332

Labeling
  depression and, **115**
  effect on mental illness of, 145
Laissez-faire parenting, **309**
Latency stage, **37**
Learned helplessness, 88, **131**
Leniency effect, **256**, 258
Lethargy, **132**–133
Libido, **7**
Life dream, **59**
Life review, **362**, 367–368
Lithium, 145, **150**
Living will, **370**
Locus of control, **62**–63, 74
Loneliness, 246, 248–249, 294
Love
  companionate, **267**
  components of, 264–265
  consummate, **267**
  destructive, 267–269

Love *(continued)*
  empty, **266**
  fatuous, **267**
  liking as, **265**
  marital success and, 275, 277, 290
  need for, 245, 246
  nonlove, **265**
  obsessed, 267–269
  parenting and, 302, 309–310, 312, 314
  romantic, **266**
  sexuality and, 219, 222, 227–228, 240
  types of, 265–269
LSD, **193**, 194, 209

Magnification, **115–116**
Major depressive episodes, **149–150**
Male erectile disorder, **232**
Male orgasmic disorder, **232**
Malingering, **154**
Manic-depressive disorder, 145, **150**, 153
Manic episodes, 143, **150**
Manipulative behavior, 106
Marijuana, **193–194**, 209
Marriage, 274–293
  communication and, 276, 283, 287–290, 291
  empty nest and, 281
  encounter groups, 283–284
  fair fighting and, 285
  irrational beliefs and, 287
  longevity of, 282–285
  masturbation and, 228
  midlife and, 358
  new couples and, 275–278
  parenting and, 278–281
  retirement and, 281–282
  satisfaction with, 290–293
  sexual behavior and, 226, 283, 290
  stages of, 275–282
  styles of, 283–285
  successful, 282–293
Masochism, **231**
Masturbation, 228–229
  birth control and, 235
  sexually transmitted diseases and, 237
Maturation, and experimentation, **16**
Mean, statistical, **18**
Media, popular
  aggression and, 118–119
  aging and, 352
  body image and, 177, 178
  eating and, 174
  feeling good and, 136
  sexuality and, 121, 238
Memory
  aids, 364–365
  alcohol consumption and, 196
  alcoholism and, 203
  availability theory and, 257

Memory *(continued)*
   drug addicts and, 210
   late adulthood and, 360–361
   studying and, 71
Menopause, **357**
Mental illness, **140–141**
   creativity and, 104
   DSMs and, 144–147
   syphilis and, 236
Mentors, **59**
   gender differences in, 61
   generativity vs. stagnation and, 353, 359
Mescaline, **193**
Metabolic rate, **176**
Methadone, **209**
Midlife crisis, 59, **353–354**
Midlife transition, **354**
   working through, 356–357
Mind reading, 116
Mnemonic devices, **71**
Modeling. *See* Social learning theory
Monozygotic (identical) twins, **27**, 174, 229–230
Moral reasoning
   cognitive development and, 31
   gender differences, 35
   Kohlberg's stages of, 33–35, 51–52
   parenting styles and, 310, 311
   superego and, 7
Motivation
   depression and, 129
   exhaustion and, 83
   goal achievement and, 378–379
   punishers and, 311
   social learning and, 42
   work and, 329–330
Motivation-hygiene theory, **329**–330
Mourning. *See* Grief reactions
Multiple personality disorder, **152**
Music, as coping mechanism, 105
Musturbatory thinking, 89, **115**, 123

Narcissistic personality disorder, **156**
Narcotics Anonymous, **210**
Need hierarchy, Maslow's, **244–245**
   relationships and, 245–246
Negative attitude, and developing relationships, 250
Negative reinforcement, **9**
   alcoholic substance use and, 203
   aversion therapy using, 161
   drug use and, 209
   learned helplessness and, 131
Nervous habits, 103–104
Neurotic, **144**
Nicotine, **192**, 206–208
Noise
   aggression and, 118
   stress and, 81

Nonoxynol 9, **237**
Noradrenalin. *See* Norepinephrine
Norepinephrine, **82**, 83
   anger and, 114
   depression and, 129
   risk-taking and, 104
   stress and, 82, 83
Normalcy, 18–20
   aging adults and, 352
   depression, clinical vs., 149–150
   emotional reacting, 46
   psychopathology vs., 141–143
Nutrition, 174

Obesity, **174**
Observational learning, **9**–10. *See also* Social learning theory
Obsession, **147**
Obsessive-compulsive disorder, **147**
   examples of, 144, 147–148
   implosion and, 161
Occupational listing resources, 332
Occupations. *See* Careers; Work
Oedipus complex, **37**
Open-ended questions, **262**–263
Operant conditioning, **9**
Opiates, **192**
Oral stage, **36**
Orgasm, **223**
   female, 225
   male, 225
   masturbation and, 228
   sexual deviancies and, 230
   sexual dysfunction and, 232, 233
Overcompensation, **39**
Overlearning, **71**

Painkilling medications. *See* Opiates
Panic attacks, **148**–149
Paranoid personality disorder, **156**
Paraphilias, **230**–231
Parenting, 300–304, 308–315
   abusive, 306, 321–322
   advantages and disadvantages of, 301–304
   authoritarian, 308–312, 321
   authoritative, 313–315
   generativity vs. stagnation and, 353
   homosexuals and, 296
   marriage and, 278
   midlife transition and, 357
   permissive, 308–310, 312, 321
   single living and, 294
   styles of, 308–315
Passing out, 196, 199, 201
Passion
   healthy relationships and, 247
   love and, 265–269
Passive-aggressive behavior, **124**–125

Passive behavior
  job burnout and, 342
  prayer and, 101
  problem-solving and, 97
Passive-congenial marriage, **284**
Passive-inactive behavior, **124**
PCP, **194**, 209
Pedophilia, **231**
Penis envy, **37**
Perfectionism
  anorexia and, 178
  bulimia and, 180
  conditions of worth and, 44
  midlife and, 353
  parenting and, 308
  superego and, 7
Performance anxiety, **78**, 240
Permissive parenting, **308–309**, 310, 312, 321
Perseverence, 100
Personal growth and adjustment, **3**
  alienation and, 249
  balanced living and, 327
  becoming a psychotherapist and, 334
  behavioral perspective of, 10
  cognitive perspective of, 11
  competitiveness and, 340, 341
  existentialist/humanistic perspective of, 13
  gender expectations and, 64–66
  goal-setting and, 377–378, 383
  marriage and, 275, 283, 284
  normalcy and, 18–20
  parenting and, 314–315
  psychodynamic perspective of, 8
  substance abuse and, 210–211
  synthesized version of, 14–15
  values and, 377, 383
  work and, 327, 330, 339
Personality disorders, **155**–156
Perspectives of psychology, **5**. *See also* Behavioral perspective; Biological perspective; Cognitive perspective; Existentialist/humanistic perspective; Psychodynamic perspective
Peyote, **193**
Phallic stage, **37**
Phenylketonuria, **27**
Phobias, 147–148. *See list,* 148
  agoraphobia, **148**–149
  simple, **147**
  social, **147**
  systematic desensitization and, 160–161
Physical peak, **58**
Placebo effect, **17**
Placebo group, **17**
Play, **343–344**, 343–348
  characteristics of, 346–347
  coping and, 104
  importance of, 344–345

Play *(continued)*
  learning to, 346
  time scheduling and, 69, 70
  workaholism and, 339
Pleasure principle, **93**, 356
Pornography
  paraphilias and, 231
  sexual arousal and, 222
Positive reappraisal, **101**
Positive reinforcement, **9**
  alcoholic substance use and, 202
  behavior modification and, 160
  caffeine and, 204
  depression and, 131
  drug use and, 209
  good feelings and, 135
  job satisfaction and, 330
  play and, 343, 345
  reciprocity of friendship as, 259
  schedules of, 160
  token economies and, 160
  work and, 343
Postconventional moral reasoning, **34**
Post-traumatic stress disorder, **80**, 149
Post-traumatic stress reaction, **80**
Potentialities, **12**
Prayer, 100–101
Preconventional moral reasoning, **33**
Predictive statistics, **17**–18
Pregnancy. *See* Reproduction
Prejudice, **256**, 258
Premature ejaculation, **232**, 233
Preoperational thought, **30**–31
Primacy effect, **256**, 257, 260
Problem-solving strategies
  angry people and, 128
  coping and, 95–99
  counseling and, 156
  late adulthood and, 360
  marital, 286, 289, 291
  providing social support using, 109
Progressive relaxation, **94**
Projection, **92**
  alcoholism and, 203
  psychodynamic psychotherapy and, 159, 160
Proximity, and developing relationships, **258**
Psychiatrists, **158**
Psychoactive drugs, **191**. *See also* Substance use and abuse
Psychodynamic perspective
  aggression and, 117
  anxiety and, 86–87, 92, 93
  childhood development and, 36–39
  cognitive distortions and, 116
  coping and, 92–93
  depression and, 130
  personal adjustment and, 7–8
  play and, 345

Subject Index

Psychodynamic perspective *(continued)*
  psychotherapy and, 159
  self-esteem and, 43
Psychogenic fugue, **152**
Psychologists, **158**
Psychomotor agitation, **149**
Psychopathology, 140–156
  abnormality of, 141–143
  defining, 140–144, 167
  example of, 144
  maladaptiveness of, 143
  personal and/or social distress involved, 143
Psychosexual development, **36**–38
Psychosocial stages of development
  child development, 38–39
  late adulthood development, 362
  middle adulthood development,
  self-esteem and, 43, 45
  substance abuse and, 210–211
  young adult development, 61–62
Psychotherapists, 158–159
  choosing, 165–166
  orientations of, 159–162
Psychotherapy, 156–157, 159–162
  behavioral, 160–161, 210
  cognitive, 161–162, 207, 210
  eclectic, 162
  efficacy of, 157–158
  existential/humanistic, 162
  psychodynamic, 159–160
Psychotic, **144**
  bipolar and, 150
  depressives and, 150
  ideations, 141
  schizophrenic and, 152
Psylocybin, **193**
Pubic lice, **236**
Punishers, **9**
  aversion therapy using, 161
  battering behavior as, 268
  drawbacks of using, 310–311
  extinction and, 40–41
  good feelings and, 135
  moral reasoning and, 33
  parenting and, 308–309, 310–312, 313–314
  self-efficacy and, 42

Racial differences, in newborns, 28
Random selection, in experimental design, **16**–17
  parenting studies and, 315
Rape, 120–121
  post-traumatic stress disorder and, 149
Rationalization, **92**, 252
Reality principle, **93**
Rebellion, in children, 309, 314
Reciprocity, and developing relationships, **259**–260

Reinforcers, **9**, 10, 40, 50. *See also* Negative reinforcement; Positive reinforcement
Regression, **92**
Relationships, interpersonal, 244–271
  communication and, 247
  healthy, characteristics of, 246–247
  need for, 244–246
  supportiveness in, 247
Relaxation response, **95**
Relaxation techniques
  alcohol avoidance and, 204
  anger management and, 124, 126
  coping and, 94–95
  sleep and, 182
  systematic desensitization using, 160–161
Reproduction
  avoiding, 233–235
  cannabis and, 194
  marital success and, 282
  midlife and, 357, 359
  sexuality and, 218, 219
  sexual response cycle and, 224
  sexual revolution and, 226–227
Reputation, **256**
Rescuing behavior, 107, 109, 267
Retirement, 281–282, 362, 365
Rewards. *See* Positive reinforcement
Rhythm method, **234**, 235
Rights, interpersonal, 246–247
  within family, 306
  within marriage, 276
Rigidity
  developing relationships and, 261
  job burnout and, 342
  marital conflict and, 286
  midlife and, 355, 357
  parenting and results of, 322
  personality disorders and, 155
Risk-taking, 183–187
  adolescence and, 184, 185
  alcohol use and, 197
  assessment of danger and, 184
  coping and, 104–105
  depression and, 187
  drug use and, 208
  hormones and, 104
  identity and, 184, 186
  impulsiveness and, 185
  peer pressure and, 184, 186
  sexually transmitted diseases and, 238
  temperament and, 184
  work and, 337
Rites of passage, **57**–58
Role models. *See also* Social learning theory
  gender differences in, 61
  observational learning and, 9
Role-playing, **161**
Rubber-band technique, **134**, 161, 182

Sadism, **231**
Safer sex, **237**–238
Sandbagging, **285**, 289
Schemas, **28**–29
  gender role, 48, 50
  group decision making and, 255
  moral reasoning, 34
Schizoid personality disorder, **156**
Schizophrenia, **152–153**
Scholastic Aptitude Test (SAT), 332
Scientific method, 15–21
Seasonal affective disorder, **170**
Self-absorption, and developing relationships, 260–261
Self-acceptance
  depression and, 132
  need for, 245
  parenting goals and, 307
Self-actualization, **12**
  need for, 245–246
  self-esteem and, 43
Self-concept, 42–51. *See also* Identity
  behaviors and, 97, 98
  child development and, 42–43
  gender issues and, 51
Self-control
  exercise and, 103
  parenting styles and, 309, 314, 315
  personal adjustment and, 10
Self-disclosure, 264, 334
Self-efficacy, **42**
  exercise and, 103
  increasing, 101
  play and, 345
  quitting smoking and, 207
  self-esteem and, 43
Self-esteem, 43–45
  anorexia and, 178
  anxiety and, 86
  child abuse and, 322
  codependency and, 214
  culture shock and, 248
  depression and, 130
  development of self-concept and, 42
  ego strength and, 248
  exercise and, 103, 132
  job burnout and, 342
  manic episodes and, 150
  marital relationships and, 276
  need for, 245–246
  parenting and, 304
  parenting goals and, 307
  self-denigrating behavior and, 245
  self-view and, 43–44
  subjective well-being and, 63
  submissiveness and, 44
  type A behavior pattern and, 340–341
  view of others and, 44

Self-esteem *(continued)*
  work and, 358
  worldview and, 44–45
Self-instruction, **101**
Self-preservation, 7, 183–187
Senior citizen. *See* Adulthood, late
Sensate focus, **233**
Sensation-seeking temperament, **184**
Sensorimotor intelligence, **29**–30
Seratonin, 129
Set point, **176**
Severe superego, **7**, 87
Sex flush, **225**
Sexism, 66, 256
Sex therapy, 232–233
  masturbation and, 229
  sexual satisfaction and, 240
Sexual abuse
  borderline personality disorder and, 155
  multiple personality disorder and, 152
  post-traumatic stress disorder and, 149
  sexual dysfunction and, 233
Sexual arousal, 220–223
  emotions and, 222–223
  erogenous zones and, 223
  gender differences in, 222, 227–228
  pornography and, 222
  reproduction and, 233
  sexual deviancies and, 230, 231
  sexual dysfunction and, 232, 233
  sexual-response cycle and, 223–225
  sexual satisfaction and, 240
  sexual scripts and, 220–223
  STD protection and, 239
Sexual aversion disorder, **232**
Sexual behavior
  children and, 231
  homosexual, 229, 230
  marriage and, 226–227, 283, 290
  one-night stands, 73
  rape, 120–121
  sexually transmitted diseases and, 235
  sexual scripts and, 220–223
  society and, 226–231
  substance use and, 121
Sexual deviancies, 230–231
Sexual dysfunctions, 232, 233
  anxiety and, 223
  attitudes and, 240
  vasectomy and, 234
Sexual identity, 218–219, 230, 240–241
Sexuality, **219**, 218–241
  date rape and, 121
  gender differences and, 226, 227–228
Sexually-transmitted diseases (STDs), 235–239
  casual sex and, 240
  condoms and, 235
  discussion of, 121

Sexually-transmitted diseases *(continued)*
   masturbation and, 229
   risk-taking and, 185, 186
Sexual orientation, 218, 229–230
Sexual preference, 229
Sexual-response cycle, 223–225
Sexual revolution, 226–227
Sexual satisfaction, 239–241
   depression and, 223
   gender differences, 239–240
   homosexuality and, 230
Sexual scripts, **220**–222
   gender differences and, 226, 227–228
   sexual satisfaction and, 240
   television and, 238
Shame attacks, **186**
Shaping, **40**
Shouldistic thinking, **89**, 123
Similarity, and developing relationships, **259**
Single living, 294–295
Sleep, 180–183
   apnea, **180**
   caffeine and, 205
   depression and, 129, 134, 149
   REM, **180**, 182
Social influence
   compliance and, 250–251
   excessive, 247–255, 269–271
   groupthink and, 252–253
   leaders and, 251–252
Social learning theory, 41–42
   aggression and, 9, 118, 119
   gender roles and, 48, 49
   infants and, 41
   parenting and, 311, 318, 322–323
   self-esteem and, 45
Social Readjustment Scale, 84, 85
Social striving, **39**
   altruism and, 107
   frail elderly stage and, 368
   goal-setting and, 377
   substance abuse and, 211
   work and, 328
Social support
   alcohol use and, 202–204
   coping and, 107–110
   depression and, 131
   drug use and, 208, 209, 210
   emotional need for, 246
   exercise and, 172
   work and, 328, 365
Social ties, 246
   excessive social influence and, 248, 249–250, 270
Social workers, **158**–**159**
Somatoform disorders, **153**–**154**
Somatoform pain disorder, **154**
Spermicides, 234, 237

Spiritual bankruptcy, **355**
Spirituality, **12**–**13**
   existential/humanistic perspective and, 12–13
   midlife and, 355
Spontaneity. *See* Impulses
Spousal abuse. *See* Battered partners; Batterers
SQ3R, **71**
Standard deviation, 19–20
Statistical significance, **18**
Staying syndrome, **390**–391
Stereotypes, **256**, 257, 362
Stimulants, **192**–193
Stimulus generalization, **8**
   fears and, 8–9
   good feelings and, 9
Stress, **78**–85
   accidents and, 84
   air pollution and, 81
   alcohol and, 196
   anorexia and, 178
   bodily reactions and, 82
   child abuse and, 322
   cognition and, 88
   conflict and, 80
   crowding and, 81
   daily hassles and, 81
   depression and, 129
   divorce and, 293
   environmental, 81–82
   illness and, 84–85, 110
   immune system and, 83–84
   internal, 81–82
   job burnout and, 342–343
   life changes and, 80, 84, 85
   noise and, 81
   pleasant events and, 136
   temperature and, 81
   traumatic events and, 79
Stress inoculation training, 122–125
Stress management. *See* Coping
Strong-Campbell Interest Inventory, **332**
Studying, 70–72
   alcohol use and, 197
   arousal level and, 82
   caffeine use and, 206
   formal operations and, 32
   time scheduling and, 66–70
Subjective well-being
   drug dependence and, 210
   exercise and, 132, 172
   hormones and, 129
   middle adulthood and, 355
   young adulthood and, 63
Sublimation, **92**–93, 137, 365
Substance use and abuse, **191**, 190–215
   antabuse and, 161
   anxiety and, 209
   bulimia and, 179

Substance use and abuse *(continued)*
  coping and, 104
  dependence, 191
  depression and, 136
  drinking games, 201
  driving and, 197, 202
  excessive, consequences of, 197–198, 215
  family relationships and, 211–213
  impulses and, 210
  intentional drinking and, 198–202
  pleasant feelings and, 136, 199
  rape and, 120
  sexual behavior and, 121, 197
  sleep and, 181–182
  withdrawal, 191, 203
Suicide
  alcohol and, 198
  child abuse and, 322
  depression and, 134–135, 149
  divorce and, 293
  late adulthood and, 361
  risk-taking and, 185, 187
Superego, **7**–**8**
  anxiety and, 87
Support groups, 164
Suppression, **92**
Syphilis, **236**
Systematic desensitization, **160**–161

Targeting, **379**–383
Television
  aggression and, 118–119
  children and, 317–319
  depression and, 136
  sexuality and, 121, 238
  sleep and, 182
Temperament, **27**
  goal-setting and, 378
  heritability and, 27–28, 51
  parenting and, 307, 315
  risk-taking and, 184
  type A behavior pattern and, 340
  work and, 335
Terminal illness, reacting to, 368–370
Testosterone, 50, 117
Test-taking
  arousal and, 82
  career counseling and, 331–332
  substance use and, 197
Time management, 66–72
Time scheduling, 66–70
Time urgency, **340**
Token economies, **160**
Tranquilizers, 181, **192**, 209
Transactional analysis, **62**
Transcendental meditation, **94**–95

Transference, **159**
Transsexualism, **48**
Trust vs. mistrust stage of development, **38**
Tubal ligation, **234**, 235
Twin studies, 27
  homosexuality and, 229–230
  weight gain and, 174
Type A behavior pattern, **340**–342

Unconditional positive regard, 162, 314

Vacations, 91
Vaginismus, **232**
Values, **21**
  congruence and, 12
  coping and, 94
  friends', 259
  goals and, 377, 383–386
  individuation and, 62
  marital status and, 295
  midlife and, 353
  parental goals and, 307
  personal adjustment and, 21–22
  play and, 345
  sexual, 227
  sexual identity and, 218–219
  superego and, 7
  work and, 333–334
Vasectomy, **234**, 235
Vicarious punishment, **9**, 88
Vicarious reinforcement, **9**
Viral hepatitis, **236**
Vital marriage, **284**
Voyeurism, **231**

Wide-Range Achievement Test (WRAT), 331
Withdrawal, physical
  coping and, 91, 342
  depression and, 129
  generativity vs. stagnation and, 353
  impending death and, 368
  late adulthood and, 361
Work, **327**–**328**, 327–338
  burnout and, 342–343
  choice of, 331–338
  coping and, 104
  parenting and, 315–317
  personal growth and, 327
  play vs., 343
  productivity, 330
  retirement and, 281–282
  satisfaction with, 328–330
Workaholic, **338**–**339**, 340

Yeast infection, **236**
Yerkes-Dodson law, **82**

CREDITS

This page constitutes an extension of the copyright page. We have made every effort to trace the ownership of all copyrighted material and to secure permission from copyright holders. In the event of any question arising as to the use of any material, we will be pleased to make the necessary corrections in future printings. Thanks are due to the following authors, publishers, and agents for permission to use the material indicated.

Page 6, figure: American Psychiatric Association: *Diagnostic and Statistical Manual of Mental Disorders, Fourth Edition,* Washington, D.C., American Psychiatric Association, 1994. Reprinted by permission. **Page 46,** numbered list: O'Connell/O'Connell, CHOICE AND CHANGE, ©1992, pp. 14–20. Adopted by permission of Prentice-Hall, Inc., Englewood Cliffs, N.J. **Page 72,** summarization: Adapted from *How to Get into and Graduate from College in 4 years with Good Grades, a Useful Major, a lot of Knowledge, a Little Debt, Great Friends, Happy Parents, Maximum Party Attendance, Minimal Weight Gain, Decent Habits, Fewer Hassles, a Career Goal, and a Super Happy Attitude, All While Remaining Extremely Cool!,* by Martin J. Spethman. Copyright © 1992 Westgate Publishing. Adapted by permission. **Page 83,** figure: Reprinted with permission from the *Journal of Psychosomatic Research,* "The Social Readjustment Scale," Vol. 11, 213–218, 1967. Elsevier Science Ltd., Pergamon Imprint, Oxford, England. **Page 125,** paraphrase: Adapted from "Dinosaur Brains: The Seminar" by Albert J. Bernstein. Presentation to Oregon Psychological Association, Portland, OR, June 26, 1993. Adapted by permission. **Page 213,** summarizations: SUMMARIZATIONS OF TEXT from BREAKING FREE by PIA MELLODY and ANDREA WELLS MILLER. Copyright © 1989 by Pia Mellody and Andrea Wells Miller. Reprinted by permission of HarperCollins Publishers, Inc. **Page 291,** figure: Journal of Marriage and the Family, "A GENERIC MEASURE OF RELATIONSHIP SATISFACTION," Susan S. Hendrick; 50:1 93–98. Copyrighted 1988 by the National Council on Family Relations, 3989 Central Ave. NE, Suite 550, Minneapolis, MN 55421. Reprinted by permission. **Page 304,** summarizations: Adapted from "Personal Relationships in the Veterinary Clinic," by Laurel Hughes and William H. Hughes, 1991, JAVMA, 198, 1748–1749, American Veterinary Medical

Association. **Page 335,** list: From "How to be an employee," *Fortune Magazine, 45,* 126–127, 168-174. Drucker, P. 1952. Reprinted by permission. **Page 362,** adaption: Adapted from ENJOY OLD AGE: A Program of Self-Management by B. F. Skinner and M. E. Vaughan, with the permission of W. W. Norton & Company, Inc. Copyright © 1983 by B. F. Skinner and Margaret E. Vaughan.

TO THE OWNER OF THIS BOOK:

We hope that you have found *Beginnings & Beyond: A Guide for Personal Growth & Adjustment,* useful. So that this book can be improved in a future edition, would you take the time to complete this sheet and return it? Thank you.

School and address: _____

Department: _____

Instructor's name: _____

1. What I like most about this book is: _____

_____

_____

2. What I like least about this book is: _____

_____

_____

3. My general reaction to this book is: _____

_____

4. The name of the course in which I used this book is: _____

_____

5. Were all of the chapters of the book assigned for you to read? _____

   If not, which ones weren't? _____

6. In the space below, or on a separate sheet of paper, please write specific suggestions for improving this book and anything else you'd care to share about your experience in using the book.

_____

_____

_____

_____

Optional:

Your name: _____ Date: _____

May Brooks/Cole quote you, either in promotion for *Beginnings & Beyond: A Guide for Personal Growth & Adjustment*, or in future publishing ventures?

Yes: _____ No: _____

Sincerely,

Laurel Hughes

FOLD HERE

NO POSTAGE
NECESSARY
IF MAILED
IN THE
UNITED STATES

BUSINESS REPLY MAIL
FIRST CLASS   PERMIT NO. 358   PACIFIC GROVE, CA

POSTAGE WILL BE PAID BY ADDRESSEE

ATT: *Laurel Hughes*

**Brooks/Cole Publishing Company
511 Forest Lodge Road
Pacific Grove, California 93950-9968**

FOLD HERE

Brooks/Cole is dedicated to publishing quality books for education in the human services and psychology fields. If you are interested in learning more about our publications, please fill in your name and address and request our latest catalogue.

Name: _____

Street Address: _____

City, State, and Zip: _____

FOLD HERE

BUSINESS REPLY MAIL
FIRST CLASS   PERMIT NO. 358   PACIFIC GROVE, CA

POSTAGE WILL BE PAID BY ADDRESSEE

ATT: *Human Services Catalogue*

**Brooks/Cole Publishing Company
511 Forest Lodge Road
Pacific Grove, California 93950-9968**

NO POSTAGE
NECESSARY
IF MAILED
IN THE
UNITED STATES

FOLD HERE